Martin Nordegg´

from Canada and United States

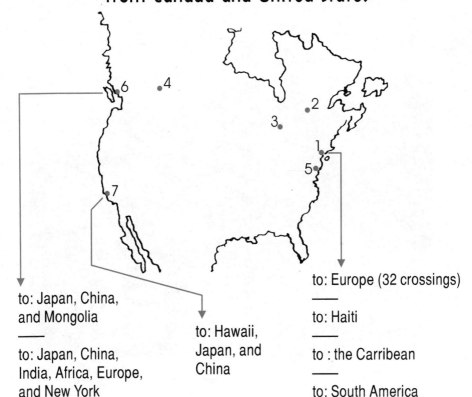

to: Japan, China,
and Mongolia

———

to: Japan, China,
India, Africa, Europe,
and New York
(around the world)

to: Hawaii,
Japan, and
China

to: Europe (32 crossings)

to: Haiti

———

to : the Carribean

———

to: South America

Points of Departure:

- ❶ New York
- ❻ Vancouver
- ❼ San Francisco

Places of Residence:

- ❶ New York
  1915-1917
  1918-1928
  1936-1948
- ❷ Ottawa
  1906-1909
  1928-1936
- ❸ Toronto
  1909-1911
- ❹ Nordegg
  1911-1915
- ❺ Atlantic City
  1917-1918

Martin Nordegg—1910

Martin Nordegg

The Uncommon Immigrant

W. John Koch

[signature: W. John Koch]

**Brightest Pebble
Publishing Co. Ltd.
1997**

First Printing July 1997 by:
Art Design Printing Inc., Edmonton Alberta, Canada

Cover design by Art Design

First published in 1997 by
Brightest Pebble Publishing Co. Ltd.
7604 - 149 Avenue
Edmonton, Alberta, Canada
T5C 2V7
Telephone (403) 457-7496
Fax (403) 475-0243

Canadian Cataloguing in Publication Data

Koch, W. John

Martin Nordegg: The Uncommon Immigrant

Includes bibliographical references and index

ISBN 0-9699669-5-4

1. Nordegg, Martin 2. Nordegg (Alta.)—Biography.
I. Title

FC3699.N67Z49 1997   971.23'3   C97-900637-6
F1079.5.N67K63 1997

Cover Landscape "Nordegg Houses" by Serena Duncan

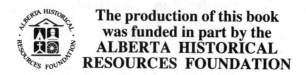

**The production of this book
was funded in part by the
ALBERTA HISTORICAL
RESOURCES FOUNDATION**

To My Wife Maria and My Son George

ABOUT THE AUTHOR

John Koch was born in Silesia, the German province where Martin Nordegg was born in 1868.

Following World War II, John studied history at the University of Würzburg before emigrating to Canada in 1954. After he obtained a masters degree in social work at the University of British Columbia in 1960, he worked in the social welfare and health-care fields in British Columbia, Saskatchewan, and since 1964, in Alberta. In 1987, John retired and has since devoted his time to writing.

John published articles in professional journals in Canada, the United States and in Poland. He is the author of *Schloss Fürstenstein,* an illustrated volume about a famous German castle (since 1945 located in Poland) and its history. He also wrote the biography of *Princess Daisy of Pless.* Both books were published in Germany in 1989 and 1991 respectively.

In 1995, John Koch and his wife Maria completed *To the Town that Bears Your Name,* a previously unpublished story by Martin Nordegg, written for his daughter Marcelle in 1912. Translated from German by Maria Koch with a short biography of Nordegg by John, this book was published by Brightest Pebble Publishing Co. in 1995, followed by the German edition *Zur Stadt, die Deinen Namen trägt,* in 1996.

Intensive research over several years spanning two continents enabled John to complete the biography of Martin Nordegg, the public persona as well as the private man.

Contents

ACKNOWLEDGMENTS

Writing the biography of a man like Martin Nordegg, who lived and worked in several countries, required research spanning two continents. In my search for the public and private persona of Martin Nordegg, I was fortunate to receive the generous assistance of government departments and numerous public and private archives in locating documents among sometimes most obscure sources. Friends and acquaintances of Martin Nordegg and their descendants and relatives and friends of Sonia Nordegg were immensely helpful in sharing their reminiscences and mementos with me.

Before giving acknowledgment to all of those who assisted me, I wish to express my gratitude and appreciation to Mrs. Martha Froelich, New York NY, the friend and attorney of the late Sonia Nordegg. Without Mrs. Froelich's interest and support, the biography of Martin Nordegg could not have been written in its final depth and scope.

I wish to sincerely thank the following for their contribution to the extended research required for my work about Martin Nordegg:

AUSTRIA

Österreichische Nationalbibliothek (Mrs. Doris Schneider-Wagenbichler); Österreichisches Staatsarchiv (Dr. Manfred Fink); Stiftung Dokumentationsarchiv des Österreichischen Widerstandes (Mr. Siegwald Ganglmair); Naturhistorisches Museum. Edith Javor; Edith Nordegg; Ebba Schober, daughter of Dr. Ludwig von Kleinwächter, all in Vienna.

BELGIUM

Bernard Gheur, grandson of Martin Nordegg's mining engineer Ernest Gheur; René van Damme.

CANADA

In Alberta: Alberta Historical Site Services; Family History Library of the Church of Jesus Christ of Latter Day Saints, Edmonton; Glenbow Archives, Calgary; *The Mountaineer* and its publisher Brian Mazza in Rocky Mountain House; Nordegg Historical Society and its project manager, Joe Baker; Provincial Archives of Alberta, Edmonton; Michael Dawe, director of the City Archives, Red Deer;. Clarence Everett, Frieda Friedli and Harriet Hudson of Stettler. I am grateful to Professor T.D. Regehr of Calgary for his useful annotations to Martin Nordegg's memoirs which he edited. I am indebted to many former residents and to friends of Nordegg, especially Anne Belliveau, Serena Duncan, John Galloway, Fred and Helen Kidd, Virginia Kidd, Dennis Morley, Elsie Veenstra and Tom Wilson.

In Ottawa: Canadian Museum of Civilization; Departments of Foreign Affairs and International Trade and of Multiculturalism and Citizenship; National Archives of Canada (Diane Duguay and others); Departments of Corporate

Services and Planning and Development of the City of Ottawa; the Ottawa Public Library; Brigadier E.G. Beament; Denis Fossberg; Andrew Haydon.

In Toronto: Henry Wellisch, president of the Jewish Genealogical Society of Canada; Lorne Ingle.

FRANCE

Françoise Ramirez, Courbevoie.

GERMANY

Heimatbund Reichenbach; Landesarchiv, Staatsbibliothek, and Standesamt Schöneberg in Berlin; Stadtarchiv Bonn (Frau Zeipel); Rheinische Landesklinik, Bonn (Linda Orth); Staatsarchiv Hamburg; Harry Amolsch, Leipzig; Professor Dr. Lothar Brandt, Berlin; Dr. Bruno & Ursula Büxenstein, Neumünster; Dipl.-Ing. Udo Korgitzsch and Dr. Matthias Otto, Berlin.

GREAT BRITAIN

Arundel Castle Trustees Limited (Sara Rogers); The Beth Din; British Library, Greater London Record Office; Office of Population Censuses and Surveys; Jewish Genealogical Society of Great Britain; Public Record Office; West Sussex Record Office. Leon Gamsa, great-nephew of Sonia Nordegg; Dr. Anthony Joseph; Michael Thompson.

THE NETHERLANDS

City Archives, Rotterdam.

POLAND

Macej Lagiewski, Wroclaw; Tomasz Wisniewski, Bialystok.

SWITZERLAND

Schweizerisches Bundesarchiv, Bern; Zivilstandsamt Bad Ragaz.

THE UNITED STATES

In New York City and New York State: Port Chester Nursing Home; Leo Baeck Institute; Convent of the Sacred Heart (Sister Mary Raney); Franklin Delano Roosevelt Veterans Administration Hospital, Montrose (Dr. Gittelson); Ferncliff Cemetery Association; Hunter College; Kings Park Psychiatric Center; Municipal Archives (Division of Old Records); New York Public Library; New York Public Library for the Performing Arts; Surrogates Court, County of New York; United States District Court. Roger Joslyn; Dr. Andrew Weissman; YIVO Institute for Jewish Rersearch (Leo Greenbaum).

In Washington DC: Department of the Navy, Naval Historical Center; Library of Congress; National Archives and Records Administration and its North-East Region in New York, the Suttland Branch and the Pacific Sierra Region in San Bruno CA (William Greene); U.S. Army Military History Institute and its branches in Carlisle PA and St. Louis MO; United States Departments of Justice and of Immigration and Naturalization Service.

In other locations: Genealogical Society and Family History Library of the Church of Jesus Christ of Latter Day Saints, Salt Lake City UT; Newberry Library, Chicago IL; Readers Digest, Pleasantville NY; Social Security Administration, Baltimore MD; State Archives of Hawaii, Honolulu; State Historical Society of North Dakota, Bismarck, ND (Dolores Vyzralek); Robert A. Furhoff, Chicago IL.

Of immense importance were the numerous personal reminiscences and mementoes shared with me by relatives and friends of Martin and Sonia Nordegg: Sonia's nephew Hyman Mizell and his wife Runelle and their daughter Barbara Deuty, Miami, FL; Sonia's niece Ruth Rothchild and her husband Sam, Tampa FL, their daughter Joyce Rothchild, Pleasantville NY, and their son Irwin Rothchild, Atlanta, GA; Dr. Paul Jordan, New Haven, CT; Dr. Sabine Jordan, Fort Collins, CO, and Dr. Cornelia Brandt-Gaudry, Montreal, PQ, daughters of Klaus and Johanna Brandt, distant relatives of Martin; Elizabeth de Picciotto, New York, NY, daughter of Frank Petschek; Gunda Taylor, Salt Lake City, daughter of Dr. Ludwig von Kleinwächter.

I wish to thank my publisher, Jim Musson, for his advice and his courage to accept yet another oeuvre on Martin Nordegg for publication by Brightest Pebble Publishing Ltd., and Phyllis Schmitt for her dedicated and meticulous editorial work.

I express, above all, my deep gratitude to my wife Maria for her never-ending patience during the years when my mind and time were forever preoccupied with Martin Nordegg. She gave me hour after hour of editorial help in the preparation of the final typescript. She shared my research work, including several trips, planned as holidays, but more than once devoted to research. Invariably, she always gave me sound, realistic advice when my enthusiasm threatened to carry me too far.

The assistance towards publication of Martin Nordegg's biography by The Coal Association of Canada, Calgary, AB, and the Alberta Historical Resources Foundation is gratefully acknowledged.

FOREWORD

This is a book about Canada, particularly about the Canadian West and its history and specifically about Alberta, my home since 1954. It is a book about a man who belonged to the generation of pioneers of the early part of our century. Too many of these courageous, determined men and women have remained anonymous to this day or are, at best, known to local historians only. Biographies have been written about some, while others kept diaries about their lives and experiences. These memoirs were never published in their lifetime. Martin Nordegg belongs to this latter group of pioneers, specifically to those whose personal lives were only rarely revealed to their contemporaries and later generations.

Much of what constituted the personality of Martin Nordegg remained hidden, or at least obscured, in the memoirs he wrote about his life between the years 1906 to 1924, which, with the exception of part of World War I, he spent in Canada. His memoirs are treasured by those who have read them or who own one of the rare copies privately distributed by Martin Nordegg to his friends—from early companions to Prime Minister Mackenzie King.

All his life Martin Nordegg was a gregarious, but intensely private person who kept much of his personal life history to himself. This was a pity because the course of his entire life from his childhood in Imperial Germany to his last years in the post-World War II United States was not only remarkable, it was also representative of its times in Europe as well as in North America.

The undeniable progress of this dynamic era as much as its disasters—two world wars, widespread political and social upheavals and persecutions—was also reflected in the fate of Martin Nordegg and in the development of the unusual person he became. The history of his life is just as much a record of the opportunities that he took hold of and explored and exploited as it is of the political, humanitarian, and moral challenges that confronted him and his contemporaries—challenges that Martin accepted, pursued, and mastered with extraordinary persistence and frequent success. His life was characterized by triumphs and defeats, by fulfillment and personal tragedies. During the later part of his life, he found a suitable partner in his second wife, Sonia, who in her own way was as remarkable a person as Martin Nordegg himself.

How did I discover Martin Nordegg—what specifically interested me in him? Martin Nordegg was born in Silesia, the province of my birth, where I grew up in coal mining country. I have always been interested in mining, and I have long been fascinated by

Canadian pioneers—especially those of the Canadian West—and by the sad fate of the short-lived existence of Alberta's mining towns, which have so quickly faded into history.

Before I discovered the original copies of Martin Nordegg's memoirs, footnotes and comments of the abridged edition of the Nordegg memoirs published by T.D. Regehr in 1970 gave me valuable pointers. But so many unknowns remained—who was the Martin Nordegg before and after his Canadian years? The search began: Ottawa; New York; Washington, DC; Tampa, Florida; Alberta, with her archives and the descendants of her early pioneers; England; Germany; Poland; France; Belgium. There were some early discoveries, thanks to the kindness of Mrs. Martha Froelich, the friend and attorney of the late Mrs. Sonia Nordegg, mentioned in T.D. Regehr's edition of the Nordegg memoirs. Some of the search, not unexpectedly, ended in blind alleys; but there were also many lucky strikes that opened up a wider vista to Martin Nordegg's life, even though to this day some mysteries remain. What has come to light, though, reveals a person of unusual talents and interests, a man driven by a sense of mission and an overpowering need to achieve—often against overwhelming odds— a man who respected people of all walks of life, a man who knew how to make and retain friendships.

This is the biography of Martin Nordegg. But this is also a book about an era which, in many respects, already seems long past. It was the famous era of the entrepreneur who, with success or in failure, pursued and exploited the opportunities of his day. It was also the era when the opening of the Canadian West and its development had entered the final stage. It is the story of a man who deeply loved his adopted country, Canada, and respected and admired its people—the miners as much as many of its political, economic and intellectual leaders.

It is also a book about Europe, primarily Germany, the country of Martin Nordegg's birth, which he left consciously because of its many political and social restrictions but whose people remained in his heart to the last days of his life.

From Berlin to the Austrian Alps and London, from Ottawa and Toronto to Alberta, from New York to Florida, I found people who remember Martin Nordegg 45 years after his death. Nearly all of them respect him; many admire him and still marvel at his initiative, his energy, and his never failing optimism. But there is not a single person who could claim to have known him, his character, and his life history in its entirety.

It is the purpose of this biography to create a composite of the many records and reminiscences, written and verbal, that I was fortunate to find in numerous archives or privileged to receive from those who remember Martin Nordegg and his second wife, Sonia. Despite the intensive, painstaking research, which so often seemed blessed with good fortune, a few blank spots remain. In a few instances, some speculation and assumptions were necessary to fill the few remaining voids in what was already known or was revealed through the many sources I examined. Otherwise, this fascinating story of Martin Nordegg is entirely based on documentation.

The result of my effort, I hope, will be the story of Martin Nordegg and his love for Canada, the story of a man who brought the best of his European heritage to the New World. Here he immediately learned to appreciate the uniqueness of his adopted country and its people and, later in his life, of the United States. This book is also intended to preserve a unique piece of Canadian history that might otherwise fade into oblivion.

Edmonton, Alberta
March 1997

W. John Koch

I

Childhood and Youth
(1868 - 1888)

"Come to Canada!.... You will never regret it!.... In Canada a man like you would have great chances! Canada needs men of your type!"

With these parting words, Colonel Onésiphore Talbot, Liberal member of Parliament from Ottawa, left 37-year-old Martin Cohn,[*] who had taken Colonel Talbot on a tour of the Technical Institute in the Berlin suburb of Charlottenburg.

Colonel Talbot was genuinely impressed with the part-time associate of the world-renowned scientist, Professor Hermann Vogel. Martin was actually the manager of Germany's largest printing house and currently "on loan one day a week" to Professor Vogel from his employer, Georg Büxenstein. Colonel Talbot had enjoyed the amiable and outgoing but obviously ambitious Martin Cohn, who had already spent some years outside his native Germany, where he had built quite a remarkable career for himself within a rather short time. But the Colonel also noticed a sense of impatience in Martin, a feeling of being restricted and stymied by the conservative conditions in Imperial Germany—a country whose restrictive political system lagged far behind its enormous industrial and economic progress.

Colonel Talbot's intuition had been correct. In 1906, twelve weeks after saying good-bye to Martin Cohn in Berlin, the Colonel greeted Martin at the railway station in Ottawa. Three years later in 1909, when Martin changed his last name from Cohn to Nordegg, he was already well known in the political and financial circles of Ottawa and Toronto and in the Canadian West, in Alberta.

Colonel Talbot's judgment of Martin Cohn would be proven entirely correct. As Martin Nordegg, Martin Cohn would grow wings in the environment of the New World. He proved to be well prepared for the challenges and opportunities that were waiting for him in Canada. He became one of the last of a generation of immigrants who not only did well in the New World but succeeded in melding their rich European heritage with the freedom and opportunities of

---

[*] Martin Nordegg was born as Martin Cohn. He went by that name until 1909, when he legally changed it to Nordegg.

their new home. This was a world of capitalism at its best and its worst. At its worst, it had many victims among the millions of immigrants streaming across the Atlantic from Europe. But it was also a world ready to receive with open arms well-educated, hard-working, self-reliant men like Martin Cohn, the courageous, imaginative, risk-taking entrepreneur.

What made Martin Cohn so eager to escape the political and social strictures of Germany for the liberty and opportunities promised in the New World? What made him different from the millions who entered Canada—and in even greater numbers the United States—after the turn of the century, only to struggle for decades before feeling at home in this different world? Often they would see only their children enjoy the fruits of the years of hard, poorly paid labour in sweatshops or on homesteads across the Continent. It was true that, unlike the vast majority of immigrants, Martin arrived in Canada well educated and supplied with considerable funds. He was not the proverbial immigrant of these years, looking forward to clearing a parcel of land and owning his own farm in the newly settled West. And it was true that Martin had already proved himself in his native country as an ambitious, enterprising man. But what motivated Martin to excel, to take risks, and to strive for and achieve success?

There were few indicators in Martin Cohn's childhood that would seem to predestine him for the life and the career he would build for himself in his adult years. He was blessed with the good fortune of having been brought up in a stable, happy family of modest wealth in a small town with a growing middle class. His life unfolded as the child of parents who believed in the importance of a well-rounded education, of parents who enjoyed the respect of their community, not because of their financial status but because of their decency as human beings and what they contributed to the welfare of their community. Martin's place of birth enjoyed a modest degree of prosperity and, unlike other more industrialized towns and cities in Silesia, was as yet untouched by the social conflicts arising from the suffering of the growing proletarian class in Germany. For the young Martin, the world must have looked, if not full of great promise, at least gentle, comfortable and safe.

The town where Martin Cohn was born on July 18, 1868, was called Reichenbach [since 1945 Dzierzoniów in Poland]. Located in the then Prussian province of Silesia, Reichenbach had a population of 13,000 at the time of Martin's birth. Its modest size did not betray the rich history of Reichenbach nor the periods of economic prominence it had enjoyed in past centuries.

Reichenbach was one of the dozens of towns and the hundreds of villages in Silesia that was founded in the earlier Middle Ages when the Polish Piast dukes of Silesia invited German settlers, farmers, tradesmen, and merchants to their lands.

The site chosen for Reichenbach was located on the eastern slopes of the Sudeten, the almost two-hundred-mile mountain range that separates Silesia from Bohemia. It was a carefully chosen location on level land close to the foothills with the high mountains behind creating a picturesque backdrop, a view that a few hundred years later would enthuse the painters of the Romantic era.

Like all other towns that sprang up during the twelfth and thirteenth centuries throughout the eastern part of Central Europe extending far into the Kingdom of Poland, Reichenbach was planned in the typical rectangular pattern of the Eastern European colonist town. It was similar to the towns of the Canadian and American West, but with a large rectangular market square in the heart of the town and an imposing city hall in the centre of the square. Close to one of its corners rose the massive nave of the Gothic town church of St. George with a tall spire that dominated the view across the roofs of the burgher and merchant houses.

The heavily fortified town was protected by a ring of high walls and watch-towers behind a water-filled moat with drawbridges that led to the four town gates through which trade and commerce flowed, especially on market days. The citizens derived many benefits from Reichenbach's strategic location on one of the important trade routes that followed the eastern slopes of the Sudeten mountains. Another trade route not far to the west of the town crossed through a pass into neighbouring Bohemia.

As was the case with many other towns and cities throughout the country, Reichenbach's fortifications were constantly restored and improved after the frequent sieges and surrenders. When the Piast Duchy of Schweidnitz-Jauer, to which Reichenbach belonged, was ceded by the Polish Piasts to the King of Bohemia in the fourteenth century, there seemed reason for the burghers of Reichenbach to hope for more peaceful times. But on Easter 1428, the armies of the Czech Hussites, driven by religious and national fervour, occupied Reichenbach after the near destruction of the town, extracting a heavy ransom from its citizens.

Recurring wars, sieges, and the Black Plague took a heavy toll of lives and disrupted commercial progress. Still, despite many trials, Reichenbach became a regionally important centre with a famous school and remarkable commercial activity, especially in cloth and linen manufacturing and trade. The burghers were proud of the Gothic Cloth Hall in the centre of the Market Square. It had been patterned after Cracow's famous Cloth Hall. Then the Thirty Years War brought destruction, epidemics, and death to Reichenbach.

Since the sixteenth century when the Kingdom of Bohemia had become part of the Austrian Empire, the burghers of Reichenbach had been subjects of the Habsburgs; and after the end of the Thirty Years War, the town began to enjoy a modest, but steadily growing prosperity. Throughout Silesia, the powerful Catholic Church erected monasteries and churches, often on a grandiose scale; and the merchants of Reichenbach built new warehouses and impressive residences as symbols of their growing wealth.

But hard times again returned to Reichenbach. In the First Silesian War of 1740 - 1742, Frederick II of Prussia invaded Silesia and took most of the province from Empress Maria Theresia. After the comparatively brief Second Silesian war (1744 - 1445), the devastating Third Silesian War (1756 - 1763) left the province and its prosperous cities in economic ruin.

Reichenbach changed hands many times between the Austrian and Prussian armies that bled the town's resources and wealth to its last drop. On August 16, 1762, less than twelve months before the end of the last Silesian War, the town was entered into the records of history when the Prussian General von Bevern led his troops into a victorious battle against Maria Theresia's Marschall Daun on the outskirts of Reichenbach.

Finally, after two decades of war and uncertainty, the peace of 1763 brought the end of destruction and deprivation, but not much more. Silesia's once flourishing centuries-old trade connections with Bohemia, Poland, and the Southeast of Europe were disrupted or severed altogether. The impoverished Kingdom of Prussia needed decades to rehabilitate the province and integrate it politically and economically. But before the efforts of the Prussian kings would show lasting results, another period of European turmoil affected the security of the Continent until it ended with a conference that entered Reichenbach into the annals of European history once again.

Russia and Austria had been at war with the Turkish Empire since 1788. Their successful campaign against Turkey, however, was perceived by other powers as a threat to the balance of power in Europe. Prussia entered into a series of alliances, first with England and Holland and later with Poland and Turkey. In spring of 1790, the Prussian King Frederick Wilhelm II moved his armies along the Silesian border to Bohemia forcing Emperor Leopold II to seek a peaceful solution. Reichenbach was chosen as the site of a conference; and for a few weeks, its burghers enjoyed the illustrious presence of diplomats and generals in their midst. In the elegant ballroom of the townhouse recently erected on the market square by the wealthy merchant Sadebeck, the Convention of Reichenbach was signed by the representatives of Prussia, Austria, Russia, Poland, England, and Holland on July 27, 1790. A few days later, the German poet Goethe arrived in Reichenbach, just in time to witness the parade of the enthusiastic burghers celebrating the successful outcome of the European conference.

Once more, again at the height of a European war, Reichenbach became a centre of historical decision-making. Towards the end of the age of Napoleon, which had brought war, destruction, and political upheaval to nearly the entire Continent, Austria joined the coalition of Prussia and Russia against Napoleon. The alliance created during yet another conference held in Reichenbach on June 27, 1813, was joined by other European states and soon led to the decisive victory over Napoleon's armies at the Battle of Leipzig between October 16 and 19, 1813. After Napoleon's downfall and his permanent exile to the Island of St. Helena, the map of Europe was redrawn during the Congress of Vienna. The Kingdom of Poland disappeared from the map of Europe altogether, while Prussia gained large territories to the north and east. After a reorganization of its administration, Reichenbach became the seat of one of the four district governments of Silesia, but only for five years. After 1820, the town returned to its former status of a smaller centre of local administration, trade, and commerce.

When the name of Reichenbach appeared in German newspapers again, it had become one of the symbols of the painful changes resulting from the beginning industrial age in Prussia. For generations, the villages to the north of Reichenbach had been centres of a cottage industry of weavers who had gradually lost their livelihood as a consequence of the introduction of mechanized mills in Silesia. After years of a precarious existence characterized by lack of work, poor pay, and near starvation, the weavers in the villages near Reichenbach rose in open rebellion that was cruelly extinguished by Prussian troops after much bloodshed.

After months of tension, the weavers' uprising had suddenly erupted when the richest of the mill owners in the village of Peterswaldau turned one of the protesting weavers over to the Prussian police. The man had sung the weavers' hymn "Bloody Judgment Day" at the gates of a mill owner's villa. Living conditions and the sullen mood were not much different in Langenbielau, the other large weavers' village outside Reichenbach, which the Prussian government had actually suspected as the source of a potential rebellion. To pacify the angry population, a public works project had been conducted during the years of 1842 and 1843, a road being built by the starving, unemployed weavers. But, if anything, the harsh working conditions under which this road was built and the unbelievably poor pay only served to increase the anger of the weavers, who named the road built by their labour "The Highway of Hunger," a designation that persisted for generations among the local people.

During successive years, the fate of the Silesian weavers, who now worked in the large mills at starvation wages, only improved marginally—and many were often out of work. Fifty years later, the human tragedy of their existence and of their rebellion was immortalized by the German playwright Gerhart Hauptmann in his play *The Weavers,* a memorial to the victims of progress during the early age of Prussia's industrialization.

Reichenbach had not been immediately and directly affected by the revolt of the weavers. Their cottages and the mills that had been erected during the two decades prior to the rebellion were located in the neighbouring villages. Reichenbach had become a centre of trade and distribution of the products of the cottage weavers and later the mills. While the town had regained a measure of prosperity, poverty persisted in the industrial villages on its outskirts and elsewhere along the Silesian mountains. The depressed living conditions of the population in the weavers' villages stubbornly refused to respond to the economic measures introduced by the Prussian government. Hunger and illness remained an enormous problem for the authorities. The desperate condition of the lower classes was aggravated by recurrent epidemics of typhoid and cholera, by the chronic lack of work, and by recurrent poor harvests. How desperate the situation finally became was demonstrated by the proclamation of "Royal Begging Days," when begging was declared legal on certain days of the week; and charity by those better off was declared a patriotic duty.

Nevertheless, as far as Reichenbach's situation was concerned, a considerable number among its population enjoyed quite a comfortable life. The town had a growing middle class of merchants, tradesmen, and civil servants. In 1859 this community was joined by Moritz Cohn, a Jewish rabbi from Rawitsch, a town located just across the eastern border of Silesia in the Prussian Province of Posen.

For a number of years prior to Moritz Cohn's arrival in Reichenbach, its small Jewish community had participated in the growing prosperity of the town. This was a relatively recent development, though, which reflected the official tolerance of the Prussian government and of the majority of Reichenbach's population.

Towards the end of the nineteenth century, an anonymous chronicler reported the history of the Jewish community of Reichenbach after its "second beginning" in a document, parts of which miraculously survived the destruction of the community during Adolf Hitler's Third Reich. Documents found in the archives of the Church of Jesus Christ of Latter Day Saints in Salt Lake City reflect the changes faced by many other Jewish congregations in Germany in that period.

> As had happened throughout Silesia during the Middle Ages, Reichenbach's Jewish community was wiped out during the later Middle Ages after generations of persecution and finally complete expulsion. But in 1811 the granting of civil rights to Jews in Prussia also included the privilege to take up residence anywhere in the country outside the few hitherto permitted Jewish quarters in certain towns and cities.
>
> In 1815, the first Jewish families arrived in Reichenbach joined by more arrivals during successive years until the group felt resourceful enough to form its own religious institutions, i.e. a house for prayer and religious instruction in 1823. In 1825, a parcel of land for a Jewish cemetery was purchased at the edge of the town where the first internment took place in 1826.

Around 1830, the Jewish community of Reichenbach consisted of nine members and their families, half of them itinerant traders, the other half businessmen established in town. It was the latter group who used the newly gained civil rights to adapt their way of life to that of their gentile environment. Even though the majority of Silesia's approximately 7000 Jews moved out of their ghettos as soon as permitted to do so, nearly all retained their orthodox Jewish faith, customs, and way of life. Others, however, sought to adapt Judaism to the modern era brought about by the emancipation of Jews in Prussia and other parts of Germany after the Napoleonic Wars. A few even converted to Christianity. For them, the granting of civil rights in 1811 would sooner or later open the door to a process of cultural and religious emancipation, in some cases near complete assimilation. This development also gave birth to the Jewish Reform Movement in Prussia aimed at adapting Judaism to modern times and to the new political freedoms and civil rights gained. It was a movement that, for a large segment of Prussia's and Germany's Jewish population, not only changed religious practices but also promoted their assimilation into the way of life of the general population. By its nature, it became a crucial influence in the adult life of Martin Cohn-Nordegg.

When integration and assimilation were only a mere shadow on the horizon, the arrival of the Reform movement became the cause

of discord and severe conflict among Jewish communities in
Prussia, often leading to a temporary or even a permanent split into
separate orthodox and reform congregations. Reichenbach was no
exception, as the anonymous chronicler reported in the annals of its
Jewish congregation:

> The Judaic Reform movement of that time did not by-pass this
> community. Towards the end of the 1840's, the Reform group of our
> congregation had grown to 22 members who insisted on religious ser-
> vices adorned by a choir singing modern hymns and on prayers per-
> formed in the German language by the entire congregation. As the older
> members were not prepared to accept such modern ideas, a separation of
> the conservative members of the congregation from the "free thinkers"
> eventually resulted in 1855. The conservatives remained in possession
> of the prayer house and the property of the congregation and also re-
> tained the cantor Mr. Löbel Naphtali, while the reformers called Mr.
> Heinrich Schwarz from Rawitsch as their new "cultus official."
>
> After a tragic split between the two congregations lasting almost
> four years, the two groups agreed in 1858 to re-unite and keep most of
> the "modern institutions" introduced by the Reformers. In order to heal
> the deep wounds of the past years, though, and to assure a new start free
> of the painful memories of past conflicts, the majority decided to retain
> neither of the two current religious leaders but to seek the services of a
> new person to head the newly re-united congregation.
>
> In 1859, Mr. Moritz Cohn from Rawitsch was called to
> Reichenbach as preacher, teacher of religion, shochet (slaughterer) and
> cantor. During his long years of service, the congregation grew consid-
> erably in numbers, strength and wealth ....

With the arrival of Moritz Cohn, the first section of the annals of
the Jewish Community of Reichenbach ends. What follows are detailed records of births, marriages and deaths—until 1874 a legally
prescribed function of all religious congregations in Prussia—and
short notations of the movements of members to and from
Reichenbach and, again and again, words of praise for the exceptional services rendered to the community by Moritz Cohn

When Moritz Cohn arrived in Reichenbach, the town was on its
way to becoming one of the most pleasant and prosperous towns of
Silesia. With the 1860s, the face of the town began to change considerably. The narrow streets of the medieval centre of town were
being more and more dominated by storefronts, and the large market
square showed more and more facades of rebuilt and expanded
houses. In the early 1870s, the city hall that dated back to the fourteenth century was modernized and vastly expanded in the eclectic
style in fashion during these years. The building received a richly
adorned pseudo-Renaissance facade; only its tall medieval tower re-

mained to dominate the town. The medieval walls with their four town gates became less prominent; many fortifications were torn down; and where the moats and outer fortifications used to tightly gird the town, a pleasant landscaped park with flower beds, fountains, and benches now surrounded the medieval core. Next to this park, Martin Cohn would spend his childhood and adolescent years.

Since 1840, the network of railways rapidly expanded throughout Silesia. It reached Reichenbach in 1855, although not with one of its major lines which probably prevented Reichenbach from becoming one of the important industrial centres of the province. But the town experienced the development of many secondary industries, especially textile and woolen mills, all locally owned, which promoted the growth of an increasingly prosperous class of factory owners, merchants and tradesmen, whose comfortable residences ringed the older part of town.

High expectations, many of them of ambiguous nature, awaited Moritz Cohn in Reichenbach. The progressive members of the congregation had readily seen in the rabbi from Rawitsch, a forward-looking man who had freed himself from the strictures of orthodox Judaism. Moritz Cohn, in turn, had quickly recognized the first task awaiting him, the crucial importance of healing the wounds caused by the conflict between the reformed and orthodox members of his future congregation. That he possessed a high degree of tact, skill, dedication, and knowledge necessary to successfully achieve his first goal, is evident in the new "Charter of the Synagogue," which, after much thought and compromise, was proclaimed in May 1863, four years after Moritz Cohn was chosen as the congregation's rabbi.

The charter is a remarkable document of tolerance and reconciliation. While truly reflecting the character of a reformed congregation, it also preserves some of the rites and customs treasured by the members of its orthodox minority. In its essence, though, the charter is a document of modern times, when the majority of Jews saw their future as one of assimilation and integration into the larger German society. New terminology permeates the charter from the first to its last page:

Adapting designations in use by Christian denominations in Germany, the charter refers to the "divine service" of the Sabbath and on the Jewish holy days; to the "consecration" or "confirmation" of newborns; to the "house of prayer" instead of the "synagogue." Men, women, and children are no longer seated separately from each other; and, except under certain circumstances, the members of the congregation are no longer required to cover their head with a yarmulke (a hat or a prayer shawl). The congregation also sing their "hymns" in the German language.

This was merely the beginning. As later records of the congregation show, "Israelite" very often replaces "Jewish" or "Hebrew"; the synagogue becomes "the Israelitic House of Prayer"; the rabbi, the "preacher" or the "cultus official"; the Bar Mitzvah is now called the "confirmation." And in the records of birth, marriage, and death, only in the cases of older deceased members is the Hebrew name entered next to the legal German name that was also commonly used in everyday life.

However, in some vital aspects, the old rites remain in force and are prominently honoured: members may say the Kaddish standing next to the pulpit. While participating in the Mitzwoth (reciting of the commandments), yarmulkes or hats must still be worn. And burial services are performed in an unchanged manner according to the "orthodox rites," although they may be followed by a sermon in German.

Tactfully, the feelings of the orthodox members are respected, but these members are also asked to compromise by restricting their "Jewishness" to the privacy of the synagogue and their home.

For the reformed members, it was of utmost importance to extinguish in the eyes of the gentile citizens the stereotype of the orthodox Jew to which belonged white silk stockings and black velvet slippers worn on the way to the synagogue. It was now prescribed that members would arrive in the synagogue in shoes or boots, which, one would assume, could then be exchanged for velvet slippers, if so desired by the individual.

The synagogue charter ends with a conciliatory statement prepared by Moritz Cohn:

> The Charter's purpose is not to reform Judaism, it is not something to be superimposed on the ancient, revered ways of our religion, but it is an institution which has its origin in this religion.... I fervently hope that this new institution will not offend in any way any pious member of our congregation.

Reichenbach in Silesia, the 18th of May 1863

Moritz Cohn
Israelite Preacher.

Were it not for the prominent position of his father and the survival of some of the records of the Jewish congregation of Reichenbach, we would know nothing about the early years of Martin Cohn other than the date and place of his birth. These were stated in several documents of a much later date—his Canadian passport from 1935 or the certificate of his second marriage in 1924 where the occupation of Martin's father is stated as "government official." While this designation was not incorrect, as all ministers, priests and rabbis were paid by the state and were thus considered civil servants, it reflected Martin's discreet attitude towards his origin and the Jewish faith in which he was brought up. And while the spotty records of the Reichenbach synagogue give us some information about its preacher Moritz Cohn and his wife Auguste, the pages with the entries about the births of Martin, his brother Theodor and his sister Malwine, crucial to the story of Martin's childhood, have been lost in the wake of the Hitler years and World War II. Only a few papers and documents from a much later period reveal that Martin was not an only child.

Thus, we will never know whether the Moritz Cohn mentioned in an unrelated record found in the Archives of the Church of Jesus Christ of Latter-Day Saints in Salt Lake City as born on May 11, 1821, in the Silesian town of Oppeln refers to Martin's father. Neither can we ascertain whether Moritz Cohn arrived in Reichenbach as a married man or whether he married his wife some time after that date. Auguste Cohn's maiden name was Teplitz, a Jewish name sometimes found in Silesia but very common in neighbouring Bohemia. It is very rare in the regions farther east, such as the area where Moritz Cohn lived prior to coming to Reichenbach in 1859. We may assume, therefore, that Martin's parents did not get married before the early 1860s.

Amongst Martin Nordegg's surviving papers and writings, there are only two brief references to his sister. The existence of his brother Theodor became known to the author only through a document from 1918 concerning Martin's first wife. Theodor was the oldest child of Moritz Cohn's family. His exact year of birth is not known. When Malwine was born in 1875, Martin was already attending elementary school.

Despite the dearth of information, it is possible with the help of the records of the Jewish congregation of Reichenbach and the author's personal knowledge of the town to create an image of the childhood years of Martin Nordegg.

As a person of Jewish descent, Martin was fortunate to be born in an era that was decidedly more favourable to Jewish persons in Germany than ever before.

When Martin was born on the July 18, 1868, as a subject of the King of Prussia, the new German Empire (the creation of Chancellor Bismarck) was already looming on the horizon. It would soon become a unified nation which, however, excluded millions of Germans remaining under the rule of Franz Joseph, Emperor of

Austria. In order to assure the hegemony of Prussia in a unified Germany, the Prussian Chancellor Prince von Bismarck had with great skill and cunning forced the Austrian Empire out of the German Federation. This process took years and included the war of 1866 with its decisive battle of Königgraetz and other military engagements, some not very far from Reichenbach just across the border in Bohemia.

Even though enjoying civil rights equal to those of all other subjects of the King of Prussia, citizens of Jewish faith were still confronted with the overt or covert symptoms of anti-Semitism. For many, the answer to this problem was rapid and complete assimilation, especially on the cultural level. This trend is easily identified in the records of the Jewish congregation of Reichenbach. Over the years, the first names chosen for newborns take on a different ring, becoming indistinguishable from and identical to those found in the birth registers of the Christian churches. Among the children born after the 1860s in the Jewish community of Reichenbach, first names of clearly Christian or Germanic origin such as Amalie and Georg, Friederike and Felix, Elisa and Oskar, Mathilde and Matthäus, Hedwig and Eduard, even Regina and Siegberth prevail. The names of the fathers and mothers–Jacob and Rebekka, Salomon and Rachel, Saul and Esther, Heiman and Ruth, Loebel and Sarah– spring from their Jewish heritage, dating back to Biblical times. Parallel to the new custom of giving Jewish children first names popular among the conservative gentile middle class, a considerable number of German Jews also adopted Christian or Germanic sounding surnames. In this context, it is not without significance, that Moritz Cohn, the Israelite preacher, chose a very Christian name for Martin and the non-Jewish names of Theodor and Malwine for Martin's brother and sister. In the birth records of the synagogue, however, next to the legal first name, a Hebrew name was always entered. A document from 1940 reveals that for Martin, his father's name Moritz was chosen as his Hebrew first name.

The Hachamowicz brothers, distant relatives of Moritz Cohn, chose the very German name of Brandt for their families after moving from Warsaw to Berlin. And, at the age of 41, Martin Cohn would adopt the very rare but striking surname of Nordegg!

Adopting German first and last names was only one of the phenomena in the complex process of assimilation that was pursued by more and more Jewish families during the nineteenth century. While the desire to escape from discrimination and confrontation with anti-Semitic attitudes was one factor, another was the steady advance and rise of the Jewish middle class, which was accompanied by the adoption of German culture. This was based on the deep admiration of everything German, especially Germany's rapid rise in industrial and commercial advancement and, above all, the veneration of German literature, art, and science. As Jewish citizens realized they were contributing to the progress and blossoming of Germany, in many aspects far greater than what they represented in numbers, an increasing number of Jewish families especially in the larger cities, felt a near complete sense of identity as citizens of the German Empire.

Nevertheless, throughout the nineteenth and more so during the twentieth century, Germany's Jews remained deeply divided as to the rightfulness and the benefits of total assimilation and especially of the not uncommon conversion to the Christian faith. Orthodox and even conservative Jews in Germany and other parts of Europe, angrily condemned assimilation as a means of gaining material and political advantages.

In one of his novels, the Austrian writer Jakob Wassermann commented that even if the Jew pushes his assimilation into the German culture to the point of denial and absolute humiliation, he is liable to be rejected by his German environment to the same degree as the Jew who carries his Jewishness to the extreme of forced self-assertiveness.

The Russian scientist Daniel Abramovich Chwolson, who had converted from Judaism to the Greek Orthodox faith in the later nineteenth century, dryly admitted that "I accepted baptism entirely out of conviction—the conviction that it is better to be a professor in the Imperial Academy in St. Petersburg than a teacher in a cheder in Vilna."

And, ambivalent about his Jewish heritage, the German poet Heinrich Heine, who tended to look down on the Orthodox Jews while at the same time ridiculing those who strove for complete assimilation, called their baptismal certificate "the passport to European civilization."

Modern German history is full of evidence of the benefits of the unique melding of German and Jewish culture, a cross-fertilization that produced a never again experienced blossoming of the arts, literature, philosophy, and sciences in the Germany of the nineteenth century and the early decades of the twentieth century.

But anti-Semitism never ceased to affect the lives of Germany's Jews. In 1912, Walter Rathenau, the renowned German industrialist and, until his assassination in 1922, foreign minister of the first German Republic, sadly confessed that

> For every German Jew, there comes in his youth that painful moment which he will never forget for the rest of his life: when, for the first time he is fully conscious of the irreversible fact that he entered

this world as a second class citizen, a position from which neither excellence nor merit will ever liberate him.

During World War I, when German Jews served with great enthusiasm and loyalty in the German armies, sacrificing their lives in numbers far exceeding their representation among Germany's total population, the German High Command ordered a census of Jews in active military service. This act proved to most Jews that the gentile population would never cease to consider them as outsiders rather than fully accepted German citizens. It remained for Adolf Hitler to demonstrate through book burnings and legislation that stripped Jews of all their civil rights that there was no place for Jews in Germany, indeed nowhere in Europe wherever the Third Reich extended its power. The dreams and hopes of several generations of Jews died forever in Hitler's extermination camps.

What writers, scientists, and politicians such as Wassermann, Heine, Chwolson, Rathenau and many others put in poignant words must not be forgotten when one attempts to comprehend the personality of Martin Cohn-Nordegg and to understand the often unusual and surprising decisions he made during his adult life while gradually evolving into the unique identity of Martin Nordegg.

But first came the years of an innocent childhood and carefree adolescence in the little town of Reichenbach, a microcosm of the change and progress of Jewish life in Germany. Gone were the itinerant traders of earlier years among the members of the congregation who, by the time of Martin's childhood, all belonged to the middle class. As did the gentile bourgeois class. The Jewish middle class instilled in their offspring, especially their male children, a deep respect for "Kultur und Bildung," which could best be defined as a thorough grounding in the humanities including classical and modern history, literature and languages, and familiarity with music and the fine arts. Young Martin was no exception. At Easter 1874, as the first step leading to the education in the humanities, the not quite six-year-old Martin started his schooling at the Lutheran elementary school of Reichenbach. Catholic schools were closed to children of Jewish faith, and the Jewish community of the town was too small to maintain its own school except for the religious instruction provided by Martin's father at the synagogue.

The congregation had grown sufficiently in numbers and in wealth to decide on the building of a new synagogue in the early 1870s. As a map of the 1880s shows, the new synagogue on the main street leading from the railway station to the centre of Reichenbach occupied a prominent location at the edge of the old town alongside the park created some decades earlier on the site of the old fortifications. Surrounded by trees and lawns, the richly adorned building reflected the new wealth and the pride of Reichenbach's Jewish congregation. It was a three-story building, which also accommodated on its main floor spacious, comfortable living quarters for Moritz Cohn and his family. With great pride, the annals of the congregation record the consecration of the new synagogue in the year 1875 on the eve of the Jewish holiday of Shawet (Pentecost).

At that time, the Jewish community consisted of only 92 persons residing in Reichenbach plus 10 members from surrounding villages. The stately building of the new synagogue was a remarkable manifestation of the prosperity of this tiny Jewish community and the dedication of its members, perhaps not more than 25 families.

Not a single word about his childhood and adolescence can be found in Martin's memoirs or in the correspondence of his later life. That Martin grew up in a comfortable, harmonious home raised by concerned, loving parents who considered themselves part of the middle class and its cultural aspirations appears certain beyond any doubt. For a child of his background, it was the expected norm to attend a secondary school. In terms of his later goals and achievements, Martin was fortunate to live in a community where the existing "Gymnasium," a high school based strictly on the humanities, had recently been modified into a "Realgymnasium," a new type of secondary school which included in its curriculum an emphasis on the growing importance of the sciences and industry in the new German Empire created by Bismarck in 1871. While the traditional gymnasium focused primarily on the classics, leading its students to full mastery of Greek and Latin as well as literature, the Realgymnasium no longer offered instruction in Greek while, in view of its importance for future studies in medicine, jurisprudence and some of the sciences, Latin was retained as a primary subject. In contrast to the traditional Gymnasium, the scientific subjects of physics, chemistry and biology as well as mathematics and geography were given equal ranking with Latin, literature, French and English.

For nine years, Martin would walk to the modern, well-equipped building of the Reichenbach Realgymnasium located alongside the town park surrounding the medieval core of Reichenbach, diagonally across the old town from his parents' home in the synagogue. Martin had the choice between reaching the Realgymnasium via the main shopping street of Reichenbach, which started at the door of his parents' home and then crossing the always busy Market Square; or he could take the pleasant, but longer walk through the park in either one of two semi-circles around the old town, between flower beds, monuments and fountains scattered throughout the park. He would pass on his way the imposing buildings of his former elementary school; the Lutheran Church built in the classic style by Langhans (the famous architect of Berlin's Brandenburg Gate); and the red brick post office with its pseudo-Gothic gables and doorways.

No records of Martin's school years have survived. He must have received a well-rounded education at the Realgymnasium, supplemented by the interests and knowledge of his devoted parents. Considering the path Martin followed so successfully in his adult life, it also seems certain that he was a conscientious, ambitious, probably superior student.

In order to be admitted to the Technical Institute in Berlin (later the Technical University), Martin had to pass the "Abitur"—senior matriculation—with above-average marks. That his high school education had given him the best of both worlds, the traditional as well as the modern advanced education, would be demonstrated again and again in Martin's later life by his easy grasp of scientific matters, even those entirely new to him; by his love to quote passages from classic Latin literature and philosophy readily and accurately even in his advanced age; by his love of the arts and his eagerness to learn about all parts of the world which he would explore in his extended travels throughout his life.

If the foregoing creates a fairly vivid picture of his daily life in Reichenbach, we know very little about the nature and the temperament of young Martin. But, again judging by the man he became, we can assume that Martin was a bright, intelligent, disciplined youngster, filled with the desire to succeed and to fulfill the expectations of his parents and make them proud of their son, always reaching for perfection in the tasks that he chose or that were assigned. We could also assume that he would follow his optimistic nature in the belief that success was attainable through imagination, dedication, persistence, and hard work in a world that was not filled with enemies and adversaries, but with agreeable, friendly human beings who would not disappoint a person as long as he possessed integrity and a positive attitude towards life and people.

With limited information and some speculation, it is possible, to create a fairly vivid image of Martin's young years in Reichenbach, but we know nothing of significance about Theodor and Malwine, the other two children of Moritz and Auguste Cohn. No birth records have survived in the annals of the Reichenbach congregation from the years 1855 to 1875, the period where Theodor and Malwine must have been born.

But there are a few entries about Martin's parents, happy as well as sad ones. The annals note that "... in the year 1884, with the participation of the entire congregation, Mr. Moritz Cohn's 25th anniversary as Israelite preacher was celebrated as a festive, dignified event."

In April 1887, Martin graduated from high school, a proud day for the Moritz Cohn family. Shortly after, Martin left Reichenbach. Returning periodically to visit his parents, he must have been concerned about their well-being. Soon, Martin experienced the first personal losses in his young life.

"In September 1890," the synagogue annals record, "Mr. Moritz Cohn resigns from his duties as Israelite preacher due to failing health. The congregation rewarded his faithful, dedicated services of so many years with an annual pension of 900 Marks."

One month later, "Mrs. Auguste Cohn, born Clara Gittel daughter of Meyer, wife of the preacher emeritus Mr. Moritz Cohn, suddenly passed away as the result of a heart seizure on October 16th, 1890."

And six weeks later, "... on December 1st, 1890, Mr. Moritz Cohn, preacher emeritus, moves to Berlin."

Moritz Cohn likely accepted his son's suggestion to live with him in Berlin. Only a few months remained for Martin to take care of his ailing father. On February 25, 1891, Moritz Cohn died of "a weak heart."

"In deepest mourning," his congregation in Reichenbach remembered its former preacher of many years in obituaries published in Berlin and in Breslau, the capital of the Province of Silesia:

> In order to honour his memory, the Board of the Synagogue decided to publish obituaries honouring the late Mr. Moritz Cohn in the *Berliner Zeitung*, the *Breslauer Zeitung* and the *Schlesische Zeitung*. It was further decided that his name would be entered into the memorial book of the congregation and that together with other deceased prominent members of the congregation, he would be regularly remembered during certain rites for deceased.

Martin's mother was only 61 years at the time of her death, while his father probably did not reach the age of 75. The loss of both parents within the brief span of four months must have been a traumatic experience for Martin, who was only 22 years of age at that time. It was the first of several personal tragedies in his otherwise so successful life.

II

FROM REICHENBACH TO BERLIN AND LONDON (1888 - 1906)

Among the people who still remember Martin Nordegg, one will look in vain for a single person who knows anything about Martin's early years in Germany, except what Martin had revealed in his memoirs of 1906-1924.

Martin will certainly have shared the story of his entire life with his second wife Sonia to whom he was so deeply devoted. But just as Martin was always reserved and tight-lipped about his background—not even his best friends dared to push him with questions in this regard—so was his beloved wife Sonia. Ready to share her reminiscences of her late husband's "public" life, especially his accomplishments in the creation and subsequent growth of the town and mine of Nordegg, Sonia was always on guard, refusing to answer any questions that might throw some light not only on events dating back to her husband's younger years but also on any speculation of what might have predestined him to become the explorer and entrepreneur whose life she had shared for more than 30 years.

In April 1963, Donald Kidd, cousin of Martin's close friend Stuart Kidd, wrote to his nephew James Kidd in Calgary about his visit to Sonia Nordegg in New York in November 1962. Knowing that Donald Kidd was collecting reminiscences about the town of Nordegg and its people, Sonia had asked Donald and his wife Mary to stop at her apartment on Central Park West in New York on their way from Washington to Ottawa.

On April 3, 1963, Donald Kidd wrote about Sonia:

> We found her very charming and intelligent. I hope to visit her again in New York later this spring and ask her some questions about Mr. Nordegg's early life.... I even have a guess how he obtained his name "Nordegg."... Mrs. Nordegg told us nothing about his early life and I felt that I should not ask her, yet....

Just as Martin's choice of the name "Nordegg" remains shrouded in mystery, the exact sequence of events in Martin Nordegg's life following his departure from Reichenbach until his decision to leave for Canada must include a degree of speculation. With the help of history and the few personal documents, however, we can re-create the milestones of these years, which included Martin's military service and further education; his absence from

Germany lasting several years; his first marriage and the birth of his only child, Marcelle; and the progress of his career during his years in Berlin until fate took him to Canada in 1906.

We must accept that the precise dating of all events in Martin's earlier life is not always possible. But for these years, it is feasible to create an image of Martin by looking at lives typical for the young men of Prussian middle class who had completed their high school education during the later part of the nineteenth century.

All young men in Prussia and throughout Germany were subject to compulsory military service. Although Germany had been unified as the German Empire by Bismarck in 1871, the traditions of the former armies of Prussia, Bavaria, Saxony, Wuerttemberg, and the other duchies and principalities were still very much alive. While soldiers and officers gave their oath to the German Emperor, they would do their duty in a military unit of that part of the German Empire where they were born or lived—in Martin's case, Prussia.

Young men of the working class were drafted immediately following the completion of their apprenticeship. After two years of military service, they were discharged to return to civilian life as labourers, skilled workers, tradesmen or lower civil servants, unless they volunteered for careers as non-commissioned officers for the duration of another twelve years. Almost inevitably, they would then turn into the proverbial drill sergeant so much hated by the young recruits and ridiculed by the general population. Striving to be treated as His Majesty's loyal soldier but lacking the accouterments, education, rank and bearing of an officer, they were invariably perceived as coarse, poorly educated and narrow-minded. In popular lingo, they were referred to as "Zwoelfender"; i.e., the stag with twelve antlers.

Everywhere in Germany, the military had achieved a pervasive presence in the lives of the country's communities and their citizens. In the perception of those who saw Germany's destiny fulfilled in the Empire of Wilhelm II, the officers corps ranked at the top of society immediately below or even equal to the old aristocracy, the exclusive source of Prussian generals and officers of higher rank. They were in charge of the traditional regiments with their long history of bloody and glorious victories, which are commemorated in the annals of Prussia's history. Much below their status ranked the line regiments, which offered an opportunity for the sons of the bourgeoisie to enter a military career leading to the rank of an officer.

Sons of the middle class with a completed secondary education enjoyed a privilege not granted to the working class. They were permitted to postpone their compulsory military service for a few years in order to further their education.

Looking at the known dates in his early life, we can assume that Martin also elected this privilege to start his education prior to serving his compulsory military service. Significantly, his post-secondary education, of which he was inordinately proud, was practically the only matter relating to his origin to which Martin ever referred later in his life. As his career demonstrated again and again, his education in engineering must indeed have been all-encompassing, ranging from practical to technical to scientific competence.

At this time, pure sciences and applied sciences had not yet attained the rank of the humanities for which universities were exclusively reserved. It is possible that prior to entering one of Germany's most prestigious technical institutes in Berlin, Martin first attended the Staatliche Hoehere Technische Lehranstalt (Higher Technical State School) in the Silesian capital of Breslau, a well-renowned educational source for those aspiring a career in engineering. Martin's ready grasp of technical matters throughout his later life appears to validate the quality of his early education as an engineer on a more practical, applied level. Developing perfect skills in drafting was one part of his training in Breslau that Martin put to good use on many occasions. We look with admiration at the precise drawing of the plan of the town of Nordegg, which Martin completed in 1911.

Where and when did Martin absolve his compulsory military service? We only know the year his military life came to an abrupt end. Reichenbach had a garrison, but it was not customary that young men fulfilled their military service in the same location where their family was living. It is likely that Martin was drafted into a line regiment somewhere in Silesia.

The number of towns in Silesia and the other provinces of Prussia that served as garrisons for smaller units or sometimes for more than one entire regiment was astonishing. Generally avoided as military garrisons were industrial towns, no doubt because of the often overt antipathy of their working class populations for King and Emperor and the military. This explains the lack of a garrison at the nearby city of Waldenburg, the centre of the Lower Silesian industrial coal basin with its large proletarian population numbering close to 100,000.

Towns that prospered because of the presence of light industry, trade, commerce and administration were favoured as locations for military units. A travel through Silesia's cities and towns demonstrated the ubiquitous presence of large military barracks, nearly always constructed in red brick, dating from the late 1870s to the turn of the century. They were the undeniable reflection of the rapid ascendancy of the army and of rapid growth of Germany's military might.

Economically and socially, the presence of a regiment or even a smaller army unit was often the life blood especially of smaller towns. The young soldiers spent their pay in the local inns on Sundays, the non-commissioned officers moved their families to the town, and the merchants delivered food staples and other goods to the barracks. The officers were considered the crème of the town's upper class; with their pride in the military readily shown, their self-assurance and their often loud joviality, they did, at least in the eyes of the local bourgeoisie, bring a little flair of the elegant world to the remote little towns. And more than one mother would hope for a marriage of her daughter to one of these dashing young officers.

The ravages of World War II destroyed almost all the regimental records from the years when Martin was serving in one of Prussia's regiments. But considering his excellent horsemanship so ably demonstrated during his years in the Canadian West, it appears certain that he had been assigned to a regiment of the Prussian Cavalry. Looking at the appearance and bearing of the older Martin Nordegg shown in numerous pictures from his years in Western Canada, it might have even been possible that for a short while Martin could have considered entering the officer corps and becoming a professional soldier.

This would not have been unusual, even for a man of Jewish descent. There were no barriers, as long as a man such as Martin Cohn would not aspire to service in one of the traditional regiments. For Martin Cohn, his Jewishness had, as for many other emancipated Jews in the Germany of that time, become an accident of birth. Jewish origin had evolved into the mere belonging to a particular religious faith of a loyal citizen of the German Empire. So Martin Cohn would not have been unique in his choice of a military career. Indeed, during World War I, the number of Jewish officers killed, wounded or surviving by far exceeded their presence among the total population of Germany.

As much as he loved his native country, when Martin arrived in North America, he had broken with those characteristics of Germany that he found burdensome, distasteful and oppressive. But what he did not relinquish was his military bearing or his love for the semi-military tunics that he preferred to wear even among cowboys, Indians, miners and engineers while exploring the wilderness of the eastern slopes of the Alberta Rocky Mountains or when travelling by canoe from Northern Ontario to the remote Hudson Bay or even while taking holidays in Banff. An outstanding example is the picture of Martin Nordegg taken in Banff in the year 1912 with the Cascade Mountain in the background. Sitting proudly astride a beautiful horse, Martin exhibits the classical pose of the military officer, erect, but natural in his posture, his right hand holding the reins lightly but firmly, the left hand placed at his hip, his eyes fixed at some imaginary point in the distance. How many men would have wished to be seen on horseback in such a perfect posture, how few would accomplish this as well and as naturally as Martin Nordegg!

The impression is enhanced by the tightly cut semi-military tunic, a slight modification of which would have turned Martin Nordegg into the perfect representative of the Prussian officer corps, except for the Stetson, which was closely modeled after the Stetson hats recently introduced to the Royal Canadian Mounted Police. The hat was a symbol of his beloved Canada but still a near-military way of Martin's preferred way to dress long after he left the Prussian army.

Whether he was fulfilling his compulsory military service or whether he had indeed become a professional officer, Martin Cohn's military career came to an abrupt end in 1894. He was honourably discharged at the age of twenty-six after suffering a compound fracture of his right arm, which made him unfit for further service. Perhaps Martin did not regret this turn of events. It is hard to imagine that he would miss military life, not because of its discipline but because of the boredom of its etiquette and its lack of challenge.

The unexpected termination of his military life permitted Martin to return to Gewerbe Institut in Berlin, where he developed his second competence through studies in photochemistry. The Gewerbe Institut was recognized as the leading educational and research facility in Germany. It was soon to be elevated to the status of "Technische Hochschule," ranking on an equal, though less prestigious level with universities teaching the humanities. After World War II, it became the Technische Universität Berlin, the foremost technical university in all of Germany.

Fate had its hand in Martin's choice of photochemistry. Studying under the famous Professor Hermann Wilhelm Vogel, inventor of revolutionary photochemical processes, would lead Martin to another outstanding Berlin citizen who would be instrumental in his travel to Canada and his career in the New World.

Born in the year 1834 in the rather obscure, small country town of Dobrilugk east of Berlin, Hermann Vogel was appointed a full professor at the Gewerbe Institut in 1879 after discovering a process of sensitizing photographic layers through certain stains and colours. This was the beginning of the famous Vogel laboratory, where more and more advanced methods of processing black and white photography and of printing colour plates were continually explored and developed.

Students and collaborators flocked to Hermann Vogel's laboratory to become famous photographers and scientists, among them the outstanding pioneer of modern American photography Alfred Stieglitz (1864-1946), who worked with Professor Vogel for several years before returning to the United States in 1890. For their motifs and their moods, made possible through the technical methods acquired under Professor Vogel, Alfred Stieglitz's photographs soon won prizes throughout the world. For decades he was celebrated as the foremost photographic artist and theoretician in the United States.

One of the far-reaching accomplishments of Professor Vogel was the "three-colour printing process," a method of superimposing the three basic colours upon each other with the result of obtaining near natural colours, which Martin Nordegg describes in the first chapter of his Canadian memoirs:

> … our great German poet Goethe was also a great scientist. He stated that there are three primary colours, yellow, red and blue, and their mixtures give all other colours. Professor Vogel succeeded in separating the natural colours by light-filters into these primary colours and reproducing them on specially sensitized photographic plates in black and white. From these negatives we make printing plates and print them in yellow, red and blue ink on paper, one on top of the other, and the result obtained is a reproduction in natural colours.[*]

The colour printing process became immediately popular among the printing and publishing industry, especially for the fine arts volumes of photographs of architecture and the works of famous painters, which were much in demand by the prosperous bourgeoisie.

This was a period of expansion of public museums and private art galleries when it was *de rigeur* for the upper classes to be seen during the openings of exhibitions of current art. Among the

---

[*] This biography contains an unusually large number of quotations from personal letters, many of which were written in haste or as means of informal communications. Spelling, casual expressions, syntax, and punctuation often do not correspond to standard English.

In order to preserve authenticity and avoid the too frequent presence of [SIC] in the narrative, it was decided to reproduce all quotations including those from Martin Nordegg's Memoirs as they appear in the original. Only in quotations from public, official, and press sources, are incorrect data, spellings, etc. identified.

painters of realism prominent at that time, no artist was more vener-
ated and honoured than the Berlin painter Adolph von Menzel, the
chronicler of Prussian history from Frederick II (the Great) of
Prussia to Emperor Wilhelm II. Through his art, Menzel also became the chronicler of the young German Empire. It was he who
captured and celebrated the vitality of the country's rapidly expanding industry for the first time. Scenes such as the fiery interior of
steel plants had never been the subject chosen by other painters.

It was said that without Professor Vogel's process of colour
printing, Adolph von Menzel would have never achieved such incredible popularity among the upper and middle class. In purchasing
the large, expensive picture volumes of Menzel's oeuvre, the aristocracy and bourgeoisie (especially in Prussia) celebrated their own
achievements and their pride in the history of Prussia. This was the
birth of what later was called the coffee table book. Soon, Vogel's
colour printing process began its victorious march through Europe
and North America. Martin Cohn took part in this development as
student and collaborator of Professor Vogel and, a short time later,
as employee of one of Berlin's outstanding entrepreneurs, Georg
Büxenstein.

One of the foremost printing plants in Berlin and, indeed, in
Germany was the firm of Wilhelm Büxenstein. His son Georg
Büxenstein, third in the family's line of printers, was its current
owner and Martin's employer. A dynamic entrepreneur and businessman, Georg Büxenstein went into partnership with Erich Vogel,
son of Martin's teacher, Professor Hermann Vogel. The two men
founded a new firm, the Georg Büxenstein & Company
Photochemigraphical Institute, where Erich Vogel developed the
colour printing process invented by his father to the point of commercial viability. The Photochemigraphical Institute quickly became
Germany's most successful producer of advertisements in colour, of
posters, and particularly of volumes of fine art presenting the paintings of such masters as Menzel, Liebermann, and Leistikow to a
receptive public.

Georg Büxenstein was born in Berlin on December 13, 1857, in
the oldest part of town in the Niederwallstrasse in the house where
his great-grandfather had established a small printing business after
moving to Berlin from the Black Forest in 1790. After graduating
from the best high school of Berlin, the Französische Gymnasium,
young Georg was not permitted to follow his dream of studying
natural sciences. Instead, following his father's plans, he started as
an apprentice in his father's printing shop where he obtained his
journeyman papers.

In order to broaden his son's horizon, old Mr. Büxenstein arranged a six-month stay in Switzerland before Georg entered the
obligatory military service. Discharged from the Silesian Curassier
Regiment with the rank of captain, Georg found his father critically
ill; and at the young age of 20, he had to assume full responsibility
for the family business. He still passed his examinations as master
printer before marrying (at age 21) the young daughter of a well-respected businessman from the suburb of Charlottenburg.

What followed was the rapid rise of Georg Büxenstein and his
printing business to the foremost establishment in Germany.
Introducing ever new printing techniques, especially in colour processes pioneered by Hermann Vogel, Georg Büxenstein also proved
venturesome in business affairs. When August Scherl (later the
newspaper king) decided to start a mass-circulation paper (the
Lokalanzeiger) along North American lines, Georg Büxenstein became his not always happy partner. Büxenstein also printed the
long-established, conservative *Kreuzzeitung* and received the privilege to print all legislation proclaimed by the Reichstag and the Parliament of Prussia.

Büxenstein's contribution to the dissemination of the fine arts
was outstanding. With his modern methods of colour printing, he
introduced old masters and modern painters to a wider public. A
lavish volume of *The Life of Jesus* earned him a private audience
with Pope Leo XIII and the Order of Pius. This volume was followed by numerous others, among them *Walhall* covering the oeuvre of Adolph Menzel and the old masters represented in the new
Kaiser Friedrich Museum. None of these publications were cheap,
but they found widest circulation throughout Germany. Georg
Büxenstein was celebrated as the senior master of German printing.

His economic success allowed Georg Büxenstein to follow numerous interests, many of them focused on sports. He brought the
first rowboat built for racing from England to Germany and founded
the Berlin Rowing Club in 1880. Later, Büxenstein started a stud
farm on an old estate he bought near Berlin; one of his most famous
horses, "Polly"—also the name of his own yacht—was purchased
by Czar Nikolaus of Russia for breeding purposes. A passionate
hunter as well, Büxenstein decided to name his elegant country
house, which had replaced the old manor house at Alt-Goln, after
St. Hubert, the patron saint of hunters.

Always fascinated by the progress of modern technology,
Büxenstein readily fell in love with the automobile. Too old to participate in car races himself, he nevertheless organized prestigious
long-distance rallies and encouraged the Emperor to introduce the
automobile into the German army. He became one of the co-

founders of the Imperial German Automobile Club and during World War I was chief of staff of the German Voluntary Automobile Corps stationed in France. And at a time when the potential for future air travel was still unrecognized, Georg Büxenstein was one of the first to travel in a semi-solid dirigible across Berlin and its environs.

Büxenstein's fascination with sports, especially water sports, horse racing and automobile sport, earned him the close contact with Emperor Wilhelm II, who shared identical interests. Even though Büxenstein was not the sycophant so typical and notorious for the Imperial Court and the Emperor's entourage and even though he did not hesitate to contradict the Emperor (something few people dared to do), the Emperor remained well-disposed towards Büxenstein at all times. It became known that the Emperor had advised the Court Marshall that "Büxe can come and see me any time," and that he should be spared the usual strict formalities preceding any audience with His Majesty.

Büxenstein was not afraid to confront the Emperor with issues such as the very unpopular censorship quite widely practiced. He succeeded in interpreting to the Emperor the negative effects of censorship, especially of press articles and political cartoons critical of His Majesty. After the elevation of the immensely rich Silesian mining magnate Fritz Friedländer-Fuld to noble rank, it is not certain whether Georg Büxenstein told His Majesty directly or via some friends that he would definitely decline such an honour for himself as "far too expensive for what it would be worth to him." But it indicates that Büxenstein was not only a successful entrepreneur but possessed a good measure of self-respect and self-assurance as well as the respect of those who counted by not relying on additional recognition by His Majesty.

In 1893, Georg Büxenstein erected a large new building with an elegant facade adorning the southern end of the Friedrichstrasse, one of Berlin's most popular shopping streets. In business circles, it soon became known as "Büxenstein's printing palace." From this prestigious address its owner sent representatives to foreign countries to introduce and market his new printing techniques. Büxenstein was also active in the "Tarifgemeinschaft des deutschen Buchdrucks" [Tariff Association of the German Printing Trade]. As its president since 1911, Büxenstein ardently promoted humane working conditions and wages. Calling for "social peace," he was at times accused by his colleagues as being in sympathy with the Social Democrats.

Büxenstein was also the co-founder of the Berliner Regatta Verein, the Berlin Regatta Association, and the German Rowing

Association; but his greatest contribution remained his promotion and support of the Berlin Club and its annual Regatta on the Havel River in the suburb of Grünau where the Büxenstein Allee still carries his name. Lovingly referred to as "the autocrat" for his determined leadership, Büxenstein also skillfully enlisted the support of Emperor Wilhelm, an enthusiast of rowing and sailing and everything maritime. Always competitive with England, the Emperor created the "Kieler Woche," the annual regatta modeled after the famous regatta at Cowes on the Isle of Wight, which he regularly attended. It was not surprising that Emperor Wilhelm lent his benevolence to Georg Büxenstein and his Berlin Regatta Association. He donated two Imperial trophies and never failed to attend the annual regatta in Grünau. The Imperial presence, which lent a special aura to the regatta, elevated this day from a sports meet to a social rendezvous of Berlin's upper class. The papers regularly reported the event in word and pictures. A photograph from 1910 shows the Emperor and the Empress on board the Imperial yacht with Georg Büxenstein at their side. It is worth quoting parts of an earlier laudatio on Georg Büxenstein republished in 1980 on the occasion of the 100th anniversary of the Berlin Rowing Club. It confirms that Martin's admiration for Georg Büxenstein, frequently expressed in his memoirs, was based on sound judgment of character.

> ... his personality surpassed everyone. Nobody could match his knowledge and competence in matters of sport. His talent for organization tolerated neither eccentricities nor cliquishness, the fiery power of his words no opposition, his sense of justice and impartiality neither inferiority complexes nor complaints.
>
> His authority was strengthened by the fact, that in his profession he was recognized as the undisputed, successful leader in his field, while for Emperor Wilhelm II. Georg Büxenstein was the representative of the sport of rowing in Germany.

When Georg Büxenstein first met Martin in the laboratory of Professor Vogel, the powerful entrepreneur and the eager student were instantly drawn to each other. Always on the lookout for bright, dynamic young men, Büxenstein hired Martin immediately upon the completion of his studies at the Gewerbe Institute. Recognizing his yet untested talent for reaching out to people in an aggressive but always pleasant and effective manner, Büxenstein decided to prepare Martin for work in a foreign country as his representative and salesman of the colour printing process developed by his firm. In January 1896, Martin left for England and Ireland. When he said goodbye to Professor Vogel, he did not realize that he would never work with this outstanding scientist again. Professor Vogel died unexpectedly on December 17, 1898.

Except for several visits to his father's distant relatives in Cracow during his youth, Martin had never left German soil before. In England, he was immediately fascinated by his first impressions of London, the centre and the heart of the British Empire, which had reached the zenith of its power and glory. While Berlin as the political and commercial centre of the German Empire was almost as vibrant as London, the German capital seemed in comparison somewhat provincial and closed off from the larger, far-away world. The gates of London were wide open to the farthest reaches of the globe. The evidence of the political and economic power of the British Empire was everywhere, as were the symbols of the monarchy, but as Martin later observed, in a much less ostentatious, overpowering way than in Berlin. Queen Victoria was beloved by her people in a different way than Emperor Wilhelm II. His constant demonstrations of his personal power quite successfully challenged the bourgeoisie to love and adore him, while the sullen masses of the working class detested the Emperor. Wilhelm clearly doubted their loyalty to him and to the monarchy.

Being as fluent in English as he was in French, Martin found it easy to understand and adopt the English way of life. He appreciated the sense of personal freedom based on a voluntary adherence to long-established rules of conduct. This code, as Martin soon decided, required far fewer laws and ordinances and the surfeit of written and unwritten rules that one encountered everywhere in Germany.

Martin fell in love with the bucolic countryside of England and Scotland, which he explored with his camera on many journeys. He was especially attracted to the gentle beauty of Ireland, which became the favourite destination of his photographic excursions. He was not blind, however, to the ravages of industry and mining that he discovered in the Midlands. Familiar with the devastating impact of large-scale industry on people and their environment from the years when he had lived next to the depressing mill towns and coal mining districts of Silesia, Martin found the lot of the armies of English mill workers and miners of much greater hardship and deprivation when it came to working conditions, wages, and social protection compared to their counterparts in Germany. Martin could not help but wonder what needed to be done to raise the quality of life of the ordinary working man to not just acceptable, but to humane levels. These were thoughts Martin never abandoned until he would find himself in the position personally to create a better world for a few thousand ordinary working people in Canada.

In May 1897, on a weekend excursion to the popular sea resort of Bognor Regis, Martin found himself seated next to a beautiful woman during dinner at his hotel. She was accompanied by three young girls of obvious upper-class background. Martin was fascinated by this attractive, elegantly dressed woman who spoke perfect English, although Martin immediately detected a slight French accent. Introducing himself in his best French, Martin received a charming smile. He realized he was falling in love with this beautiful French woman. Her name was Berthe-Marie Brand. She was to become Martin's first wife.

Berthe-Marie, Martin's wife for twenty-seven years, was not the only important person in his life whom Martin failed to mention in his writings. Only through secondary sources are we aware of her existence and the crucial part that her complex, unhappy personality played in Martin's life. Apparently no relation to Martin's distant relatives from Warsaw who had just moved to Berlin and changed their name from Hachamowycz to Brandt, Berthe-Marie had recently moved to England from her native France. Of German descent, she had been born in Paris on November 21, 1867, as the daughter of the merchant Gustave Guillaume Brand and his wife Charlotte Marie Louise née Dieterich. Berthe-Marie's father had been born in 1837 as the son of a notary in the Prussian city of Dortmund. Her mother, a teacher prior to her marriage, had been born in 1836 as a teacher's daughter in Göttingen in the Kingdom of Hannover. Guillaume and Charlotte Brand had three sons and three daughters. Berthe-Marie was the third oldest child in the family.

A document of far later years when Berthe-Marie had reached the age of fifty describes her as 5 feet 4 inches tall, weighing 150 pounds. Her complexion was stated as fair, her hair dark-brown, her eyes blue and her features "regular." Four fingers of her right hand were "crippled or deformed." It was noted that Berthe-Marie was "highly intelligent and refined," an impression confirmed by her attached photograph. However, one cannot fail to notice the blankness in her eyes, the bitterness expressed in the deep lines surrounding the downward corners of the mouth. The once-beautiful face was ravaged by illness, depression and unhappiness.

This, however, was not the Berthe-Marie that Martin was courting soon after their first meeting at Bognor Regis. He had learned that she was employed as a governess with the Middleton family at Tortington House. The Middletons were renting the manor house at Tortington from the Duke of Norfolk whose medieval castle with its powerful bastions at Arundel was easily visible from Berthe-Marie's room at Tortington House.

Not finding it easy to break out of the loneliness imposed upon her by her duties as governess and the comparative remoteness of Tortington House, Berthe-Marie quickly responded to the charm of

Martin and his radiant personality. Both felt happy to have found each other and were deeply in love.

In early December 1897, Berthe-Marie confided to Martin that she was expecting his child. She was grateful for his apparent joy of becoming a father; and after a relatively brief courtship, Martin and Berthe-Marie got married on December 15, 1897. in Brentford, Middlesex. Berthe-Marie's sister Louise Brand and Martin's brother Theodor Cohn were present as witnesses. Theodor, incidentally, was another of the relatives Martin never mentioned in his memoirs or letters.

The young couple found a comfortable house at One Whitehall Gardens in the charming neighbourhood of Gunnersbury near the London suburb of Richmond. Martin had been very successful as Büxenstein's representative and now enjoyed a secure income. Not only could Marie and Martin furnish their home according to their taste and desires, they were also financially comfortable enough to enjoy the cultural aspects of London life and travel to the seashore for brief holidays. But Berthe-Marie could not accompany Martin on his occasional business travels throughout England and Ireland. These were weeks when Marie missed her husband very much, feeling a sense of loneliness and abandonment which, as a single woman, she had never experienced before. It was a feeling she would encounter more and more in the future; and she would react to it with sadness, depression, and finally with anger. It remains to be seen whether it was her anger and her depressive mood or whether it was Martin's growing sense of adventure and the constant drive to seek new challenges that caused him to leave the vulnerable Berthe-Marie so often. Perhaps it was her increasing passivity, her growing inflexibility, and a fear of life in unknown countries that prevented her from accompanying Martin to the wilderness of Western Canada. If one considers how much Martin cherished the challenge of exploration and discovery in which Berthe-Marie seemed neither willing nor able to participate, her reluctance was a tragedy.

But these unhappy years still lay far in the future. These were still the months of marital bliss. Martin curtailed his business travels to an absolute minimum and became as caring and protective of his wife as never again in their later years. Berthe-Marie cherished her husband's attention and care; both delightedly looked forward to becoming parents.

On July 20, 1898, Marcelle Florence was born, a healthy, sweet-looking baby girl. She had jet-black hair, the greyish-blue eyes of her mother and the darker complexion of her father. Marcelle's birth was registered on August 6 at the Chiswick sub-office of the General Register Office. Physically well after a normal, uncomplicated birth, Berthe-Marie nevertheless suffered through a period of an abnormally deep post-partum depression. Martin remained as caring and solicitous as ever. It did not occur to him that Berthe-Marie's prolonged state of depression might herald an unhappy future for Berthe-Marie and affect their marriage as well.

But Marcelle gave them great joy. She was an easily cared-for baby, always content, never plaguing her parents with frequent crying spells or tantrums. Her smile was sweet but rare. Martin was too busy being the happy father to wonder whether his daughter might have inherited not just the physical beauty of her mother, but her sad disposition as well.

Despite Berthe-Marie's mood swings, these were the happiest years of Martin's first marriage. He also remained most successful as the representative of Georg Büxenstein, who enjoyed visiting the young family during his business trips to England. In January 1902, he arrived in Gunnersbury with an honourable offer for Martin. It concerned the future plans of Erich Vogel, who, after his father's death, had returned to Berlin to resume his position as technical manager of the Büxenstein Photochemographical Institute. After deciding to accept the offer of a professorship at the Technical Institute, Erich Vogel had asked Büxenstein to release him from his contract with the Photochemigraphical Institut. There was only one man Georg Büxenstein could think of as Erich Vogel's replacement: Martin Cohn. Delighted with the honour of being chosen by Georg Büxenstein, a hard-headed businessman, Martin followed the call to Berlin, but not without some trepidation at the thought of having to relinquish the cherished freedom and autonomy he had so enjoyed in England. He knew he would miss the liberal way of life that he had learned to appreciate so much.

In July 1902, Martin and Berthe-Marie Cohn arrived with little Marcelle in Berlin. Martin started his work as manager of the Photochemigraphical Institute immediately. Gratefully, Martin accepted Büxenstein's suggestion that he spend one day a week in the Vogel laboratory at the Technical Institute, recently re-named as the Technische Hochschule and elevated to the rank of a university. Erich Vogel had resumed his father's research in the laboratory, which had been closed since his father's death. This arrangement was not only advantageous for Georg Büxenstein's business, it would also influence Martin's career and, indeed, his entire life in unexpected ways.

Martin was astonished by the changes that had occurred during his absence of only a few years. He discovered everywhere the evidence of an incredible economic boom.

After the unification of the German states in 1871, when the capital of the Kingdom of Prussia became the capital of the new German Empire, Berlin had started out on a breath-taking, at times rollercoaster-like development of its industries, commerce, and trade. The reparations flowing from defeated France to victorious Germany after the Franco-Prussian war of 1870-1871 gave the economy of the young Empire an enormous boost, which was concentrated economically and financially in Berlin. But Berlin also suffered repeated boom and bust cycles during the following two decades. It also became the focus of political and social tensions resulting from the large influx of an undereducated proletariat that flooded into Berlin from the depressed rural areas of the eastern parts of the country.

This dramatic transition from a conservative, quite old-fashioned capital to the centre of one of Europe's largest and most powerful states seemed to take an accelerated pace towards the end of the nineteenth century. After a visit to the Russian capital, St. Petersburg, in 1888, Lady Randolph (Jenny) Churchill, mother of Winston Churchill, observed with a critical eye the lifestyle of the ultra-fashionable circles of the city's upper society and their role at the Imperial court as "lavish in its extravagance, barbaric in its splendor." By comparison she found the German Imperial capital of Berlin "unpretentious and, perhaps, a little dull, but full of traditions and etiquette . . .signs of the all conquering and victorious army were everywhere; everything military was in the ascendant."

Only fifteen years later, Lady Randolph would have found the presence of the military even more pronounced, but the German capital greatly changed, its vibrant economic and cultural life so much different from earlier years. Some of that change was due to the influence and the role of Emperor Wilhelm II.

Young and forceful, daring and impetuous, the young Emperor seemed to embody the modern Germany storming relentlessly under his leadership towards a glorious future. For many Germans, that future had already begun. They were ready to follow their Emperor in his quest for the creation of a powerful Germany, seeking her deserved "place in the sun," if necessary by the threat of force. A latecomer among the richer nations of Europe, Germany had not found her rightful place among the powerful of the world. Traditionalist in some ways and progressive in others, the dynamic, multifaceted personality of Wilhelm II appealed to widely differing segments of the population. To the military, to the civil service, and to the majority of Prussia's landed aristocracy, the Emperor represented continuity of tradition; the burgeoning class of industrialists and entrepreneurs praised Wilhelm II for his interest in science and technology, which helped promote the flourishing German trade and commerce throughout the world. Finally, the pomp and circumstance of Wilhelminian Germany excited the petit bourgeois while it led many an artist to a sycophantic, often tasteless celebration of the Emperor and the German Empire.

But the young German Empire was nevertheless confronted with major problems. There was still much poverty among the working classes and the rural proletariat. The Social Democratic Party represented a growing political force, which was deeply distrusted by the bourgeoisie, feared by the establishment, and detested, if not hated, by the Emperor. Young writers and poets openly expressed criticism and dissent. On the surface, however, the majority of the people seemed content and optimistic; and most parties and groups, even the Social Democratic Party, professed their loyalty to the monarchy. Strangely absent was a general awareness that most of the cherished Prussian traditions had ceased to determine the course of events of the new Germany, even though Bismarck, the creator of the Second Reich, had been a Prussian conservative par excellence. But Bismarck was no longer at the helm of the Empire. One of his first decisions, of fateful consequence for the direction Germany would take from then on, was Wilhelm II's dismissal of the German chancellor.

The Countess Catherine Radziwill, widely read but not liked because of her frankness as the astute observer of the European scene, noted that

> ... the general public imagined that nothing had changed; they failed to realize that after the triumphs of Sadowa and Sedan neither the Emperor nor his ministers could proceed upon the same lines as before. No longer were they heads of a mid-European state; their territory was now of wider significance; their eyes were lifted towards the hills, and in the consummation of 1871 they saw the beginnings of an Empire which should be wide-spreading in territory, far-reaching in power, and knit together by a love for the fatherland which should make the German Empire supreme in the councils of Europe.

While the growing class of industrialists, entrepreneurs and merchants of the upper bourgeoisie was generally free of a militaristic outlook, it still supported in its optimism and pride the new identity of Germany which the Emperor Wilhelm constantly fostered in his frequent speeches and political pronouncements from which this class benefited economically.

In these years, Berlin assumed not only the function of the Imperial capital, but of the political, economic and cultural centre of Germany as well. In the eyes of the world, Germany and Prussia seemed synonymous. But in many areas of the country, people still felt as Bavarians, Saxonians, Swabians and Hessians first and only second as citizens of the German Empire. Next to the growing military strength, however, it was largely the unprecedented economic dynamism that promoted the identity of the young Empire and the loyalty of most of its citizens to the crown. It provided the force that welded the country together. In his *History of Germany Since 1789*, the German writer Golo Mann, son of Thomas Mann, surveyed the development of the country in all its astonishing facets:

> In 1870, German industry had not yet overtaken France; better military organization, not a superior industry, gave the Germans their victory. Thereafter the curve rises noticeably more steeply; first under Bismarck and then even more so under Wilhelm II. Like a speck of grease in a plate of soup the pompous Imperial regime floated on a stream of prosperity created by others.
>
> Between 1848 and 1914, the population of Berlin increased tenfold, from 400 000 to four million. [And the Second Reich], this nation state without responsible government, without internal unity, was one of the greatest centres of energy there had ever been, its population increased annually by almost a million, its industry was surpassed only by that of America and its army was second to none.

Having his powers of observation sharpened by life and travel in foreign countries, Martin could not help being overwhelmed by the incredible progress of Berlin. Sleepy villages which had surrounded the capital since medieval times were growing overnight into autonomous cities connected to the core of Berlin by wide avenues and a rapidly expanding system of transportation of subways, elevated trains, and streetcars.

Adored by many and detested and hated by others, nowhere was the Wilhelminian Age with its pomp and its crass materialism more pronounced than in Berlin. Other capitals in Germany like Munich, Dresden, Stuttgart, or Karlsruhe, although retaining their predominant role in the arts but no longer being the centres of political power they once had been, experienced far less drastic changes. In Berlin, however, the economically powerful upper bourgeoisie celebrated itself and its successes in the elegant new neighbourhoods of the Westend and of the Grunewald in the Southwest. The northern and eastern districts of the city were dominated by huge factories of world-renown, surrounded by a sea of grey, overcrowded tenements where the working population subsisted in deplorable conditions. Situated between the East and the West of Berlin—two distinct worlds forever remaining apart—the centre of the city accommodated the Imperial Court and the seat of the Prussian and Imperial German governments, neither of which succeeded in forming a link between the upper classes residing in the Westend and Southwest and the sullen, suffering proletariat on the opposite side of Berlin.

Significant for Martin's station in life, his economic security and his sense of belonging to the comfortable middle class was the particular district of Berlin he chose for his young family. The city directory of 1903 lists the residence of Martin Cohn as Leibnizstrasse 32 near the fashionable, tree-lined Kurfürstendamm in an elegant section of the suburb of Charlottenburg. The Cohn family's flat was located on the third floor of a five-storey apartment building with a facade richly adorned by a mix of Renaissance and Baroque elements so popular at this time. It was a spacious flat of four rooms with bay windows and balconies. Elegant shopping and a large number of establishments of culture and entertainment ranging from the sublime to the frivolous were around the corner–from the German Opera to theatres offering serious to light fare and from elegant nightclubs to houses of questionable fun. The nearby famous Zoological Garden must have been a place much enjoyed by little Marcelle. Nor was the vast park of the Tiergarten very far. The Technische Hochschule where Martin Cohn continued his research was within walking distance. And within minutes, the new subway would bring Martin to his place of work in the Friedrichstrasse in the heart of the city.

Georg Büxenstein became Martin's hero and model and mentor, perhaps even a father figure. For Martin, Georg Büxenstein was a true representative of the modern, progressive Berlin and its dynamic class of industrial, commercial and financial entrepreneurs. Büxenstein did not operate on quite the illustrious level of industrialists like Siemens, Borsig or Rathenau or the owners of the huge department stores of Wertheim, Tietz and Grünfeld or the big publishers Ullstein, Mosse and Scherl, or the heads of the large banks such as the Deutsche Bank, the Fürstenberg Bank and other powerful private financial institutions. All of them had their share in transforming Berlin from an industrious but somewhat sleepy royal capital into the leading industrial, commercial, and cultural centre of Germany. It was the country's only true metropolis and was increasingly recognized as such by the rest of Europe and the world. In his own way, Georg Büxenstein contributed his share to the commercial and social life of the city; in his personality, his business acumen, his drive, and his multitude of interests and financial and personal pursuits, he ranked with the best of them.

Towards the end of his life, Georg Büxenstein would look back on memberships (often as president) in more than 200 organizations of professional, social, and humanitarian nature; for his services and accomplishments, he was decorated 13 times. Of imposing appearance, tall and robust, with a high forehead and a huge moustache, Georg Büxenstein was nevertheless an easily approachable man. He was always liked by those working for and with him, even though he had a tendency to be rather autocratic at times; but then, this was part of his success for which everyone respected him. And he was always on the best of terms with the decision makers and power brokers of Berlin's commercial and financial circles, his reputation for honesty, integrity and business acumen always standing him in good stead.

No wonder Martin admired this extraordinary man. Nor was it surprising that Georg Büxenstein became so fond of Martin in whom he discovered many of his own qualities and aspirations. Mutual respect and high regard for each other's character and talents soon grew into a lasting friendship.

Like a dedicated mentor, Georg Büxenstein had over the years guided and educated Martin, fostering his competence and self-confidence. In direct and in subtle ways, he had influenced Martin's decisions more than once. But neither man realized the far-reaching consequences when Büxenstein selected Martin as host for a distinguished visitor from Canada on a bleak November day in 1905. Büxenstein's choice was, as usual, an appropriate one. Martin Cohn immediately impressed the visitor from Canada, who asked to be shown the facilities of the Technical Academy.

A tall, lanky figure, Colonel Onésiphore Talbot was fascinated by the vivacious German man who had such a powerful presence despite his short, but stocky physique; by his dark, expressive eyes, his quick mind and his excellent command of English and French languages, which both men used during the tour of the Technical Institute and, later, at the Hotel Bristol where Colonel Talbot had invited Martin for dinner. During the evening, Colonel Talbot realized that he had met in Martin the man his country needed: healthy and physically strong, highly intelligent and well educated, dynamic, curious, courageous and adventuresome. Martin was the perfect example of the person Canada's Prime Minister, Sir Wilfrid Laurier, sought to attract to his country in order to realize his vision of making Canada a great, populous, and prosperous nation. He not only needed farmers and toilers, but also educated men capable of opening up the vast resources of Canada, especially its Far West.

Animated by Colonel Talbot's description of Canada and its opportunities, Martin admitted that, although successful and respected in his present position, he missed a sense of fulfillment and satisfaction. In Colonel Talbot he found "a sympathetic listener...this encouraged me to open my heart and tell him how difficult it was for me to acclimatize myself again in Germany after so many years abroad."

Colonel Talbot's frank response became an immediate challenge for Martin:

> In Canada a man like you would have great chances and if you had some capital, you would have tremendous opportunities. You would be welcome. Canada needs men of your type....You will and must discover your chances yourself, or else I should be greatly mistaken in you. But I will help you where I can. I am a Liberal Member of Parliament and a personal friend of Prime Minister Sir Wilfrid Laurier, and I shall introduce you to him and to many other important people who will be of great use to you.

Martin was momentarily lost for words. A window to the world seemed to open suddenly. While its view was radiant and challenging, the conflicting emotions rushing through Martin's mind were frightening.

"... like a flash I felt the urge of going there. 'I will come to Canada,' I said."

What did he know about Canada other than her languages and what he had learned in his geography and history lessons in school at Reichenbach! But Canada looked inviting, a land of opportunity bathed in a romantic glow. A poem that he used to recite in school came to Martin's mind—*The Savage* by the German poet Johann Gottfried Seume: "It described how an honest Canadian redskin was tricked by a white trader—and the Indian repaid evil with good." Canada began to look like a good country to Martin.

His mind struggled with many thoughts, challenges and fears, and at night he lay awake for hours. What should he do about his wife and his young daughter who both, he knew, needed him so much? Could he, husband and father, dare to rob them of his presence, protection, and security while he searched for opportunities in a far-away country? The painful questions were endless and the answers still to be found, but decisions would have to be made. Martin knew he could not afford to wait.

> What should I do in Canada? I repeated the Colonel's words, that I must discover chances myself. Was this accidental meeting perhaps the great chance of my life? Had I not read only lately that opportunity knocks only once at the door?
>
> But then, there were the practical questions. Should I give up my secure position to chase after the will o'the wisp? And where and how could I get the capital? Who would advise me?

After a sleepless night, a pensive, preoccupied Martin sat across from a worried Berthe-Marie at breakfast in the dining room flooded

by the early morning sun. Berthe-Marie could not fathom the roots
of a sudden anxiety. Never had Martin, always so cheerful at the
start of a new day, appeared so distant and removed from her. With
worry in her heart and confusion in her mind, she noticed how
Martin descended the wide staircase at a pace slower and heavier
than usual. Nor did he look back to wave to Marcelle, who was too
little and too innocent to have noticed how somberly her father had
looked into her eyes after he had kissed her good-bye.

There was "only one capitalist" Martin knew: Georg Büxenstein.
He resolved to approach him immediately. But not until the afternoon was his employer available. In agony and anxiety, Martin decided to have a message sent to his wife that he would not be home
for lunch. Not until a decision had been made with Georg
Büxenstein's blessing and support would he have the courage to
face Berthe-Marie and Marcelle. Barely able to attend to his duties,
Martin rehearsed over and over again how to present his plan to
Georg Büxenstein. By the time of the appointed hour, a feeling of
enthusiasm for Canada and its opportunities had gripped Martin,
who felt at ease when he noticed how his own excitement was transferring itself to his employer and mentor. Georg Büxenstein was far
too wise and experienced an employer to try to hold Martin back or
appeal to his gratitude for the mentorship and the opportunities he
had given to him. Rather than raising new guilt feelings, which vis-
ibly plagued Martin already, Büxenstein responded in two ways: as
the fatherly advisor helping Martin rein in his burgeoning enthusiasm and realistically weigh the pros and cons of leaving a secure,
respected position for an uncertain future; and as a businessman
identifying the factors that would make Martin's adventure a success. Büxenstein agreed that with certain provisions Martin's plan
looked reasonably promising and profitable. What happened next
caught Martin by surprise!

As he intensely reviewed Martin's plans, Georg Büxenstein
found himself caught by a sudden enthusiasm and a yearning for
challenges far away from his place of business in Berlin. Rather
than envying the younger, less experienced, and perhaps also more
impulsive man, he spontaneously made Martin's plan his own and,
eventually, a common venture shared by both men. In Büxenstein's
mind and even more so in his feelings, Martin became his alter ego,
ready to strike out and leave its mark in the New World! Returning
to the cool, rational thinking required at this crucial hour, Georg
Büxenstein advised Martin that he would see him the next morning
for a final decision as to his support and participation.

No doubt, as a businessman, Büxenstein was also challenged by
the chance of success in a venture so dramatically different from his

past and present pursuits. Interestingly enough, in his later memoirs
Martin describes Georg Büxenstein, in addition to his many interests
and hobbies, as "...an enthusiastic card player, a member of several
clubs in which the elite and rich bankers gambled." So Georg
Büxenstein was, after all, not only a cool businessman who saw and
used opportunities as they offered themselves, he was also like
many other successful entrepreneurs attracted by ventures involving
great risk.

The desire to help Martin, now coupled with the prospects of financial gain, attracted Büxenstein as much as the excitement of taking the risk of placing money in Martin's hands for yet undefined
projects in a far country on the soil of which neither he nor Martin
had ever set foot. Büxenstein had full confidence in Martin's energy, intelligence and courage. He knew that Martin would, as always, seek and listen to his advice. And he knew he could place his
trust in Martin without any reservations. Before Martin had left his
employer's office, Georg Büxenstein had already decided to raise
the funds needed to enable Martin to go to Canada to seek his own
and Georg Büxenstein's fortune.

What happened at Büxenstein's club during the evening of this
day says as much about Büxenstein as about the venturesome atmosphere prevailing in Berlin's business circles. Early next morning,
Büxenstein called Martin into his office and related the events of the
previous evening to him:

> In my club there are mostly bankers. When I got there yesterday, I
> shouted across the room that I wished to tell the members something of
> great interest. They all stopped their games and listened: 'I want to say
> something about Canada. The manager of my plant received a most cor-
> dial invitation from a great Canadian who just visited him here.... He
> wants him to go there and make his fortune. The trouble is, as usual,
> he has no considerable capital. What do you say, if we finance him... I
> am willing to subscribe $5000.00 out of my own pocket. If you join
> me, we will make a syndicate, and I am willing to be the President of
> it.' In half an hour, I had $60,000 together.... All you got to do now,
> is, to go to our bank...and be off to your promised land, and good luck
> to you!

One week later, a meeting of the "Deutsches Kanada Syndikat"
was called where shares of a total of $100,000 were issued. Martin
was overwhelmed.

> ... It seemed to me that they were ... counting the venture already a
> success. How could I doubt that these benevolent gentlemen who
> entrusted me with a quarter of a million Marks, deserved from fate
> anything else but great profits.

Three weeks later, Colonel Talbot's eagerly expected confirmation arrived from Ottawa. "He was highly pleased with the news; he had expected nothing else from me; he had already spoken with the Prime Minister who said Canada needed men and money."

Colonel Talbot suggested, however, that Martin should wait for four months rather than depart for Canada immediately. April would be a much more favourable time than the country's harsh winter.

Although Martin was most eager to set out for the promised land, the extra months gave him an opportunity to train his successor and in his free hours devour book after book about Canada. The knowledge about his new field of enterprise would turn out to be immensely useful and profitable, as Martin would realize immediately after his arrival in Ottawa.

If there was one reason why Martin wished to leave for Canada as quickly as possible, it was the daily agony of facing Berthe-Marie who was in a state of shock about the approaching departure of her husband. Even though Martin patiently explained to her again and again that he would continue to work for a group of German businessman, that he would remain part of the Berlin business community, and that he would return as soon as his venture had grown to a certain level of stability, Berthe-Marie sensed that something of far-reaching consequences had taken hold of Martin's mind. She suspected that he never gave much thought to what he was doing to his marriage. She had to agree with Martin, though, that it would be premature, even foolish and irresponsible, for him to take his family along to Canada at this time.

Berthe-Marie was not a strong woman, and Marcelle was far too young and vulnerable to face the rigours of growing up in another country where Martin would not even know where he would ultimately make a home for his family. In the end, Martin moved his own anxiety and guilt about the burden he was placing on his marriage and his family out of his mind. And Berthe-Marie wished she could believe her husband's plan to return to Berlin within less than one year. "I was walking constantly on clouds...The weeks went by far too slowly for me. At last, April came and I said good-bye to my President. He said to me:

> Never forget that I am entrusting you with my money and that of my friends. I rely on your honesty. Use common sense in whatever you may do, and if you are doubtful, think what I would do in your place. My reputation for my good judgment and your success is in your hands. And now, go with God and come back with many good Canadian Dollars.

Early on May 3, 1906, Martin departed from the Lehrter Bahnhof in Berlin for Hamburg and Cuxhaven where he boarded the German steamer *Blücher* on the following day. On the platform of the Lehrter Bahnhof, Martin had left behind a sobbing, disconsolate Berthe-Marie, who was clutching a handkerchief in one hand and in the other the tiny hand of an excited Marcelle who, as every morning, waved goodbye to her father with a sweet, innocent smile.

III

FIRST STEPS IN THE NEW WORLD
(1906 - 1910)

After a "rough crossing" of the Atlantic, Martin arrived at New York on May 14, 1906. Unlike the majority of the passengers, who were poor emigrant families from Russian Poland and Austria-Hungary crowded into the steerage of the German steamer *Blücher*, Martin shared a comfortable first-class cabin with a friend of Georg Büxenstein, the 48-year old Eduard Lehr. While Mr. Lehr hardly left their cabin during the ten days on the *Blücher*, Martin had almost cherished the rough seas. During his years in England, he had crossed the Irish Sea numerous times and "was now well trained not to get seasick." But when the Statue of Liberty and Lower Manhattan's skyscrapers rose above the horizon, Martin could hardly wait to touch the ground of the continent which would eventually become his home for the rest of his life.

The next eighteen years would turn into the most adventurous period in Martin's life, successful beyond expectations, but not free of disappointments and heartbreak. But no defeat would cause Martin to abandon his vision or turn away from Canada, the country he learned to love so much. So important were those years of achievements and defeats that Martin in his later life wrote his memoirs of the period from 1906 to 1924. Even though he entirely excluded his personal and family life from his writings, his memoirs assist us to follow his dreams and actions, his triumphs and defeats through the years that brought him the greatest fulfilment.

While not the typical immigrant, Martin nevertheless belonged to the millions of Europeans who chose the United States or Canada as their destination. They hoped to find either a life of freedom from want or, as in Martin's case, a life of opportunities and challenges no longer existing in the Old World. The majority of immigrants, uneducated and often illiterate, would face years of deprivation and hard labour and often only their children would benefit from the opportunities in education and employment the New World offered. But among the millions, there were always a few thousand who were well educated, fluent in the English language and, if not already well off, at least well prepared to master the challenges of the New World and become successful and prosperous within a few years.

When Martin arrived in the New World, the United States had reached a pinnacle of growth and economic and industrial expansion. During the decade in which Martin entered the United States, the country's population grew by almost 16 million people from roughly 76 million in 1900 to nearly 92 million in 1910. This population boom was fuelled by the masses of immigrants arriving from Europe. Six times during the first decade of the twentieth century, the number of immigrants arriving in the United States, primarily in New York, had exceeded one million per year. In 1900, approximately 14 percent of the population of the United States were foreign-born. The first years in the New World brought incredible hardships for many immigrants. But the expanding economy of the United States, although held back by recurrent recessions, had developed into the largest and most powerful in the world and seemed to have an almost unlimited capacity to absorb the millions of new people arriving mainly from Eastern and Southern Europe.

New York, more than any other city in the United States, reflected the dynamic nature of this huge country. It was also the city where the arriving masses first sought shelter, comfort, and support in the ethnic neighbourhoods where they could feel at home. But this was also the city where the economic power, along with the wealth created by it, was openly visible in the streets lined by elegant stores and large commercial buildings, by the country's major banks and headquarters of industrial enterprises around Wall Street, and by the elegant mansions of the truly rich along the east and west sides of Central Park.

Martin was overwhelmed by the vitality he sensed everywhere in this city of almost four million. But his mind was set on the much younger country to the north where he saw opportunities that had been already exhausted in the United States. Although his briefcase was filled with letters of introduction, he made use of a few only. And no matter how much he was urged to stay as a guest of Georg Büxenstein's business friends, Martin was impatient to reach the country of his destiny. After only a brief stay of three days, Martin left New York on the Grand Trunk Railway. He crossed the Canadian border at Morgan Junction and arrived in Ottawa in the morning of May 18, 1906.

Neither in New York nor on the train to Canada did Martin feel out of place. Again, he realized the tremendous advantage of having lived in England and Ireland for several years. As always, Martin habitually absorbed impressions; he observed his fellow passengers waiting for a seat in the dining car and later preparing themselves for the night on the Pullman coach; it was a ritual he would follow numerous times during his travels over the next decades!

After the teeming metropolis of New York and the string of towns and villages of the Hudson River Valley that the train had passed after leaving New York, the first impressions of Canada on this spring day were not inspiring.

> I saw a flat, dreary country with very few houses and barns. The train stopped at every station, where few people were to be seen. They seemed to me to be railway employees, and occasionally I noticed some carriages which were called democrats. So it went on for hours …

But Martin had read enough about Canada to know that spring came late to this vast country, which accommodated almost every kind of topography and climate other than tropical or subtropical. He was aware that, later than the United States, Canada was now entering a period of growth and expansion. It was fostered by Prime Minister Sir Wilfrid Laurier, who envisioned masses of sturdy immigrants breaking the soil of the still thinly populated West at a time when free land was becoming scarce in the country to the south.

In 1887, the first transcontinental railway, the Canadian Pacific, had been completed. While the first groups of settlers in the West arrived from Central Canada and the United States before the turn of the century, the colonist trains from Halifax and Montreal soon carried large numbers of immigrants from Central and especially from Eastern Europe to the prairies. This massive influx significantly contributed to the remarkable population increase of 34.2 percent during the first decade of the century, the highest rate of growth ever recorded for Canada. In some years, more than 300,000 immigrants entered Canada, many of them destined for homesteads in the West. Between 1901 and 1910, 1.5 million immigrants helped increase the country's population from 5.4 million in 1901 to 7.2 million in 1911, a remarkable rate of growth which geographically, however, was rather unevenly distributed. While the number of residents of the Atlantic provinces remained stagnant or, in the case of Prince Edward Island, even decreased and the growth in Central Canada was concentrated in urban areas, the increase of the rural population in the West was dramatic. Saskatchewan alone grew from 91,000 to 492,000 people within the short span of ten years! By 1905 both Alberta and Saskatchewan gained provincial status.

When Martin had begun in 1905 to read everything about the New World he could find in the libraries of Berlin, he realized that opportunities in Canada would be far greater than in the United States, not only for his goal of achieving financial success, but also for his adventurous spirit. Eagerly, his eyes searched for Colonel Talbot when the train entered the station in Ottawa in the late morning. "Pressing my face against the window, I noticed the Colonel, searching with his eyes along the Pullman car. I waved to him, and he smiled."

Martin could not have asked for a better person to introduce him to Canada, particularly its capital, Ottawa. Colonel Onésiphore Talbot was a staunch Liberal, proud of the role his party, under the leadership of Sir Wilfrid Laurier, played in the dynamic development of Canada since the Liberals had assumed power in 1896. The once mighty Conservative party under John A. Macdonald had lost much of its drive after its leader's death. If Colonel Talbot did not hesitate to characterize John A. Macdonald as a visionary, he also commented on his personality, typical for a late Victorian of Scots descent. In contrast, he enthusiastically described Sir Wilfrid Laurier, the epitome of the elegant Victorian, eloquent, superbly dressed. His tall, slim figure, his sharp features, and his flowing white hair left an indelible impression. Colonel Talbot pointed out that Macdonald's and Laurier's goals to build a great Canadian nation reaching from sea to sea were almost identical.

Now the Liberals under Sir Wilfrid Laurier were blessed with an era of general prosperity and economic development throughout the industrialized world. There was capital, foremost in Britain, but also in the United States and to a lesser degree in France and Germany, waiting to be put to work in Canada, only recently discovered as a country of opportunity. Sir Wilfrid Laurier and his ministers were superb salesmen, attracting capital as much as they attracted settlers. Both were crucial to the creation of a Canada strong and independent of the United States. Martin learned how the energetic promotion of the West not only brought people to the still empty plains but also fuelled an economic boom to the benefit of the entire nation. A second transcontinental railway with numerous new branch lines spreading across the prairie provinces was bringing about the birth of thousands of villages and hundreds of towns with their huge requirements for construction materials, machinery and tools. Martin had arrived in Canada at the right time!

If any doubts about the vibrant spirit that had seized this country were still lingering in Martin's mind, they were quickly dispelled within the first days of his arrival in the Canadian capital. What happened during the first 48 hours suited Martin perfectly. The quick pace and the uncomplicated way in which he was introduced not only to important people but also to the ebullient mood so characteristic for this time in Canada brought out the best in Martin. Everybody was welcoming him and would immediately respond to his inquiries with advice, with sincere interest, and with a genuine desire to assist this astonishing man who had just arrived from Germany. Martin impressed people by his frankness and curiosity.

He also created the impression of being knowledgeable, informed, competent and dynamic. He appeared optimistic and enthusiastic, but self-assured enough to admit his ignorance where it existed. Nor did he hesitate to ask for frank advice. From the beginning, Martin did not encounter any problems of credibility that might have planted caution into the minds of the people to whom he was introduced. What Martin found were not only open doors and open minds but, especially around Parliament Hill, the mood and pace, the flexibility and imaginativeness he had been hoping for.

Fortunately, Colonel Talbot was as quick of mind and body as Martin. After having taking his charge immediately to the Russell House Hotel, the best hotel in Ottawa at that time, Colonel Talbot allowed Martin only a few minutes to have his bags taken to his room to get ready to meet his friends at the Laurentian Club. Martin caused a great surprise when he explained that he had come from Berlin in Germany rather than Berlin in Ontario [renamed Kitchener in World War I], as everybody assumed.

This was also Martin's introduction to Canadian drinking habits. He had already noticed the strong odor of alcohol permeating the lobby of the hotel. Emanating from its famous lounge, the aroma pervaded the entire main floor of Russell House. After the many drinks of unknown strength offered to him in the Laurentian Club, Martin was only too glad to follow Colonel Talbot's suggestion that he might wish to rest in his room for a while. It was fortunate that he did as the Colonel called on Martin just a couple of hours later to announce that Prime Minister Laurier would meet with them in the early evening after dinner.

If Martin was no longer puzzled about Canadian drinking habits, he faced another surprise when, despite his very adequate French, he had noticeable difficulties in understanding the French Canadian members of Parliament the Colonel introduced him to on their way to the visitors' gallery of the House of Commons. After listening to debates that would make sense to him only months or years later, Martin prepared himself for the crucial event of the day while having dinner with Colonel Talbot. Incredibly, within 16 hours of entering Canada and less than ten hours after arriving at its capital, Martin Cohn was introduced to Sir Wilfrid Laurier, the country's Prime Minister! "We waited in the anteroom of the Prime Minister and were then ushered in. Sir Wilfrid arose from his chair behind a large desk; his beautiful white hair, his searching penetrating eyes impressed me very much."

Sir Wilfrid Laurier seemed equally impressed with his visitor: "Oné, you have done well," he said to Colonel Talbot after listening attentively to the latter's introduction.

What followed was a rapid-fire exchange of questions and answers between the Prime Minister of Canada and the immigrant from Germany, interspersed by advice from Sir Wilfrid. Martin was astute enough to rein in his enthusiasm, presenting himself as flexible in his ideas and eager to accept advice. Looking at someone whose aspirations were of apparent value for his country, the Prime Minister not only frankly offered advice but skillfully steered Martin in the direction he considered most advantageous and useful for Canada. Thirty years later, Martin recorded this fascinating encounter in his memoirs from notes and memory, no doubt, quite accurately:

> "What do you intend to do here?"
> "I do not know yet and want to ask your advice."
> "Have you got large capital?"
> "I am being financed by substantial interests."
> "Have you any preference?"
> "No, sir."
> "Well, as you are a scientist by profession, and in a very obtuse science, there may be chances for you, if you drop that science," and he smiled. "Let me see. There is Forestry, Agriculture and Mining. Which would you prefer?"
> "I do not know, sir. Where would be the best chance of investing money with great opportunity?"
> "Forestry seems already very much disposed of, as we have given our best lands away. Agriculture is being financed by banks and land companies, but what do you think of mining?"
> "I should like to become interested in mining."
> "All right then. I shall inform the Minister of Mines. Oné, you better take your friend to Templeman. You may come to me from time to time and report how you are getting on."

An audience of fifteen minutes at the end of his first day in Canada had steered Martin in a new direction. Without fully realizing it, Martin had taken his first, decisive step away from the "obtuse science" of photochemistry towards an entirely different career—prospecting, mining, business, and entrepreneurship.

The day of decision had not yet ended. The same evening, Colonel Talbot and Martin went to see the Honourable William Templeman, the Minister of Inland Revenue, who was also responsible for mining regulations. The rapid course of asking questions, giving advice, and making decisions in the Prime Minister's office only an hour ago was repeated:

> "What kind of mineral would interest you?"
> "I do not know. In which kind of mining could one make money and quickly?"

"There is a great nickel field at Sudbury, and the newly discovered cobalt-silver field at Cobalt, North of Temagami."

The thought flashed through my mind that the great steel works of Krupp in Germany were using nickel for hardening steel:

"I should like to be interested in nickel."

"All right, I will speak to the Director of the Geological Survey to give you all information. You may call on him in the morning."

Already advised by the Minister, the Director of the Geological Survey, Mr. Alfred P. Low, proved most helpful. He called in Dr. Alfred E. Barlow, who immediately offered to take Martin to Sudbury himself, having his own personal reasons as he would prove later. Mr. Low gave his permission; and the next evening, Martin and Barlow left by train for Sudbury. Three days after arriving in Ottawa with little idea of what to do and where to apply his energies and funds, Martin set out for his first Canadian venture in mining, something he had not even thought of until Sir Wilfrid Laurier directed him towards this particular field of opportunity.

Martin's good fortune persisted, at least in making useful contacts and finding people who would work with him for many years to come. Some of them would become life-long friends.

The journey to Sudbury in the company of Barlow turned into a sobering disappointment for Martin, who was overwhelmed by the horrible destruction the fumes of the huge Sudbury smelter had wreaked upon the surrounding countryside for miles around. Furthermore, Barlow also advised him that "I had come many years too late, as all known nickel deposits had been taken up years ago."

It is at this point that one cannot help but wonder whether Martin, who considered himself fortunate to have the advice and guidance of a man of Barlow's competence, was perhaps less cognizant of Barlow's secret plans for himself. Barlow must have been fully aware of the fact that there was no territory left for Martin to enter the exploration business in the Sudbury area with any hope of success. Why did he then accompany Martin to Sudbury without telling him in advance of the futility of the trip? But Martin was not sorry to leave the desolate Sudbury area and return to Ottawa to develop new plans. On the train, however, Barlow directed Martin's attention to opportunities well known to him in the new cobalt-silver field northeast of Sudbury. Naturally, Martin's interest was easily aroused, and Barlow could move to the next step in his strategy. He had quickly come to appreciate Martin as a man he would like to work with; and perceiving an unexpected chance to fulfill his own aspirations, Barlow confided to Martin that he had wanted to leave the Geological Survey for some time. How would Martin like to engage him as his geological expert in future explorations?

I felt that without the help of experienced Canadians I should make only
very slow progress, knowing neither the country nor the people, in fact
it would be impossible for me to make any success. But here, by a real
chance, I had the opportunity of engaging an expert...

While Martin spent the next days at the Geological Survey in
Ottawa, Colonel Talbot undertook discreet inquiries about Barlow,
which produced excellent results. Colonel Talbot also suggested that
it was now essential for Martin to engage legal counsel and introduced Martin to his solicitor Andrew Haydon, once more directing
Martin to another man of competence and integrity. Haydon would
become not only his trusted, effective legal counsel, but also his reliable political and personal advisor, his protector in difficult times to
come, and until his untimely death in 1932, his closest friend in the
Canadian capital. Unexpectedly and rather quickly, it seemed to
Martin, Andrew Haydon also introduced him to another Canadian
custom, within days calling him by his first name and insisting that
Martin call him "Andy." This "seemed very unusual to me ... I was
proud to have gained the confidence of a stranger so quickly..."

Of almost the same age as Martin, Andrew Haydon was born on
June 28, 1867, not far from Ottawa in Ontario's Perth County.
Raised as a farm boy, he became a teacher, but soon turned to law.
After graduating from law school, Haydon first practiced in Lanark
and soon after entered into lifelong partnership with Harold
MacGiverin in one of Ottawa's most prestigious law firms, which is
still in existence today. In 1922 Andrew Haydon became the organizer for the Liberal party and in 1924 was appointed to the Senate.
Haydon was not only a competent lawyer, but he also had the
personality of the true politician and, as such, would prove himself
most useful to Martin on countless future occasions.

Andrew and Martin were ideally suited to each other by character
and temperament; both men were guided by intelligence and obser-
vational skill and by practical minds that were ready to make sound
decisions whenever needed. Andrew realized that it was time to prepare a legal and financial base that would provide Martin with a
more attractive image and the status of representing an international
corporation. With Martin's consent, Andrew immediately proceeded
to register a company under a Dominion charter as a sister corporation to the Deutsches Kanada Syndikat in Berlin. Martin chose the
name German Development Company Ltd. He gladly followed
Andrew's advice to choose a prestigious address for his new company on Ottawa's busy Banks Street.

It was only the beginning of June, but much had been accomplished in laying the groundwork for the future. Martin had made
many contacts with persons of power and influence. He felt he had a

fairly solid understanding of the dynamics of the Canadian political and economic scene. He had registered the German Development Company in Ottawa; and he had hired Barlow, an experienced Canadian geologist and mining engineer who was familiar with most of the country. Martin felt ready to sail for Germany to report his first accomplishments in Canada to Georg Büxenstein and the shareholders of the Deutsches Kanada Syndikat. But again, Barlow had different ideas. Even a brief trip to Germany would take away precious weeks from the time required to make a prospecting trip to Northern Ontario profitable.

Giving in to the persuasive Barlow, Martin agreed with some reluctance, although he suspected that Barlow had prepared his plans without involving Martin, as it took only two days for Barlow to complete all the necessary preparations. If Barlow acted in part in his own personal interest, he also affected Martin's enthusiasm and love for Canada in a most decisive way. The trip, his first venture into the Canadian wilderness, became an unforgettable experience to which Martin devoted three chapters in his later memoirs.

Barlow introduced Martin to experiencing seemingly endless bush country of Northern Ontario–travelling on the (for the novice) treacherous canoe for countless miles; portaging canoe, baggage, equipment and supplies for long stretches through dense bush to the next body of water; living and working, eating and sleeping in a country infested by billions of hungry mosquitoes and nasty black flies. Martin would also meet the people–the miners and prospectors–who crowded the train on its way to North Bay and who would talk about nothing else but the riches they would soon discover. Martin had doubts about some of his fellow passengers, but he was highly pleased to notice the respect with which Barlow was treated by the mining engineers on board the train.

After crossing miles of bleak country with vast, desolate sections of burnt-out forest, Martin was overwhelmed by the quiet beauty of the Temagami area and its beautiful lakes farther to the north. He took out his camera equipment to take pictures of the country and its people, as he would do a thousand times more during the coming years. For the first time, he was introduced to Indian culture and its way of life when the five canoes of the prospecting party were loaded with the equipment and supplies for a long journey. As comfortable as Martin was on horseback, to the same degree did he feel insecure in the light canoe; he did not have an inkling of the hardship of portaging.

> After paddling about two hours, we drew near the shore. Barlow explained to me that this would be our first portage. Had I known what this meant, I would not have welcomed it as I did. Sitting, half lying

on the bottom of the canoe, I had become very stiff. Every time when I wanted to change my cramped position, the Indian steersman back of me said 'Care'. Barlow ... told me not to move at all, as a canoe is easily upset. I felt the cramping arms and legs and, slowly, imperceptibly stretched them from time to time.

At last, the party reached the first portage. Fascinated, Martin watched the portaging routine:

All the canoes had landed, they were being unpacked, and the contents piled on land. I saw an Indian swinging the first emptied canoe high over his head, upside down, and then carrying it on the hardly visible trail, he disappeared between the trees. The others unwound their tumplines, which had a brown thick leatherband sown on the centre. They tied the bundles together with these lines, knelt down, slipped the leather band across their front, and by getting up, raised the load to the back. They followed the canoe-men on the trail into the woods. Barlow and I stayed with the remaining boxes. The first men returned already and carried the remainder into the forest. All that was left now, was Barlow's and my own bundles. He said, he had no respect for men who did not carry their own belongings and I took the hint. I hoisted my bundles on my shoulder, and Barlow said, that this was the way, but he would get me a tumpline, as it would be much easier. I thought, anything easier would be highly welcome, because after a few hundred steps, I had to stop and shift the bundles from one shoulder to the other. With many stops we reached at last the end of the short portage. I longed to sit again cramped into the canoe.

This was an entirely new experience for Martin which, thanks to his good health and rugged constitution, he mastered exceedingly well, if not without pain and anguish. He gained enough expertise and practice to soon travel with success and pleasure through uncharted territory as far as the Hudson Bay and the Canadian Rockies. And always, he was enchanted by the beauty of untouched nature: "The sun was sinking. The blue Mediterranean sky with cirrus clouds reflected in the quiet surface of the lake. The dark green of the pine forest formed a beautiful background..." And in between, he wondered how best to conduct himself among these strong, experienced woodsmen and gain their respect.

I debated with myself, what would be better: to have an Indian carry my baggage over the many portages of which Barlow had told me, or to carry them myself and be respected. I decided eventually, I would rather suffer and be respected. I regretted this decision very often while on the portage, but I felt proud when the agony was over at the end of every portage. I made up my mind, however, to eliminate from my belongings everything that was not absolutely essential... I admired the strength of our men... I never had any physical exertion since leaving the German army years ago.

Martin learned fast and developed confidence very quickly, but there was much to learn. Forever curious and not ready to call it a day after he had, for the first time, been taught how to set up his tent and make his bed, Martin went off on his own:

> I went for a walk, unobserved, and followed the trail. I walked on, it got dark, because I suddenly found myself in thick undergrowth with fallen trees and saw no way out. Then I thought of the direction in which the camp would be, instinctively turned my face towards it, started to walk through the thicket, and was soon on the trail again. I heard voices in the distance, calling my name, and soon met some of our men running towards me, shouting, headed by Barlow. They were sure that I had been lost in the wilds. Barlow reproached me for having left the camp alone and told me of the great danger. It had never entered into my mind that I could not find my way back to the camp. Thus I discovered that I possessed the invaluable gift of finding my way everywhere, even in unknown territory: a gift which cannot be acquired. It stood me in great stead in my roamings and made me entirely independent....

After several days of hard canoeing and even harder portaging, the party reached beautiful Lake Evelyn, the destination chosen by Barlow. After dividing the party into two, "we started tramping with them over difficult ground, until he [Barlow] finally placed them [the two groups] for prospecting." It was time, Barlow suggested, to return to Temagami and set out for their next venture. If Martin knew how to conduct himself in the wilderness, Barlow still seemed in charge:

> I felt that the best thing to do, should be to let him have his way.... He allowed me to experiment with the paddle. I soon got the knack. We made excellent time...

A short train ride took Martin and Barlow to Cobalt, the centre of Ontario's current mining boom. This became Martin's first exposure to the excitement, fever, and skullduggery of prospecting and mining, which had repeated itself in thousands of locations throughout much of the United States and Canada since the 1840s. The discoveries in Northern Ontario came at a relatively late stage in North America's mining history, which had always been fuelled by the sense for adventure, hope for riches and, often, plain greed. Hordes of prospectors would move from one mining territory to the next, once their hopes were squashed. They were nearly always single men who caused towns to spring up. The settlements often mushroomed overnight to a population of several thousand and, with rare exceptions, folded just as quickly and sometimes disappeared altogether within a few years.

Cobalt was an experience more disturbing than anything he had seen so far in Canada. Martin was glad he had Barlow with him. As previously in North Bay, Barlow was respected everywhere "as a great authority" by his colleagues and by the prospectors in the area.

> We were received everywhere with lavish hospitality. As soon as his presence had become known over town, he was beleaguered by prospectors who showed him samples of rocks and asked for his valued opinion. We tramped over the claims in and around Cobalt. It was a rough, hilly country with bare rocks and burnt-over forest, swamps and new growth.

Martin was horrified by the character of the town and its rough and tumble appearance. If he did think of going into mining at some future time and building a town, it would have to be radically different from what he saw in Cobalt! Perhaps the seeds for Martin's idea of a mining town like Nordegg went back to his days at Cobalt. Barlow related the history of Cobalt where only a few years before

> ... the first discovery was made by accident, by a railway gang, cutting through a rocky hill. A French-Canadian blacksmith, La Rose, found a small chunk of black ore, and on the side of it, there was pink colour. He tried to smelt it in the open fire, but did not succeed. He sent the ore to the Provincial geologist, Professor Willet Miller of Toronto. He recognized it at once as silver and cobalt-bloom, travelled up to the railway cut, met La Rose, and advised him to stake a claim. Others followed him at once. The news of this discovery spread like wildfire and from all parts of the country prospectors rushed there and in an incredibly short time the surrounding country was staked and development work started.

What Barlow described to Martin at least in part explained the appearance of Cobalt and the nature of its population. But nevertheless, while fascinated by what he observed, Martin could not help disliking this

> ... wooden town, which looked so temporary, rose from rough ground over night. Stores, pool rooms, restaurants, drugstores, boardinghouses and cottages, all hastily constructed and ugly looking, formed the new town of Cobalt. The Provincial Government forbade the sale of liquor, but plenty of whisky was to be had on a doctor's prescription, and this was a welcome, perhaps the most or only remunerative income of the medical profession, of which there were already far too many representatives....
>
>   The silver rush was on. There came mining men and geologists from all over the world, there came promoters from the East and West of the United States, human hyenas who tried to benefit from the experience of the innocents by gambling and betting and selling worthless shares for the hard-earned savings. Business men from Toronto,

Montreal and Ottawa came to convince themselves with their own eyes, if the glowing newspaper reports and the pressing tips of the stockbrokers were actually true. Nothing is easier than to make enthusiasts of doubting Thomases by taking them over the ground and showing them prospects and actual ore, and when one of the greatest mines laid bare the famous silver sidewalk, the excitement knew no bounds. Many brokers established offices in Cobalt, and in Toronto new brokers' offices grew like mushrooms. The country became silver-mad. Fortunes were made and lost. How I kept my head cool in this whirlwind, is difficult to describe. The money belonging to my friends was of course, sacred. And I had no money of my own. And thus I remained only a very interested observer of this wild scramble.

Hopes were raised when a messenger from the prospecting party arrived asking Martin and Barlow "to come and see." But there was very little to see. One party had laid bare a thin quartz vein showing "some yellow spots" while the other party had found nothing at all. Frustrated, Martin returned to Cobalt.

The summer was going. We had seen around Cobalt all that was to be seen. I had many chances offered, but I did not take any, because I was afraid of the risk. However, I learned a lot about mining and financing and speculating and saw that it was easier to lose money than to gain it. But later on, when the rush for stock gained a very rapid momentum, it was difficult to lose money, if one was a little careful, only I was too careful.

Perhaps it was time to leave, but upon Barlow's suggestion, Martin returned once more to the wilderness to shoot a moose at Bear Island. With great excitement, Martin shot his first game. It was also "a bloody experience," in which Martin was confronted with the ambivalence of killing just for the sake of killing. In future, Martin would substitute his camera for his gun and only kill when game was needed for food. And he would always remember Bear Island for its beautiful nature.

The pest of insects had disappeared, and the beautiful autumn began with cold nights. The leaves began to colour after the first frost, and soon there was a riot of colours, ranging from pale yellow to the deepest red. At night the stars appeared to be brighter, and once Barlow awoke me from sleep to admire the Northern light—the aurora borealis. I watched it fascinated for hours, till it disappeared....

At the Ronnoco store, Barlow was waiting with the news that the prospecting parties had returned and had nothing to report.

"I was highly disappointed. We left for Ottawa."

Martin returned to civilization without even a promise of success. But personally, he felt greatly enriched by a wealth of experience gained during the weeks in the wilderness, which, he realized, would stand him in good stead in future. The time had arrived for him to make his own decisions. And now, it was time to sail to Europe!

Martin, nevertheless, felt quite uneasy about arriving in Berlin practically empty-handed. He would not be able to report the discovery of potential riches to the shareholders of the Deutsches Kanada Syndikat. But he was determined to face them honestly, as someone who instead had gained a sound knowledge of the Canadian economic and political scene and made important connections with men of influence. And he had learned much about the dynamics of prospecting and mining, for which he was indebted to Barlow. Martin decided to take Barlow along to Germany.

This was Barlow's first ocean trip. The Atlantic was rough throughout their journey, and Barlow was seasick nearly the entire week. The stay in Berlin, however, made the trip worthwhile for him. Barlow, who had up to this time worked in scientific and civil service circles, was overwhelmed by the self-assured, generous and expansive nature of the shareholders of the Deutsches Kanada Syndikat, all of them successful businessmen or bankers. They, in turn, were slightly taken aback by the appearance of Barlow who was neither dressed very elegantly nor seemed to represent the image the German shareholders had of an educated, successful Canadian. Even Büxenstein had expected someone quite different after what Martin had written him about Barlow. Martin hurriedly assured everybody that Barlow " ...was not the Canadian type, but a great expert."

The shareholders meeting went exceedingly well. In absolute honesty, Martin reported everything he had learned during these few months in Canada—and this was considerable. But he also freely admitted his own disappointment in not having located a promising, sure source of investment. Martin conceded that he might have missed some opportunities because of having been overly cautious, but he received only praise from the shareholders for his frank report.

The news of the boom at Cobalt had also reached Berlin, and some of the shareholders had almost been persuaded to invest in ventures that Martin, from the experience he had gathered, considered quite risky. Barlow's opinion and his recommendations were also respectfully listened to, and the meeting closed to both Martin's and Barlow's satisfaction.

At the lavish banquet that followed the meeting, Barlow felt overwhelmed in the company of these millionaires. But Martin explained to him that in Berlin, "no business of importance would be concluded without plenty to eat and drink." And had the shareholders not fully approved of Martin's choice of Barlow as his geologist to be paid by the Deutsches Kanada Syndikat? And did the shareholders not congratulate him for forming the German Development Company? Martin and Barlow could leave for Canada with the sense of full support of the shareholders of the Deutsches Kanada Syndikat.

Less happy were the hours Martin spent with his family. The main reason for his visit to Berlin was the meeting with the shareholders and receiving advice and support from Georg Büxenstein who had planned for almost every hour of Martin's stay in Berlin.

Martin found his wife Berthe-Marie in a depressed, almost morose state of mind, while little Marcelle had much to tell about her days in school. But was it only Martin's imagination or perhaps a sense of guilt that he felt that even Marcelle seemed less affectionate than before.

Martin left his home on Leibnizstrasse with a heavy heart. He sensed that Berthe-Marie did not believe his assurance that at the end of his next visit to Berlin, the entire family would move to Canada. On the morning of his departure, Marcelle was in school and Berthe-Marie declined Martin's wish for her to accompany him to the Lehrter Bahnhof. Martin did not protest.

Even though it was late fall, the crossing from Bremen to New York was really very pleasant, at least for Martin who returned to Canada much assured by the outcome of the meeting in Berlin. But Barlow, although not seasick at all this time, appeared in a brooding mood. On the train from New York to Ottawa, he confided to Martin that he was very discouraged by the results of the past season and now was "most anxious to show results even during winter." He proposed that Martin send out a party on snowshoes to the Abitibi region north of Cobalt for a report on the geological formations there. Martin agreed and in January 1907 even accepted Barlow's suggestion that he, the great lover of nature, must experience "the beauty of the wild country at this best month of the long winter."

Barlow was eager to meet with the geological party he had sent out, but for Martin, the trip became an ordeal which nevertheless taught him valuable skills of surviving in "deep snow and permanent sunshine." As he later wrote,

It did not take much persuasion to induce me to accompany him [i.e. Barlow]. Had I known what it meant, no persuasion, however glowing, would have induced me. But I did not know, and it seemed to me a novel experience, and adventure.

An adventure it became indeed! The unspeakably poor food in North Bay where Martin was forced to share a bed with a huge, bearded, snoring giant of a lumberjack who smelled to high heaven; the freezing cold during an endless sleigh ride which, at hindsight, seemed comfortable after Barlow and Martin had to change to snow-shoes in order to reach, with the help of a compass, the camp of their party; the strained muscles unused to the gait required for snowshoeing and sleeping in deep snow in a sleeping bag that was barely warm—these all tested Martin's endurance and resilience to their limits.

In comparison, the days at the party's camp were most pleasant. Martin and Barlow slept in a comfortable tent and were served the best food since Ottawa. But the outcome of this strenuous trip al-most broke Martin's heart. "The geology was hardly promising...as no minerals or indications had been noticed."

Martin decided to end this unfortunate adventure. Everything on the return trip served to make Martin's mood bleaker. He had reached the low point of his Canadian activities. He felt and, he was sure, looked like all the other downtrodden prospectors who spent the winter in hopeless, unsuccessful search for minerals.

> I had been in my clothes for so many days. Washing had been spo-radic. In fact, I had only rubbed my face and hands with oily cream. I did not dare to use a looking glass. I believe I must have smelled like my former bedfellow.
> Snow began to fall, which meant higher temperatures. This pro-duced perspiration and I was wet through when we returned to our start-ing point.... We just made the train South, and caught the nighttrain at North Bay. Of course, we wanted to ride the Pullman, but we must have looked like tramps because the porter hesitated in admitting us, until we showed a roll of dollar bills. In Ottawa I soaked for hours in a luxurious warm bath.

Martin decided against any further ventures in Northern Ontario before spring and cherished instead the comforts and pleasures of Ottawa's winter season. The capital's social life, however, Martin found rather stiff and boring, but the remaining winter months, be-came a time of intense learning and of making vital decisions. Martin knew the time had come for him to look elsewhere for opportunities that would satisfy him and the shareholders in Berlin. But where would he find the promised land? Martin spent every day in the of-fices and reading rooms of the Geological Survey, poring over maps and reading reports completed by geological surveying parties across Canada during the last decades. He regularly attended the sessions of the House of Commons, learning more and more about Canada and the political and economic issues of the day. His friend and partner Andrew Haydon introduced him to many members of the House and the Senate.

> ... their conversations taught me a great deal... Gradually I learned there much of the problems of this great country and began to find interest in politics.

Martin's admiration for Sir Wilfrid Laurier rose from week to week. He realized that the Canadian Prime Minister had taken a liking to him. Martin was more than pleased when Sir Wilfrid recognized him in the halls of the Centre Block and invited him to Government House. Remembering several private visits, where "the conversation was always highly interesting" Martin wrote later:

> I admired this great statesman enormously.... He completed the Confederation and his life's work was the reconciliation of races and creeds. He stood for freedom, justice and toleration. He remained Prime Minister for 16 years, until the campaign for reciprocity with the United States gave the Conservative party a chance for defeating him in the elections of 1911. He was the first statesman to raise the question of autonomy of Canada within the British Empire. His philosophical outlook on life and on European politics made me admire him more than ever.

One debate Martin followed intensely during his hours in the visitors' gallery of the House of Commons concerned the question of reciprocity in trade with the United States, part of the entire tariff policy which remained a key issue throughout Laurier's years as Prime Minister. Only the prairie farmers were strongly in favour of reciprocal trade arrangements with the United States, while the fear of American competition caused the Conservative party, the young industry of Central Canada, and British business interests, especially in Canada's budding railroad systems, to oppose strongly any opening towards freer trade with the United States.

Although Laurier managed to diffuse some of the opposition by fostering a system of preferential tariffs that were designed to give advantages to countries (such as Great Britain) that offered favourable tariffs to Canada, the issue remained contentious. In 1911, Laurier decided to call an election primarily on the issue of reciprocity. Its outcome was the defeat for the Laurier government. While in Ontario the anti-reciprocity forces remained dominant, Quebecers distrusted the Liberal party because of what they perceived as too strong an allegiance to the British Empire and its causes around the world. Only in the Prairie provinces did the Liberals gain votes, mainly because of their stand on reciprocity. But the age of Sir Wilfrid Laurier came to an end in 1911.

It was during the winter of 1906-07 that Martin became interested in issues of trade and commerce, quite independent of his own objectives of profitably investing the moneys of the Deutsches Kanada Syndikat in Canada. At this time, Canada's position in the world, especially as a trading nation, became a separate issue for Martin, who soon would be recognized as quite an expert in this field. When he submitted memoranda on issues of international trade to the Government or promoted contacts with German businessmen and experts, Martin received a favourable reception. Having a foot in both countries and on both continents, Martin's offers of opinion or advice were recognized as useful and significant. If what he proposed did not necessarily result in immediate change or action, this was merely a reflection of the Canadian preference of leaving matters unchanged, even though in the case of foreign trade, action seemed pressing in the interests of the country's prosperity.

It appears useful to follow Martin's activities in this field during the next few years. They ran parallel to his primary goals in exploration and mining, which he had chosen soon after his arrival in Canada.

It was Georg Büxenstein who encouraged Martin to create the German-Canadian Economical Association with its headquarters in Toronto. It rather promptly found its German counterpart in a Deutsch-Kanadische Wirtschafts-Interessengemeinschaft in Berlin, which Georg Büxenstein loaded with prominent bankers, lawyers, industrialists and financiers. Martin advised Sir Wilfrid Laurier immediately of this new group when he met him on Parliament Hill in November 1908. And within three weeks, Martin demonstrated the prestige and effectiveness of the new association on both continents when he asked Sir Wilfrid by cable from Toronto on December 12, 1908, whether the Honorable Fielding, Minister of Finance, on his forthcoming tour of Europe would accept an official invitation to Berlin, as

> ... our most influential German Canadian Association ... intends to give a banquet in his honour... Imperial German Government representatives will take part ....

Martin saw in Sir Wilfrid's positive response an important milestone in the gradual alleviation of the strained economic relationship between Germany and Canada, which had reached the proportions of what Martin described as a trade war. It was an issue on which he was prepared to work patiently and persistently, eventually with considerable success.

On August 3, 1909, Martin wrote to the Prime Minister advising him that through his intercession, the Honorable George F. Graham had received special permission from the German Foreign Office to inspect the installations of the Kiel Canal in northern Germany and the Treptow Canal near Berlin as well as several technically advanced features of the German railway system. Martin was pleased to report to Sir Wilfrid that

> ... the Hon. Graham has been received by the German Foreign Office in the most amiable manner, although, according to his special wish, he was received not officially. All permissions he asked for, have been granted at once and most extensively, and he has expressed his highest satisfaction for the way he has been cared for.

Perhaps Martin wanted to place his personal efforts in a favourable light. But there is no doubt that his efforts were genuinely aimed at improving the frosty and often suspicious relations between Ottawa and Berlin in the hope of eventually gaining important economic and political advantages for Canada. Martin did not fail to point out his own importance to the Prime Minister and to Canada when he closed his letter to Sir Wilfrid with the remark that

> I have no doubt, that this information will be gratifying ... especially as permission was refused only recently to the chairman of the Montreal Harbour Commission who had recommendations from the Government and the German Consul in Montreal.

On September 8, 1909, Martin asked the Prime Minister to receive Dr. Brauer, the assistant to the German Secretary of Economic Affairs, who had just completed a tour across Canada. On September 11, Sir Wilfrid's private secretary, M. LeMaire, advised Martin that Dr. Brauer had met with the Prime Minister and "before leaving expressed himself as highly pleased."

Only three days later, on September 14, Martin confidentially approached Mr. LeMaire in an almost conspiring tone that

> ... the Secretary of the German Canadian Economical Association which you will remember I founded for the purpose of ending the tariff war between Germany and Canada, is coming over to this country for a short visit. This Secretary, Dr. Neisser, I would not recommend to Sir Wilfrid by any means, in fact, I would be greatly obliged if you would prevent him from approaching Sir Wilfrid.... Dr. Neisser is absolutely incapable ... and he might damage ... negotiations which are carried out by other people....

More was happening behind the scenes in the delicate, sensitive building of contacts, which eventually would lead to success. In the summer of 1909, when Martin was already deeply involved in the exploration in the West and in the planning of the development of coal mines, he entered into his first and only serious activity of mediating between Germany, the country of his birth and Canada, his adopted country.

Martin was concerned about the loss of economic opportunities Canada suffered because of the poor trade relations that had existed for some years, especially after Canada refused to grant Germany most favoured nation status, even after the British House of Parliament had given special customs privileges to the Dominions of the Empire. When in response, Germany erected high tariff barriers against Canada, Canada retaliated in like manner, which resulted in what Martin described to his friend Andrew Haydon as "a trade war between the two countries." Haydon, who always had free access to the Prime Minister's office, took Martin to Parliament Hill to speak with Sir Wilfrid Laurier, who openly welcomed any initiative that could improve the commercial relations between the two countries from which Canada could only benefit. Martin should discuss his ideas with the Minister of Finance Fielding, who angrily insisted that

> "... as Germany had started the trouble, it was up to her to make the first approach." I replied that I would see what I could do in Berlin.

Martin devoted an entire chapter of his memoirs to this issue, which places him in the light of the experienced lobbyist who knows how to utilize his connections on the highest level. Again, it was Georg Büxenstein who opened the doors for Martin in Berlin. He took Martin to the Foreign Office where a highly placed official, "a fat Saxon," rudely insisted that as long as he was in the Foreign Office, Germany would never approach Canada in this matter. But Büxenstein won in the end by approaching the Emperor. And "The Emperor ... worked quickly."

Two days later, Martin and Büxenstein were asked to come to the Foreign Office where the new German Consul General for Montreal, Dr. Lang, was introduced to Martin. In the most conciliatory manner, Martin was asked to assist Dr. Lang in discussing the sensitive matter of trade relations with the Canadian Government.

A few weeks later in Ottawa, Martin met a rather nonchalant Dr. Lang, who did not hesitate to downplay Martin's usefulness in any forthcoming negotiations with the Canadian government. But he nevertheless expected Martin to request that the Finance Minister Fielding extend an invitation to him. Martin managed to arrange a meeting between the minister and the consul without giving either party the sense that they had taken the initiative for the meeting. Fielding asked Martin to be present, and it is obvious that Martin had briefed Fielding much more extensively than Dr. Lang, who subsequently accused Martin of having acted in the interest of Canada against Germany.

Canada was indeed the greater beneficiary of the agreements eventually reached. An angry Dr. Lang pointedly failed to invite Martin to attend the signing of the treaty about which an informed Martin had already sent a cable to Büxenstein who in turn advised the not yet informed Foreign Office in Berlin. "That ended all relations between the German Consul General and myself."

As he sometimes did in his memoirs, Martin likely described this episode somewhat "larger than life." But although he never tried to become involved in German-Canadian relations again, Martin would be called upon to assist the government of Canada in similar matters on more than one occasion, which gives the description of his role in the ending of the German-Canadian trade dispute a considerable measure of credibility despite its colourful account.

No doubt, Martin's personality and appearance attracted the attention of persons of similar character traits. One of these was Guglielmo Marconi, the Italian inventor of radio telegraphy, who took an immediate interest in Martin when the two met at Russell House in the winter of 1906/07. Marconi had just opened a relay station at Glace Bay, Nova Scotia, from where test messages were sent across the Atlantic to Ireland. During his stay in Ottawa, Marconi had just proclaimed the birth of a new era when "there will be no more cables lying on the bed of the ocean." But, as Martin found out through the inquiries of Colonel Talbot, everyone in the capital looked upon Marconi as a charlatan.

The two men freely shared their experiences and aspirations; and when, after three strong Tom Collinses, Martin admitted that so far success had evaded him in his search for opportunities in Canada, Marconi offered him a partnership in his venture in a very aggressive way. As Martin relates this conversation, Marconi had immediately recognized Martin's qualities, naming them one by one in a most persuasive manner as in a résumé.

> "I like you, young fellow. I could use you very well here in Canada. You know something of science. You speak languages. You are quick in understanding things. I got a Canadian charter. I have a station in Glace Bay, and that is where messages are being received. You might be my representative in Canada."

No question, Martin was flattered, but he also wondered about his obligations to the Deutsches Kanada Syndikat and to Andrew Haydon, who had encouraged him to form the German Development Company. How could he "quit them for something better!" Marconi had a somewhat cynical answer for that problem as well. "... You return their money which will now probably be more, than they will ever see again."

Marconi gave Martin only hours to decide, claiming to leave Ottawa within hours. Not without significance, though, was his willingness to delay his departure when Martin insisted on more time sufficient to consult his lawyer.

If it had not been for the quick inquiries of Colonel Talbot and the outspokenness of Andrew Haydon, Martin might have accepted Marconi's offer and would have never realized his dreams in Canada. When Martin assured Andrew Haydon that in spite of three Tom Collinses, Marconi had been sober, nor did he smell of alcohol the next morning. Andrew Haydon exclaimed

> Well, then the matter is worse than I thought. That fellow is not a drunkard, he is a lunatic. Imagine, sending messages across without a cable! You keep your hands off him.

Martin felt "very humiliated" and gave Marconi his decision over lunch. Marconi's answer was only a curt "You will be sorry." He never returned to the subject, even though Martin spent another three hours with him and saw Marconi off at the train station. As it turned out, Marconi was wrong about Martin; and Andrew Haydon was wrong about Marconi. It was years later that Martin Nordegg and Guglielmo Marconi met by chance at the Savoy Hotel in London. Both men could report success for which they respected each other. And Andrew Haydon had long since recognized the genius and the vision of Marconi.

Marconi had left and with him the temptation for Martin to seek his fortune elsewhere rather than with the German Development Company. But where did his future lie? With spring approaching, Barlow agitated again to send another survey party to Northern Ontario. But this time, Martin firmly refused to finance another exploration venture in an area that had brought him nothing but disappointments.

Finally, a ray of hope appeared when Martin discovered the reports of George M. Dawson, the renowned geologist and director of the Canadian Geological Survey between 1895 and 1905. George Dawson's surveys in the Yukon had contributed to the Klondike gold rush; and the capital of the Yukon, Dawson City, was named after him.

When Martin came across the mention of coal strata that George Dawson had noticed in the Yellowhead Pass west of Edmonton on one of his return trips from the North, his mind immediately started to work on a new vision. Only a week before, he had followed the debates in the House of Commons concerning the two new transcontinental railways that were to cross the Rocky Mountains via the Yellowhead Pass!

> My mind got active.
>
> Coal would be very useful for the two transcontinental railways which were planned to use that pass. I thought I should take time by the forelock and see if I could provide coal for the railways. The question was, would coal be there in satisfactory quality and sufficient quantity? How could one get it? I knew the great value of coal from my native province, Silesia.
>
> I asked Barlow, who were the specialists on coal in the Survey who knew the West.
>
> He replied that he had the very man for me, and there was none better. He took me to the room of D. B. Dowling, introduced me and left us alone.
>
> At once I took a great liking to this charming man.

Once more, Martin was blessed by good fortune. Dowling was not only an expert in his field and a man of imagination, he was also temperamentally to Martin's liking. Dowling was impressed with Martin's modesty, his admission that he knew nothing about coal but that he had a vision of its importance for the rapidly developing West. Dowling recognized that he was not talking to "a born gambler" when Martin explained that his interests were no longer with precious minerals and valuable ore bodies of which he and Barlow had found nothing yet, but with coal, especially "good steam coal for the railways."

Pulling a large map of Western Canada from a shelf, Dowling explained that the two new transcontinental railways "will have to get their coal from Vancouver Island, then further east they will get it from Canmore on the mainline of the Canadian Pacific Railway, and from the Crowsnest area. Of course, that means expensive freight!"

Realizing that he was on the right track, Martin exclaimed

> ... But they are several hundred miles away from the new transcontinentals... Allow me your ruler... If coal is down there, and coal is up here, why should there not also be coal between along that line?

Dowling was somewhat surprised that Martin had read Dawson's earlier report and intimated that his own official report would be soon forthcoming describing his findings gathered on a surveying trip a year ago to the very area Martin had pointed out on the map. Even though he could not permit even a glance at his report before its official release, Dowling did give Martin valuable advice about a number of legal hurdles he would have to clear. The area Martin was so interested in was still unsurveyed Crown land for which the Dominion government had not yet issued regulations with respect to coal mining. Dowling urged Martin to speak to the Minister of the Interior before taking any further steps.

Intrigued by Martin's determination, but also worried about Martin's eagerness to rush ahead, Dowling decided to protect Martin from another failure like he had suffered in Northern Ontario. Yes, Dowling confided, in the particular region along the Eastern slopes of the Rocky Mountains that Martin considered a strategic location for mining coal for the two transcontinental railways, there would be "semi-bituminous coal, good for railway fuel!"

Martin rushed to the office of Andrew Haydon who cautioned that there was as yet no railroad within a radius of almost a hundred miles of the region Martin planned to explore for coal. But Martin was flying high and merely exclaimed, "All right, we will build one!" Andrew Haydon could not help but admire such "spunk and imagination."

Good fortune stayed with Martin on the following day. In the morning, Andrew Haydon introduced Martin and Dowling to the Honourable Frank Oliver, Minister of the Interior and member of Parliament from Edmonton, capital of the province of Alberta.

"The Minister permitted me to go into the foothills of the Rocky Mountains, stake coal under the quartz-mining regulations, and to purchase claims containing coal from the Dominion Government... I did a lot of hard thinking that night..."

Much of Martin's hard thinking centred on Dowling.

"... the only course to pursue would be to travel into that unexplored country with an expert of coal, preferably one who knew the Rockies. What better man in the whole world could I find but Dowling. I would try to engage him..."

Engaging Dowling proved a difficult task. After some lobbying with the Minister of Mines, Martin went to see Mr. Low, the Director of the Canadian Geological Survey. Half laughing, half annoyed, Low received Martin with the words

> I know what you want. The Minister has phoned me. Now you want to take Dowling from the Survey after you took Barlow away from us... You cannot engage Dowling ... But the Minister has told me ... to assist you in your intentions... You can have Dowling under certain conditions: he must agree to work for you this coming season... You can have him only for this season.

Surprised but pleased that the Minister thought so highly of him, Dowling accepted Martin's offer without hesitation. He only requested to remain on the payroll of the Survey while Martin should reimburse him for his extra expenses. "I agreed joyfully; we shook hands and I went home very happy."

Dowling would lead him into an area where he saw his destiny unfolding. During the next six months, he was going to learn a great deal from Dowling, and by the time of Dowling's departure at the end of the summer, he would be ready to stand on his own two feet.

"I did not want to be always under the tutelage of Andy and the Colonel. I wanted to be independent and work out my own salvation. After all, the idea was mine and nobody had helped me to develop it."

The next three months would be filled with preparations for the exploration of the wilderness of the Alberta Rocky Mountains and its resources. This expedition would require vastly different equipment and personnel than the travel through the wilderness of Northern Ontario. Not canoes, but horses would be the means of transportation. For once, Martin was grateful to the German Army; it had made a good horseman out of him. Detailed plans were made; much correspondence went back and forth between Ottawa and Alberta. Dowling kept Martin busy with making most of the arrangements he had decided on and a pleased Martin wrote:

> Dowling found me a very interested and docile pupil ... He advised to inform my friends abroad that I would be gone about four or even five months, and that they could not reach me during that long time by letters or cables.

A feeling of confidence and certainty about the new direction his plans had taken convinced Martin that he was ready to bring his family to North America. He sent a cable to Berthe-Marie and to Georg Büxenstein in early February and on short notice booked his passage from New York to Germany.

For the year 1907, Martin had already mapped out his life. Now he made plans for his family in a rather unexpected way. He decided that Berthe-Marie and Marcelle should live in New York rather than in Ottawa. And if his daughter's future would lie in North America, it was necessary for her to master the English language as quickly as possible and receive the best possible education in a private school. Martin chose the Academy of the Sacred Heart in New York, which taught its pupils in both English and French. This would assure Marcelle, who was already fluent in French, an easier start in North America.

In contrast to his last visit in Berlin, Martin approached the meetings with Georg Büxenstein and the shareholders of the Deutsches Kanada Syndikat in a victorious mood. Not only could he present a solid plan based on geological and economic reports, he was also able to report on the support he had received from more than one minister of the Canadian government.

Martin also looked forward with much greater ease to returning to his family. This time, he would not leave an angry Berthe-Marie in Berlin. Marcelle was excited about the forthcoming trip across the ocean. But Berthe-Marie did not seem to be overjoyed about leaving Europe and was deeply disappointed when Martin explained to her that time would not allow to arrange for even a brief visit to Berthe-Marie's parents in Paris. He had already booked passage on the steamer *Kaiserin Auguste-Victoria* leaving Cuxhaven on March 30. But he promised to take Berthe-Marie along on his next trip to Europe immediately after his return from Alberta in fall and include a leisurely visit to Paris.

The family landed in New York on April 8 after a very pleasant crossing of the Atlantic. Berthe-Marie had enjoyed the comfort and the luxurious surroundings of the *Kaiserin Auguste Victoria*. For the first time in years, she appeared free of her resentment of Martin's egocentric lifestyle. She felt she could now believe Martin's reassuring words that he cared very much for her, after he had, without her knowledge, arranged and paid for Berthe-Marie's parents and her brothers and sisters to come to Cherbourg where the *Kaiserin August-Victoria* landed for a few hours.

The first day in New York already brought the tragic circumstances of the Cohn family, dictated by Martin's restless life and his plans in which neither wife nor daughter had a place, to the surface. The entry in the passenger arrival list said it all.

The data under the column of residence in the United States stated the following:

Martin Cohn—merchant—Waldorf Astoria, New York
Mrs. M.Cohn—wife—Meyer's Hotel, New York
Marcelle Cohn—daughter—Belvedere House New York

For himself, no doubt for reasons of prestige, Martin had chosen the Waldorf Astoria, as he had arranged several business meetings for his brief stopover in New York. Meyer's Hotel, Berthe-Marie's first home in the New World, was a renowned hotel preferred, especially by wealthy Germans, for longer stays in New York. And Marcelle was taken by Martin and Berthe-Marie to Belvedere House, the residence for out-of-town girls attending Sacred Heart Academy. The origins of the Academy, today located on the Upper East Side at Central Park, go back to the Society of the Sacred Heart founded in France early in the nineteenth century. Upon the request of the Catholic bishop of the Diocese of New York, three nuns were sent from France to New York where they opened their first school in 1843 on Houston Street. After several moves and transitions, the Academy of the Sacred Heart was officially founded in 1881 as the first independent school for girls in New York. Although conducted as a Catholic institution, it was noted that the Academy also accepted girls of different faiths.

Martin did what he saw as best for Berthe-Marie and Marcelle. But after being reunited for less than four weeks, the family was split again. Marcelle would remain a student at Sacred Heart Academy until the age of fourteen. Berthe-Marie would never adjust to life in the New World, whether in the United States or in Canada.

Martin suppressed anxiety and guilt about leaving his wife and daughter once more and returned to Ottawa. He could hardly rein in his sense of coming adventure.

> I was in a permanent thrill, and could hardly wait for the day of our departure for the West.

IV

FINALLY, THE WEST
(1907 - 1909)

Colonel Talbot and Andrew Haydon wished Martin and his companion Dowling "luck and success" when the transcontinental train pulled out of the Ottawa Union Station on May 1, 1907. Waving good-bye, Martin fervently hoped that he would return with good news to his "two loyal and good friends in Ottawa."

> The coloured porters shouted 'All aboard' and with constant ringing of the engine bell, and the deep hooting of the siren, which sounds like wolves' howlings, the long train pulled slowly out of the station which I was not going to see again for a long time.... Yet, nothing could dim my adventurous spirit.

Martin's eyes, ears, and mind were wide open. This was his first trip on the Canadian transcontinental train, which he insisted on exploring immediately in its entire length—the elegant Pullman cars, the quite comfortable tourist sleepers, and the day-coaches with their "manifold odors." Martin concluded that "money also here made a class distinction," and Dowling concurred "that the European idea of American equality in the 'one class' trains was a chimera."

Next morning, Martin rose early to spend most of the day on the observation platform at the end of the train. Only occasionally was he driven back into the coach by "clouds of dust, and spells of rain and even hail and snow."

For the entire day Martin was overwhelmed by the bleakness and desolation of the country:

> We noticed deserted huts ... sometimes we saw a sparse settlement, but not a human being or an animal. Every four or five hours the train stopped at divisional points, towns with a dozen or so of wooden houses, and on the platform stood a few men, women and children to whom the daily trains afforded the only diversion.... We skirted the shore of Lake Superior, which looked very beautiful. However, there were no steamers nor sailing boats, rarely a few Indian canoes....

The picturesque area around the Lake of the Woods and the town of Kenora offered a welcome change. Soon after, "... the scenery changed. The small foliage trees got scarcer and scarcer and we entered the prairie. The former round clouds changed into flat and long stretched clouds.... The prairie looks very much like the Siberian tundra," Martin wrote, remembering the endless plains of the Russian Empire he had crossed on his way to China. Nor could he help comparing the delicious food he had enjoyed in Peking and in Shanghai to the terrible slop he had been served in a Chinese restaurant in North Bay!

Martin's mind was set on the Rocky Mountains, where he hoped to find the riches the prairie failed to offer. Besides, he had always been in love with mountains, with the pleasant hilly countryside near his birthplace in Silesia, and even more with the Austrian and the Swiss Alps. But he was still struck by the strange beauty of the prairie and its vastness and emptiness. Faithfully, he entered his impressions in his diary every day.

> Its formation, soft rolling hills and plateaus, no tree or even shrub, shows a startling analogy to the Siberian tundra. There were a few isolated houses and barns, but every station, however small, had its own elevator for grain, and coalsheds; a few houses stood back of the station, mostly stores, and a poolroom. They showed a square front, but this was only a bluff. Behind this make-believe front, there was the sloping roof....

But Martin was surprised and greatly impressed by the city of Winnipeg. He walked from "the splendid Royal Alexandra Hotel...along the broad avenue, called Main Street, laid out in hopes for the future which intended Winnipeg to become the Chicago of Canada."

Everywhere, Martin sensed the excitement of the newly opened, rapidly developing West and the dynamism of the people who had built Winnipeg. This prairie city had been established by the French Canadians as Fort Rouge at the confluence of the Red and Assiniboine Rivers in the middle of the eigthteenth century. It then became Fort Garry and finally in the early 1870s, the settlement of Winnipeg.

> The incredible expansion in less than 40 years of a village with 240 inhabitants into a thriving city of about 100,000, is expressed very well in the change from the fortified trading post of the Hudson's Bay Company to its large and imposing Department store. The former traders of the pallisaded post, dressed in skins, exchanging pelts against rifles, ammunition, beads, baubles and firewater, have changed into a large staff of employees, and immaculately dressed floorwalkers direct the shopping crowd to the counters, filled with merchandise from all corners of the world.

There was pride among those who had succeeded in this dynamic city and hope in the eyes of those who had just arrived or were passing through on their way further west.

> We returned to the station and looked at the motley, truly cosmopolitan crowd, in which the colour of the skin ranged from the pale white of the Scandinavian to the deepest black of the African. Peacefully, they sat side by side. And their costumes—Scots in kilts, and Parsees and Hindus in turbans, Malayans and Bohemians, Chinese, Japanese and Greeks, all friendly together, seeking a new home in hospitable Canada. They sat on their baggage, patiently waiting for the train which would take them to their ultimate destination, as settlers.

The romance of the West had captured Martin. Probably, there were fewer people from Asia and Africa in "the motley crowd" waiting for their train in Winnipeg than Martin later seemed to remember. But without intending to do so, the forever hopeful, optimistic, and visionary Martin accurately characterized the composition of the millions of immigrants later in this century seeking a better life in "hospitable Canada."

Regina, the capital of the young province of Saskatchewan, which the train passed in the middle of the night, left no impression on Martin. Martin entered a note in his diary about Medicine Hat,

> where the lamps, fed by natural gas, burn day and night, and the squaws of the Sarcee tribe sat placidly on the platform, trying to sell their beadwork and sweetgrass baskets to the tourists.

And finally, when the train stopped at Gleichen on the Blackfoot Reserve

> I saw in the far distance the serrated silhouette of the Rocky Mountains, and as the sun was setting behind them, his rays gilded the clouds which changed again from flat bodies to round ones.

Martin was close to his destination, Alberta and its Rocky Mountains. These were to become his destiny. This was the country where he would spend the most fruitful, exciting, and meaningful time of his life, a country which would never let go of his imagination.

Alberta was truly a province in the heyday of its pioneer era. Created in 1882 as one of four districts of the North West Territories, Alberta gained provincial status in 1905 after much political wrangling. Edmonton was chosen as its capital, much to the disappointment and chagrin of the people of Calgary and the politicians representing the southern half of the province.

Edmonton was a much older settlement. The first trading post and fort, Edmonton House, had been established in the area in

1795. Because the fur trade, initially the primary economic activity in the area, was concentrated in the northern half of the later province of Alberta, Edmonton gained prominence much earlier than Calgary, which was founded only in 1875 as a fort of the North West Mounted Police.

When soon after it was decided to build the first transcontinental railway along the southern route rather than through the Yellowhead Pass farther north via Edmonton, Calgary began to boom, not unlike Winnipeg a couple of decades earlier. Not until Edmonton became the seat of the provincial government did Calgary find a competitor to the north. In the meantime, Calgary had grown rapidly, remaining for years the feeder point for Edmonton via the Calgary-Edmonton Trail first, and from 1891 on via the Calgary and Edmonton Railway. Ahead of Edmonton, Calgary was incorporated as a town in 1884 and became a city in 1892.

After travelling hundreds of miles through the empty prairie, Martin was surprised to find a well-developed city with paved streets, excellent hotels and elegant stores. And Calgary's main street, Stevens Avenue [Eighth Avenue], was lined by respectable brick and sandstone buildings. There was already a prosperous upper class, who had begun to build their mansions on the hillsides above the city centre. But the flavour of the West and its pioneer days was still prevalent: cowboys, Indians, ranchers, and newly arriving settlers crowded the city's downtown streets.

Two days in Calgary and a short train ride west to the Stoney Indian Reserve at Morley were to be the last contacts with the comforts of civilization for Martin and Dowling for months to come. From then on, Martin would fill page after page of his diary with facts and poignant observations about the nature of the country and its inhabitants. He was fascinated with the way of life of the Stoney Indians, their social structure, customs, habits, and dress, which he would describe in minute detail in his memoirs thirty years later, preserving an image of an era which by then would have changed beyond recognition.

Not that there was any lack of studies, reports, stories and memoirs about the Canadian West. There were many at that time and more to come, including numerous scientific articles and historical monographs. Martin would not tell informed readers anything new. But in addition to his other talents, in his memoirs, letters, and other writings, he proved himself a writer of remarkable gifts—outstanding powers of observation, retention of events and impressions, and a talent to put everything on paper in a rapidly flowing, entertaining but nevertheless highly informative form.

If Martin seems to go into every detail, he never does so to the point of boredom. Detail after detail in a never-ending chain of images, he admirably succeeds in creating a composite picture that comes to life immediately in the reader's mind, as if one were looking at a photograph of the scene he so vividly describes.

Martin was neither a historian nor an anthropologist by training; but his writings and reports, especially his memoirs, are of remarkable accuracy and depth of characterization. And what helped Martin to create breadth and depth in his writings was his curious, gregarious nature which never stopped him from reaching out to people and learning from them at all times—and, of course, relating to the best of them and making them his advisers, partners, and friends!

Martin and Dowling now entered the crucial phase in their expedition; and Dowling proved himself invaluable as a resourceful advisor, introducing Martin to the country and its people and, of course, eventually to one of its primary resources–coal.

Hardly having stepped off the train at the little station of Morley, Martin was introduced by Dowling to a man who was to become his trusted, loyal partner, and faithful friend,

> ... the factor Stuart Kidd, in charge of the general store, who sold to the Indians, cowboys and ranchers all they could afford to buy. I liked his looks. He had such true eyes.... I watched him carefully in his dealings with his difficult customers, white and red, and they all seemed to like him. We became great friends; later I engaged him and he stayed and still stays with my company. He remained loyal to me, when the war made me an outcast, and we remained friends ever after.

As Stuart Kidd's son Fred wrote in a short biography of his father:

> My father was born in 1883 on a farm about 25 miles East of Ottawa.... His parents were James Kidd and Catherine Stewart (Kidd). The Kidds ... settled on this farm in 1818, having come from the south of Ireland.... The Stewarts came from Perthshire, Scotland and settled nearby.... Dad finished grade nine, then left to assist his father on the farm....
> In 1902 Dad came west to Saskatchewan on a harvest excursion, workers were given free passage to help in the harvest.... He liked the west and came to Alberta ... homesteading ... about four miles ... from the present Calgary city limits on the west branch of Nose Creek.... Dad's shack was in the creek valley but from the height of land on the east side of the valley he could see the Rocky Mountains. He told me he could not resist their attraction and moved to Morley in 1907. There he became the storekeeper and ranch manager ... replacing his brother Fred who had run the store from 1902 to 1907. Fred Kidd became great friends with Donald Bogart Dowling, a Dominion of Canada geologist

who named a mountain on the south side of Ribbon Creek "Mount Kidd" after Uncle Fred....

Dad learned to speak the Stoney Indian language at Morley, and he took lots of horses in trade with the Indians.... Martin Nordegg ... used Morley from 1907 as a starting point for coal exploration.... Dad and Mr. Nordegg became good friends and in 1910 Dad took a job as purchasing agent for Mr. Nordegg....

Gazing at the nearby Rocky Mountains, Martin was eager to start for the Bighorn and Brazeau River country to the north. He wanted to find his coalfields. But Stuart Kidd required at least a week to get all supplies together and to ready the packtrain. Martin welcomed Dowling's suggestion that they head west instead of waiting on the reserve. That way, Martin would not have to wait any longer to get to the Rocky Mountains, which he had longingly looked towards from a distance for almost a week. Besides, on their way to Banff, he could inspect the coal mines supplying the Canadian Pacific Railway in Canmore and Bankhead before embarking on his own exploration for coal deposits. Always aware of his own ignorance when it came to coal, Martin was more than grateful.

Introduced by Dowling, I was received most heartily everywhere, and with his explanations I was able to learn a lot about Western coal and mining methods.

The preparation of the packtrain destined to take Martin and Dowling to the Bighorn Basin took longer than expected. At last, the head-packer arrived, a rather colourful man whom Martin observed with anxiety and mistrust. Not until the first days on the trail did he fully recognize and appreciate his remarkable qualities:

... while we partook of some more cool beer in the cellar, somebody stumbled down the ladder. In strutted an old cowboy, dressed in buckskins, the famous Tom Lusk, our headpacker. He spent his life in Texas and had come North only a dozen of years ago. Tom squatted on the floor... pulled from his chaps a large bottle of whisky, took a very long drink, interrupted by girgling, and then smacked his lips. When he took the bottle out of his face, I saw that the contents had dwindled to nearly half. He wore a Stetson hat, and a red bandana decorated his neck. The silver spurs on his high Strathcona boots tinkled like bells. His leather belt was studded with silver nails. He looked like a figure from a Wild West show.

As long as we were in Morley, his eyes appeared to me glassy, and I began to believe that this was their natural appearance. But when I noticed the copious drinks he took so frequently, I had doubts and asked Dowling. He replied, that Tom never took a drink on the trail for several reasons. Bottles are too fragile, and the weight of many cases had to be taken into account, as they would have required several more packhorses. But at the finish of the season's work, all these reasons did not exist any more, then he invests his hard earned wages in liquor and retires with many cases to his cabin near Morley. The Indian agent and the neighbours watch the smoke from his chimney. When that stops, they pay a courtesy call to see if they have to relight the fire or just prepare a funeral. Tom is very methodical in his habits. He divides his cases and bottles into the six winter months....

As the preparations for the trip continued, Martin felt more at ease about Tom Lusk. During the day

> ... he was only moderately drunk, which enabled him to concentrate on this important business, in which nothing must be forgotten. But when the evening came, the time was his own, and he made full use of it... He wobbled like a ship in a storm.... In the morning he was perfectly sober, and then I saw, that his eyes were not glassy but steel blue! Instead of breakfast, he took a good size drink.

No matter how inebriated he became, Tom Lusk treated Martin as a gentleman, which speaks well for Martin who had barely spent a year in Canada and only a few days in the West. The old Texan had quickly gained great respect for Martin, but he also made it clear that he was the boss. Politely, he asked Martin to lay out in three distinct piles all the possessions he wanted to take along on the trip to the Bighorn. Reshuffling things again in order to reduce them to what Tom considered absolutely necessary, a heart-broken Martin saw his gear dwindle to one tiny bundle, small enough to be squeezed into one dunnage bag. Only a change of underwear did Tom Lusk grant, because Martin was "a gentleman... Tom declared me a good scout, and I felt proud."

On their last day at Morley, Tom introduced Martin to his horse Bessie. Martin knew that he was in a different world when Bessie indignantly turned her head away when Martin offered her a lump of sugar. Martin would learn much more from Tom—that these "cayuses" of the wilderness had never known sugar but would appreciate a lick of salt instead.

Because of a late start, the first day of the expedition, mainly along what Martin described as "almost a wagon road" turned out to be easy and short. Only the unaccustomed Mexican saddle caused Martin much discomfort. But after a few days, the wagon road changed into a narrow trail; and as the party climbed higher and higher in the mountains towards Pipestone Pass, the going became more and more difficult. It was often extremely strenuous because of the numerous deadfalls where the trees, intertwined in all directions, at times seemed insurmountable.

There was no end to what Martin had to learn—making his bed from boughs each night, reining in and packing the horses in the

mornings, crossing the frequent swamps on horseback, stopping his
ornery but clever horse from pushing him against the rough trees on
the narrow trail, and enduring rain and snow in clothing that never
seemed to dry. In all, Martin was the perfect disciple. For him, this
was a time of adventure and new experiences from which, thanks to
Tom Lusk, he learned much that would prove invaluable on his future expeditions when he would be the boss and decision-maker.

> Tom Lusk became a good friend of mine. He was high in the sixties.
> He carried two revolvers and a large bowie knife. On the revolvers he
> showed with great pride several notches, indicating the number of men
> he had shot, as he said. Dowling thought this possible, because Tom
> had to leave Texas very suddenly and never wanted to go back there.
> Tom was high-tempered. For the slightest reason he flew into a rage
> which caused most picturesque, very descriptive and emphatic language.
> He scared men and beast. He loved horses but addressed them always in
> the most terrible swearwords. They didn't seem to mind them from
> him, but not from the packers to whom they showed absolute indiffer-
> ence....
>   The horses were badly mannered. They knew all the tricks of the
> trade of making life easier for themselves; they rubbed their packs
> against every tree so that the cinch would get loose, and in consequence
> they had to be relieved of their load for a while.... The saddle ponies
> followed different tactics. Before mounting, they pirouetted and danced
> ... and made some attempt at bucking.... If unsuccessful, they tried a
> sitdown strike, roll over and one had to be very quick taking the feet out
> of the stirrups....

Despite the unaccustomed strain of travelling through such
rough territory on horses that were a far cry from the horses he had
ridden while in the German army, Martin was involved in this expedition with heart and soul. The days were long and the sunset late.
Each evening before nightfall, he entered detailed notes into his diary. And as a skilled photographer, he made constant use of his
camera. Some of the copies of his later memoirs and some personal
albums contain photographs of great descriptiveness and beauty: of
mountains and valleys, of rivers and creeks, and of the people of the
packtrain. Among them, the pictures of the Pipestone Pass and the
crossing of the North Saskatchewan River are the most impressive.
    What excitement his first experience of travelling with a pack-
train through the Rocky Mountains brought to Martin is illustrated
by the lengthy and detailed descriptions of this trip in his later
memoirs. They convey such a vivid picture that their readers will
complete these passages with a sense of having been there in person, having learned about packtrains and riding through wilderness
territory, much as Martin did in the spring of 1907.

Martin had approached the Canadian Rocky Mountains with the romantic notions of the European traveller well familiar with the Austrian and Swiss Alps. What he found was awe-inspiring, but very different. What Martin later wrote about his first impressions echoes the reports of thousands of European tourists travelling through the Canadian Rockies to this day:

> Although comparisons are odious, it is natural that a European should compare the Alps with the Rockies. The structure of the Rockies resembles that of the Dolomites. But even the bare Dolomites show in their lower regions the presence of man; there are villages, barns, fields of hay and clover, cows, sheep and goats grazing peacefully in the meadows. The Alpine flowers, roses, gentians and other flowers bring a vivid colour into that lively and living landscape. The Rockies appear in their bareness and solitude majestic and awe-inspiring. There are flowers in the valleys and passes, but not of vivid hues. And over them hang the towering crags and rocks. While the Alps are full of melodious sounds, the Rockies are silent. There are birds, but they are mute. The forests, mostly pines, extend up the mountains to the tree-limit — but often they are burnt over and the trunks point despairingly to the firmament. For a pioneer, there is the great thrill of penetrating a region which hardly a human foot has trodden before him.
>
> A great silence reigns in the Rockies. Only the creaking of the saddles and leather straps, sometimes the neighing of a horse disturbs thoughts. In the higher mountains, one is startled frequently by the sudden whistling of a curious marmot which disappears as soon as one looks in its direction.
>
> At night, the noises are more prevailing. Wolves are howling in the distance. In a strong wind fallen trees, rubbing against each other make ghostlike noises, shrieking, squeaking. But no other sounds....

This was a poignant characterization of a remote territory of the Rocky Mountains experienced even today by only a few hardy hikers. It is quite different from the more accessible country around the much-frequented Banff, the destination of most tourists visiting the Canadian Rockies. On his later trips to the high mountain country, Martin learned that there was a short season when the Alpine flowers high up in the Rockies did break out in a riot of colour, but his first crossing of the Pipestone Pass in 1907 preceded that season by several weeks. The overwhelming experience of solitude and silence that surprised Martin so much in the spring of 1907, hits the hikers of the back-country even today. There were daily challenges of following hardly visible trails, crossing one windfall after the other, travelling across passes above the treeline in rain, sleet and snow.

> Little did my shareholders or I myself imagine the hardships that were ahead of me. But what were these physical hardships, compared to the mental ones I had to endure to make a realization of a dream? These

were the thoughts when encountering hindrances in the mountains. Strange to say, I did not even miss news from the outside. No letters, no cables, no newspapers for weeks and months. I concentrated on the happenings of the day, on the difficulties of the trail and hopes for the future, building castles in the air.

To ride from one of the luxurious hotels in the mountains on well-trodden trails, over wooden bridges spanning rivers and creeks, over corduroy roads covering swamps—for sport, fishing, hunting, camping—that is a great pleasure. But travelling for months into the virgin wilderness, with a determined purpose which must be a success, looking for a trail made by hunting Indians long ago, or cutting new trails, through windfalls and muskegs, across rivers, in every weather, sharing the responsibility for men and beasts, and large expenditure, that was a totally different matter....

The dichotomy of struggling to survive the challenges of the hitherto unknown wilderness and the worry about the ultimate purpose of this expedition tormented Martin night after night. There were hours when this harsh, lonely country and its desolate, overpowering mountains took on the character of hostile territory to Martin. It was at times uninviting to the explorer who hoped to find and develop riches for the benefit of a civilization that seemed more and more remote every day.

Finally, riding ahead of the packtrain to the top of a bare mountain, Martin looked "... down on the mighty Saskatchewan ... a wonderful panorama of this wide valley."

From the Pipestone Pass it took another two days and, for the inexperienced Martin, a hair-raising crossing of the treacherous North Saskatchewan River before Tom Lusk announced time for a prolonged rest for men and horses. The group had reached the Kootenay Plains, the wide, open valley where, to Martin's delight, flora and fauna were so much richer than in the high mountain country. Martin had a first inkling that he could grow to love this country, not yet knowing that one day he would wish to build his permanent home not far from the present campsite.

But he also sensed that the day was close when Dowling would replace Tom Lusk as his most important companion. Dowling had explained that they were only a couple of days from the Bighorn area where he had discovered some coal during an earlier trip. Martin was very tense. The burden of knowing that he would soon have to report the findings of his exploration trip to Georg Büxenstein and his German shareholders in Berlin rested heavily on his mind.

Far too remote from any area of settlement, the Bighorn was still a territory that no one had considered worth exploring. Instead, for the past twenty years, the search for coal deposits and their subsequent development had followed the building of railways and the opening up of land for settlement in what became the province of Alberta in 1905.

It all began in the young town of Lethbridge where Sir Alexander T. Galt established the North Western Coal and Navigation Ways in 1882. Below the town, in the deep valley of the Oldman River, Galt's company opened its first mine, shipping its coal by steamer to the Canadian Pacific Railway at Medicine Hat. In 1890, the Canadian Northwest Coal and Lumber Syndicate began to supply coal to the C.P.R. from its new mines at Canmore west of Calgary at the entrance to the Rocky Mountains. Within a few years, additional coal mines were opened at Bankhead and Anthracite, close to Banff. When the Canadian Pacific Railway built its Crowsnest Pass line in 1897, the International Coal and Coke Company established the town of Coleman to be followed by a string of more than half a dozen coal mining towns throughout the length of the Pass.

The search for coal was also on to the north, where the Canadian Northern Railway had reached Edmonton in 1905 and was rapidly working its way towards Jasper and the Yellowhead Pass when Martin began to search for coal in the Bighorn area to the south. Soon, a second transcontinental competitor entered the race, the Grand Trunk Pacific, which ran its line to the West Coast on an almost parallel course to the CNoR.

While the Canadian Pacific was well supplied with coal from the mines near Banff and in the Crowsnest Pass, Martin envisioned tremendous opportunities for coal producers to serve the two northern transcontinental lines that were also laying numerous branch-lines throughout the Prairies. While some of these branch-lines could be supplied at least in part by small local coal operators, the bulk of the coal required for steam locomotives still had to be transported from Vancouver Island or from mines in the East.

Martin and Dowling's party had now reached the Bighorn, where Dowling had discovered promising coal deposits during an earlier exploration:

> This is good steam coal and probably the best grade for coke. The fuel ratio places it at about the grade of Blairmore and Frank coal [in the Crowsnest Pass], though it seems to have less ash.

Martin hardly noticed the beauty of the dual cascades of the Bighorn Falls [Crescent Falls] next to which Dowling had decided to set up camp. He urged Dowling to begin the search for the coal immediately the next morning.

We walked along the river. Suddenly Dowling stopped and showed me on the other bank long horizontal black bands in the creamish rock.

'Is that coal?' I asked.

'No, that is shale. But below we are sure to find coal. This will be our first coalfield.'

'How will we find the coalseams?'

'I will show you tomorrow.'

Next morning we set out, accompanied by the men with picks and shovels ... to start driving a tunnel....

In the afternoon, while Dowling was completing the trace of our travelling on his fieldmap, one of the men came running down and brought a chunk of coal. There was great excitement.... I believe I was the most excited of all.... On the logfire ... it immediately started burning with red flame....

This first chunk of coal that the elated Martin held in his hand came from a trench his men had dug on the hillside less than a mile above the upper Big Horn Falls—and that trench is still faintly visible to-day!

During the next days the men worked hard. Dowling shifted them to other places and they uncovered six workable seams, ranging in thickness from 4'6" up to 13'. In the meantime, we started staking, taking the top of the double fall as a landmark, and in a few days covered altogether several thousand acres. My dream had come true! I could not sleep quietly any more. I only saw mountains of coal. Dowling was happy with me and whistled all day long with contentment and excusable pride.

For several weeks, the party worked in the narrow valleys of the Big Horn Range, slowly making its way through the densely covered, mountainous country to the northwest. The work was hard, but the weather was perfect, and there was plenty of game and good feed for the horses, which "looked sleek and plump." But Martin remained in an unsettled, anxious mood. They were struggling through rugged mountain country where any possible coal deposits were too deeply located in the disturbed geological strata. Martin and Dowling impatiently pushed on, always riding ahead of the packtrain, only to report to the rest of the party each evening that no coal had been found.

Finally, high above the banks of a little creek, a tributary of the South Brazeau River [Blackstone River], Martin and Dowling noticed clearly visible coal-bearing strata. Camp was set up immediately for further explorations, digging trenches, driving tunnels into the hillside, and testing the unearthed coal. After two weeks, Martin jubilantly reported in his diary that

... we found eight workable seams varying from three feet to 12 feet,
and the coal seemed to be of the same excellent quality as the Bighorn
... testing ... proving it to be a coking coal.

In the happiest mood in many weeks, Martin Nordegg baptized
the little creek "George Creek" in honour of Georg Büxenstein, his
mentor, friend, and boss.

Martin's enthusiasm was dampened, however, by worry about
the problems he would face after his return to Ottawa. Where could
he raise the necessary cash for the purchase of the discovered coalfields? Dowling advised him to stop exploring and staking—there
would be enough coal for generations to come. But Martin refused
to listen. During his weeks in the Cobalt area, he had learned
enough to realize the importance of protecting his claims against future intruders. He was determined to continue his explorations.

Although Martin admitted to Dowling that he could not afford
further staking of claims, he insisted on making use of the time left
to the maximum. Dowling eventually agreed to an exploration of the
area to the north so that when Martin returned in the following
spring he would be able to stake additional claims quickly.

What followed were several weeks of wretched life for the small
party of Martin, Dowling, Tom Lusk, and a few other men. While
the rest of the group remained at George Creek with explicit instructions for the uncovering of further seams, Martin and his party experienced nothing but disappointments and hardship. No coal of acceptable quality was discovered anywhere, the weather was rough,
and neither game nor fish were found. When one packhorse nearly
drowned while crossing a swollen, turbulent river, all the staple
food supplies—coffee, tea, bacon, etc.—were lost and the men became nervous, irritable, and testy. Martin sensed they were close to
a mutiny, when even Tom Lusk became so difficult that Martin had
to stay out of his way.

> Next day we were all ready to explode when we heard some shots, and
> two hours later ... one packer brought in the liver and tongue of a
> young moose.... This seemed to have changed our luck, because we
> found not only fish but also coal.

But Martin did not dare to stake more claims. He would return to
the upper reaches of the South Brazeau River the following year after having raised more money. This turned out a grave mistake, as
Martin realized the following spring: "I wished I had not been so
circumspect that time — it would have saved us a lot of trouble... "

But for now, Martin was more than happy to return to the camp
at George Creek where the men had worked hard driving tunnels
into the mountainside. When he watched Dowling carefully inspect-

ing samples from various seams, an idea sprang up in Martin's head: What more convincing evidence could he present to his investors in Germany than a large chunk of this excellent coal! After much deliberation, Martin selected "... a block of shiny black coal, weighing at least thirty pounds ... to impress my friends abroad."

Tom Lusk constructed "... a little coffin for the chunk ... and chose his most gentle and obedient horse to carry it."

The cool autumn nights had arrived, and Martin was ready to leave for Morley. During the return across the Pipestone Pass, there was enough time for Martin to calculate the capital he would have to raise for developing the coal deposits he had discovered. With Dowling's expert advice, he arrived at a sum that looked astronomical to both of them—$2 million for the mine and $6 million for the railway! Martin was shocked and troubled, but his optimism eventually gained the upper hand: "We had the coal, and the railways needed it, and therefore I knew that by some miracle the money would have to come."

After the hardships of the past months, the Indian reservation at Morley "appeared like paradise." But Martin was eager to return East and depart for Germany as quickly as possible. He could hardly wait to report his success to Georg Büxenstein and his investors. And he also badly needed to calm his mind that the shareholders of the Deutsches Kanada Syndikat were prepared to raise sufficient capital that would enable him to secure his claims and proceed with the opening of the coalfields he was so proud to have discovered.

Martin left Tom Lusk in charge of the horses for next year's expedition. Everything was packed for his journey. There was one last big party. Martin went to bed contentedly but could not fall asleep. Perhaps in somewhat grandiose words, but still reflecting the true feelings in his heart, he wrote thirty years later:

> That night the thought occurred to me that I had really now a stake in this great country. My ties with my native country had been severed already many years ago, when I emigrated ... to England; and when Colonel Talbot visited me in Berlin, I had only been a few years there again having been recalled from London to manage the plant. I was now more at home in Canada than I had ever been in Germany. Here I had succeeded in making great friends too—I felt very happy here and not so oppressed as in Germany. There was no question in my heart. I would adopt this great country, hoping that it also adopt me.

During these beautiful, sunny fall days of 1907 in Alberta, Martin's love affair with Canada had come into full bloom. It was a love that would never diminish, although more than once, it would be put to a severe test. By circumstances of war and eventually by his own choice, his loyalty would extend to the United States, finding its expression not only in pioneering ventures but also in more and more friendships with people of all walks of life, from the uppermost circles in politics and finance in Ottawa and Toronto, Washington, and New York to the working class. It speaks strongly for the qualities in Martin's personality and character. He had a strong sense of loyalty; and he knew not only how to form meaningful relationships, but also how to nurture and maintain numerous friendships over a lifetime.

Conversely, it was this latter quality in Martin that bound him irreversibly to the land of his birth through numerous tangible and less tangible ties to Europe, foremost to Germany. Martin's pronounced identification with Canada and later the United States, with their democratic system and their tradition of freedom of the individual, gives credence to his frequent criticism of the political climate in Germany and everything "Prussian," which he hated too much to ever want to live in Germany again. On the other hand, Martin never relinquished his deep admiration of German culture, always trying to interpret to his friends and to Canadian and American politicians and businessmen what he perceived as the best in the German character.

There is no question that Martin possessed a strong sense of self-worth and self-importance. Some people might even be inclined to judge his political involvement in the affairs between Canada and Germany and later between the United States and his country of birth as a source of nurture of his sense of self-importance. But in Martin's words and actions, there is an undeniably genuine concern for the welfare of people, individuals as well as specific groups. This became evident after World War I and more pronounced during the Hitler years when political conditions in Europe, especially in Germany, Austria, and Czechoslovakia, became increasingly precarious. In this respect, Martin proved himself the courageous humanitarian, at times even at considerable risk to his own personal safety. Deep in his heart, he always retained a strong sense of loyalty not to Germany as a nation but to the German people. Still, his love for Canada and the personal freedom and respect for the individual inherent in North American civilization and its traditions became the guiding force in his life.

How tragic it was, though, that Martin never succeeded in creating a sense of stability and permanence for his wife and his daughter. There was no legal breakdown in his marriage, but after the first happy years in England, it never became a happy, fulfilling union again. If Martin was successful in helping hundreds of friends and strangers to a better life in the New World, he singularly failed to do the same for his first wife and his daughter.

When Martin travelled to Europe after the successful summer of 1907 in the Bighorn country, he took along a reluctant Berthe-Marie, who felt guilty about leaving her nine-year-old daughter at the boarding school in New York. She was happy to see her own family again in Paris. But her days of being with Martin were exceedingly short. After the crossing of the Atlantic, Martin left Berthe-Marie in Paris and immediately continued his journey to Berlin.

In Berlin, a triumphant Martin placed the box containing the thirty-pound chunk of coal from Alberta on the desk of Georg Büxenstein, president of the Deutsches Kanada Syndikat: "… this is our coal, and I have bought the coal fields from the Canadian Government."

Staring at the shiny block of coal in surprise and confusion, Büxenstein exclaimed, "But we have so much coal ourselves here in Germany, at the Ruhr and in Silesia!"

It was easy for Martin to reiterate that "… this is our coal to be needed badly by the expanding railways in Western Canada," but much harder to confess that to make the possession of these rich deposits of coal profitable would require enormous outlays of capital. "The President's face grew pale. He was speechless for a minute."

But true to his nature, Büxenstein allowed his sense of opportunity to gain the upper hand. To Martin's relief, he was willing to call a meeting of the stockholders of the Deutsches Kanada Syndikat as soon as an expert opinion of the coal's quality was obtained.

Büxenstein chose Professor Potonié, a French scientist working at the Prussian Academy of Mines in Berlin, who was considered the foremost authority in this field. Potonié, who had just published a highly respected volume on *The Origin of Coal*, seemed the ideal person. But when Martin entered Potonié's office with the chunk of coal from the Bighorn in his arms, he had no inkling of what was about to happen:

> A gaunt, tall figure with silver-white hair and a long white beard rose from behind the desk.
> "Not there, on the floor!"
> I did as I was told.
> "What is that?"
> "A sample of coal from Canada."
> "… show me on the map where it came from." He never even asked my name.
> He turned to the wall, where many maps were hanging … one … labelled British North America.

I found the Rockies, but could not reach so high up and grabbed a ruler on his desk to point on the map.

He tore the ruler from my hand, slammed it on his desk, took a long bamboo pole from behind the map and stretched it out to me. Meekly I took it....

I found the Saskatchewan River and pointed to a spot North of its source.

"That must be a mistake.... The Rocky Mountains, young man, are Cretaceous, are they not?"

"Yes...."

"Oh no, my young friend, that coal never came from there...."

He took a book from his desk....

"See here. This is my book about the Origin of Coal. On this page you find, that there is no coal in the Cretaceous.... You are one of the most impudent swindlers and imposters I ever heard of.... Out you go, or else I kick you out."

He came towards me with his long bamboo pole, and I fled out of the door....

Then came a crash. The Professor had lifted my precious coal and he threw it through the door to the landing, and it broke into several pieces— and it nearly broke my heart ... tears welled in my eyes....

In his memoirs, Martin described the episode in the Prussian Academy of Mines over several pages in colourful detail, probably somewhat larger than life. But a reader familiar with the exalted position academics enjoyed in Germany and their belief in the unquestioned possession of the ultimate truth will be intrigued by Martin's account. Although Potonié was French, Martin detected in him all the traits so typical of the German professor at that time: from the description of the professor's appearance and superior demeanor to his habits, his manner of speech, and his obvious lack of respect for Martin, who may have been knowledgeable about coal, but as a non-academic, not worth the time listening to but only lectured to.

What saved Martin's career in Canada from a premature end was Büxenstein's absolute faith in him and his honesty and integrity, which superseded the belief Büxenstein had for Potonié's expertise. Now, the question was how to obtain absolute proof of the origin of the coal sample Martin had brought to Berlin. Only the Canadian government could help! Büxenstein directed Martin to dispatch a cable to Ottawa immediately, requesting confirmation of the location of Martin's coal discovery.

While the statement received from Ottawa was unequivocal and to the full satisfaction of Georg Büxenstein, the tragi-comedy surrounding Professor Potonié had not yet ended. Haughtily, the professor refused to meet with Georg Büxenstein, the respected Privy-

Councillor. But he could not refuse the order to appear at a conference the clever Büxenstein had arranged with a member of the Emperor's civil cabinet, Privy-Councillor Abbe. True to the stereotype of the German professor who will treat anybody below his status with disdain but will immediately fall into a posture of deeply respectful demeanor in the presence of a high government official, Potonié "...bowed deeply. He was full of apologies when he read the cable from Canada.... He insisted on seeing the occurrence in person, as there must be a mistake somewhere."

Privy Councillor Abbe assured Potonié that he would personally make arrangements for a visit to the coal fields in question as early as next spring and that the professor had "better get ready to go to Canada."

An amused Martin, now feeling the winner, noted how "the Professor shook hands with the President and bowed deeply. But he made a very stiff bow towards me, without shaking hands." Martin could not wait to introduce the professor to his domain in Canada.

Martin had won the battle, but he still had to face his President with the request for approximately $8 million for the realization of his Canadian dream. He did not need to worry. Firmly committed now to Martin's project, Büxenstein opened the meeting of the board and shareholders of the Deutsches Kanada Syndikat by asking Martin to give a report on his discoveries and the opportunities for coal produced in Western Canada. After Martin's enthusiastic presentation, it was easy for Büxenstein to raise $40,000 on the spot. But this was only a pithy amount.

On the following day one of the shareholders arranged a meeting between Martin and Fritz Friedländer-Fuld, one of Upper Silesia's great coal magnates and a well-known investor in new industrial ventures. Friedländer-Fuld's reaction was not what Martin had hoped for: "You have found some coal out there in the wilderness. Hand it over to somebody else, after you have helped yourself to a nice profit."

To Martin's relief, Büxenstein had another ace up his sleeve:

England is the mother-country of Canada. That is where we should get the money. I will speak to one of our big bankers and induce him to go to London. You better be off to Canada, and we will cable to you.

On February 10, 1908, Martin left Berlin from the Potsdamer Bahnhof, where Georg Büxenstein embraced him in an emotional farewell, congratulating him once more for what he had achieved in Canada in less than two years.

Martin, hurried as always, had sent a cable to Paris asking Berthe-Marie to meet him in Cherbourg where they would board the

SS *Kaiser Wilhelm II*. It was not a happy journey to New York. Berthe-Marie seemed deeply distressed. She was looking forward to seeing Marcelle, but did not hold back with her resentment about resuming the lonely life without Martin in her small suite in Meyer's Hotel in New York.

It seemed as if Martin wanted to escape from New York, unable to tolerate the feelings of guilt about leaving Berthe-Marie and Marcelle on their own once more. The *Kaiser Wilhelm II* had arrived on Thursday, February 26. On the following Monday morning, Martin boarded the train for Ottawa.

In his office on Elgin Street, Büxenstein's cable awaited Martin with the news that Lazard Bros. of London had bought 20,000 shares and also assured further interest in financing projects of the Deutsches Kanada Syndikat. Martin could hardly wait for the opportunity to see Colonel Talbot and Andrew Haydon. With the funds raised in Berlin, he explained, he could not only pay off his debts to the Canadian government for the coal leases obtained, but with the assured involvement of the well-known Lazard Bros., he could also quite confidently proceed with his further plans.

Büxenstein was indeed right in turning to London for financing the ventures of the Deutsches Kanada Syndikat in Alberta. For decades, British investments in the Dominion of Canada far exceeded those of all other countries. In 1906, they were still triple of those invested in Canada by sources from the United States, while investments from Continental Europe did not represent more than 10 percent of those originating in Great Britain, or less than 7 percent of all foreign investments in Canada. While the presence of foreign capital in Canada would continue to increase sharply during the following years, reaching a total of more than half a billion dollars prior to World War I, the proportion of funds originating in Continental Europe remained stagnant, never exceeding a maximum of 7 percent of all foreign investments in Canada.

In this light, the investments of the Deutsches Kanada Syndikat and its European partners during the following years were quite substantial. With its Canadian branch, the German Development Company Ltd., the Deutsches Kanada Syndikat began to receive some attention in Canadian financial circles, which were primarily based in Toronto. For reasons of access to the financiers and entrepreneurs of Toronto as much as for prestige, Martin decided to open a branch office of the German Development Company on 53 Elm Avenue in Toronto in March 1908. The headquarters of his company remained at the prestigious address of 19 Elgin Street in the country's capital. Too much was at stake for Martin in securing his ventures in the West. Too many of them had political implications.

In 1908, another event took place that demonstrated again how Martin found ways to meld his personal interests with those of his adopted country. This was the invitation to visit Canada that Georg Büxenstein had extended to Professor Potonié, Martin's adversary in Berlin. As Martin knew only too well, he had to impress upon the critical professor with all possible means that he was a respected figure in Canada. Nothing would be more impressive than an official invitation extended by the government!

But even Martin's always resourceful friend Andy Haydon was at a loss how this could be arranged. It was the Honorable Charles Murphy, later to become one of Martin's best friends in Canada, who was ready to help. He was the Postmaster General of Canada at that time and later, between 1909 and 1922, the Secretary of State for External Affairs. He remained a member of Parliament until his appointment to the Senate in 1925.

Murphy, whose Irish sense of humour found Martin's colourful story of his encounter with Potonié hilarious, promised to see Sir Wilfrid Laurier immediately. A few days later, Martin received the good news: the Canadian government had decided that the Canadian Mining Institute would convene a congress of mining engineers from the United States and several European countries, among them Germany, Great Britain, and Belgium. After the conference in Quebec City, this illustrious group would be taken on a cross-country inspection tour from the Atlantic provinces to the West. And Professor Potonié was to receive a special invitation from the Prime Minister.

When the congress was opened in Ottawa in early summer, Martin had already gone West and had asked Barlow to be Potonié's host. At the train station in Calgary, a bemused Martin was greeted by an exuberant Potonié with the words "The possibilities of Canada are truly great," which turned out to be the slogan that Martin discovered on the banners fastened to the sides of the coaches of the special train carrying the more than fifty mining engineers across the country.

While the group continued to the mines in the Crowsnest Pass, Potonié left the train in Calgary to inspect "… the coal in the Cretaceous" along the Rocky Mountains.

In Ottawa, the convening of mining engineers from two continents had been termed "a success from every standpoint." And Martin who unintentionally had some part, if not in the success of the conference, but certainly in its inception, took pride in the fact that over fifty mining engineers from five different countries were shown Canada's mining developments all across this vast country. But the presence of his old foe Potonié brought him the greatest personal satisfaction.

And there was the experience of sweet revenge as well! From the first day after their arrival in Morley, Martin did his utmost to please the professor in every way, earnestly trying to make what would no doubt be strenuous days as easy for the professor as possible. But Potonié's inexperience and his physical weakness and his ineptitude for life in this rugged country far from the comforts of Europe caused problem after problem.

Out of consideration for Potonié, Martin had chosen to take the professor to his claims in the relatively easily accessible Kananaskis, which was much closer than the remote Bighorn country. Martin's crews had just exposed another substantial coal seam near Mount Allan. But to reach even this coal field, so close to Morley, proved to be an incredible ordeal for Potonié, who had never ridden a horse or slept on the ground in a tent. In the end, he covered the second half of the ride into the Kananaskis and the entire return trip to Morley on foot. He was grouchy and very unpleasant and obviously resentful of having to submit, not by choice but by necessity, to Martin's leadership and authority.

Martin was careful not to show his feelings. But in his memoirs, he devoted an entire, albeit short chapter to this memorable journey, describing in great detail and with obvious delight Potonié's discomfort, helplessness, and anger; his stubborn insistence of breaking a chunk of coal out of the side of the tunnel Martin's men had dug; and his angry denial of his weakness when he failed to swing the pick with the sufficient force required to break loose the sample he wanted to inspect. Martin triumphantly quoted Potonié's exclamation

"There is coal in the Cretaceous. I must rewrite my book." ... He never apologized to me nor did he speak at all that night....

Indeed, for the remainder of his stay, the insight he had gained through never-before-experienced pains and tribulations, left Potonié in a gruff mood right up to his departure from Calgary, much to Martin's regret. But, as he wrote later, Potonié

... furnished to the President such a glowing report that our engineers and geologists felt very small reading his enthusiastic opinion. I never saw the Professor again in my life.

As optimistic and energetic as Martin felt after Potonié's departure, he was actually going through extremely stressful and anxious months. All of a sudden, there was great interest in exploring the

Eastern slopes of the Alberta Rocky Mountains for coal, even right in the area that Martin had considered his own, undisputed territory, as all his stakings from the summer of 1907 had been properly registered with the government in Ottawa.

But already in January of 1908, Martin heard learned that a new syndicate formed in Toronto had sent out a party to Alberta late in the previous fall and had done extensive stakings in the Bighorn and Brazeau areas, in some instances right over Martin's registered claims. Martin, who correctly suspected foul play rather than an oversight, rushed to Andrew Haydon's office; and again his good friend Andy knew how to help. After speaking with Sir Wilfrid Laurier, Haydon took Martin to the office of the Hon. Frank Oliver, Minister of the Interior. He suspected that, as a member of Parliament from Alberta, Oliver would be vitally interested in the energetic but harmonious development of his young province's resources.

In the West, Frank Oliver had gained early fame as the dynamic, often controversial publisher of Edmonton's first newspaper, the *Edmonton Bulletin*. He represented Edmonton in the Territorial Government and between 1896 and 1917, in the House of Commons in Ottawa. From 1905 to 1911, Frank Oliver served as Minister of the Interior, a stroke of luck for Martin.

Before becoming personally involved in settling the conflict, Oliver insisted that Martin himself first seek a compromise with the Toronto syndicate. With foreboding in his heart, Martin travelled to Toronto, where he faced five powerful, overbearing men who rode roughshod over the German entrepreneur, for whom they showed neither interest nor respect.

> It was my first attempt at negotiating an important business transaction in English in a foreign country. I did my best. But apparently my pleading had very little effect, or was it all a game of poker? I had watched this game, but had never learned to play it, yet I knew all about poker faces. I felt handicapped.... I returned to Ottawa crestfallen.

Again, Sir Wilfrid interceded and the Honorable Frank Oliver decided that from then on stakings made in unsurveyed territory must first be surveyed before purchase would be possible. Martin had gained some time, but he remained very anxious for months. He wished he could go to the West immediately, but this was impossible, as the work required could not be done in the midst of winter. Some weeks later, Martin was confidentially informed of the Government's new decision to no longer allow purchase of potential coalfields, but only their lease for twenty-one years with possible extensions. In this new policy, Martin immediately saw new opportunities. Leasing would require far less capital than outright purchases!

But another disappointment awaited him. At a time when Martin needed Dowling's advice and assistance and his endorsement more than ever before, Dowling advised him that he could not join him on the next expedition to Alberta, which, in view of the conflict with the Toronto syndicate, was of crucial importance. But Dowling did not desert Martin without finding a replacement in James McEvoy who used to work for the Geological Survey and also knew Alberta well. "... 'If you can get him, you are in the best of hands.' The same night I went to Toronto, engaged McEvoy, brought him back with me to Ottawa, and we three worked together for several weeks... "

Martin's mind was frantically busy. He envisioned an empire of strategically located coal mines, which would eventually enable him to supply most of Western Canada's railways:

> We decided to stake more coalfields to the North, so that we would cover practically all the territory between the Canadian Pacific and the other two Transcontinental railways.
>
> Counting already on a large coalfield on the Kananaskis River, further on the purchased fields on the Bighorn and the South Brazeau, and hoping for fields to be staked further North, I felt that our company would be in a strategic position to command the supply for a great part of the prairies....

This was the absolute high point of Martin's far-flung plans which, in spite of all his later success, never fully became reality. Neither time nor financial resources were adequate to realize such enormous dreams, not least, as T.D. Regehr suggested in his condensed publication of Martin's memoirs, because "Nordegg was a better manager than a financier."

In early spring of 1908, Barlow again encouraged Martin to go to the Cobalt area for further prospecting and staking.

> I had lost interest in Barlow's attempts in Ontario, I had this excellent, but very expensive geologist on my hands, and it would have been unfair, not to give him all the chances he advised.

Once more, Martin and Barlow went to Northern Ontario, this time much farther north from Cobalt. "The whole of the United States soon sent their men to this district," and Martin was in a real conflict, his ambivalent mind being bombarded by Barlow's insistence "... that the Cobalt district would show this year an unprecedented boom."

Martin's heart and hopes were in the West, where McEvoy was already working on his behalf. Eventually, he put the decision in the hands of his President, Georg Büxenstein, who sent a respected German expert, ostensibly to give the needed advice whether to pursue work in Northern Ontario or sell all claims there. But to Martin's frustration, this man "… never answered any questions, neither did he ask any. He just looked and examined."

Not until the very last moment, when the German expert stepped on the waiting train in Cobalt did he whisper in Martin's ear in German: "Do not invest one cent in Cobalt. The silver will all be exhausted in ten years."

To the end of his days, Martin had doubts about his decision to follow the German expert's advice:

> His advice made me overcautious, and I lost many opportunities. But strange to say, the expert was absolutely correct in his prophecy. The thing which he did not foresee, was, that the silver mines of Cobalt produced not less than 400 million ounces before they were exhausted.

Martin never completely lost his interest in this area; he even discussed a partnership with William Mulock, at that time a Chief Justice of the Exchequer Division at the High Court of Ontario, in a company to be formed by Martin. And after the Great War his men would still be prospecting and staking in Northern Ontario. But in the spring of 1908, Martin had only one wish: to return to Alberta and build on the successes of the past year.

> I saw McEvoy off for the West, with heart-aches because I was not able to accompany him to the mountains which I loved. The longer the distance, the greater the love. I forgot all the hardships which I suffered there.… I was happy when at last I boarded the train for the West.

Martin set up his headquarters at the Banff Springs Hotel from where he could travel across the Pipestone Pass to the Bighorn area whenever McEvoy needed him. At the hotel, Martin made the acquaintance of Sir Elly Kadoorie, the immensely rich financier and entrepreneur from Hongkong and founder of the China Light & Power Company. Elly Kadoorie had been born in Baghdad as one of six children of poor Jewish parents. Still a very young man, he moved to India and later to Hongkong. He became a British subject and quickly managed to build a fortune. While he knew how to live well, he never forgot the poverty of his own youth. Kadoorie became one of the most committed philanthropists in the Middle and Far East, building schools and hospitals in Iraq, Iran, Turkey, Syria, and even in India, Portugal, and France. In 1926, he was knighted by King George V. Martin became very fond of Lawrence and Horace, the sons of Sir Elly. After their father's death, Lawrence and Horace were also knighted for continuing and expanding their father's philanthropic efforts. After 1948, they assisted tens of thousands of refugees from Mainland China through their inventive resettlement schemes in Hongkong.

It was mainly Sir Elly Kadoorie's humanitarian outlook that attracted Martin to this unusual man, who held the firm belief that "wealth is a sacred trust to be administered for the good of society."

From then on, Martin would spend some weeks with Sir Elly and his family every summer at the Banff Springs Hotel. His later trips to China were in part inspired by Sir Elly.

In 1908, Martin met another remarkable man, Tom Wilson, to whom he was introduced by the famous Jim Brewster who was building his transportation empire in the young Banff National Park, which was attracting more and more tourists every year. Tom Wilson's men were taking messages between Martin and McEvoy back and forth across the Pipestone Pass.

Tom Wilson had already left his mark in the history books of the West. Born in 1859 near Toronto, he worked as a young man in Fort Benton on the Missouri River, but returned to Canada to serve one year with the North West Mounted Police detachment stationed at Fort Walsh. After 1881, he became the guide to Major Rogers, who had explored a route for the Canadian Pacific Railway through the Rocky Mountains, including the pass that was later named after him.

After serving in the Riel Rebellion of 1885, Tom Wilson started a guiding and outfitting business that he later moved to Banff. In the annals of Rocky Mountain history, he is remembered as the first white man to lay eyes on Lake Louise, the jewel of Banff National Park. Tom Wilson also owned a large herd of horses used for the tourist services provided by Jim Brewster. In the fall, they were taken across the Pipestone Pass to the Kootenay Plains. With their comparatively mild winters and lack of snow, the Plains provided ideal winter quarters for Tom's horses. Near the small Indian Reserve occupied by Peter Wesley's band, Tom set up his trading post on the banks of the North Saskatchewan River. There, the Indians traded furs and sheepskins for the supplies Tom had brought over the Pipestone Pass from Banff and Laggan, the railroad station later called Lake Louise.

Through Tom Wilson, Martin Nordegg became friends with the Bighorn Indians. From them, he received invaluable advice on many occasions. Originally, this group was part of the Stoney Reserve at Morley, the starting point of Martin's first expedition to the Bighorn country. Peter Wesley had taken a number of families across the mountains to the Bighorn country in the hope of escaping the changes that had begun to affect the lives of the Stoney Indians at Morley. Martin had great respect for this small band that had retained its traditional ways in the remoteness of the Bighorn country. But outsiders were beginning to invade the area!

Late one evening, the messenger Martin had sent across the Pipestone returned from McEvoy's camp to the Banff Springs Hotel, handing Martin a small piece of paper "full of perspiration and grease" with McEvoy's urgent message "You better come quick. Trouble!"

With one packer and three horses reluctantly provided by Jim Brewster, Martin hurried across the Pipestone Pass to learn from McEvoy that a party, obviously sent by the Toronto syndicate, had pulled up most of the stakes Martin had placed the year before and had substituted them with their own.

Martin found McEvoy in a most peculiar frame of mind. McEvoy was deeply alarmed, but seemed elated at the same time. Not only had he spotted the rival party but he had also discovered another, most promising coal field further north of the South Brazeau River. Martin decided to stake this field immediately.

With his arrival at McEvoy's camp, Martin entered a life of challenge, risk, trial, and conflict in the remote, unexplored wilderness. Now, there was no Tom Lusk to guide and protect him. He was entirely on his own, the undisputed leader of a party of men he had to lead through this wild country, relying entirely on his own wit and courage and his limited experience from the past two years.

Restaking old claims and staking new claims according to the new leasing regulations of the government caused much trouble even for the experienced McEvoy. But, as established later in Ottawa, McEvoy had done superb work. There was the hostile party sent out by the Toronto syndicate to stake in the territory already claimed by Martin and the struggle to reach the yet unclaimed area to the northwest as fast as possible. Martin's party was trailing "the enemy like an Indian," observing and guessing his next movements; hiding from the rival party and living for days in the rain without daring to light a fire; and finally, being discovered.

Sensing that both parties were heading in the same direction towards the same coal fields, Martin and McEvoy decided to "make it a race"–a race that almost ended in disaster when both parties became engulfed by an enormous forest fire that threatened the lives of men and horses. Even though the fire was still raging in the vicinity, Martin and McEvoy continued staking. In the end, Martin and McEvoy won, staking their new coal field ahead of their competitors, who moved farther to the North. The exuberant McEvoy called the new claim "Race Creek." "And Race Creek it was. It had been a race between us and our competitors, and we had won the race."

Truly grateful, Martin said goodbye to McEvoy. Although incredibly tired and physically and mentally exhausted, his mind was now at ease. On his return to Banff, he was capable of enjoying his beloved mountains again.

> ... the plateau which was the Pipestone Pass and the source of the river... was covered with a mass of wild flowers. The Northern sides of the mountains closing in on the pass were still covered with snow, and in the distance we saw the glacier with its mass of bluish ice. I dismounted, leading the horse and picking some flowers....

Four years later, in the comfort of his suite in the Banff Springs Hotel, Martin wrote:

> After all these trips in the mountains, I had the right to consider myself an old trail-rider and was as such recognized in Morley, Banff and Laggan. I looked with a sneer on the greenhorn tourists who attempted a short ride over the wide trails near these beautiful mountain hotels. They, of course, never knew the hardships, privations and exertions in the mountains, in all kinds of weather, through virgin forests, windfalls, muskegs, over rolling stones, fording deep and swift rivers which carried trees with them—and often going hungry.
>
> I started to dislike the life in these luxurious hotels with all their comfort and I longed for the trail. I was waiting for McEvoy.

The remaining days of summer 1908 were spent with McEvoy in the Kananaskis, where Martin inspected "... the beautiful bed of coal which our party had opened up."

Winter arrived unusually early, bringing with it constantly low temperatures and one blizzard after another. Martin decided to call all his work crews from the Kananaskis, the Bighorn, and the Brazeau back to Morley. He paid his men and returned with McEvoy to Ottawa. But when he filed the surveys and descriptions of his stakings with the Department of Mines, he was informed that his rivals had already done the same two weeks earlier.

The fact that staking by the two parties had taken place in unsurveyed territory caused endless conflicts and seemingly insurmountable complications. Only McEvoy's skill and intensive search for invariable landmarks eventually secured the leases of the northern fields for Martin when the official survey of the area was completed two years later. In the meantime, however, Martin felt confident enough to cable to Georg Büxenstein that "... the Bighorn and the Race Creek fields are definitely ours."

Barlow had also returned to Ottawa after dismissing his work party. It had been another summer of disappointment. As much as Martin tried, Barlow's unshakable belief in the potential of Northern Ontario prevented him from closing down this particular venture.

Without arriving at a solution, Martin left for Berlin from New York in November 1908, taking Berthe-Marie along for an extended stay with her family in Paris.

In Berlin, Martin gave the report of his success in Western Canada to a very pleased group of shareholders and to the Board of the Deutsches Kanada Syndikat. On December 1, 1908, he informed McEvoy by letter that he would not be back in Ottawa until the early spring of 1909. "After my successful report, the President gave me a three months' holiday which he said I deserved fully."

Martin needed to detach himself from the pressures and uncertainties of the past months in Canada. For the next two months, he returned to the roots of his European background.

> I travelled to the South of France, spent some days in Avignon, Nimes, Carcassone and then went into Spain, returning via the Riviera. All that was known territory to me, because we students had hiked there, following the route of Hannibal from Spain crossing the Alps. We always chose historical routes, like Napoleon's march across the Saint Bernhard; another time the Roman Limes from the Danube to the Moselle.

Berthe-Marie had been reluctant to accompany Martin on his journey through southern France, and she definitely refused to come to Spain with him. In the end, she did consent to spend two weeks with Martin at Nice. But she did not show any interest in Martin's enthusiastic account of his adventurous days of travelling through Spain.

Martin desperately realized once more how far he and his wife had drifted apart, how little was left of what they once shared in interests and aspirations. Impulsive as ever, Martin told Berthe-Marie that from now on they would live together in Canada, not in small-town Ottawa but in the large city of Toronto, where he had already planned to relocate his office this year. Berthe-Marie agreed more passively than happily, not even protesting that Martin had not included Marcelle in her move to Canada.

Martin and Berthe-Marie left Cherbourg on March 16, 1909, on the SS *Kronprinzessin Cecilie*. In New York, Marcelle seemed curiously unaffected by the news that her mother was moving to Canada. Why did Martin not choose the common sense solution to reunite the entire family in Toronto? One is inclined to wonder whether he had made the conscious decision to leave Marcelle at the Sacred Heart Academy in New York. Could his daughter grow into a healthy, happy, optimistic child in the care of her always complaining, unhappy, and often depressed mother? He knew he would be absent far too often to balance the negative influence of Berthe-Marie on Marcelle. One cannot help admiring Martin's psychological strength having to come to decisions affecting his family—the best possible under the circumstances but still far from what he must have wished for—and constantly worrying about where the millions were to come from for the development of his claims in Alberta.

Always filled with far-flung dreams, he still managed to concentrate on the here and now and direct his energy to attack the immediate problems of the day. This, more than anything else, explains Martin's seemingly inexhaustible courage to confront, to compromise, to beg, to deal with countless officials, advisors, friends and foes day after day, never taking no for an answer while never feeling solid ground under his feet.

At night, after the fruitless negotiations and dashed hopes, he often wondered how he could go on as literally a one-man operation. The biggest tasks and challenges were still ahead of him, this impressive and dynamic man from Germany with his excellent English but a still pronounced German accent, which readily identified him as a newcomer and an outsider. After his move to Toronto, he would have to stand up to the top financiers and promoters in Canada. Martin decided that he would enter the business world of Toronto with a new last name—a name of European sound, but not of Jewish origin, a name that would be unique to Canadian ears and not easily forgotten.

In April 1909, Martin Cohn's name was changed by order in council to "Nordegg." Both his wife and daughter were included in the change. Unfortunately, the legal records of the change of name are lost. At any rate, they would not have stated the reasons for Martin's choice of the name of Nordegg. It is a German name that is most unusual and extremely rare in the German-speaking countries of Europe.

Martin's particular choice remains a mystery. Nevertheless, his new name appears to have symbolic significance in several respects. To the biographer, it appears clear that the change of name was Martin's final act of becoming a permanent resident of his adopted country, signifying his new identity. Only in Alberta is there still a degree of awareness of Martin's original name of Cohn, primarily from old records, newspaper clippings, and the memories of the former residents of Nordegg, the town Martin founded. When the author established contact with numerous relatives of Martin's second wife, whom he married in 1924, not one of them was aware that Martin had been born with the name of Cohn; and all of them were surprised that Martin had been born a person of the Jewish faith.

If one wants to solve the enigma of Martin's adopted name of Nordegg, it is logical to explore literature and scan city directories and telephone books.

There is one bibliographical reference L. von Nordegg, the author of the book *Die Berliner Gesellschaft*, published in Germany in 1907. However, an inquiry at the State Library in Berlin revealed that L. von Nordegg was the pseudonym of the author Adolf von Wilke. An entry of "Grete Nordegg, actress" in the 1913 city directory of Berlin turned out to be a stage name. Not in a single one of the current directories of the large German cities, from Berlin to Hamburg, Cologne, and Munich, is there a listing under "Nordegg." Only the Vienna directory of 1995 includes three Nordeggs. None of them revealed any connection to Martin and at least two of them are the result of a legal change of name.

The rarity of the name of Nordegg becomes even more obvious when the two German standard works *Deutsche Namenkunde* and *Etymologisches Wörterbuch der Deutschen Familiennamen* are consulted. The first does not even list "Nordegg," while the latter refers to the origin of the name of "Nordeck" in Hessia in the twelfth century. Finally, the huge index of family names compiled by the Church of Jesus Christ of Latter-Day Saints in Salt Lake City, Utah, contains only three "von Nordeggs" but not a single "Nordegg."

Martin must have come across the name "Nordegg" in Germany or Austria. If his mother was indeed born in Moravia, where the ancestors of at least two of the Nordeggs currently living in Vienna came from, it might also be possible that Martin became acquainted with this name much earlier in his life during visits with the relatives of his mother.

Martin's writings refer more than once to his enduring love for the Austrian and Swiss Alps and, even more frequently, to his love for the Alberta Rocky Mountains, where he intended to make his permanent home. It may be of significance that in the area where the Alps of Germany, Austria, and Switzerland meet, geographic locations and settlements with names ending in "egg" such as "Scheidegg" are quite common ["egg" meaning "Ecke" in High German or "corner" in English].

Martin's experimental garden of Alpine plants imported from Switzerland to Nordegg and his design for a home in the Alpine style above the future town of Nordegg all point to his dream of re-creating some of the character of the European Alps in this corner of the Rocky Mountains. North means "Nord" in German, and for Martin, the two syllables, Nord and the ending of egg combined into "Nordegg," perhaps expressed perfectly his aspirations for creating a new life for himself in this "northern corner" of the Rocky Mountains.

In April 1909, Martin Cohn became Martin Nordegg. True to himself and his private nature, he shared the reason for choosing the name Nordegg with no one except perhaps his wife Berthe-Marie.

In 1909, Martin was forced to shift his attention to the Kananaskis. Like a replay of his troubles of 1908, Martin faced a new competitor, this time for the rich coal fields in the Kananaskis, which he intended to exploit as a source of coal to be sold to the Canadian Pacific Railway. His competitors, a group of promoters from Edmonton, were applying for a lease of the coal field at Mt. Allan. They claimed

> ... that theirs covered the outcrops while ours covered the hills, in other words, that they had entry to our seams. This was very serious, because it would have necessitated our sinking deep shafts to reach the coal ... too expensive to compete with Canmore.... There was nothing else to do than to rush West....

In Calgary, Senator Lougheed introduced Martin to R. B. Bennett, later the Prime Minister of Canada. There were suspicions of unethical conduct by a prominent member of the provincial bureaucracy. Not for entirely altruistic reasons, Bennett offered his help to Martin. With his already well-developed political instincts, Bennett saw an opportunity to embarrass the Alberta government. Neither he nor Martin succeeded in dislodging the Edmonton promoters; but this was the start of a friendship and occasional partnership that began because of "coal" and would end abruptly about fifteen years later, again because of "coal." Ironically, neither the Rocky Mountain Collieries in the Kananaskis field, which Martin leased after beating out the Edmonton promoters, nor Martin's later ventures into coal deposits east of Nordegg brought any profits to Martin or to Bennett. Their failed ventures only destroyed their friendship.

Martin's life during the summer of 1909 was peripatetic. After spending only two weeks in the Alberta coal fields, Martin found it necessary to rush to Calgary and Edmonton, Vancouver, then to Ottawa, New York, Toronto, and Ottawa again—all for the purpose of gaining certainty of his coal discoveries and the badly needed leases.

When Martin was certain that the rich fields of the Bighorn and Race Creek were safely in his hands, he sailed for Europe. During the entire passage across the Atlantic, Martin worked over his report again and again, as he assembled charts, diagrams, tables, and a set of photographs carefully selected from the rich inventory of his camera work of the past years.

Well briefed by Martin's letters about the need to proceed to the next stage, namely, the energetic development of the coal fields, Georg Büxenstein showed the usual perfect sense of timing. He expanded the meeting of the shareholders by inviting members of Berlin's financial community and arranging for Martin to give his presentation in the prestigious setting of the Ethnographic Museum to 300 carefully selected persons. Martin performed at his best, raising a great deal of interest among his audience, which included the chief of the Emperor's civil cabinet. Three days after Martin had earned much applause from this select group of important men, Büxenstein was advised that His Majesty wished to see the President of the Deutsches Kanada Syndikat and his representative in Canada.

Martin was dressed in morning coat and striped trousers, which he had to borrow from two different friends in order to meet the etiquette of the Imperial Court, when he and Georg Büxenstein ascended the splendid marble staircase of the Berlin Stadtschloss, the Imperial residence. In the ante-chamber, Martin had time to reflect on the irony of waiting to be received by the most important man of Germany.

Martin had never cared for the Emperor and his well-known idiosyncrasies—his vanity, his egotism, and his tendency to lecture rather than to learn from those he wished to see. What Martin reported about his audience with the German Emperor was strikingly similar to the accounts of most of his contemporaries:

> Entering the room, the President bowed low, and I did the same. I felt very uncomfortable in the borrowed clothes.
>
> The Emperor, dressed in a general's uniform, came forward and shook hands with the President. The President then introduced me as the German pioneer in Canada, and the Emperor extended his hand to me. The Emperor reeled off all he had read or better what he had been prompted that morning. He interjected his speech with a few really pertinent questions regarding Canada, which fortunately I was able to answer satisfactorily.... He made it really very easy for me. He asked repeatedly:
>
> "Is this or this not so?"
>
> And I was very glad to reply every time:
>
> "Certainly, Your Majesty,"
>
> with which he seemed very pleased, and it saved me a lot of explanations.
>
> At the end of the audience, the President craved permission to report what we had done in Canada. The Emperor looked at me, but I do not know if he listened.

"That is good work. We will give this young German pioneer a German order as a reward" and he bestowed an order on me, which I never wore, although I had many an occasion....

We bowed our way out, walking backwards.

As fatuous as it might have felt for Martin, the audience with the Emperor gave Büxenstein extra ammunition. He had no trouble getting the enthusiastic approval of the shareholders. But it was a different story at the meeting of the Board of Directors the morning after the audience with the Emperor:

"And now, that we have the coal, what are we going to do with it? Now when we actually possess these large coal-fields which could only be compared to the Silesian and Westphalian, what good are they unless we mine them and sell the coal?"

... the whole matter looked entirely different. In fact there was great consternation when they heard that several million dollars were required. There was considerable grumbling. The President, however, never lost his presence of mind, told the Directors, as several of them were prominent bankers, it was up to them to advise how and where these sums were to be obtained....

The outcome of the meeting was the decision to dispatch Martin to London immediately to obtain the greater part of financing from the Syndicate's British shareholders as, after all, "Canada was a British Dominion and consequently London should contribute...."

The directors of Lazard Bros. in London were sympathetic but refused to commit any funds unless Martin "... could sell the output of coal for some years."

Still on uncertain ground in matters of high finance, Martin returned to Berlin deeply dejected. But Büxenstein found this view "quite correct" and told Martin to go on his annual vacation "and think it out."

Martin indulged in his love of history again travelling to Greece and Turkey, and then to Egypt, across North Africa, and across the Mediterranean to Spain. In Gibraltar, he received a cable from McEvoy that the former president of the Crowsnest Pass Coal Company, which belonged to the American railway magnate James Jerome Hill of the Great Northern Railroad, was interested in buying a substantial number of shares in the German Development Company.

Martin saw stars when he read the name J. J. Hill! He immediately returned to Germany and took the next steamer from Bremen to New York, but the meeting with Hill's representatives produced nothing but the distinct impression that this group was only interested in a take-over of Martin's promising company.

Martin was disappointed but not disheartened. He knew he had "to sell coal" now; nothing else was of importance. Later, he must have thanked his stars for the strong dose of persistence and self-confidence he possessed and which he soon would need more than ever. Martin did not find it difficult to meet with those who held the financial and economic power of Canada, but invariably he had to realize that when it came to the knowledge of who controlled what part of the expanding Canadian economy, he was woefully ignorant. And he had not even reached the stage of bargaining and negotiation!

Martin did not know one person who could teach the intricacies of the financial world to him, as Dowling, Barlow or Tom Lusk, kind and unselfish men, had introduced him to the wilderness of Northern Ontario and Western Canada.

Conscious of the financial restraint he faced, Martin aimed at developing the Kananaskis deposits first because of their closeness to the transcontinental rail line of the Canadian Pacific. Costs would be much less, compared to the miles of railway through unsettled territory to reach the Bighorn and South Brazeau deposits. The Kananaskis plan led Martin to Sir William van Horne who frankly explained to Martin that he had come to Canada twenty years too late and, instead, should invest the funds of his company in Cuba, where Sir William was opening huge iron ore deposits. When Martin insisted that his destiny was Western Canada, the president of the Canadian Pacific Railway called his advisors together. They convinced Martin that the Canadian Pacific was well serviced through contracts with existing companies and "... did not need our coal... This was highly disappointing, ... because I had built great hopes on the Canadian Pacific Railway."

The response from the Grand Trunk Pacific Railway designated to reach the Pacific on a northern route through Edmonton was equally disappointing. There was interest in coal, but Martin's company would have to build its own railway from his coal fields to the Grand Trunk, whose exact route was not even certain yet. Senator Béique, who encouraged Martin to raise the required capital in Canada, referred him to Sir Herbert Holt, the president of the Royal Bank of Canada. But as Martin learned to his embarrassment, Sir Herbert was also a director of the Canadian Pacific, as was Senator Béique. Martin felt he had come around full circle, although Sir Herbert thought he could interest some friends, provided Martin's company was prepared to sell sufficient shares to them so that they would gain control of his company. This was out of the question, of course, but Martin at least felt that there were Canadians, after all, who "... believed in the success of my Development Company, which gave me great courage."

If Martin learned anything from his experience of going from door to door "like a greenhorn" with a promising product but no capital, it was the need for his company to build its own railway to promising markets. With no idea where the enormous funds required for the financing of such a railway would come from, Martin applied for a charter for a railway to be called "The Canadian Northern Western Railway Company." At least, a charter granted would assure a government subsidy of $6,000 per mile.

Martin persisted in "thinking big." There was only one large railway company left in the Prairies, the Canadian Northern Railway. It was owned by Mackenzie, Mann & Company, which had already earned a dubious reputation for taking enormous risks in the rapid expansion of its rail network, especially in the West, where it was pushing its main line to the Pacific Coast in direct competition with the Grand Trunk Railway. Martin's friend Andy Haydon was shocked to hear that Martin had decided to approach Mackenzie & Mann: "Who sups with the devil must have a long spoon. But, of course, the coal must be sold. We will talk to Talbot."

Talbot immediately arranged a meeting with Billy Moore, the parliamentary lobbyist of Mackenzie & Mann. Martin liked Billy Moore and felt he could trust him. And Martin was in luck. Mackenzie and Mann were expected in Ottawa the next morning, but would return to Toronto in the evening. Billy Moore suggested that he procure an invitation for Martin to accompany Mackenzie and Mann in their private car to Toronto. If the "highly intelligent," frank, and easy-going Billy Moore represented Mackenzie & Mann in Ottawa, he was not representative of what Martin was to be confronted with when he met William Mackenzie and Donald Mann and their party on the train to Toronto the next evening.

A great deal has been written about William Mackenzie and Donald Mann, some of it quite uncomplimentary. Although William Mackenzie's name became a household word across Canada because of his spectacular business ventures, his enterprises and financial activities were looked upon with caution, distrust or even suspicion of unethical practices. He was thought to have dealt deceptively with the government, seemingly proven later by the failure of the Canadian Northern in 1922, leaving an enormous problem to be solved by the Dominion Government.

As an individual, William Mackenzie did not seek publicity. By nature a private person, he wrote few letters, did not keep a diary, and often travelled without a secretary. What remains undisputed, however, is the impact Mackenzie and Mann left on the economic development of Canada. In addition to the transcontinental Canadian Northern Railway, their empire included steamship lines, several large street railway companies (including those in Toronto and Winnipeg), and enterprises reaching as far as Rio de Janeiro and

Sao Paolo in Brazil comprising utility companies and extensive gas and timber rights. For some years, Mackenzie & Mann also owned *La Presse*, Montreal's largest and most influential newspaper.

William Mackenzie was advisor of three Canadian Prime Ministers. In 1911, he was knighted by King George V. Although he had accumulated an enormous personal fortune, at the time of his death his estate was practically bankrupt after the collapse of his Canadian Northern Railway.

Little in the early lives of William Mackenzie or Donald Mann predicted their spectacular careers. William Mackenzie had been a school teacher in Ontario before taking over the management of a local country store. Donald Mann was working as a blacksmith for the Canadian Pacific Railways when the two men first met; they immediately agreed to form a partnership.

With not more than $500 between them and borrowed money, they entered into their first venture, the building of snowsheds for the Canadian Pacific in the Rogers Pass. They succeeded in completing this difficult job ahead of time and without cost overruns. Increasingly larger construction jobs quickly brought profits and led to the purchase of a bankrupt short rail line in Manitoba, the beginning of Mackenzie and Mann's railway empire. After acquiring more short lines in Manitoba, Mackenzie and Mann announced their intention of building yet another transcontinental railway, which led to the unique situation where three lines ran close to one another through the largely unsettled bush country of Northern Ontario. This phenomenon was repeated in the West, where both the Grand Trunk and the Canadian Northern laid their tracks from Edmonton through the Yellowhead Pass almost side by side.

Since this is the story of Martin Nordegg, it appears appropriate to quote in detail Martin's opinion of William Mackenzie and Donald Mann and his experiences with these two powerful men. They were Martin's most important partners for years and were instrumental in the realization of his plans in Nordegg. Ultimately, they were also the destroyers of his cherished dreams.

Martin's (at times, critical) characterizations of Sir William Mackenzie and Donald Mann do not differ greatly from those of other contemporaries. But one aspect is worth noting. While he was permanently forced into a position of defensiveness by the confrontational Donald Mann, Martin never wavered in admiration and respect for Sir William Mackenzie. These feelings were returned by Sir William to an astonishing degree.

During the crucial period of World War I and afterwards, Martin knew that Donald Mann had done nothing to protect his interests. But he never doubted William Mackenzie's loyalty during the entire length of their partnership and right to Sir William's untimely death in 1923.

> Their successes aroused the envy of others and their reputation began to suffer. It was said, for instance, that their construction work consisted in just laying rails on the flat prairie. I can testify that there must have been something true to this, because travelling on their railway meant physical agony. As to their reputation in financial and economical matters, it was attacked right and left. They were supposed to deal harshly and bargain in the most unethical way; their financing was supposed to be done on a shoe string. They were reputed to get the best of everybody. Their system was, that Mackenzie bargained first, then shunted the party over to Mann, who tried to improve on it further; at last their lawyer Zebulon Lash, K.C., had to take the party in hand and improve on the bargain. Altogether there was not one of my acquaintances and friends in Ottawa who did not warn me against them.
>
> I asked the manager of my bank. He said, that these men bond every mile of railway, then Mackenzie goes to London and sells the bonds. He considered Mackenzie a most original financial wizard ...one of the shrewdest financial promoters. Mackenzie looked after the finances and organization, Mann after the technical part and their staff. Their first assistant was T.B. Hanna ... the canny Scot....
>
> In spite of all the warnings, I was most anxious to meet these two men, whose star was in the rapid ascent. They belonged to and were part of the heroic age of Canada...and I was proud to witness this wonderful period....
>
> Mackenzie and Mann boasted that they built one mile of railway every day, and their system started already towards the East, with branches to the North and feeders to the American railways in the South....
>
> Great opportunities were naturally offered to these men and they cannot be blamed if they grabbed everything in sight, at their own price and terms. This naturally aroused great envy and jealousy and while many reproaches may have been justified, many others were mere slander.

Whatever warnings Martin received, he knew he had no choice. As he wrote later,

> All this information tended to make me extremely cautious. On the other hand, if I did not succeed in an arrangement with them, I had no further chance of selling the output of our mines to any railway; in fact, I could not think of financing until I had a contract for the disposing of the coal for many years.
>
> I was therefore forced to "sup with the devil."

Years later, the memories of what Martin experienced on the train between Ottawa and Toronto, sitting next to a jovial William Mackenzie in the latter's private rail car, and on the following day in the Toronto office of a totally changed Mackenzie, would still bring perspiration to Martin's brow. This was his last chance. Desperately, he marshaled all his courage, wit and knowledge, all the time realizing that he was no match for Mackenzie, Mann, and their associates. Somehow, Martin managed to stand up to the two men and their cohorts. He did not win, but the bargaining leading towards a partnership had been opened. Martin knew that nothing would disrupt the process, if he only played his cards right. What he offered was neither money nor financial wizardry, but energy, determination and common sense, and a vision of profit which, Martin sensed, neither Mackenzie nor Mann would be able to resist.

What began in Toronto that day took Martin on a high road that ended successfully some weeks later when the start of building his coal mine and his town was within close grasp. How excited and elated Martin was is evident in his recollections of the tough negotiations in MacKenzie's office. They were deadly serious, but their account is peppered with Martin's colourful, sometimes hilarious descriptions.

> I boarded their private car late in the evening and found already about a dozen men in the lounge. I knew some of them, being members of Parliament, and when Billy Moore saw me standing at the entrance, he took me to Mackenzie, introducing me jokingly as the representative of the German Emperor. Mackenzie introduced me to Mr. Mann who smoked his famous fat black cigar. This jocular remark about my connection with the German Emperor made me a marked man and I suffered in consequence many an insult and harrowing investigations after the war broke out....
>
> Mackenzie asked me to sit next to him, and tell him who I was, where I came from, what I had been doing here and what I intended to do. I compressed the desired information into a few sentences and asked him whether he would permit me to see him on business the next morning. "Certainly ... drop in any time."
>
> I was surprised.... But I found the explanation.... His visitors actually ... had often to wait for hours and hours and other influential men dropped in and took preference over ordinary mortals. Later, after becoming a partner of these two men, I had the privilege of entering their private office, no matter who was in there....
>
> I must confess that my heart went pitter patter when I appeared in the office armed with my reports. I was immediately ushered in, and found Mackenzie busy ... discussing railway problems. He just beckoned to me to sit down. I listened with surprise how easily he disposed of the expenditure of thousands of dollars.... I told him of our coal fields. He sent for a large map ... and seemed satisfied with the names of Dowling and McEvoy....
>
> "How many miles of railway have you got to construct?... 'Oh, about 160."

> "Then you will find the money to build the railway?"
> "I am sure, you will."
> "No, I don't think so."
> "I offered you all I had to offer. You build the railway. We equip the mine and sell you a minimum of coal of three hundred thousands tons per year for five years...."

Martin tried to keep up with Mackenzie's sharp mind, which worked incredibly fast. There was baiting and flattery alternating with threats of withdrawal. It was now time for the next step in the Mackenzie-Mann routine:

> "I did not know that Germans were so smart.... We have two coalfields in Alberta, and we do not need your coal. But ... I do not want the Canadian Pacific or Grand Trunk to get your coal. We will amalgamate your coalfields with ours and form a big coal company."

Martin refused to even consider the idea of amalgamation. Now, Mann got into the act, and after some threatening comments, declared that "... we really make you a present of them [i.e., their coal fields], and I don't see why we should."

Martin was speechless, looking to Mackenzie for help, but Mackenzie followed the well-established routine: "Don't let us lose time. We better call Lash."

The famous lawyer appeared and, within minutes, turned Martin over to Judge Phippen. And while Martin was in the midst of explaining his plans and offers to yet another powerful, but uninformed member of Mackenzie's empire, Judge Phippen was called into Mackenzie's office "for instructions."

> I waited with baited breath a quarter of one hour.
> "Mr. Mackenzie says you are the hardest fellow he ever dealt with."
> ... it was such a bargaining, as I had never experienced. In fact, I had never made any bargain at all. The outcome was that two companies were to be formed, one in the North comprising our Northern fields and those of Mackenzie, Mann, and one in the South for our Kananaskis field, that the shares of both companies were to be divided 50-50 between us, and that my Development Company was to receive additional bonds ... and a sum in cash....
> Mackenzie took one look at the proposed contract:
> "You are just crazy. I will never agree to that."
> And Mann seconded as expected:
> "I call it crazy."

Martin gathered all his courage and wits:

> We began to bargain afresh. I saw that I was facing three very strong opponents. Yet I had the feeling that they wanted to close the

deal under all circumstances, and I stood by my guns, as long as I could.

Martin had one more ace up his sleeve. He thought he would get along much better if he could only dislodge Mackenzie from his allies. It was up to his President Georg Büxenstein to sign the accord. Rather than send it over to Berlin, as Mackenzie suggested, Martin had a better suggestion to make to Mackenzie:

> "You told me that you were sailing for London in a week. Why not go with me to Berlin and have it signed there?"
> "That is not such a stupid idea. I always wanted to see Berlin. We will go together."
> A heavy stone dropped off my chest. I felt that I had not been a match for these three traders, and yet I had reached my goal.... I remained most friendly with Mackenzie. I ... found that Mackenzie invariably made a harsh deal.... But having agreed to something he never broke his word. When he wanted to go back on his word, he used his partner Mann—and appeared to stand up against him, till he finally appealed to my kindness asking me if I wanted to break up his partnership with Mann. This I could not do, of course, and thus Mann was victorious. But I got the better of the bargain later on, until the war broke out and made me defenceless.

Together, Mackenzie and Martin sailed to Europe. Perhaps the undisturbed days on the boat away from the interference of the Toronto office resulted in Martin's favourable opinion of Mackenzie that never changed until his partner's death. By letter and cable, Martin had carefully prepared his President in Berlin for the encounter with Mackenzie and the crucial final phase of negotiations.

Georg Büxenstein met Martin and Mackenzie at the Lehrter Bahnhof. Martin described the arrival as

> ... a regal reception.... One dinner followed another, one was more sumptuous than the other. There was no talk at all about business....

Büxenstein confided to a puzzled Martin his strategy "... to first make a good impression on the honest Canadian."

Mackenzie was impressed with the respect shown to his German host at the opera, at Berlin's best restaurants, indeed everywhere. In one of the most powerful automobiles Mackenzie had ever ridden in, Büxenstein, the first president of the German Automobile Club, drove his two visitors to his country estate "Hubertushöhe," picturesquely located at the shore of a secluded lake two hours from Berlin. "...the reception on entering the grounds was like entering a baronial castle," Martin remembered.

By now, Büxenstein felt he had sufficiently impressed his future Canadian business partner and started to talk about business. Martin was relieved to be no longer the lone player in the negotiations.

Now, they were two against one, the tables were turned.
Fascinated, he witnessed how Georg Büxenstein in fluent English
and

> ... with old-world diplomatic methods got gradually the better of
> Mackenzie, the shrewd trader of the new world. Whenever the President
> got into a tight corner, he professed not to have heard very well, which
> made Mackenzie repeat his phrase, which he naturally did, but in a dif-
> ferent phraseology. Another little trick was to pretend that he did not
> understand a sentence, and he asked me to translate it. That gave him
> time to think over his reply. But when he was absolutely cornered, he
> did not reply to the question or statement, but took one word from the
> sentence, and associated it most cleverly with one of the many jokes for
> which he was famous and so well liked by the Emperor.
>
>   It was during the discussion of valuing our coal fields against
> Mackenzie's. Amongst the fields, I mentioned Race Creek....
>
>   "Speaking of Race Creek, I want to tell you a funny story. The
> Emperor to whom I told this story, made me repeat it to your King
> Edward, when he as Prince of Wales attended the yacht race at Kiel,
> called the regatta, and Prince Henry was also present. And, I assure you,
> they screamed with laughter."

The anecdote, used by Büxenstein as a diversionary tactic, did
not fail in its effect on the dour Mackenzie. Here was a man of
power and such absolute self-assurance who did not hesitate to tell a
story in which no one else but he was the butt of the joke:
A few years previously in London, Büxenstein had entered a
German team in the Henley Regatta. After a sumptuous dinner the
night before, the clerk of the Savoy Hotel had failed to awaken
Büxenstein who, without breakfast, in frock coat and top hat, ran to
the Thames Embankment but missed the boat which was to take the
guests of honour to the regatta. Fortunately, he discovered another
motor boat marked "Henley Regatta," where he introduced himself
to the captain as the President of the German Rowing Clubs and
persuaded him to take him to the Henley as fast as possible. After
some hesitation, the captain's face lit up. He agreed to take
Büxenstein, provided he would stand in the bow of his boat once
they neared Henley. Büxenstein related how

> The river was full of crafts, and the captain sailed into their midst,
> blasting his siren. The people turned when they saw me, they pointed at
> me, shouted to each other, laughed and waved their arms.... I lifted my
> top hat and bowed to all sides, the more I bowed and smiled, the more
> they screamed with joy, quite unusual in the English character.... I
> thanked the good captain and asked how much I owe him. "There is no
> charge," he said, "I have to thank you and I am highly honored for deco-
> rating my boat."

I thought he referred to the orders I wore on my breast. But when I boarded the committee-boat, where everybody pressed to shake my hand and laughed and laughed, they turned me round to look at the boat which had brought me, and with consternation I read on the banner at the side, printed in large letters:

"This is the man who took Beecham's Pills."[*]

Mackenzie laughed till tears came into his eyes, he slapped his thighs and it took a few minutes before he calmed down. The story put us into an excellent humour.... We signed the agreement then and there.

Büxenstein had by no means exhausted his schedule of impressing Mackenzie. For the next day, he invited Mackenzie to the Regatta in Grünau.

I am going to make a special performance for you. You look at the Emperor and myself. You watch us both. When I see you, I will look straight at you and as a sign that you have seen me and are looking, just wave your hand. And then, I will put my arm around the emperor's neck.

An incredulous Mackenzie admitted that he "would like to see once the Emperor.... I do not want to be presented at all, I only want to see him."

Martin took the excited Mackenzie to Grünau. From the first row of the box reserved for dignitaries, they watched the scene on the Emperor's yacht happening exactly as predicted by Büxenstein the night before.

Whether the event, related with so much delight by Martin in his memoirs, took place as described, only Martin could answer. But a photograph of the 1909 Grünau Regatta in an illustrated Berlin newspaper shows Georg Büxenstein next to the Kaiser on the bridge of the Imperial yacht. It is entirely possible, that after appropriate explanations by Büxenstein, the Emperor would allow "Büxe" to put his arm around his shoulder in public. As Martin wrote, the Emperor's entourage was mortified by this unheard of display in public. But Georg Büxenstein and a few others close to the Emperor—men and even a few women courageous enough to be frank and honest with their monarch—had noticed that in the right mood the Emperor, who upheld etiquette and pomp to the point of ridicule, could also throw all etiquette overboard. And, as Martin intimated, Büxenstein also used the opportunity to remind the Emperor, who loved to see his country politically and economically in the forefront, that he had brought the "Railway King of Canada to Germany to sign an agreement to buy their coal in Canada from me."

---

[*] A popular laxative.

The Grünau episode also helped Büxenstein put the Board of Directors of the Deutsches Kanada Syndikat into a cooperative mood. Martin received much praise. "I only then perceived what I had accomplished, and began to get a higher opinion of myself."

As the following days would show, Martin needed all the self-confidence he could muster. The board members voted to entrust the financing negotiations in London to Martin. But first, Martin was sent to Brussels to lobby with the prominent banker Eugène de Wassermann, a cousin of one of the board members. It is of interest that he was the brother of the German pathologist August von Wassermann, the discoverer of the blood serum test that revolutionized the diagnosis of syphilis.

Eugène de Wassermann, the "cousin" in Brussels, lived in luxury of dimensions Martin had not even imagined. Wassermann was not only an art collector, he also enjoyed good food and wine and, above all "lovely ladies," whom he chose, one at a time, as companions on his business trips.

But Wassermann also turned out to be a shrewd financier. He practically forced Martin to choose the South Brazeau over the Kananaskis as the site of Martin's first mine development. In vain, Martin explained that the spur line into the Kananaskis would cost only $600,000, while access by rail to the South Brazeau would require several million dollars.

Wassermann left Martin no choice, especially after he learned that William Mackenzie was the major partner of the German Development Company. Martin had to admit to himself that in matters of international high finance he was quite ignorant and naive after Wassermann impressed on him that

> You do not understand the matter. It is easier and more profitable for me to find several millions than a few hundred thousand.... If you people do not agree with me, you can go elsewhere!

At the Société Général, Martin began to comprehend "the cousin's" tactics. "You let me do the talking. Just watch me."

Wassermann easily convinced the director of the Société Général that he was doing him a favour, but could not let him subscribe more than one million dollars, as "I must reserve the rest for London, Paris, and Berlin."

Wassermann applied the same approach in Paris, in Berlin, and in London, the first stop for Martin, Wassermann, and his entourage.

> I was surprised to see that our party had increased to six persons. There was one of the charming ladies whom I had met at the cousin's dinner. Then there was her personal maid, his valet and his secretary. It was my

first experience that somebody took care of my tickets and baggage, and
the luxurious manner of travelling just made me wonder. What a difference from the pack-train!

In London, Wassermann's strategies worked as successfully as
in Brussels. But against his original plan, Wassermann had to con-
cede that Lazard Bros. of London would become the leaders of the
financing syndicate.

> Then our cavalcade of six set out for Paris. The negotiations there
> started with a sumptuous luncheon ... at one of the finest restaurants, at
> which two bankers and the cousin's lady attended. They were directors
> of the Banque de Paris et Pays-Bas. It took three gala dinners and two
> more luncheons to settle the matter, which ended in great success....
> The whole cavalcade travelled to Berlin.
> The Germans were more careful, they felt offended that my German
> syndicate had not been offered yet a participation....
> I could not help being convinced that we had already made a success
> in Canada, because people complained that they had not been asked to
> subscribe.
> It had taken the cousin not more than three weeks to raise the mil-
> lions required during a tour of four European capitals, which concluded
> in Berlin. To Martin, the cousin's trip seemed to be more pleasure than
> hard work.
> The Brandenburg Gate was, figuratively speaking, adorned with gar-
> lands....
> But ... I felt very small, because I had not done anything else to-
> wards this success than listen to the cousin.

Did Martin really respect Eugène de Wassermann? After introducing Wassermann to his readers, Martin persists in calling him
merely "the cousin." In vain, one looks for the reverence with which
Martin invariably refers to Georg Büxenstein as "my President" or
to "Sir William Mackenzie."

Whatever respect Martin might have developed for Wassermann,
it was shattered by the bill "the cousin" presented to Martin before
leaving Berlin for Brussels:

> Travelling expenses to London, Paris and Berlin—$50,000.
> Commission for effecting the finances: a considerable part of the
> shares of both coal companies. Further a commission for financing the
> railway.

For once, Martin was even shocked by Georg Büxenstein's reaction:

> I ran to our President in my excitement. He said, there was no need
> for excitement, because the banker had accomplished his deal. It would
> not come out of our own pocket. It was up to me to dig out sufficient

coal and pay for it. Anyhow, we should discuss it with Mackenzie, and the president was ready to go to London on his arrival, but, of course, at the expense of our German company. How I had saved every cent in Canada, and how thousands of dollars were spent here with apparent justification!

Somehow, Martin preferred what Mackenzie said to him in London, while the two were waiting for Büxenstein's arrival:

"I am glad, that the bankers have left us at least a part of our coalfields." Following that sarcastic remark, Mackenzie instructed Martin to pay "the cousin" in Brussels.

As always during negotiations of that nature, the nightly dinners and jovial festivities did not preclude bitter disputes and heated altercations between Büxenstein and Mackenzie the next morning. Martin felt like a helpless bystander, but

> My President won out in the end.
> The business was finished. I was to return immediately to Canada, select the place in the South Brazeau field where the mine was to be opened; work with the railway surveying party to choose the best route. I was told to call on moneys from the banking syndicate as and when I wanted.

These exhausting weeks had taught Martin much about "high finance and some of the dubious attributes of capitalism." Thirty years later, an experienced and much wiser Martin closed the chapter "I Learn High Finance" of his memoirs with unmistakable criticism:

> From the net profits, the directors received first a certain percentage for their services. The rest went to the Berlin syndicate again, considering the transferred amount as profit, deducted a fee for its directors, who incidentally were actually the same as those who had already received their director's fees.
> Apparently they deserved it for doing nothing else than attending some meetings and signing their names. The work, the responsibility and the hardships were mine, but also the pride of accomplishment.
> The financial discussions showed the greed of all and I felt that I did not belong there, in fact that I did not belong to Europe any more. Even the luxury and comfort, with all its artificiality, had no attractions for me. I belonged to Canada. The air there was not so contaminated. I was happy when I was on board the steamer which carried me to New York.

V

THE DREAM COMES TRUE
(1910 - 1914)

In the spring of 1910, the work crews of the Grand Trunk Pacific, William Mackenzie and Donald Mann's competitors, had pushed the steel of their transcontinental railway as far as Wolf Creek, 121 miles west of Edmonton. Today a tiny settlement of only a few people, Wolf Creek grew overnight into a rip-roaring, wild railroad camp, which accommodated the large construction crews building the bridge across the deep McLeod River gorge and laying the tracks through the muskeg country to the west. As Harold Fryer reports in his book *Ghost Towns of Alberta*, Wolf Creek boasted a business section that included

> ... a bank, half a dozen stores, and a dozen or so restaurants and stopping houses. Then there were several poolrooms, barbershops, blacksmith shops, livery stables, real estate offices, a drug store and two buildings used by the North West Mounted Police ... and ... of course, the more clandestine businesses that mushroomed in every construction camp—the brothels, the bootleggers and the gambling joints.

At its height, up to 2000 people lived in Wolf Creek, and plans were made for a town with a bright future. Such hopes never materialized, as the engineers of the Grand Trunk Pacific decided to develop a divisional point 9 miles further west, the new town of Edson. Within the next decade, the coal deposits southwest of Edson were opened; and the area became known as the "Coal Branch." One of the branches of this railway reached 60 miles into the foothills ending at the town of Lovett, while its other branch climbed to a height of 6000 feet to the town of Mountain Park at the edge of the Rocky Mountains. Mountain Park laid claim to being the highest settlement in all of Canada.

With a large party in the summer 1910 Martin crossed this unexplored and as yet unsettled area. The financial backers of Martin, mainly Lazard Bros. of London, had insisted on the assessment by a recognized expert of all those Alberta coal fields that Martin had recommended for immediate development, especially the field near the headwaters of the South Brazeau. Upon Martin's suggestion, Charles L. Hower from Johnstown, Pennsylvania, was selected "as the best known coal mining engineer." The relationship between these two men, who by character and background could not be more different in almost every respect, was not to last. But Martin placed great trust in Hower's experience and competence. Hower had been in Alberta before in 1910, when Martin had engaged him for the preparation of a report to the German Development Company on the coal fields previously explored by Martin, Dowling, and McEvoy.

Martin and his family had gone to Europe in February 1910. Berthe-Marie and Marcelle stayed in Paris while Martin went to Berlin and later to London, where the decision about hiring Charles Hower was made. Martin began preparations for the expedition with Hower immediately. From the SS *George Washington* on its way from Southampton to New York, he telegraphed Stewart Kidd in Morley, asking him to prepare a large packtrain consisting of "… coal-miners, cooks, packers, a timber cruiser and assistants, an engineer with another outfit, about thirty eight horses in all."

According to Charles Hower's report the final party was made up of "… 32 men, 2 freight teams and 38 pack and saddle horses."

On May 18, Hower and his large party left Wolf Creek travelling upstream along the McLeod River. Martin joined Charles on July 19. Ira Gray of Rocky Mountain House remembers Hower,

> … red, or sandy complexion; weight about three hundred pounds. The Brewsters gave him the largest riding horse they had…. Hower never dismounted uphill or downhill….

Charles Hower stood over six feet tall, while Martin measured only 5 feet 6 inches. Hower must have had some difficulties coming to terms with Martin's personality and temperament. His image of Germans was likely formed by the gentle, conservative Amish (the Pennsylvania Dutch), who had settled near Hower's place of birth. Nor was Hower as educated in the broad sense of the word as Martin was. He was an excellent man in his own field but lacked the background and the social graces of Martin. Besides, Martin kept wearing his semi-military tunic, which seemed to have aggravated Hower to no end. He had no choice but to accept Martin's authority and decision making but did not like it.

Martin probably tried to bring Charles Hower around to his side in various ways. With a sense of humour, although with ambiguity, he gave a picture taken of Hower and himself the tongue-in-cheek caption "The Big Party."

The expedition seemed very well planned but was plagued with problems. Hower complained in his report that one of the parties sent to the Race Creek area was lost for almost two weeks and

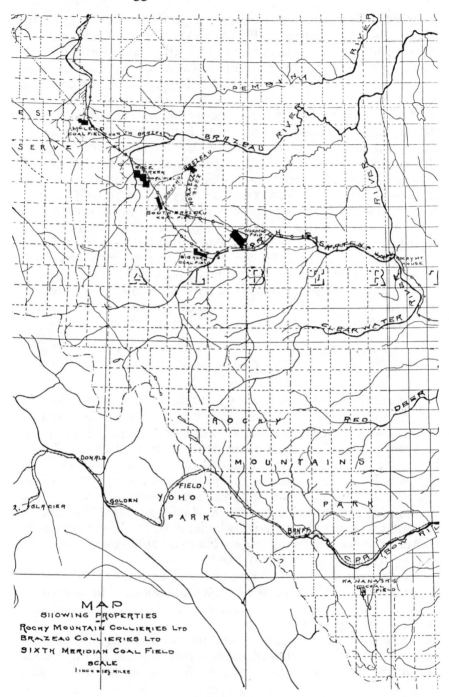

Taken from Martin Nordegg's *Memoirs* Vol. 2

achieved absolutely nothing. Its leader had contracted typhoid fever. There were also numerous other problems of shortages of food, equipment and tools; and the suitability of some of the men left much to be desired. As Hower observed,

> Pack train work is picturesque but scarcely lends itself to the commercialism of modern working methods. Used by the nomads of the frontier, to whom time is no factor, it follows the line of least resistance which means slow progress and small accomplishment. Indispensable for exploring it meets the early demands of a new mountain country that is inaccessible by ordinary means of transportation.
>
> Packing is a survival, not a development, and the men who follow it are those whose love of outdoor life and hate of responsibility, poorly equips them for work on ideas of order and progress.

Hower was particularly frustrated with the leisurely pace of the those men who had experience in mountain country and for whom time meant nothing; on the other hand, most of those coming from organized working conditions often turned out to be completely helpless in the wilderness; finally, those who were hired as packers disliked the work at the South Brazeau site, where Hower immediately assigned them to trenching, digging tunnels, cutting timber and constructing log buildings.

Despite all these problems, Hower accomplished an enormous task during these few weeks. When he left the South Brazeau, there was the beginning of a mine, the future location of its various buildings had been determined, and a town site had been laid out.

Olaf Thomasson ... one of four Norwegians hired as helpers recalled how

> ... we prospected and laid out a townsite ... never developed. Most of the time I was out with a CNR engineer, Mr. Murray Hill, to locate possible railway routes to the claims. We made three trips, of twenty to thirty miles each, around the valleys and mountains.

First with the help of Tom Lusk and then on his own, Martin had managed well during his earlier exploration trips. The agenda for the trip of the summer of 1910, however, was infinitely more complex. Martin would have never achieved what the experienced Hower described in his report forwarded from Johnstown, Pennsylvania, to Martin in Toronto on December 31, 1910. Hower included a detailed assessment of all properties and leases from the Kananaskis to the South Brazeau and Race Creek, including numerous maps, geological drawings, and the plans for the underground tunnels of the South Brazeau mine, all surface buildings and a complete plan of the town.

With his remarkable document, Charles Hower helped Martin enormously in advancing his development plans. Following Hower's advice, he had already started a regular string of packtrains from Rocky Mountain House to the South Brazeau, transporting machinery and equipment for the mine, which included everything from boilers and hoist engines to cement, lumber and nails. The distance from the nearest station at Innisfail on the Edmonton-Calgary railway to the mine site was 162 miles, almost two-thirds of it unsettled territory, the last third of it on the other side of the Bighorn Range.

Hower prescribed that " ... at least five tons of freight must move to the destination each week."

Charles Hower's *Report on the Properties of the Rocky Mountain Collieries Ltd., Brazeau Collieries Ltd., and The Sixth Meridian Coal Lands* was most favourably received in London and Berlin, where it was published by Georg Büxenstein. Of the three original copies typed by Charles Hower, only one miraculously survived. It was found by an alert citizen on the garbage dump in Red Deer and is now kept in the archives of that city.

Returning to civilization, Martin and Charles Hower travelled with their party to the Bighorn River. Martin had always left the Bighorn country via the Pipestone Pass to the southwest. This time, however, Martin entered unknown territory, taking for the first time the trail to the east towards Rocky Mountain House. He had no idea how crucial a decision he was making at this moment. It is best to let Martin tell it in his own words:

> On the second day out from the Bighorn River, we were travelling on an old hunting trail at the side of a mountain which looked like an extinct volcano. Ahead of us we saw a gap. I was riding alone, far ahead of the packtrain. Just before reaching the gap, I saw a pretty lake below me, from which a creek was running through the gap. On the lake I saw four wild geese. I took my mauser carbine out of its sheath, hanging on my saddle and loaded it. When I reached a point just above the geese on the lake, I dismounted, dropped the reins of the horse and the horse stood still. I estimated the distance five hundred yards. I knelt on one knee, aimed and fired. I saw a splash in the lake about twenty yards short, and screaming the quartet rose and flew to the South; I fired once more and missed again. I did not fire again, because three shots were the signal for distress, and the geese were already far away.
>
> I knew that the slow moving packtrain could not arrive for half an hour or so. I sat down and looked around. To the North, the Coliseum Mountain, looking exactly like an arena, rose from a green meadow into the blue sky. Towards the East, the two mountains forming the gap, hid the view. To the South, there was the lake, reflecting the blue sky with a few cirrus clouds, and I saw reeds on the shore. Beyond,

there were the forests of leaf and needle trees in the rising ground. Then I looked at the southern mountain, forming the gap. It showed horizontal dark streaks, similar to the ones of our coalfields in the West. I wondered, if these strata were not the same indications of coal. The more I looked, the more I became convinced that they were. When the packtrain reached me, I asked Hower for his binoculars, and I told him that I had fired two shots at wild geese. They had heard them and wondered what I may have been shooting. I let the packtrain pass me. Then I looked through the binoculars. There was now no doubt any more. These were decidedly coal strata. I made a hurried sketch of the lake, the gap and the hill with the strata. Then I mounted and cantered after the packtrain. I decided to keep my observation to myself.

We camped that night outside the gap, near the creek which came from the lake. We had passed a wicked muskeg in a pine forest, and it was very hard on the horses and men. Then we had to ford the creek innumerable times. When we reached the next day the mouth of the creek which runs into the broad Saskatchewan River, we turned east following the river on a high bank. This was often intersected by creeks which cut deep gullies into the clay, we got off and led our ponies down and up again, which made travelling very hard.... In three days we reached the ruin of Rocky Mountain House, an old fort of the Hudson's Bay Company....

No matter how hard the travelling, how loud the swearing of the exhausted men, or how irritated the snorting of the overdemanded horses during these last days of his expedition, Martin was gripped by intense excitement that allowed him hardly any sleep. There was no one with whom he could share his anxiety about his newest discovery, which seemed so much more promising than the remote South Brazeau fields. In vain, he tried to banish his dreams of a mine and a town that had sprung up in his mind as soon as he had noticed the dark strata through Hower's binoculars. It was his discovery alone, but would it turn out to be worthwhile? Martin needed Dowling and McEvoy more than ever.

Exhausted, Martin's party reached the ruins of the old Fort Rocky Mountain House on October 25 "... on a Sunday, cold and wet—the summer of 1910 was characterized by a considerable amount of rain," as Ira Gray remembered. Ira had come to the area with his parents, Thomas and Minnie Gray, and his three brothers from North Dakota in 1907. His father opened the first general store west of the North Saskatchewan River in 1909.

On October 25, Ira Gray and his brother Eph

... rode four miles down the river to visit the family of my uncle who was operating the ferry boat. On arriving at our pasture gate the sight I saw was of about fifty head, or more, of saddle and packhorses in our pasture and many tents near our house.

This was the party of Martin Nordegg of Brazeau Collieries Ltd. (German Development Co.) which had been prospecting for steamcoal and had found a coalfield on the Blackstone River, some forty miles west of the present day town of Nordegg....

This event marked my first meeting with Mr. Nordegg, Stuart Kidd, a company agent, and the Brewsters.

That night the party camped at our place. Mr. Nordegg and some of his party, including a Mr. Corry Weatherby, who later was the first mine manager at Nordegg, slept in our house, had supper and breakfast there, as it was a treat to have decent accommodations after many days of following the packtrains and living in damp tents and damp bedding.

The purpose of the horses roundup by Eph and me was to make up three teams to haul the Nordegg party to Innisfail, Alberta, a distance of some seventy miles. Two days were required for this trip to the railway town on the C.P.R. Calgary-Edmonton line....

At Innisfail, after a lot of handshaking and farewells, Mister Nordegg and party took the train to Edmonton.

In his further recollections of the years 1910 to 1913, Ira Gray continued to write about his work for Martin Nordegg. His story becomes a parallel record of Martin's memoirs, complementing them in some instances but, more importantly, confirming and substantiating what Martin wrote about his activities in the area in greater detail and often in such an exuberant manner that some readers came to the conclusion that not all life, people, and events had been as dramatic, humorous, and colourful as Martin liked to describe them.

For the admirer of Martin Nordegg, it is gratifying to discover how Ira Gray's recollections not only parallel but practically mirror what Martin writes in his memoirs. In the chapter "To Our Coalfields," Martin describes at great length, the son of a good friend from Perth, Ontario, whom Martin had engaged as his aide-de-camp for the expedition of the summer 1910. This young man had just graduated from the Military Academy in Kingston with a promising résumé, but turned out to be rather ill-prepared and ill-equipped for the rough life of a prospecting party in the Far West.

With humour but also with noticeable exasperation Martin describes in great detail the problems, commotions and near disasters the young man caused, making himself the butt of jokes and source of anger. If every large party has to have a weakling, an innocent, a greenhorn, the young Easterner filled all roles to the ultimate, becoming the subject of many jokes, scares and finally a mock trial put on by Martin's crew and presided over by Charles Hower.

During the entire summer, the young man never seemed to learn anything. And at the end of the expedition, he still stood out large enough in this party of many men which Ira Gray took to Innisfail later that day:

... he was a queer-looking fellow as well as dumb-acting, and wore city clothing and very thick glasses. As we parked on the gravel bar on the east side of the river, I noticed this fellow took his toilet case, dig into his duffle bag for towel and soap and went away downstream ... to perform his toilet.... When the entire outfit had gotten across on the ferry, Stuart Kidd counted noses, as a final check before resuming the travel. I heard him remark "There is someone missing. Who could it be?" I remarked, "there is one man down there who had his top shirt off and toilet articles spread around on the bar." Stuart gave one of his sharp shouts, calling the fellow's name, "You have been a nuisance on this whole trip and here you are again holding up everything. Gather up your belongings, get in that wagon, and stay there till I tell you to get out," and to me, "Boy, watch him; we're apt to leave him behind anywhere."

Martin had not exaggerated his drastic description of the young man at all!

Martin was eager to return to the East. On the train from Edmonton to Ottawa, a journey that seemed longer than ever, a very anxious and troubled Martin could not take his mind off the image of the lake with the fleeing geese and the mountain behind it. Hardly settled in Ottawa, Martin immediately searched the library of the Geological Survey for

... a possible intimation of similar occurrences in the neighbourhood. I found nothing. Yet it appeared to me very strange that such great geologists, like Dowling and McEvoy, who had passed over the same trail as I did, should not have seen what I believed to be coal measures. Hower had also looked in the same direction as I did, when I borrowed the binoculars from him, and yet he never noticed anything. I began to feel more and more uncertain, and confided at last in friend Dowling.

Dowling was the only person other than Andrew Haydon that Martin dared to take into his confidence about his exciting discoveries east of the Bighorn field. Dowling believed Martin's description, but as this particular coal deposit "...was further East than the Bighorn and Brazeau fields, it would in all probability be of an inferior quality."

On the other hand, Dowling did not deny the economic advantages of mining coal so much further east with its considerable savings in the costs of railway construction and, ultimately, the savings in the reduced cost of every ton of coal shipped.

Dowling was quite willing to come west and give his opinion. However, this would not be before the end of summer 1911, a date for which Martin could not afford to wait. Should Dowling pronounce Martin's discovery as of suitable quality and volume, hundreds of thousands of dollars would have been spent uselessly on the South Brazeau field. Even the work of the railway surveying party would have been for naught. Martin decided he must go on his own as early next spring as possible. Instead of Dowling, he would engage McEvoy.

There was not too much left to do for Martin but wait for the early spring expedition. But first, he had to go to Berlin and obtain approval of the new development from Georg Büxenstein and the board members of the Deutsches Kanada Syndikat. It was certainly premature to take Mackenzie and Mann into his confidence. But without informing the head office in Toronto, Martin advised Stuart Kidd to suspend temporarily the freighting of supplies and equipment to the South Brazeau, where Stuart had left an older man as guard. Ira Gray remembered that five months later, "Stuart returned with the old gentleman, who was pretty nearly dead from scurvy."

In Berlin, Martin again realized how fortunate he was in having Georg Büxenstein as his "partner." Always enjoying adventure and a certain measure of risk taking, Büxenstein easily managed to overcome the objections of a cautious board of directors and authorized Martin to proceed with the development of the newly discovered coal deposits, once they were found to be profitable.

Martin wanted to return to Canada immediately, but Georg Büxenstein convinced him that he could wait for spring in Europe just as well or better than in Canada. It was time for another trip for the two of them, through the Mediterranean and the Suez Canal and through parts of Africa. This exciting proposition put Martin in a painful quandary. For the first time since coming to Canada, he was able to look forward to three or four months free of urgent work. Berthe-Marie had been very happy to hear that finally they would have time for each other, spending a quiet winter in Toronto interspersed with trips to New York to see Marcelle.

Not surprisingly, Martin's unquenchable desire for adventure and travel around the world won out again. He wrote a long letter to Berthe-Marie, explaining that he had already booked passage to Le Havre for her and Marcelle. In March, the family would be reunited when he would join them in France. He insisted that it would be inadvisable to refuse his president's generous offer to join him on a trip to Africa.

Travelling with Georg Büxenstein was as stimulating and rewarding as always. Martin arrived in Paris in an excellent mood, which transferred itself to Marcelle and even Berthe-Marie. After having enjoyed the early spring at the French Riviera, the three left Europe on April 1, 1911, on the SS *Rotterdam* from Boulogne.

By the end of April, Martin departed for Alberta to join McEvoy, who had already started further exploring of the Kananaskis field and was ready to go with Martin to the Bighorn country.

Whether Charles Hower had expected to remain with Martin for the completion of the mine at the South Brazeau is uncertain. As yet, Martin had not made him a definitive offer. There was too much that made the relationship between these two, in so many ways, incompatible personalities unpleasant.

Whether Hower was angry at Martin for not being rehired or whether he had any inkling of Martin's discovery of another coalfield which Martin had kept from him, he vented his anger in a letter to Stuart Kidd, written on March 7, 1911, in Johnstown, Pennsylvania. Full of sarcasm, Hower gave free rein to his hostility towards Martin:

> My dear Stuart:
> ... By this time you have probably heard from Nordegg. I had a letter just prior to his going to Africa. He was just as erratic as ever. There is no doubt but that he will need you this coming summer, someone will have to go in and bring the old man out [i.e., the cache guard at the South Brazeau mentioned by Ira Gray]. This will probably fall to you, but I imagine that Nordegg will have precious little to do with the real development of the Northern property when it is developed, which will probably be several years.
>
> I am satisfied that whoever has to bear the burdens of that organizations foolishness will find in you an able and willing helper. I wish my own plans were in such shape that I could make you an offer.
>
> If I ever have any future connection with Nordegg, it will be in an advisory capacity, where I will not be responsible for results. Some other poor devil can bear the brunt of the responsibility and the censure for the other ones stupidity. No more for me thank you.
>
> I want however to correct an impression you may have. I am not sore on the Brazeau. Merely satisfied that I could not do myself justice working under their conditions. And I want to say now they will either change policy or just be another Northwestern mining failure.
>
> In the meantime I am with kindest regards
> Yours very truly
> Chas. L. Hower

Stuart, whose faith in the competence and integrity of Martin Nordegg was unshakable, must have been deeply shocked by Hower's invective against Martin Nordegg. Stuart decided he had to share Hower's letter with Martin, especially after he had read the page Hower had attached to his letter, which in even stronger words betrayed Hower's hatred for Martin Nordegg:

> ... You well know the little dutchman's [i.e., Martin Nordegg] weak head and weaker heart. A man who uses his whole brain to remember

small things is never going to handle big affairs. His own ignorance makes him gullible and his conceit makes him vulnerable. A man of his kind can never be trusted and he will attempt always to gain by craft what others would accomplish by honestly sustained effort... He will never appreciate loyalty let alone sacrifice...
Yours
Hower

What must have gone through Hower's mind during the rough months of sharing the trail, the food and the tent with Martin Nordegg! There is no other even remotely similar characterization of Martin in letters or comments by other people who knew Martin well.

Only after his return from Europe did Martin receive the copy of Hower's letter, which Stuart had sent him confidentially to Toronto. After reading Hower's invective over and over again, Martin breathed a sigh of relief for not having renewed Hower's contract and having severed all connections with Charles Hower in time.

What a pleasure and comfort it was to have McEvoy at his side. Together, they travelled from the Kananaskis to Innisfail "...where our large party was getting impatient to start out West."

Martin waved goodbye to McEvoy and his men and left for Banff where he would be close to both the activities at Kananaskis and at the South Brazeau. But his stay at Banff turned out to be less than a day due to the telegram he found upon his arrival at the Banff Springs Hotel. Georg Büxenstein advised him that a Mr. Zuckermandl was on his way to Montreal. Zuckermandl was one of the directors of the private bank of Schlesinger, Trier & Co. in Berlin, which was expected to invest heavily in the projects of the German Development Company. Büxenstein asked Martin to meet Zuckermandl in Montreal and accompany him on a cross-country trip by rail to Vancouver. Nothing could have been more inconvenient for Martin at this time. He was most anxious to determine the value and potential of the coal deposits he had discovered east of the Bighorn River in October. He was also increasingly worried about other possible parties prospecting in the area. But "orders being orders, there was nothing left but to travel East at once."

Martin met Zuckermandl in Montreal. They had hardly boarded the train when Martin's worst fears seemed confirmed. A Calgary paper left by another passenger carried a brief item announcing the return to Lacombe of a prospector who had discovered a large coal deposit at the Baptiste River. A quick look at the Alberta map he always carried in his bag confirmed Martin's worst fears. The Baptiste River was only a few miles northwest of the "Gap"! *

> I became so excited, that my hand trembled, and my companion asked me if I was sick. I pacified him.... I hardly slept that night, nor the following...my companion insisted on spending one day in Winnipeg. The night before ... I had made up my mind: I would telegraph to Fraser....

Norman Fraser, a mining engineer from the Crowsnest Pass, had been hired by Martin for the work at Lusk Creek in the Kananaskis. He was the only man Martin entrusted with the work he had planned to do himself at the Gap that spring. In Calgary, the train stopped for one hour; every minute was needed to discuss with Fraser the task that Martin reluctantly and with a good deal of apprehension assigned to him.

> Having learned already to be most careful and not to trust anybody until I knew him well, and sometimes not even then, I was confronted with a great difficulty. How could I send a man whom I did not know, into an unknown district, with instructions to stake a coalfield ... in his own name ... and depend on his honesty to transfer afterwards the leases into the name of my company.
>
> I remembered the stories ... I thought of claim-jumping.... But what was I to do? I took a chance.... I should have, of course, accompanied Fraser. But I could not, as it would have been against my Berlin orders. Then I thought with relief, that in this case Fraser would have probably thought the exploration extremely important. No, the best would be to be appear casual. My companion had already become impatient. I said goodbye to Fraser, wished him good luck, asked him to report to me immediately when he had found anything.
>
> I knew it would take him and his party about one week to reach the place, and this again gave me a chance of riding in very quickly, once I got rid of my banker....
>
> I felt very uneasy when the train rolled out of Calgary towards the mountains. In fact, I was tense with excitement. My companion thought my nerves were in bad condition.... If I could only tell the old gentleman why I was so nervous!... One day in Banff, another in Lake Louise.... At last,... we pushed through to Victoria. The banker took the night boat to Seattle ... at last, I was free.... I took the train to Calgary.

But in Calgary, a telegram from Mackenzie called Martin to Toronto immediately. Mackenzie wanted to discuss various financial matters before going to London. Martin "had just time to jump again on the train." As it turned out, Mackenzie wanted Martin to accom-

---

* The location of the future town and mine of Nordegg.

pany him to London. Martin knew what was at stake for him and delayed his response to Mackenzie day after day until early one morning a page brought him a telegram:

> "Have found the stuff. Going to Calgary to land agent filing claims. Fraser."
> My hand trembled holding the telegram. I read it over and over again, and could hardly believe that my dream was fulfilled.... I must inform Mackenzie at once. I rushed to his office. He had not yet arrived. The waiting appeared to me like years.... At last Mackenzie came.
> In my great excitement I stammered. I explained to him what this discovery meant for us, for our coal company, for the railway. He was visibly impressed, and congratulated me warmly.

Martin had tears in his eyes of joy, of pride, and of gratitude for Mackenzie's recognition of his success. For once, he felt an equal to Mackenzie, but not for long. Mackenzie coolly advised the "thunderstruck" Martin that one half of this new field would belong to the German Development Company and the other half to Mackenzie, Mann & Company! "Don't you remember what your President arranged with me in his hunting lodge? All business regarding coal in the West should be done half and half?"

Martin brought all possible arguments to the fore, he alone had done all the work of exploration on the field he had discovered on his own, while Mackenzie's company "did not do anything at all." Martin's success would save the railway 40 miles of track through difficult terrain saving at least $2 million in construction costs and 40 cents for every ton of coal transported.

Martin stood his ground in the heated argument so well that Mackenzie found it necessary to resort to the old routine of calling Donald Mann and Judge Phippen. Mann "took up the cudgel at once" while Phippen threatened a law suit if the "gentlemen's agreement" between Büxenstein and Mackenzie would not be honoured. On the verge of losing his nerves in his battle with three men who were notorious for driving a bargain to the extreme and invariably winning in the end, Martin felt on very uncertain ground.

> I was scared. We did not have the leases yet. I did not know anything about the quality of the mining conditions of the new coal. I bit my lip. I should not have mentioned it at all. But it was imperative....
> I said: "If my President has promised such an arrangement, of course it will be carried out.... I cabled Berlin ... and travelled West again.

Martin had no inkling of the "Great Trouble" awaiting him in Alberta!

Everything started out well. Martin travelled in a light wagon from Innisfail to Rocky Mountain House, where an Indian hired by

Stuart Kidd waited for him with three good horses. They travelled fast, through muskeg and on high ground, reaching the Gap in record time. In the falling darkness, they saw a spiral of smoke, the location of Fraser's camp.

Leaving his horse in the care of the Indian guide and refusing to bother with supper, Martin listened to the exciting reports of Fraser's successful exploration work. He pored over the detailed map Fraser had drawn showing the claims he had staked, and the outcroppings of coal, all of which were to the south of the lake where Martin had shot at the geese eight months ago.

> I sat up with Fraser until late at night, in front of the fire in which big chunks of beautiful coal, our coal, were burning with a bluish flame. They came from the two seams which had been uncovered.
>
> At last I was on the ground which meant the fulfilment of my dreams. To think that I had found it myself—that I had noticed what trained geologists and coalmining engineers had passed by, that I had saved two million dollars in the construction of the railway, all that made me very proud. Is it surprising that I could not find any sleep that night? I was lying on the very ground where in the future a large coalmine was to operate, where hundreds of men would work, where I would build a town with pretty houses, not slums, but a town of which I could be proud. My heart was drumming and I built castles in the air....
>
> I thought already of a place for the townsite, halfway between the lake and the mine. I imagined how happy I would be to live there.

Martin was up before sunrise, ready to start the inspection tour with Fraser. He was incredibly happy on this beautiful morning. But there was something in Fraser's demeanor that made Martin uneasy. Fraser had done a competent job of exploring the future mine site. But vaguely, he referred to some difficulties at the land agent's office in Calgary because the claims were still in unsurveyed territory. Also, and this alarmed Martin, Fraser could not clearly explain why he had failed to take a coal sample to Calgary for assaying. Martin knew he had to leave for Calgary immediately.

Clear, dry weather allowed for fast travel to Rocky Mountain House. At Thomas Gray's place, Martin met Ira Gray with a large packtrain with supplies destined for the party that was surveying the railway line to the South Brazeau. A bemused Martin wondered when he would be able to finally tell the men travelling back and forth between Rocky Mountain House and the South Brazeau that their new destination would be the Gap rather than the current location 40 miles further to the north.

Martin expected a restful time in Calgary. The assaying of the coal samples would take at least three days. He would see the land agent and hire a competent surveyor and send him to the stakings as quickly as possible. But unexpected trouble confronted Martin when the land agent suggested that Martin share the costs of surveying with another party that had been staking during the past weeks in the area of Martin's claims.

> I was thunderstruck. The blood left my face. In a very small voice I asked him to let me see the staking sketch and description of the other party. The name of the applicant was unknown to me. I had just paid all the men in Fraser's party, and that name was certainly not among them. Who could that be? How could he have found that spot? Why did Fraser not tell me anything at all about it? I asked again for the description of the land and copied the name and date....
>
> The assay showed the coal to be of an excellent quality.... I should have been overjoyed. I was not. I was terrified that we should have a competitor close to us who would benefit besides by our railway. That would be great competition and while, of course, the needs of the Canadian Northern Railway would be entirely taken care of by our mine, yet there was a great market for steamcoal on and East of the Calgary-Edmonton line, on which I had counted. Now I would have to fight for it. My imagined monopoly was gone. I raced back to Fraser's camp with a heavy heart, and the trip was miserable through heavy downpour.

Very much on guard now, Martin decided to take the surveyor he had hired with him and keep him at his side at all times. Under no circumstances would he leave him alone with Fraser.

Martin's account of the events following his return to the future mine site has the character of a spy story. Fraser seemed overly eager to show the development work his men had completed during Martin's short absence. The next morning, Martin took Fraser to the rising ground west of the lake where, according to the sketch he had brought from Calgary, he expected to find a stake. A few yards from where the reeds of the lake ended, there was indeed a stake and "Fraser seemed highly surprised. He asked me how I knew it."

Martin explained the discovery he had made at the land agent's office in Calgary.

> I watched his face closely. He never moved a muscle.... I found the other stakes easily. Then he said, that when he returned from Calgary, his men had told him of having noticed a camp there ... and found a party of three men who were staking. When I asked him why he had not mentioned this to me during my previous visit, he replied with embarrassment, that he must have forgotten it. We walked silently back to camp....

Martin was certain now that Fraser had deceived him. In order to retain his chances, he would have to either buy these claims or take

Fraser to court. But he needed more proof. Fraser became more and more uneasy but did not resist when Martin requested seeing his diary. It turned out that, contrary to his earlier account, Fraser had stayed in Calgary for a full week. The next entry in the diary further confirmed Martin's suspicions: the staking of the competing claims had been done the day after Fraser's return from Calgary!

Martin needed advice and support from someone he could trust absolutely. He left for the South Brazeau immediately to take McEvoy into his confidence. McEvoy was elated about the news of Martin's coal discovery and its advantages over the more remote South Brazeau field. He even grew more enthusiastic after reading the assay report from Calgary.

McEvoy whistled when he learned the name of the staker: "...We would have to do some detective work... We were up against one of the worst rascals."

From his Crowsnest days McEvoy already knew this man who lived in Fernie. Martin was desperate, but McEvoy told him not to worry. One way or the other, they would succeed in taking over the competing claims. In the meantime, it was futile to spend even one more day of work at the South Brazeau. The time had arrived to transport the men and all the equipment to the Gap and commence work at the new site with all the forces that could be mobilized. Gratefully, Martin accepted McEvoy's advice and gave the necessary orders before departing from the South Brazeau. If there was going to be a town of Nordegg, it would be located at the new site near the Gap.

At Fraser's camp, McEvoy did not hold back with his praise of Martin, who had discovered coal deposits of high quality that neither he nor Dowling had suspected in this area. On his own, McEvoy spent a great deal of time talking to Fraser's men. He did not hesitate to scare them about being under suspicion of aiding illegal activities. "Cross-examining" the men, McEvoy eventually established that Fraser had often been seen talking in private to the staker of the competing party, who turned out to be Fraser's relative. On his way to Calgary, Fraser had taken along a message from this man to be telegraphed to Fernie. Fraser became more and more evasive but did not deny that he had travelled to Calgary via Red Deer.

The journey to Red Deer seemed endless and the nights on the trail brought Martin little sleep. What would he have done without the even-tempered, always optimistic McEvoy who actually seemed to enjoy playing the detective. With cunning, he persuaded the station agent in Red Deer to show him the telegram to Fernie: "It was signed not by Fraser but his relative at the camp."

Martin and McEvoy took the next train to Calgary from where Martin cabled to Andrew Haydon not to let the Department act on the competing claims until he made a report. Next, Martin rushed to Edmonton to engage a lawyer to accompany him to Fernie, picking up McEvoy on the way in Calgary. In Fernie, the "rascal" was easily located. Although he refused to transfer his claims, he was ready to sell them for $5000. "He had a relative working on the neighbouring claims for Fraser who had informed him...of some valuable coalfield, he should come up at once and stake, and he promised to divvy up with him."

When confronted by Martin's lawyer with the dishonesty he had been involved in, the "rascal" turned out to be a very tough opponent, refusing any settlement and only shrugging his shoulders when threatened with a lawsuit against him and his relative as well. Martin, McEvoy and the lawyer travelled to Lethbridge where a subpoena was issued for both the "rascal" and his relative to appear at court in Lethbridge. Still, it was imperative to be crafty and surprise the opponents. Martin sent a messenger to Fraser's camp ordering the "rascal's" relative under some pretext to come to Red Deer, where he was served with the subpoena. Two days later, Martin wondered whether the ruse had been necessary and whether he had really caught the man by surprise. At the opening of the proceedings, Fraser unexpectedly turned up in the court room in Lethbridge. Martin gathered that Fraser must have known his game was up.

Fraser immediately asked to speak to Martin in private, assuring him that he could arrange for a settlement out of court. Court was recessed; and Martin's lawyer went into action, threatening Fraser's relative and the "rascal" from Fernie with jail. He was not aware that both men already had a prison record and would, if convicted, indeed face heavy jail sentences. The "rascal" remained quite stubborn but the man from camp who had a large family dependent on him quickly broke down. Upon Martin's whispered urging, the lawyer reluctantly effected a settlement and the case was dismissed. Martin did not allow the relative to return to camp, where under the watchful eyes of Martin and McEvoy, Fraser finished his work. Two days after Fraser's departure, Dowling arrived, examined the field and "became very enthusiastic." After the stress of the past weeks, his words were music to Martin's ears:

"Of course I must report this great discovery at once to the Provincial and Dominion Government. It is a very large deposit and we will name it The Nordegg Coal Basin."

This it was called by the Dominion and Provincial Government in their publications and records, and the Geographical Board of Canada named the South branch of the Brazeau River, Nordegg River. I was elated.

For Martin, the "great trouble" was over; the season's work in the West was finished with complete success. The location of his first mine in Canada was now determined. Although the trace for the railway to the South Brazeau had already been cut, the mine to the north would have to wait for development at a future date. With Dowling and McEvoy, Martin returned to Ottawa.

In Ottawa, Martin was able to relax in the happy atmosphere of the home of his friend Andrew Haydon for a few days. Good-naturedly, Andy teased Martin for being too kind-hearted and not having sent the two men to jail. If he wanted to succeed in future, he would have to become much tougher and less trusting. Martin promised to be more cautious from then on but wondered whether he really could change his nature.

For Berthe-Marie in Toronto, he had more than just the good news of his success in the West. He was opening a new office in the building of the Canadian Northern Railways at One Toronto Street, only a few steps from their home at 19 Toronto Street. Much work expected him at his office, and for the first time in many years, he would come home from work every evening, as he had done in London and in Berlin.

Berthe-Marie was not as overjoyed as Martin had expected. Two weeks later, her chronic pessimism was justified once more. By cable, Mackenzie requested Martin "to sail by the first steamer to London." There was trouble with the bankers, who were reluctant to agree to the purchase of the Nordegg claims before the older claims had produced any tangible results. Martin should also cable to Georg Büxenstein, asking for his presence.

In London, Martin had to suffer through two weeks of intense negotiations. Although only a bystander most of the time, Martin's presence proved to be crucial. He absolved himself extremely well when the bankers literally interrogated him for hours about the entire history of his coal explorations and discoveries, especially the most recent one in the Nordegg basin.

Day after day, Mackenzie's and Büxenstein's negotiations with the tough representatives of the banks in London, Brussels, Paris, and Berlin continued, sometimes until after midnight. And when Martin, dead tired, had retired to his room, he was called to Mackenzie's or Büxenstein's suite to witness another "private fight" between the two. He had come to regard Mackenzie highly and had absolute trust in Georg Büxenstein and marvelled at their ability to take common front against the bankers. But he felt buffeted between

Mackenzie and Büxenstein when the two became enmeshed in heated quarrels during their own meetings.

Eventually, agreement was reached with the bankers. Brazeau Collieries, now heavily financed by Lazard Bros., would buy the Nordegg claims for cash and bonds,

> ... and thus, all seemed to end in harmony between the bankers and ourselves. But this proved not to be the end. Now a private fight started between Mackenzie and the President. The latter naturally insisted on receiving the lion's share of the purchase price, as it had been acknowledged by the bankers and also by Mackenzie, that the discovery was due to my work on behalf of the German Development Company. Mackenzie insisted on 'sharing fifty-fifty.'
>
> Another heated struggle ensued and I saw everything in danger. But at last, to my surprise, Mackenzie gave in to the convincing arguments of the President, both seemed happy and content, and an aide-de-memoire was drawn up and initialled.
>
> This called for another celebration by ourselves and the bankers whom the President invited....

But not everything was over by any means. During the festive dinner, the question of the Dunsmuir Collieries came up. Büxenstein expected to participate in the venture of buying the collieries on Vancouver Island, based on the old agreement with Mackenzie that everything in the West would be shared between Mackenzie and the German Development Company. Mackenzie resorted to a number of arguments including one that has not been settled to this day: Was British Columbia part of "The West" or was "The West" comprised of the three prairie provinces alone. Despite heated arguments, Mackenzie stood his ground and

> ... this closed the fight, the President coming out second victor. I had the feeling that the former very friendly feeling between the two had been seriously disturbed, and the future proved this to be correct. We had to pay for this very heavily later on.

Martin accompanied Georg Büxenstein to Berlin, staying there for only a few days before returning to Canada. In Toronto, he immediately enlarged his staff in order to complete all plans for the building of the mine and townsite. Much time was spent on the logistics of continuing construction throughout the winter. Martin was determined to fulfill his promise to Mackenzie that 100,000 tons of coal would be waiting to be shipped east, once the first coal cars of the railway line under construction would reach his mine.

Upon the recommendation of the Société Général in Brussels, Martin had hired a Belgian mining engineer, Ernest Gheur who turned out to be one of the best men professionally and personally that Martin had ever hired for his Nordegg project. Gheur immediately drew up detailed plans and specifications for the mine itself. In September Martin and Gheur went to Chicago, where a contract was signed with the Roberts & Schaefer Company, Engineers and Builders for the construction of the mine.

Everything seemed to proceed well and for a few weeks, Martin was flying high. But when Mackenzie was presented with the first of several notes of $200,000 in favour of the German Development Company, Mackenzie flatly refused to honour it. When Martin became insistent, Mackenzie called Mann; and once more, the well-known disagreeable routine ensued with Mann acting in "his brusque way." Lacking the authority or power to act decisively, Martin could only cable to Berlin for help. Over the next weeks, telegrams flew back and forth between Toronto and Berlin, eventually ending at a curiously significant stage in the life of William Mackenzie and Donald Mann. When Martin informed Georg Büxenstein that the two partners had been knighted by the King, Büxenstein advised him

> ... to tell Sir William Mackenzie and Sir Donald Mann nothing else from him than 'Noblesse oblige,' and that he would only congratulate them after they had paid their notes plus accumulated interest.... I found both knights in best humour, which encouraged me to show them the cable. They both laughed aloud, and Sir William said: "That German is no fool" and asked me to cable the President, that they were both "very poor knights." I did not let this opportunity pass without striking the iron while hot, and negotiations ensued which ended by settling all previous notes by a very large payment with a considerable discount of the accumulated interest.
>
> But this matter, as well as the success of the mine, resulted in a manner which was very helpful to me, even during the war and after it: a sincere friendship between Sir William Mackenzie and myself, which ended only with the death of Sir William.

Time was pressing. But Martin was thriving on the challenges he was facing: planning the mine and the townsite in his office in Toronto and travelling to the head office of Roberts & Schaefer in Chicago several times; ordering and purchasing equipment for his mine in the West; mapping out the schedule for shipping the mine equipment to the West; engaging dozens of men for the packtrains needed to transport everything to the actual site of construction; anticipating the changing means of transport available—trains to the junction north of Red Deer from where the Canadian Northern Western Railway was gradually making its way towards Rocky Mountain House; scheduling packtrains, wagons and sleighs through the undeveloped country to the mine site; moving equipment, construction materials and food supplies in relays from one depot or "cache" as it was called in the West, to the next. The tasks were hundredfold. But Martin was cheerfully entering what became the most gratifying, fulfilling, and successful period of his life and endeavor in the Canadian West!

> I was aware that the most important work of my life was now ahead of me. Only by incessant and organized work would I be able to make it a success. To do this, I had to be on the spot, which meant spending every day, even the whole winter and the following seasons on the ground, in the Rockies. I made my plans accordingly....

But Mackenzie crossed Martin's plans again sending him on short notice to London to sign the bonds to be issued in his capacity as Vice President of Brazeau Collieries. Without unpacking his bags, Martin completed the onerous task of signing thousands of bonds "...continuing for two days from early morning till midnight, and I returned by the same boat to New York, catching immediately a train to Toronto and for the West."

From the boat, Martin had telegraphed to New York asking Marcelle to meet him at the pier and accompany him by taxi to the train. Marcelle was grateful to see her father, but with tears in her eyes and disappointment in her heart watched him wave from the departing train. Would he keep his promise to take her to the West next summer?

In Toronto, Martin was spared another rushed goodbye. Berthe-Marie had already left for Egypt accompanied by Maria Fuhrmann, her maid from Vienna. A few months before, Martin had shared his worry about Berthe-Marie's increasing respiratory difficulties with her physician, who cautioned against another winter in the raw, damp climate of Toronto. A mild, dry climate was urgently indicated. The physician agreed with Martin's choice of Hélouan, the resort in the desert of Egypt, which Martin had visited with Georg Büxenstein. Martin himself caught the next train for the West, where "Snow flurries in Calgary heralded the coming winter." Again, the Nordegg family was split up for months to come.

It is doubtful that without his by now thorough familiarity with the West, Martin would have succeeded so splendidly in realizing his plans in the months and years ahead. He had traversed the difficult terrain between Rocky Mountain House and the mine site several times and had experienced the unpredictability of its climate. He had gotten to know the people in the area and understood their nature and habits. He had developed relationships with people of power in the East as well as in Alberta. And last not least, his orderly mind, his talent for organization and his ability to inspire people and win and retain their loyalty and trust, all contributed to the realization of his dream.

Martin engaged the Brewster Brothers for the transports between Red Deer, Rocky Mountain House, and the mine site. He also opened a temporary head office in Red Deer. Stuart Kidd was appointed as purchasing agent and was requested to move to the mine site and build a cabin there, the first permanent structure on the mine site with Stuart becoming the first permanent resident of the future town.

In Rocky Mountain House, snow was falling heavily and the temperatures were unseasonably cold. But Martin was grateful for the cold weather. He was delighted to see the mountains of equipment and supplies waiting for transport to the mine. A number of heavy sleighs were constructed for carrying machinery and supplies upstream on the frozen North Saskatchewan River as far as Mire Creek [now Shunda Creek] from where the trace of the railway to be built was used to reach the mine site. The local people and the railway engineers only shook their heads about Martin's plans. But despite frequent accidents of sleighs and horses breaking through the ice of the river, the need to lessen the load for each sleigh carrying the heavy machinery, and frustrating weeks of helplessly waiting for the temperatures to turn colder and for the ice to become stronger again, the Brewster crews did manage to move back and forth along the transport route for most of the winter.

Stuart Kidd saw the impatience in Martin's eyes and rented a Ford automobile at Red Deer in order to help Martin save precious time in his continuous trips back and forth. Travelling by car seemed a vast advantage in comfort and speed, but for only a few miles, until the sharp edges of the river ice cut the tires to shreds. Ropes wrapped around the wheels performed even better than rubber tires, but eventually, the Ford had to be abandoned and the journey continued on foot until Martin and Stuart caught up with one of the sleighs.

Martin remembered the beautiful sunshine during most of the winter days, but never forgot the intense cold, which several times reached minus fifty degrees Fahrenheit. At the mine site, temporary log buildings and a cookhouse had been erected. But despite the intense cold, Martin preferred sleeping in a tent under heavy bearskins rather than among the miners in the log cabins, which were filled with "foul air" from overcrowding and the smell of old straw. In the morning, he proudly took his first photographs of the log cabins and his tent with ten smiling men, including a beaming Martin with his pipe in his hand. Another picture taken from a hill looks down upon Stuart's cabin again and a teepee surrounded by heavily wooded terrain. A year later, Martin would take more photographs of the area, by then a large, busy construction site—the beginning of an incredible transformation of this hitherto untouched wilderness.

Construction continued at a fast pace. Ira Gray was in charge of moving building materials to the site:

> Jack [Brewster] put me in charge of the outfit and told me to move the freight from the cache at Mire Creek into Nordegg. We were to load each team with 1600 lbs. of freight and take three days for a round trip ... it took us a good while to put all the freight into Nordegg ... a heavy amount of horse feed was used on the job. The sleighing was very poor. Then we camped at Nordegg and skidded and hauled the logs up to the building site, up near to where the tipple was later built. The logs were cut on the side hill ... we arranged them in order on the sites where they were to be erected, endlogs and sidelogs in place for each building. Later, ... the buildings were raised by rolling the logs into place.
>
> The buildings consisted of the following: office buildings, large cookhouse and mess, bunkhouses, two warehouses, stables, and feed storage. Lumber was freighted in for the roofing and the flooring. As manpower increased, ... packhorses were used to pack needed supplies into Nordegg.

Ira also mentioned running into "the headpacker Old Dutch in his moosehide suit." Old Dutch (Dutchie) was by no means an old fellow, but a character well known among the people in the area and later a good friend and collaborator of Martin.

During the winter of 1911-1912, Martin travelled back and forth between Alberta and Toronto, where he worked on his vision of the "modern and pretty town" to be built next to the mine.

The trained draughtsman Martin completed an album of sketches that he "looked at with greatest pleasure over and over again."

There was to be a main street lined by public buildings of stores, hotels, churches and a miners' recreation hall. For a well-equipped hospital, Martin sought advice from medical authorities of the University of Toronto.

In late March, Berthe-Marie returned from Egypt, her lung condition noticeably improved. But within a few weeks, the Toronto climate began to show its effects again. Berthe-Marie expressed the desire to return to Europe soon. Martin booked passage to Europe for his wife and, according to her wishes, arranged for a stay in the German spa of Wiesbaden to precede her return to Hélouan.

Berthe-Marie left for Europe in May, and Martin went West again. Since work at the mine and the townsite was running according to schedule, Martin decided on the Banff Springs Hotel as his temporary headquarters. From there he would make frequent trips to the mine across the Pipestone Pass and to his office in Red Deer by train via Calgary. He also found time for hiking in the mountains and, the fulfilment of a long standing wish, reached the foot of Mt. Assiniboine, the Canadian Matterhorn, where he took some exceptional photographs.

Martin's railway, the Canadian Northern Western was slowly creeping westwards, having reached the half-way point between Blackfalds and Rocky Mountain House. Travelling in a freight car, Martin endured a bumpy ride on the still unballasted track and after the second derailment changed to horse and buggy. It was a difficult trip on wet, muddy trails. Indeed, the entire summer of 1912 was to be very rainy and wet. Martin prayed for a sunny, dry September, the month he intended to take Marcelle across the mountains.

A surprise awaited Martin near the North Saskatchewan River ferry west of Rocky Mountain House, where he spotted a party of surveyors of the Canadian Pacific Railway. To his distress, Martin learned that the CPR had bought an old charter for the purpose of building a bridge across the river. That meant two bridges would cross the river next to each other! Martin saw an opportunity to save his railway at least a quarter million dollars!

But Mackenzie, who did not want to hear of negotiating with the rival railway, said that "The Canadian Pacific had always shown a hostile attitude and that I might save myself all the trouble."

Undeterred, Martin rushed to Winnipeg to see Sir George Bury, the vice president of the CPR. While initially taken aback by the proposed joint use of the bridge, Sir George eventually took to Martin's idea, actually much more readily than did Mackenzie. In the end, after many telegrams going back and forth between Toronto and Winnipeg, Martin did win. The negotiations resulted in a grant to the Canadian Northern Western Railway of the running rights across the bridge, which was the indispensable link between Rocky Mountain House and Martin's town and mine.

In the summer of 1912, Martin finally made the acquaintance of "the murderer from Germany." This hard-working, but very reserved and elusive man was called "Dutchie" or sometimes "Dutch" by the locals. Although Dutchie had been employed as a head packer during the summer, Martin had never managed to meet him until one day, when riding through the bush west of the mine

> ... my horse suddenly jumped to the side and I nearly fell off. There, between two cottonwood trees, stood a short, stocky fellow. A slouch hat, buckskin jacket with fringes, high boots. He was leaning on a rifle. I was annoyed at him for scaring my horse.

Dutchie became one of Martin's most loyal and stalwart friends. But the beginning of their relationship was most difficult, even for the outgoing Martin, who managed so well with almost every person he met. Dutchie was gruff and uncommunicative, although he accepted Martin's invitation to dinner that same evening. The camp cook was horrified when Martin asked him to prepare a good meal for his guest whom the cook easily identified as Dutch, the guy who had to flee Germany after he had murdered someone there. The dinner went well, although Dutchie did not reveal anything about himself and only smiled once when he accepted a pair of binoculars from Martin as a special gift. Dutchie merely said thank you and disappeared. Two weeks later, the two men met again and Dutchie finally revealed his story, after Martin pleaded with him to become friends. After all, they were the only two Germans for miles around.

Dutchie, who had never murdered anybody, had become too tired of being teased by the locals about his German accent. Besides, with only a few men in the area, women were just too interested in him. So Dutchie decided to protect himself from their attention by describing himself as a murderer who might be liable to commit another murder if people would not know better than to leave him alone.

As Martin relates in his ten-page chapter on "Dutchie," his new friend had been born in Hamburg. During his military service, he fled Germany practically overnight after he hit his sergeant in an altercation that was certain to result in a court martial.

As with many other persons mentioned in his memoirs, Martin did not reveal much about Dutchie, who was born as Conrad Bernhard. What we know about Dutchie and his work for Martin comes from Dutchie's own diary, a small part of which survived.

From Germany, Dutchie had first gone to the United States where, until 1904 he worked in North Dakota near the villages of Pratt and Eckman, both of which have long disappeared from the map. A Christmas card from "your sister Grace" in Zenith, Alberta, written in 1914, led the author to the area south of Stettler in Alberta. At the site of the former village of Zenith, which no longer exists, Clarence Everett remembered Conrad Bernhard as the friend of his father, who had also come north from North Dakota a few years before Dutchie took out a homestead just east of Zenith.

Canadian immigration records indicate that Conrad Bernhard entered Canada from North Dakota on May 7, 1904, already a United States citizen. So Dutchie, who was born in the year 1880, must have left Germany as a very young man. In Red Deer, Dutchie applied for a homestead patent near Zenith on July 4, 1904. Later homestead records indicate that Dutchie fulfilled the obligations of clearing sufficient land each year, building a 12 x 16 ft cabin, a barn and a henhouse. He owned three horses and raised some chicken and pigs.

On August 31, 1909, Dutchie became a British subject and during the same month received title to his land. But Dutchie was not cut out to be a farmer. Three years later, he sold his quarter section to a neighbour. He had already moved to the foothills west of Rocky Mountain House and become a forest ranger.

Recognizing Dutchie's personal qualities, his conscientiousness, loyalty and, above all, his numerous talents, Martin succeeded in persuading Dutchie to give up his job as a forest ranger and become his all-round man. Upon Martin's direction, Dutchie started an experimental garden with the seeds Martin had brought from Europe. Not only did Martin want to establish that a future population could successfully grow various vegetables in the rather harsh climate with its comparatively brief growing season, he also dreamt of an alpine garden of Edelweiss and Alpenrosen around his own future house.

In all the jobs assigned to him, Dutchie proved himself as very resourceful and adept. His initial distrust of Martin was soon replaced by unquestioned loyalty. But then, as a German, Martin was a different man, not like all other mine owners and industrialists, whom Dutchie hated as greedy exploiters of the poor labourers. Nor did he have any respect for politicians of any stripe, "...who could not or would not make an honest living otherwise."

Martin did not spare his praise for Dutchie.

> He was scrupulously clean and had everything in apple-pie order. Whenever and wherever an odd job was to be done, Dutchie did it and did it well.... He built a neat loghouse, with silk curtains, a shining nickel range, a small but good library, mostly scientific books, had a grammophone with only red seal records....

The person Martin described in his memoirs is mirrored in Dutchie's diaries. For years, they show a number of standard entries including the daily entry of the day of the week, temperature and weather conditions and, Sunday after Sunday, the identical entry "...cleaned house, washed clothes, had a bath."

With very few exceptions, namely the wives of the few friends he had, Dutchie distrusted women. But those he respected, he remained fiercely loyal to, even though their education, sophistication and station in life was usually far superior to his own. Martin's daughter Marcelle was only fourteen years old when Dutchie was introduced to her. He remained her devoted friend and correspondent wherever Marcelle happened to live.

For the late summer and early autumn of 1912, Martin had for the first time in his life reserved an unusually long period of time to be spent with his daughter. Nothing, neither his business nor orders from Toronto or Berlin, should interfere with the journey that Martin had carefully planned for Marcelle. He wanted Marcelle to experience the country he loved so much and see the growing mine and the beginning town of which he was so proud.

For seven weeks, Marcelle received her father's undivided attention. It was most significant that, contrary to his usual habits, Martin did not mix business and his personal pleasures with fulfilling his long-neglected family obligations, which at this time, however, did not include his wife. These weeks, dedicated to his daughter alone, became an incredibly rewarding experience for both, which Martin preserved in an album of photographs and a lovingly written story for "My beloved daughter Marcelle as a memory of the days in the Rocky Mountains in September 1912."*

Written in flowing, but meticulous German, which does not leave out any detail in the vivid description of the thousands of things seen and experienced, the story is a document of early life in Canada, especially in Alberta. It readily captures the reader's imagination and stimulates his or her curiosity from beginning to end. Throughout Martin's story, his deep love for Marcelle shines through in the way the father cares for his daughter on this arduous trip; on the trains through a large part of Canada; on horseback through a wild part of the Rockies in sun, rain and snow; in pointing out to Marcelle the countless things worth remembering; in picking delicate alpine flowers on top of the Pipestone Pass to be dried and placed under cellophane in the album for Marcelle, in taking numerous photographs of the country and its people; and again and again, of Marcelle in various poses, most of the time without her being aware of it.

Martin had fetched Marcelle from New York to Toronto where his story begins:

My Dear Child —
Now that you are fourteen, you are capable of absorbing memorable impressions and retaining them for your entire life. For this reason, I took you along to the Canadian West to show you this vast country which is only at the beginning of its development. On the one hand, I was aware that this would require some renunciation and privation on your part during the stages of this long and varied journey—in the pullman, on the freight trains and, finally, with cowboys and Indians on horseback. But, on the other hand, I was convinced these hardships would disappear from your memory and only the greatness

* Published in English (1995) and German (1996). Refer to Bibliography under Nordegg, Martin, *To the Town....*

and the beauty of what you had seen will remain in your memory forever.

On the last day of August 1912, Martin and Marcelle left Toronto. Whether it was the seemingly monotonous country the train traversed before reaching the mountains, the ever changing cloud formations, the composition of the passengers that betrayed that this country was not a classless society after all, the imposing appearance of Winnipeg's Hudson's Bay store and the city's elegant Royal Alexandra Hotel, the masses of newly arrived immigrants from all parts of the world huddled in the railroad terminal, the first mounted policeman on the platform in Medicine Hat next to the Sarcee women selling Indian handicrafts, the first faint outline of the Rockies the excited Martin pointed out to Marcelle, the story reads like a very complete and very personalized travelogue.

In Calgary, Martin met Ernest Gheur, the new mining engineer from Belgium, who was to accompany him and Marcelle to the mine. An educated and charming man, speaking both English and German, Gheur proved to be good company. Edmonton was the next stop with a rather dirty hotel full of drunks and unpleasant smells. It was also the stop where Marcelle had to divest herself of most of her travel clothing and comforts, changing into gear appropriate for mountain travel on horseback. Not more than what would fit into one bag to be carried by horses would be permissible, Martin explained to his daughter, a routine of packing Martin had practised many times since his initial introduction to mountain travel on horseback by Tom Lusk in Morley five years before. One week later, an amused Martin noticed that Marcelle had managed to smuggle her silver mirror into her travel bag!

After the crossing of the North Saskatchewan River on the rickety, overcrowded streetcar, they boarded the train in Strathcona, the sister city of Edmonton on the south bank of the river. In Blackfalds halfway to Calgary, Martin, Marcelle and Ernest Gheur had to leave the comforts of civilization behind for nearly three weeks. A special railway car was expected to wait for them at the rail line of the Canadian Northern Western a few miles to the south. The line had just reached Rocky Mountain House a few weeks earlier and was not yet ballasted. There was no special railway car in sight, as this car had been hopelessly derailed before reaching the meeting point, a lone water tower in the midst of nowhere. What was available after hours of waiting was a short freight train, where Martin and Marcelle sat between sugar bags and, at night, slept in the cramped dome of the caboose. In most colourful words Martin described this train ride and its intriguing passengers of cowboys, miners and cooks. To reach Rocky Mountain House, "… it had taken two days and two nights for 65 km, and eight times the cars had jumped the tracks."

A little more comfort awaited the travellers in Rocky Mountain House, where on the next morning Marcelle "held court" on the steps of the local general store. By now, Martin Nordegg was a well-known, important personality for the townspeople, and the news of the arrival of his daughter brought everybody to Main Street to inspect the young lady. One wonders what went on in Marcelle's mind. On some photographs, she looks almost like an adult; on others, we see a young girl sitting on the steps of the store playing with the dog of the proprietor.

Marcelle immediately took to Stuart Kidd like to an older brother. But with Dowling who was on his way east, she conversed like a young lady. And she conducted herself perfectly when interviewed by the editor of the local weekly.

In its September 17, 1912 issue, the *Rocky Mountain House Echo* published an extensive story on Mr. Nordegg and his party, quoting Martin's report of the development and future of the mine and his announcement that his daughter was "...to christen the first coal mining town west of Rocky Mountain House."

Martin also waxed enthusiastically about their forthcoming trip across the Pipestone Pass,

> ... a delightful ten days trip with mountain scenery that is unsurpassed even in Switzerland, and he thinks this will be a favourite route for tourists in the next year or so ... Mr. and Miss Nordegg will return to their home in Toronto and ... then take a trip to Europe; Miss Nordegg will remain abroad for three years, attending schools in England, France and Switzerland.

Not all of Martin's predictions made during this interview came true. Tourists would not come in great numbers into this area for at least another 50 or 60 years, certainly never to the Pipestone Pass; and Marcelle would never attend an expensive boarding school in Europe.

With the departure from Rocky Mountain House, all the comforts Marcelle had been used to all her life had to be left behind. From then on, travel was on horseback or on foot, tents were used for sleeping, boughs from fir trees for mattresses. Food came from supplies carried on packhorses, and fires provided warmth at night and, more than once, a chance to dry rain-soaked clothing. But Marcelle astounded not only her father but everyone on the packtrain with her stamina, good humour, and unexpected horsemanship.

Martin was delighted with his daughter and very proud of her. The ride on horseback to the Nordegg Basin and from there across the Pipestone Pass to Laggan and the hotel at Lake Louise was by now familiar to Martin in every aspect. But not one of the many trips he had taken along this route he had described in as pertinent, colourful and enthusiastic words as in the story of this unforgettable journey with Marcelle. He finally was able to show her what a good father he could be and what a successful man he had become as an explorer, entrepreneur, and manager of a large enterprise.

Day after day, Martin was struck by the maturity of his daughter, who had turned fourteen only a few weeks before; but to him she appeared like a child, happy to be looked after by her father with special treats at meal times and with being tucked into the heavy blankets in the evening, with listening attentively to his many descriptions of the countryside, the flowers, the animals, and the history of the local people. But to the people she met on the trip and those she shared the journey with, Marcelle was a mature, well-bred young lady.

Marcelle conversed in fluent French with Ernest Gheur, the mining engineer from Belgium, while she displayed an astonishing knowledge about scientific and historical matters when talking with Mr. Coulthart and Mr. Caldwell from Toronto, both very well-educated men. And she quickly changed to German when the party arrived at the mine site, and she was introduced to Dutchie.

The last days before reaching the mine had been especially hard, and Martin had been intrigued how Marcelle's presence had resulted in hitherto undisplayed behavior among the packers of the party. No matter how difficult the terrain, how obstreperous the horses, there was none of the usual swearing—nothing but good humour and praise for Marcelle's agility on horseback and her even temper despite the rough going on the trail.

> ... We followed the old trail of the trappers of the Hudson's Bay Company.... We crossed the river which in that area is surrounded by swamps on both sides, and ascended the hills to the south. The first sign of the civilization I had transplanted there was the experimental garden which I had created at an altitude of 4,000 feet.... A few minutes later, a dog's barking welcomed us, and, riding through a dense grove of spruce trees, we suddenly spotted the first house in the town that bears your name. Did your heart beat like mine?

Marcelle had indeed endured the onerous travel in remarkably good mood and without a single complaint. At the mine site, though, she enjoyed a few days of rest. Martin took her to the top of Coliseum Mountain above the mine and the next day guided his wide-eyed daughter through the first mine tunnels. Marcelle was impressed, but having grown up in Berlin and New York, centres of culture and civilization, she was also overwhelmed by the primitive and incomplete nature of everything, even when her father proudly showed her the rows of stakes indicating the layout of the streets and crescents of the future town.

After the departure from the mine, the party consisted only of Martin, Marcelle, Stuart Kidd, Tom, and two Stoney Indians from the nearby Bighorn Reserve. During the first three days, "a heavy storm broke out" more than once and a concerned Martin watched his daughter riding on without a complaint. But he sensed that for Marcelle, his beloved Rocky Mountain wilderness still looked foreign and overpowering. Remembering his own bewildered feelings during his first trip across the mountains, Martin hoped his daughter would, during the days of crossing the Pipestone Pass, discover the unique character of the Rocky Mountains, so beautiful but also so elusive to the newcomer. How happy Marcelle made him when she began to observe things and ask about their significance and when she accepted the cold nights and the long days on horseback in good stride.

> The horses sometimes called each other with their neighing and soon, we recognized yours by its lighter sound. From the first day on, you had gotten used to your horse, but you were disappointed when it did not want to take a piece of sugar as a reward. It was still an unspoiled child of nature that did not know the charms of luxury. You rewarded it by patting and stroking and made friends with him, and with confidence about your absolute safety in the saddle, you followed my example and absorbed the beauty of the mountains, the clouds and the blue sky. You looked left and right, far into the distance, and you learned to look out for yourself, to look around and ask. And when you began to get tired in the saddle, you changed your position, turning one leg over to the other like a lady in a side saddle, which I also often did and this way, you could look even backwards. Since I had awakened your interest in botany, we never rode past the smallest flower to which you would not draw my attention and often, I quickly jumped off the horse to pick one of the flowers for you. Do you remember when I showed you where the upper line of growth of vegetation was? It was there that I picked a few flowers and pressed them in my notebook for you....
>
> We had just climbed over another mountain and descended into a long valley.... I showed you the old tracks of lynx and wolves, also a few newer ones of a little grizzly bear and, finally, very fresh ones of a herd of mountain sheep....
>
> The cold wind hitting our faces interrupted our chat and we climbed higher and higher in the valley.... The sun disappeared behind clouds of rain, and a light shower sprinkled down on us; it already was mixed with snow flakes.... We now hurried to unsaddle the horses, unload the packhorses, pitch the tents, all before darkness fell.... A snowstorm broke out which within a few minutes blew everything upside down and covered it with snow.... I tore down the half-pitched tent and spread it

on the ground to secure a small dry spot for us...and cut wood so that you could quickly get warm and be protected in the teepee and could dry your things....

The next morning turned out to be a very miserable one.... It was a bad one for humans and for animals.... Our horses crawled as slowly as the minutes pass in this icy wind.... On the ground, I noticed a rock which showed the imprints of plants and I succeeded in distracting you for a short while. I put it into my pocket, and now it sits in front of you serving as a paperweight. May I remind you, my dear child, that even the most difficult hours pass. And there were really tough hours which you stood very bravely.

The wind almost blew us over the sharp ridge (8400 ft) and we looked down into the long valley the Pipestone River occupies,... which runs into the Bow near Laggan....We got the last rays of sunshine directly into our faces.... And the prospect to see the railroad again at the end of it, a real hotel ...with beds and baths ... and clean clothes! These were probably the thoughts that passed through your little head; they were mine too....

After we had eaten supper, the moon was already high up in the sky.... You went into the tent ... and when you did not return, ... I cautiously peeked inside. While unpacking, you had fallen asleep, and I only covered you with both blankets in order not to wake you.... When the first rays of the sun woke me and I in turn had to wake the others, you were still sleeping soundly and even the commotion following, rounding up the horses, breaking camp, cooking, eating breakfast did not disturb you. Until we finally took down your tent and carried it away and the sun laughed into your face and so did we!

Impatient as so often, Martin decided to ride with Marcelle ahead of the group to reach Laggan [Lake Louise] before nightfall, thus almost bringing this unforgettable journey to an unpleasant end:

I could not make out our trail any more.... Then we encountered a windfall which necessitated so many detours that we lost our tracks again. The trees were piled denser and denser. We had already dismounted and were drenched with perspiration from climbing over the trunks.... The horses had become weak and stumbled over every root, but still, we moved on. The sun was slowly setting, and again we came up against a swamp, and this time I hopelessly lost the trail.... Then it began to get dark. I sensed how you began to lose your courage, although you did not say a word.... That was when our troubles were at their worst, I admit. At that moment even I feared that I would have to spend the night with you in the forest.

In my mind, I was already cutting branches for fire and thinking the two horse blankets would be sufficient to keep you warm. I quickly reached into my pocket to convince myself of the presence of our last chocolate bar when suddenly, the howling of a locomotive sounded from the distance. Our courage returned instantly. We jumped like electrified, I asked you to stay behind while I once more went looking for the path ... and to my great joy found the summer path.... I hurried back to you and your horse, then rushed back to get mine.

The poor, exhausted horses started to trot on their own. The path widened, we crossed a wooden bridge, then soon after, three abandoned houses appeared ... and in the rapidly growing darkness, we finally saw the lights of the station at Laggan.... The lights of the hotel served as our guide, because it had turned pitch-dark in the meantime.

We galloped into the yard of the hotel and jumped off our horses.... I was assigned our rooms and received a big package of letters ... from which—after opening them with a pounding heart—I learned to my great joy that your mother was well.... I turned around to give you the good news ... and finally discovered you behind a pillar at the entrance of the hotel. You were hiding because you did not want to be seen in your "clothes of the wilderness" by the guests of the hotel, who were mostly wearing evening dress.... I ordered through room service a meal ... and with a bottle of champagne we finished our repast toasting our happy homecoming....

After the first bath ... we felt reasonably clean and went to bed. But neither of us slept very much....

As usual, we got up very early, then the suitcases arrived which we had shipped from Edmonton by train, and with the clothes of civilization we dared show ourselves to the astonished folk in the hotel. Only now did I notice how tanned you were. While we were on the terrace of the hotel, admiring the grandiose panorama of Lake Louise and the Victoria Glacier, Tom and Stuart appeared, still in their cowboy suits! They hardly recognized you, and when they later adopted the clothes of civilization, you confided in me that they had looked much nicer before!

The following days in Banff were pure enjoyment. This was Marcelle's second visit to Banff where she met her friend of four years before, Dora Wilson, Tom's daughter. Martin took numerous pictures of Marcelle, at the Bow Falls, in front of the Banff Springs Hotel, in the hotel pool and many more.

After a few days, Martin and Marcelle continued their journey by train to Vancouver, Martin again pointing out to Marcelle the beauty of the mountains, the feats of engineering at the spiral tunnel near Field and the long snowsheds at the Rogers Pass. Martin remembered everything in his story for his daughter, also the brief, unexpected encounter at Glacier with Mr. Hanna, the vice-president of the Canadian Northern—at that time still Martin's good friend—to whom Martin proudly introduced his daughter.

More pictures were taken in Vancouver—Marcelle in the depth of Stanley Park, swimming in the tidal pool at the edge of the park. An interview with the *Vancouver Sun* was published in the morning edition of Saturday, September 28, 1912, quite enthusiastic if not always accurate in the names of places Marcelle had just experienced:

Little Miss Here From Thrilling Trip—First Woman Over the Pipe Stem Pass

Arriving last evening at the Vancouver Hotel, charming little Miss Nordegg, daughter of Herr Martin Nordegg, a German capitalist of Nuremburg, recounted to a Sun reporter the story of her thrilling trip across the Pipe Stem pass in the Rocky Mountains, a route never previously traversed by a white woman....

Ten hours daily in the saddle, an exhausting feat even for the hardy rider of the plains, was the feat accomplished by Miss Nordegg. At an altitude of 8,400 feet blinding sleet storms and blizzards were encountered.... The little Fraulein withstood the strenuous onslaught of the elements and arrived in Laggan with the flush upon her cheeks that only the windswept vastness of the Rockies can bring.

'Were you not the littlest bit frightened at the danger and the storms?' curiously queried the reporter as Miss Nordegg finished her story.

'Just once, when the horse stumbled and I lost my hat over a 1000-foot cliff,' smiled the girl as she concluded the interview.

It is obvious the reporter was charmed by Marcelle, alternately characterizing her as a woman or as a little Fraulein or as a young girl.

Soon, Marcelle's memorable journey across Canada came to an end. The last page of Martin's story for Marcelle is filled with pride in Marcelle and gratitude to her. For once, he had truly achieved the fulfilment of his role as Marcelle's father.

Later, we took the steamboat to Victoria and Seattle and then travelled by train five nights and four days back to Toronto. A short time later, we started on the big trip from New York via the Azores, Gibraltar, Palermo and Naples to Genoa where you were happy to embrace your beloved mother after months of separation.

The trip half around the world—from the Pacific Ocean to the shores of the Mediterranean—had ended. You had travelled the long rail- and ocean journeys so often that they hardly offered anything new to you. But on this trip, you took part in the strenuous ride into the wilderness, your eyes viewed the wonders of the lonely mountains, you learned to bear tiredness without complaining, to be satisfied with the simplest food and to try out the spice of hunger after heavy physical effort, to let the 'categorical imperative' affect your at times quite rebellious mind, to subordinate your will to the discipline of the packtrain, to wrap your blankets around you in the evenings without missing the soft bed, to weather dangers without batting an eyelash and, last not least, to have to depend on your own resources and not depend on others. All this, I hope, my dear child, made an indelible impression upon you. You learned to overcome pain and discomfort in silence and you demonstrated that you, a child still young, could bear what strong men shy away from, only because they lack willpower and energy.

And when years later, these pages and pictures come to your attention again, then let all of us who enjoyed your company come to life again—the stoical Indians, the prudent Stuart, the cheerful Tom and, last not least, the one who loves you so much, your

Father.

With utter happiness, Martin once more enumerates the qualities in Marcelle's character that he had observed day after day. That some of them were very much like his own must have made him especially proud.

But Martin's beautifully written story is not free of shadows. He had constantly been aware how much Marcelle was missing her mother and how much she worried about her mother's health. As a father, Martin understood very much what Marcelle experienced being so far from her mother and, for many weeks, unable to communicate with her by letter or by telegraph. In this very private document, Martin does not hold back with expressions of love for his daughter and his sympathy for her sense of being separated from her ailing mother by thousands of miles. But at no point does Martin reveal his own feelings for his wife. Berthe-Marie is never mentioned by him as "my wife," only as "your mother" or, as is quite customary in Germany, "our mother." The distance between Martin and Berthe-Marie was not just one of geographic nature.

Was Marcelle suffering under the distant, cool relationship between her mother and her father, who shared so little of their lives with each other? From an early age on, she must have been conscious of their unfulfilled marriage and of her own dual burden of being a support to her depressed, ailing mother and of being her father's competent, courageous daughter. Martin loved Marcelle very much, even though, with the best of intentions, he challenged her far too early in her life.

Marcelle passed the severe tests and challenges life had presented her with at an early age. That she paid a price seems revealed in many of the photographs in Martin's 1912 album. One cannot escape the serious expression always present in the face of this very attractive fourteen-year-old, who looks so much more mature than her age. Marcelle rarely shows a smile.

Much space has been given in this biography to Martin's Canadian journey with Marcelle. This was done intentionally. Martin's 1912 story is the only one of his writings in which the relationships with his daughter and, in an indirect way, with his wife play a part. But even in this intimate story, Berthe-Marie remains almost anonymous, her character shrouded in mystery, while in

Martin's memoirs, the existence of neither Berthe-Marie nor Marcelle is even acknowledged.

Berthe-Marie had come to Genoa to return with Marcelle to Egypt. The three sailed to Naples, where Martin said goodbye to his wife and daughter and boarded a steamer for New York.

An early winter in 1912 found Martin in Alberta again, where work at the Brazeau Collieries and its town, still without a legal name but already called "Nordegg" by the local people, continued at a rapid pace. "Work went on incessantly. The contractors made the men work until nightfall..."

Before Martin's eyes, his town was taking shape according to his plans, which had progressed from a dream to a manifestation of his inventiveness and his humanitarian spirit.

This would not merely be another one of the thousands of dreary mining camps and towns that dotted the American West from Alaska to Mexico. The future citizens of his town deserved decent homes in a well-planned, pleasant community, favourable to the raising of families and the recreation of its hard-working miners. Under such conditions, the invariably multi-ethnic population would live in harmony next to one another. Martin was determined to prove that people of various ethnic and social backgrounds could be helped to live together without prejudice and jealousy. With thoughtful management, his town would be as free as possible of social and economic strife.

In his enthusiasm, Martin seemed to reach for the stars. Eventually, his vision became reality. But first, there were problems which Martin had to face. Already, the arrival of so many new residents from all parts of Europe had become a topic of concern in the area. Although normally very well disposed towards Martin Nordegg, on February 17, 1913, *The Rocky Mountain House Echo* reflected the rumblings among the local population:

> Much dissatisfaction is being caused by the introduction of foreign labour. In September last, Mr. Nordegg issued orders that only English-speaking men should be employed and at the present time fully two-thirds of the employees are foreigners. It is hoped that Mr. Nordegg will soon be on the ground and adjust matters.

That the sudden influx of foreigners had raised some strong feelings among the local population was also reflected in the diary of Father Voisin, the Catholic priest from Red Deer who regularly visited Rocky Mountain House and later Nordegg as well. Born in the city of Le Havre in France in 1875, Father Voisin came to Canada in 1904 as a highly educated man. After establishing a French settlement north of Castor, he started with the building of a Catholic church and a convent in Red Deer, where he took up permanent residence in 1908. At the same time, he served the entire district north, south, and west of Red Deer, saying mass in various settlements and newly founded towns and villages and building churches in many of them.

Father Voisin loved his work and the people he served, but he had a horror of the wild country to the west of Red Deer and around Rocky Mountain House, which he described in his journals as

> a country disinherited where the big woods alternate with marshes, full of mosquitoes, a country with early frosts and so desolate that it is astonishing that there were some settlers to occupy it....

To Martin, Father Voisin voiced serious doubts, mixed with barely disguised mistrust, about some of the people passing through Rocky Mountain House on their way to the mine: "Miners, they did not know culture and their progress was slower ... almost infallibly contaminated by socialism."

Martin had deep respect for Father Voisin. But like any philanthropist and social reformer, he could not share Father Voisin's low opinion about the newcomers. He had witnessed the stark poverty in the slums of England's mining districts and the mining camps in Alberta, but he sincerely believed that the miners and their families arriving from all parts of Europe—some of them literally from the edge of civilization—would thrive in the environment he was going to create for them.

Most people saw in Martin the energetic entrepreneur and businessman who was inclined to watch his pennies. What he planned for his mining town now seemed utterly ridiculous, utopian, and certainly impractical. But he would not listen or change his mind. His town was going to be unique in the West.

During his years in England, Martin had seen the "garden cities" promoted and developed by the social reformer and town planner Ebenezer Howard. Assisted and supported by philanthropists, Howard built a number of model villages and towns for the working class, some of them in a circular design surrounded by agricultural land. Another example Martin had found in Montreal, where the Canadian Northern had designed a section of the Mount Royal district in a similar circular pattern.

It was this pattern that Martin adopted for his town plan of Nordegg. Laid out on a slope gently rising towards the hills, five semi-circular crescents were crossed by the axis of the town—Centre Street—the location of stores, offices and other businesses. The railway tracks separating the upper section of the town from its much larger, lower section, formed the base of the five crescents accommodating the houses for the miners. At the lower end of town adjacent to the crescents, Martin had envisioned the larger houses of the administrators and their families, a location he considered particularly charming in view of the closeness to the lake. But Martin encountered unexpected resistance:

> The great problem of the higher officials' houses and their location gave reason for many a heated debate between the interested parties. As the town was built below the railway, and the ground towards the north, bordering the lake on which I had shot the wild geese, was sloping, I had to give in to the arguments for building an upper town for the officials' cottages. The railway separated it from the lower town. Instinctively I had the feeling of approaching disaster. But I could not offer any reasons for it. Next to the pretty and comfortable officials' cottages we built the hospital, the policeman's cottage and the officials' club, all overlooking the town.

An idealistic Martin was forced to accept what he had tried to prevent at all costs. Yielding to the wishes of his administrators, he reluctantly modified his original town plan. As every other company town, his town would also consist of two sections. The "upper classes" would reside in the upper town, while the lower, the working class would live on the proverbial "other side of the tracks."

What Martin created for the people on the other side of the tracks, though, was nevertheless exceptional for a mining town of that era:

> It was my intention to build a modern and pretty town; I insisted on having every cottage fitted with a bath but met with the greatest objection from the experienced engineers. They told me that I would create trouble with this unheard-of idea. The outcome of our discussion was as usual a compromise: the four room cottages were to be without, the five room cottages with a bathroom....

This was truly a revolutionary idea, not just in this part of the world, which Father Voisin characterized as "...the extreme outpost of civilization in the Rockies west of Red Deer." Even in the industrialized areas of Central Europe where housing for the working classes had been built everywhere before World War I, bathrooms in miners' cottages or flats were practically unheard of until decades later.

Martin also wanted a town pleasant to look at not only by the shape of its cottages lining the crescents, but by their colours as well. Avoiding the proverbial white with green trim typical for this time, Martin

> wanted to show a variance of colour, and refusing the crude colours which the superintendent liked, I selected soft pastels which proved very

pleasing to the eye. The selection was not easy, as clashes with the landscape had to be avoided....

The pastel colours chosen for the cottages, ranged from washed blue and green to hatched umber. The water tower above the town, built on a prominent elevation that was completely bare because all the trees around it had been cut down, became a special challenge for Martin:

> I wanted it to be hidden, as its shape looked ugly. I experimented with various shades of green until we really found one which hid it so completely, that one could not see the tower at all, unless one knew its location.

A few decades later, the tower had disappeared in the new growth of spruce trees.

Martin was proud of the town's hospital, its miners' club, movie theatre, and the other facilities. He distributed free flower seeds to encourage the miners' wives to do their share for the beautification of the town on which he had spent so much time and thought. In front of his eyes, Martin's town was rising out of the ground, the workmen of the Red Deer construction firm of Baird & Mckenzie erecting one row of houses after the other. No other mining town in Alberta came even close in its layout, appearance and quality of its houses to the uniqueness of Nordegg. Only in Brulé, at the edge of Jasper National Park, did the company build for its miners a few blocks of row houses, which were moved 200 miles east to Edmonton after the closing of the town. Interestingly enough, after decades of offering modest, inexpensive housing in the Oliver district of Edmonton, two rows of the former Brulé miners' houses were considered attractive enough in their appearance to be "gentrified" in the 1990s, offering the type of housing near the city's core preferred by the well-to-do.

Martin also left his stamp on the town through the names he gave its streets. Not without significance, Martin chose the name of his daughter Marcelle and the designation of "avenue" for the most prominent residential street, where the administrators and their families lived. Streets and crescents lined by the miners' cottages were named after Martin's friend Stuart Kidd (Stuart Street), the Belgian engineer Ernest Gheur (Ernest Avenue), and his wife Marthe (Marthe Avenue), while the meaning of three other streets, Elizabeth Avenue, Lilly Avenue and Kate Drive remains obscure. Since Cherie Avenue is running parallel to Marcelle Avenue on the other side of the railroad tracks, one can assume that Martin named Cherie Avenue after Berthe-Marie, his French-born wife. The town's designations also included Martin's name: the little stream running along the eastern edge of the town, Martin Creek, was dammed up above the town to create a reservoir to ensure a reliable supply of clean water.

Once the reservoir was filled with crystal clear water, it turned into an idyllic little lake surrounded by dense forest, its trees reflected in the still water. Martin loved its quiet beauty, so far removed from the bustling town and the noisy mine. This was to be the site of his future residence. Fate would never allow Martin to realize this dream. The plans he designed for his permanent home in Nordegg had been kept in the offices of the Brazeau Collieries in Nordegg for many years. Sadly after the closing of the mine, they disappeared, together with many other valuable papers and documents. A few of the former Nordegg residents remember having looked at the plans Martin had designed and drafted for his charming Swiss chalet and its terraced rock garden reaching to the shore of the lake.

One cannot help compare Martin's design for the town of Nordegg with the standard, utilitarian and unimaginative town plan that Charles Hower had laid out for the South Brazeau mine—a plain grid 14 blocks long and 8 blocks square close to the mine. No wonder Martin was immensely proud of his accomplishments when the town of Nordegg was nearly completed in the summer of 1914. Years later, he wrote:

> I had reached my goal, I had seen my Fata Morgana become reality. I was proud and happy.
> I thought of the day four years ago, when I first saw the lake with its wild geese and the mountains enclosing that valley. Nature in its beautiful loneliness—and now awakened to pulsing life through the arrival of many men, women and children....

In the study *Nordegg Historical Resources,* completed by Brian Melnyk for the Alberta Government in 1981, special reference is made to the character of Nordegg as a mining town. Martin would have been pleased to read that

> Nordegg's status as a product of capitalist philanthropy can be well established. Martin Nordegg was thus in the same tradition as other garden city promoters... Irrespective of the origin of Nordegg's ideas on planning, the community he created was Alberta's most ambitious attempt at integrative town planning during the pre-World War I period.

In poetic words, Martin also wrote about his other achievement, the Brazeau Collieries of Nordegg:

> Men working into and below the earth, bringing out coal from these mountains which had guarded the treasure of warmth for eons.

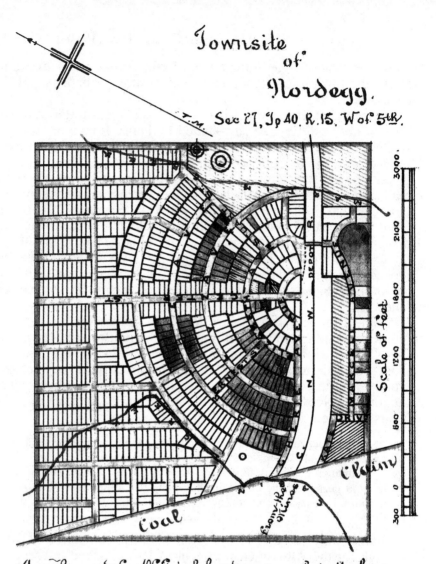

Townsite of Nordegg.

Sec 27, Tp 40, R. 15, W of 5th.

Scale of feet

3000 · 2400 · 1800 · 1200 · 600 · 0 · 300

·Area Reserved for Official Residence washed Umber
·Areas   do   Forestry Department   do. Purple.
·Area   Hotel   hatched Umber
·Areas   Other Purposes   do Red.
Workmens Cottages   washed Blue.
Cottages (5 Room)   hatched Green.
Residences   washed Green.
Bighorn's Warehouse, Stores & Stable washed Red.
Boarding House & Hall hatched Blue.
Other Buildings washed Yellow.
Hospital Hatched Black.
Schools washed Black.
Laundry, Mortuary, Payne's Stable thus :- ○ ◎ ⊕

And this preserved heat brings now warmth to thousands of hearths in the prairies, it drives hundreds of engines which pull the products of the prairies towards the Atlantic and Pacific Oceans and to the boundary of the United States.

I had created something to the benefit of mankind—and that made me very happy indeed.

The mine had begun producing coal at a very promising rate. Martin experienced no serious problems with either equipment and machinery or with the miners. An effective administrative structure with very specific lines of authority had been put into operation by the head office of Brazeau Collieries in Toronto, which Martin communicated in a memo to the senior staff including Stuart Kidd, on April 28, 1913. Ranging at the top are Sir William Mackenzie, President, Martin Nordegg, Vice-President, followed by the Directors (one Canadian, two Germans, one British, and one French), Sir Donald Mann, Gg. W. Büxenstein, Emil Bärwald, A.J. Mitchell, and L. Jadot.

Ernest Gheur, who reported to the vice president, was put in charge of the Western Office in Red Deer, which consisted of three departments: (1) The Operating Department in charge of Mr. Weatherbee. (2) The Provision and Supply Department in charge of Mr. Kidd. (3) The Accounting Department in charge of Mr. Perry.

The memo of three legal-size pages closed with the request that

... all officials of the Company are asked now, to work harmoniously together to further the interests of the Company.
Martin Nordegg.

Shortly after, Martin placed Stuart Kidd in charge of the company store, the Bighorn Trading Company. He also used his influence in Ottawa to secure Stuart's appointment as Postmaster and Justice of the Peace in Nordegg. In addition, Stuart was also responsible for Dutchie, who proved himself diligent and useful in numerous tasks, including the provision and maintenance of a reliable supply of horses.

"I must also say," wrote Stuart Kidd to Dutchie on November 24, 1913, "that your work during the past season has been most satisfactory in every way and our horses never were handled better or finished their season's work in such good condition...."

The Western Office of Brazeau Collieries in the H.H. Gaetz Block in Red Deer had become the busiest company office in town, a fact the local press referred to regularly. On December 12, 1913, the *Red Deer Advocate* published another enthusiastic article:

The Brazeau Collieries Limited, after months of patient waiting, are beginning to see the realization of the important development enterprise upon which they embarked in the opening up of the new coal fields west of Red Deer.... The railway is now built within seventeen miles of the mines ... and the laying of steel is being proceeded with very fast. The first shipment of coal is expected to take place before the end of January.... Before the end of 1915, the present capacity of the two mines under development will be reached and it is expected that a daily shipment of 1100 tons will then be realized regularly.

In February 1914, Martin advised the Head Office of the Canadian Northern Western Railway in Toronto that all work between Rocky Mountain House and the mine was completed and that the line could officially be taken over from the contractors. This announcement was followed by the official opening of the line on March 3, one of the happiest days in Martin's life. Sir William Mackenzie asked Martin to make all travel arrangements and meet the official party in Red Deer.

> I accepted with joy.... While it had been very cold in Red Deer, it was springlike at the mine ... a special engine pulled the private car of the General Manager. We travelled very fast ... and on arrival at the mine, we were received in state by our officials. The arrival of the train meant for me the crowning of my work, the fulfilment of my dream. Yet it also meant for me the end of romance and of adventure, which I loved so much.

The Red Deer photographer Fleming, who had been invited to accompany the party, took a large number of photographs, one of them is particularly memorable. It shows the arrival of the official party at Nordegg. All the dignitaries except one are standing at the foot of the private rail car, while Martin stands on its rear platform, dressed in his semi-military khaki suit, hand at his hip, his eyes gazing towards the mine, like a general overlooking the location of his venture which culminated in such a splendid achievement.

A day of perhaps even greater personal satisfaction for Martin followed two weeks later:

> I received a telegram from Sir William MacKenzie He was coming West and I met him in Edmonton. He had already received a very favourable report from his engineers about the coal and the mine. It did not take me long to convince him that a trip to the mine would be most desirable and two days afterwards we travelled there again in a private car. He was surprised to see what we had accomplished and congratulated me most enthusiastically.
>
> Then he said, I was the first man in his experience to have kept his word in finishing construction work in time and well within the cost estimated. Further to have the promised 100,000 tons of coal ready for shipment. He stated as far as he knew, no mine had ever been producing such a quantity of coal before the advent of the railway.

All that deserved a reward. He had decided to erect a monument to me which would be living and more lasting than one made out of stone or bronze: to name the town after me.

The painters appeared soon and put my name on the station building, railway tickets were printed and maps arranged to show my name....

The last two paragraphs quoted from Martin's memoirs present somewhat of a puzzle. At least informally, the town had been referred to as "Nordegg" for quite some time, even in the press such as in the report of the *Red Deer Advocate* from December 12, 1913. One can only speculate that Sir William Mackenzie gave his blessing to a choice made by the people and decided to give the town its name of "Nordegg"officially.

After the triumphs of the opening of the rail line and Sir William's visit to Nordegg—his only one ever—Martin decided on the spur of the moment to go to Berlin and celebrate the success of the German Development Company and the Deutsches Kanada Syndikat with his President. He had not crossed the Atlantic for more than one year. In 1912, Berthe-Marie had gone to France for the first time on her own. And at the time of Martin's celebrations in Nordegg and in Berlin, Berthe-Marie, Marcelle, and the maid Maria Fuhrmann were again in France. It is interesting to note that after a short stay with Berthe-Marie's parents, the three women resided at the posh Hotel Edouard VII in Paris.

The surviving records of transfers of moneys from Martin's account at the Commerz Bank in Berlin to Berthe-Marie indicate that as usual Martin was a conscientious and generous provider to his family. But it appears certain that he did not even once meet his family during this hurried trip to Europe. He had already returned to Nordegg when Berthe-Marie, Marcelle, and Maria Fuhrmann boarded the SS *France* in Le Havre on April 25, bound for New York.

Back in Nordegg, Martin felt for the first time that he was not hounded by the pressure of time in completing the town and mine, the worry about beating the odds of bad weather, and the competition from others seeking their fortune in coal. Now that everything was running well, the period of excitement and "romance" had come to an end. There was finally time to contemplate his achievements and to enjoy at leisure the beauty of the country Martin treasured so much.

"On Sundays, I rode alone towards the Bighorn Mountains, mostly on the well-trodden trail on the high bank of the Saskatchewan River, towards the Bighorn Falls."

There were always problems to solve, of course; but they were now of a very different though often unexpected nature. Martin wrote about some events with amusement and glee, but about others with disappointment and frustration. He realized he still had a mission to accomplish with his intention to help the new citizens of Nordegg live together in harmony as families and as a community and to enjoy what he had created for them with so much thought and imagination.

> Into the cottages of the officials moved the manager, the assistant manager, the doctor, the manager of the store, the chief accountant and lastly myself. My feeling of hesitancy regarding the separation from the lower town proved to have been true. It created a caste of supermen and even more so, superwomen. The ladies would not mix socially with the women living below the railway line, and all my attempts to level this separation failed utterly.

Martin learned how insurmountable the invisible but rigid barriers between upper and lower town were maintained. He had been invited for tea by the schoolmistresses who, by virtue of the location of the school, had ended up residing in the lower town. Surprised that the teachers had never socially met the mothers of the children they taught every day, Martin decided to resolve this matter and

> … introduce the teachers officially to high society. I called immediately on the leader of this high society and met a decided rebuff. That was the first time that my word was not acted upon without hesitation, and worse still, that a request from me was absolutely refused.

Martin was not prepared to give in to this ridiculous class structure. When the town's theatre on Centre Street was opened with a special show and a dance afterwards, Martin had five seats reserved among the three front rows designated for the upper crust and separated from the common folk by a rope. To the consternation of the ladies from upper town, Martin triumphantly led the teacher ladies to the reserved front section. At the reception afterwards, Martin introduced the teachers to the ladies and during the following dance, the young lady teachers were the preferred dancing partners of the officials. "… the ice was broken and they were accepted into society. But this exception was only extended to the teachers, not others living in lower town."

The problem continued to fester like an open wound, especially among the officials of middle rank living in the lower town, such as the station master and the mine surveyor. When Martin encouraged the shy Stuart Kidd to marry "a pretty Scotch girl working in his store," Stuart's new wife was readily accepted by high society of the upper town because, as store manager, Stuart lived in the upper town. But this did not include the sister of Stuart's new wife, who had married the station master who lived on the upper floor of the station building which, unfortunately, was located on the south side of the tracks and therefore was considered part of the lower town. After weeks of delicate manipulation on Martin's part,

> ... the station-mistress was officially accepted as a member of society in Nordegg. Everything then was harmony. In fact, the ladies formed a tennis club, a curling club, and later a golf club. They even permitted the inhabitants of lower town to play on certain days and hours. But they would not mix with them.

Up to a point, these class distinctions were never fully extinguished and, in a small way, remained a sore point throughout the life of the town. Although in the reminiscences of the former residents and their descendants this was truly a community proud of the harmony among its citizens, some do remember the occasional bitter feelings about being excluded from the life of the upper town, even though by education and professional competence, they felt equal to the families living on "the right side of the tracks."

Perhaps differing customs brought from Europe, lifestyle, and sophistication were partly responsible for the split between upper and lower town. Martin also had to learn that some of his visions had been far too idealistic. Still dejected years later, he wrote about

> ... the failure of my greatest pride: the installation of bathrooms in the five-room cottages for the miners.... I thought my eyes deceived me. I saw that a family was using the white enamelled bathtub for storage of coal, and the foreman told me that they used the watercloset for bathing the babies. Another cottage showed the same mistaken use, and the foreman suggested that the neighbours may have consulted each other about the possible utilization of these hitherto unknown appliances and had to come to an unanimous decision. The families hailed from Galicia, Poland, Italy and Roumania.

Martin called upon the doctor, asking him to instruct the families in proper hygiene. Although willing, the doctor did not have much hope.

> After a few months he reported to me, that the futility of his efforts was evident, and the foreman transmitted to me the wish of the tenants to have the installations removed, so that they would have another bedroom. I had to give in.

Ironically, almost all the families that gave the idealistic Martin so much grief came from countries he had visited in the course of his far-flung travels. Only now did he realize that he had spent his time in their countries admiring historical and architectural monuments. Hardly ever had he come into contact with the common people in their homes. Now these people were sincerely grateful to Martin for homes they never had enjoyed before; they faithfully planted gardens with the seeds Dutchie had distributed to them; but their backyards were a disgrace. It made no difference whom Martin engaged to help, the doctor, the teachers, the officials. They were all unsuccessful–until the bears appeared in late fall and began to rummage through the refuse in the backyards of the miners cottages. A happy Martin noticed how the miners cleaned up their backyards immediately. He was sure he had won the battle. "However, they only cleaned them in winter time."

Martin also had to listen to the complaints of Father Voisin, who came to Nordegg once a month to say mass in the miners' club. Father Voisin refused to use the Methodist church, the only church in town, and he did not mind consecrating the miners' club before each mass until Nordegg had its Catholic church. Some of Father Voisin's complaints survived in his diary which, after his death in 1934, was sent with all his belongings to Rome, according to the tradition of the Fathers of St. Mary of Tinchebray. In Rome, it was translated from French into a slightly awkward English and summarized as a "notice biographique" by Father Renut.

Father Voisin liked Martin, but did not hold back with criticism. Why had Martin not built a Catholic church first instead of a movie theatre and a dance hall, which resulted in

...socialist tendencies and finally alcohol abuse with the fights and disorders which are the consequences ... where the people dance and amuse themselves. Isn't that the essential beginning of all Western cities? ...

Father Voisin deplored how

Alcohol made terrible ravages. Bottles and barrels arrived by hundreds at each train.... Penetrating in the houses ... the priest always found numerous company, men and women feasted, bottle in hand, without glass, and in a corner a bottle pile waiting to be emptied, and it didn't take long for that....

The kids abound ... and they are the worst kind, emancipated of the checking of their parents, learning the bad before anything else. One catechism class organized by the priest must be revived at each of his visits: the toil is tough, also the good willing who have accepted that mission are discouraged rapidly....

Father Voisin did discriminate between the various ethnic groups, though: "We have to say also that the Slavonic population has more kept her religion, that she drinks less, that she loves religious service and is more pious."

Neither Martin nor any of the former Nordegg people mention such horror stories. For Father Voisin, however, "... this mining milieu was new," as the translator of his diary observed.

But in all his anger about the immoral living he had observed in Nordegg, Father Voisin did not mention the lady Martin reports about. She "... established a tent camp, constituting a red light district.... Suddenly, out of a clear sky, a new and threatening matter arose...."

As she had located her camp outside town, nobody could prevent the lady and her companions from conducting their business.

> The female population was horrified. And there was for once unanimity between upper and lower town, and a deputation of both towns called on me ... far from satisfied with the interview, as they were under the impression that I looked on the tents as a desirable addition to the town.... I often saw the ladies of the town inspect the tents from a respectable distance....

Martin took recourse to the forestry officials and to the police. But nothing could be done. With glee, Martin reports that

> ... there was no law forbidding the ladies camping in the woods, and gentlemen visiting them. I had the husbands of my complainants explain to their wives the view of the Forestry and Police.
>
> What happened in their households I do not know, but the tents became and remained a great attraction for the ladies, who were so inquisitive, and the manager of the store reported to me with evident glee, that the sale of the same perfume used in the tents increased enormously to the female population of Nordegg who made a run on them.

No doubt, Martin could not help but enjoy a sense of sweet revenge while listening to Stuart Kidd's account of his thriving perfume sales, especially to the ladies of the upper town who had caused him so much grief just a few months ago.

Did Martin cherish his role as the father of the town the residents had apparently assigned to him? Certainly not always! He needed to escape the pettiness he was too often confronted with. The officials he had appointed last spring worked efficiently and in harmony. Martin felt he had earned a holiday.

On a beautiful day in early June, 1914, Martin crossed the Pipestone Pass on his way to the Banff Springs Hotel to spend a few leisurely weeks with his friend Sir Elly Kadoorie and Herr von Uslar, a nobleman from Germany.

He had no inkling what lay ahead. When he returned to Nordegg in September 1914, the world, and with it his own life, had changed irreversibly.

VI

THE ENEMY ALIEN
(1914 - 1918)

Long after the ravages of World War I, Europeans still remembered the singularly beautiful summer of 1914. Many countries had reached the peak of prosperity. If not most, at least a larger number of people than ever before enjoyed a life of contentment and security. Perhaps there was an unease about the deteriorating political situation, but it was barely perceptible. For too many people, open conflict and war seemed unthinkable.

The Banff Springs Hotel was an island of peace and international harmony during the first half of the summer of 1914. Guests from all corners of the world filled its halls and social rooms. As in previous years, Martin found Sir Elly Kadoorie and his family among the guests. He introduced Herr and Frau von Uslar to Sir Elly explaining that he had been asked by the German government to assist Herr von Uslar, a high official in the Prussian government, to explore opportunities in the boom that had gripped Calgary after the recent discovery of oil and gas south of the city. As Martin cheerfully wrote, "… with other friends and acquaintances we formed a very interesting circle."

In the middle of June, the Viceroy of the Dominion of Canada, the Duke of Connaught and his wife, the daughter of Prince Friedrich Karl of Prussia, arrived by special trains with their daughter Princess Patricia and a large retinue. They had already received the von Uslars at their official residence when the latter passed through Ottawa on their way West.

The royal party had expected to spend most of the summer in Banff; but on the evening of June 28, a note was posted at the reception desk of the hotel announcing the assassination of Archduke Franz Ferdinand of Austria, successor to the Habsburg throne, and his wife in Sarajewo. Martin remembered, how

> The news of the assassination of the Austrian heir at Sarajewo brought great excitement to Banff. Herr von Uslar had also returned from Calgary and we discussed the political situation in Europe. We decided that a war arising from this incident was out of the question. Sir

Martin Nordegg 1868-1948

1. Business Card, 1912.

Mr Martin Nordegg
Vice President of
Brazeau Collieries Limited

Canada   *Nordegg, Alta.*

2. Banff, 1912.

3./4. In Northern Ontario, 1906 and 1907.

Martin Nordegg 1868-1948

5. With Alfred Barlow (right) and crew in Northern Ontario, 1907.

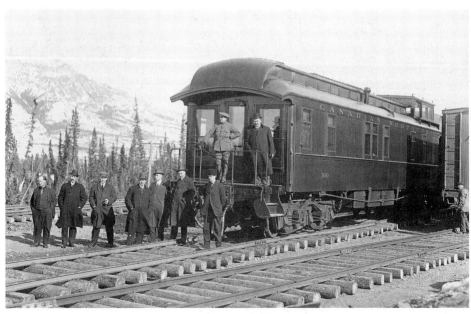

6. First passenger train with official party arriving in Nordegg on March 3, 1914. Martin on rear platform.

Martin Nordegg 1868-1948

7. Martin and Sonia on the Indian Ocean, 1926.

8. Baghdad, 1935.

10. Mausoleum, Ferncliff Cemetery, 1997.

9. With Sonia in St. Moritz, 1927.

11. First crossing of the Pipestone Pass, 1907.

12. Crossing the North Saskatchewan River, 1908.

Exploration and Mining in Alberta 1907-1922

14. Near Rocky Mountain House with Marcelle (left) and Stuart Kidd (right), September 1912.

13. First diggings at Bighorn River, 1907.

15. With Charles Hower (left) at South Brazeau.

16. Site of the mine and town that were never built (South Brazeau, now Blackstone River, 1995).

Brazeau Collieries Nordegg 1911-1954

17. First building in Nordegg, winter 1911-12.

18. First car of coal mined at Nordegg, 1911.

19. Brazeau Collieries, early 1920s.

20. Coal processing plant, 1985. Thirty years after closure, nature is returning.

Progress

21. Number 2 seam entrance, 1913.

22. Number 2 seam entrance, 1920.

23. Mine train electrified, 1922.

The Town

24. Nordegg across the lake, 1920s.

25. Elizabeth Street, 1921.

26. Railway depot after the name change from Nordegg to Brazeau, 1921.

Marcelle Nordegg 1898-1945

27. Martin's daughter
Marcelle, Nordegg 1912.

28. Berthe-Marie Nordegg
née Brand (1867-1924),
Martin's first wife and
Marcelle's mother, 1918.

29. With her father on the way to
Nordegg, September 1912.

30. In detention at
Angel Island, San
Francisco, 1918.

Marcelle Nordegg 1898-1945

31. New York, 1919.

32. In China, 1926.

33. With her son in Ottawa, 1930.

34. Departure, Ottawa, 1930.

35. Last known picture, Bonn 1936.

Sonia Nordegg 1890-1970

36. Atlantic City, 1917.

37. Water Gap, Delaware, 1919.

39. New York, 1937.

38. Forsyth Street on New York's Lower East Side, 1996. Sonia's first home in the New World.

Sonia Nordegg 1890-1970

40. In Harlech, 1927.

42. and 43.
From Sonia's acting days.

41. In China, 1926.

44. At the border between Syria and Iraq, 1936.

Sonia Nordegg 1890-1970

45. New York, 1947.

46. Presentation of Martin's memoirs to the National Archives of Canada (Ottawa Citizen, November 22, 1955).

47. Last visit to Austria, Bad Gastein, 1967.

The Relatives

48. Martin's sister Malwine and her daughter Bertel with Sonia, Hamburg, 1924.

49. Sonia's father Isaac Meisel.

50. Sonia's mother Rachel Meisel, Ottawa, 1935.

The Relatives

51. Martin's nephew Klaus Brandt, New York, 1959.

52. Sonia's sister Anna Meisel with her great-niece Joyce Rothchild, Newark, New Jersey, 1940's.

53. Anna Wolgiel in the United States Coast Guard, Elizabethtown, New York, 1944.

54. Anna Wolgiel's mother Fanya with her son Lev, Grodno, Poland, summer, 1939.

Sonia's Cousins

55. With Sonia Tokar-Lampert, Baghdad, 1936.

56. Emma Gamsa, London.

57. Fanya Wolgiel (left) and other relatives, Grodno, 1935.
(They all perished in the Holocaust.)

Nephew and Niece

58. Sonia's niece Ruth Rothchild with her father, Sonia's brother Harry.

59. Sonia's nephew Hyman Mizell (r) with Martin, Carla Fliegel and Sonia, Elizabethtown, New York, 1947.

60. Hyman Mizell, Florida, 1980.

Martin's Friends

61. Stuart Kidd.

62. Dutchie (Conrad Bernhard) flanked by Stuart Kidd (left) and Wilfred Gray (right) at Shunda Creek Gap east of Nordegg, 1912.

63. Senator Andrew Haydon.

Martin's Friends

64. Georg Büxenstein.

65. Georg Büxenstein (left) with Emperor Wilhelm II. on the Imperial yacht during the 1910 Regatta at Grünau attended by Martin and William Mackenzie.

66. Dr. Ludwig von Kleinwächter entering the White House, 1946.

Martin's Friends

67. Franz and Janina Petschek, Lodz, 1927.

68. Tom Wilson at his cabin in the Kootenay Plains, 1906.

69. Ernest Gheur.

Public Figures

70. Sir Wilfrid Laurier.

71. William Lyon Mackenzie King.

72. Richard B. Bennett.

73. Agnes McPhail.

Public Figures

74. Sir William
Mackenzie.

75. Sir Donald Mann.

76. David B. Hanna.

77. Andrew William Mellon.

78. Emperor Wilhelm II.
of Germany.

Martin's Homes

synagogue.

79. Martin's birthplace Reichenbach with its synagogue, 1925.

81. Marcelle Avenue in Nordegg with Martin's house (right), 1914.

80. One Whitehall Gardens, in the London suburb of Gunnersbury, 1996.

Martin's Homes

82. 28 Range Road in Ottawa, 1930.

83. The Green Salon.

84. The Chinese Room.

85. The Austrian Room.

86. The SAN REMO on Central Park West in New York, 1996.

Elly Kadoorie who joined our deliberation said that financially no nation could stand the strain of a long war.

Far from the rising tension in Europe, none of the guests at the Banff Springs Hotel seemed too concerned about the immediate future. The Duke of Connaught and his family, the Kadoories, and others continued to enjoy their stay, and Herr von Uslar returned to Calgary. But Martin decided to ride to Nordegg and assure himself everything was quiet among its population. Understandably, he was worried about the fact that a considerable number of the miners in Nordegg had come from countries immediately affected by the events in Sarajewo. Martin was especially thinking of the people from Serbia, Russia, Austria-Hungary, and Germany.

But everything was quiet in Nordegg. Martin tried his best not to disturb the peaceful atmosphere. There was only weekly delivery of mail and newspapers and the public telegraph line to Nordegg was not yet in operation. The telegraph of the railway was reserved for company business, for communication with Martin, and for emergencies.

When news of the Austrian ultimatum to Serbia reached him by railway telegraph, he swore the stationmaster to secrecy and asked him not to post the news in town. Martin would immediately ride to Banff, hoping to return to Nordegg with reassuring news and then prepare a bulletin for the people of the town, summarizing the recent events.

Martin was unaware how rapidly the events in Europe progressed from one crisis to another towards the ultimate catastrophe of war.

When I reached Laggan [Lake Louise] ... the station agent told me that the Vice-Regal party had suddenly left Banff in a special train for Ottawa. I was puzzled and so was the whole hotel in Banff.... Sir Elly Kadoorie told me that there were strange movements on the stock exchanges of Europe.

On July 28, the news of Austria's declaration of war against Serbia arrived in Banff. But everybody still hoped for a localized conflict on the Balkans. Unconcerned, Herr von Uslar left for Calgary again, planning to return on August 4. But on that date, he would already be interned, for Germany had declared war on Russia on August 1.

On the following day, Germany entered the Duchy of Luxembourg without diplomatic explanations. On August 3, Germany declared war on France, entering Belgium as a route into France. The violation of Belgium's neutrality brought England into the war on August 4. Between August 4 and August 12, Austria-

Hungary declared war against Russia, Serbia against Germany, and France and England against Austria-Hungary. Within less than two weeks, Europe became enveloped in a war into which more and more countries would enter, bringing about a world war affecting five continents.

Martin remembered the first day of war, how

> ... in the afternoon my secretary rushed to the room and exclaimed 'War has been declared.' I could not believe it. I ran downstairs to the lobby where many guests stood reading a bulletin posted—they gesticulated and discussed the unbelievable news in an excited manner. I tried to push my way through the small crowd until I could read myself the unbelievable news that Germany had declared war against Russia. I was shocked and stunned and jostled my way out. I ran against Sir Elly Kadoorie, who had read the bulletin. He said, there is no doubt that France and England must join Russia to defeat Imperial Germany, once and for all. I was moved too much to enter into any discussion. The night brought no rest. I could not imagine a war between these great nations....

Several generations of historians, political scientists and philosophers, statesmen, politicians and military men have written numerous volumes about the constellations and causes that led to the outbreak of World War I. Some wrote serious, well-researched and documented books while others published their diaries and memoirs from the war years.

Analysis of the European political constellation prior to 1914 and interpretations of the events and the decisions that contributed to "Europe sliding into war" vary greatly. But the existence of certain political and social currents in pre-war Europe and their tragic consequences are generally accepted:

1. The legacy of the Franco-Prussian war of 1870/71, in particular the strong trend in France to regain Alsace-Lorraine ceded to Germany in 1871.
2. The British distrust of Germany's economic expansion and especially Germany's continuing build-up of a powerful navy perceived as a threat to Britain's dominance of the seaways of the world, while Britain, as Winston Churchill wrote,

> ... got all we wanted in territory, and our claims to be left in unmolested enjoyment of vast and splendid possessions, mainly acquired by violence, largely maintained by force, often seemed less reasonable to others than to us.

3. The relentless growth of German industry, manufacturing, and economic power following the Franco-Prussian War and the creation of the Second German Empire in 1871.
4. The ambiguous image of the German Emperor who proclaimed a Germany in "shining armour" insisting on its rightful "place in the sun," while at the same time presenting himself to the world as the "Emperor of Peace."
5. The growing sense of national and ethnic identity among the numerous Slavic populations of Austria-Hungary. Ideologically supported by Russia, but not accepted by the politicians of Austria and even less by those of Hungary, and their reluctance to make concessions until it was too late.
6. The politically labile internal situation of the Czarist Empire of Russia.
7. The fateful absence in Europe's political landscape of truly gifted statesmen of outstanding ability guided by deep humanistic convictions.

As Lloyd George described the drama of Europe after the end of the war:

> Nobody wanted war, but … there was no arresting voice anywhere to call a halt; no dominating personality to enforce attention or offer acceptable guidance amidst the chaos. The world was exceptionally unfortunate in the quality of its counsellors in this terrible emergency. Had there been a Bismarck in Germany or a Palmerston or Disraeli in Britain, a Roosevelt in America, or a Clémanceau in authority in Paris, the catastrophe might, and I believe, would have been averted.

The men in power

> … were able, experienced and conscientious and respectable mariners, but distinctly lacking in force, vision, imagination and resource which alone could have saved the situation. They were all handy men in a well-behaved sea, but helpless in a typhoon.…

It was impossible for Martin to appreciate that the notice he read on the bulletin board signalled the beginning of a relentless change in his life; how a declaration of war in far-away Europe would destroy his plans and aspirations in Canada; and how, because the war would last much longer than anyone predicted in August 1914, his life situation would become utterly precarious and unpredictable.

Still, after the sleepless night following the news about war in Europe, Martin concluded that he was safe in Canada. He had devoted almost eight years of his life to the country he adopted as his homeland. And in turn, Canada had given him great opportunities for which he was truly grateful, as he was for the many friendships he had made since coming to Canada.

There are no indications that Martin felt anything else but loyalty to Canada when Germany entered the war. He had no thought whatsoever of leaving this country. However, he had no idea how difficult it would soon become for him to maintain the strong identification with his "adopted country." He had relinquished his allegiance to Imperial Germany, but not his sympathy for the German people. This idealism—or perhaps naiveté—must be recognized to understand Martin's repeated spontaneous attempts, all of them unwise in hindsight, to help German citizens in difficulty without realizing the problems he might cause for himself. Whether he was prepared to recognize it or not, in the eyes of some Canadians, Martin had become overnight the expatriate, even the enemy alien.

On August 7, Martin learned that Herr von Uslar had been interned in Calgary as a spy. Frau von Uslar insisted that Martin telegraph the Duchess of Connaught, asking her to intervene. Although puzzled and provoked by Frau von Uslar's reaction, Martin agreed to help.

> I expected a nervous collapse. Nothing of the kind happened. On the contrary. She [Frau von Uslar] said that she was happy in the thought of her husband and herself contributing by suffering their share towards the war which perfidious Albion had forced on their country.

Two days later, a telegram from Ottawa advised that the von Uslars were free to leave the country. Martin accompanied the formidable German lady to Calgary where Herr von Uslar had already been released. In deep thought, Martin watched them take their seats in the train to Spokane—they did not even wave goodbye. He knew he no longer belonged to their world. He had nothing in common with the von Uslars, who represented everything Martin disliked about Germany and some of its people.

How safe was Berthe-Marie in Toronto? Martin had begun to worry about his wife after Herr von Uslar had told him about the many Germans he had met in the internment camp near Calgary. Berthe-Marie carried a German passport. Would her French origin protect her? Martin decided that it would be much better for Berthe-Marie to spend the next months in the United States, whose neutrality in the European conflict was not yet in question. He cabled his friend and solicitor Herbert Brussel in New York, asking him to get in touch with Berthe-Marie and make all the necessary arrangements for her move to New York. He thought it best to exercise caution and not contact his wife until after she had left Canadian soil.

Martin now felt in jeopardy himself. Everywhere in Canada, German nationals and citizens of Austria-Hungary were being interned in large numbers. Most were quite ordinary people, while Martin was conscious of his relatively high profile. He needed to secure his freedom somehow if he wanted to carry on with his work as vice president of the Brazeau Collieries and representative of the Deutsches Kanada Syndikat. He realized that he was now completely on his own in trying to protect the interests of his German investors in Canada. It was still possible to maintain communication with Georg Büxenstein in Berlin via New York, but Martin wanted to keep any contacts with Germany to a minimum in order to avoid unnecessary attention.

As in all countries embroiled in the war, enemy aliens were readily suspected of spy activities. Even their most innocent actions or harmless pronouncements were liable to be misunderstood and quickly exploited by a sensational press. British papers reported about the spy mania in Germany under which innocent subjects of the British Crown suffered; but in the London dailies, one could also find numerous stories of equally inane actions on the part of the British authorities, caught up in the general uproar among the public.

On August 15 Martin had already approached the Minister of Militia and Defence, General Sam Hughes, in Ottawa requesting "... to be protected from arrest or molest on account of being a German citizen."

Martin was greatly reassured by the Minister's immediate, unequivocal response:

Ottawa, August 18, 1914.

Dear Sir,-

I am in receipt of your letter of the 15th instant, relative to your desire to be protected from arrest or molest on account of being a naturalized German.

In reply I beg to state that, if anyone says anything at all, all you have to do is refer them to me.

Trusting that this will be satisfactory.

Faithfully,
Sam Hughes

Martin was relieved that he still had influential friends in Ottawa who would speak for him. As the future would demonstrate, he certainly needed such persons in high places, who would always remember his loyalty to Canada and remain well disposed towards him throughout the war with its increasingly bitter and hostile mood prevalent in the country. Although Martin was eventually asked to leave Canada for the still neutral United States, the protected and privileged status that he retained in either country throughout the entire war was indeed extraordinary.

How much Martin needed that sense of being respected and of feeling free to travel about the country became evident soon enough when a "terror-stricken" Martin received a telegram from Lazard Brothers in London that

> ... on account of the war, London could not collect any more payments from the continental bankers, and consequently there would be no more payments until the end of the war. I was absolutely bare of large funds. I had just sufficient money in the bank to provide for the next two payrolls.

Besides, a note of $250,000 in favour of Roberts & Schaefer in Chicago, the builders of the Nordegg mine, was due on September 1. Wherever Martin turned for help, the response he received was negative, often openly hostile. The bankers in London and Paris refused any credit. Trying to hide his desperate situation from the head office of the Brazeau Collieries, Martin had postponed approaching Sir William Mackenzie until there was no alternative left. But Sir William cabled that his companies "... had to husband their resources and could not pay."

Martin had already requested a horse from Tom Wilson for his return to Nordegg. Instead, Martin packed his bags and took the first train from Banff to Toronto to appeal to Sir William in person.

> Arriving in his office I noticed an icy atmosphere, where formerly I had always been a welcome visitor. It did not enter my mind that I suddenly had become an alien enemy, and as such considered hostile to Canada. My feelings towards the country of my adoption had not changed. How could I be thought to be an enemy. But I soon was to learn more. Sir William Mackenzie was out of town. I wanted to see Sir Donald Mann. For the first time he made me wait a couple of hours. There was no warm greeting and the hearty usual handshake....

Martin got the distinct impression that Mann was eager to exploit to the fullest the weakened position in which Martin found himself. As usual, Martin was no match for the wily Sir Donald. Losing his temper, Martin painted the picture of the impending bankruptcy of the Brazeau Collieries unless Mann would help. For Mann, this was only the welcome signal to call in Judge Phippen who joined in the game by suggesting that the railway should take over the mine! Still disgusted years later, Martin described how "Sir Donald took his fat cigar out of his mouth and said: 'I wonder if that would not be the best thing for all concerned.'"

Martin sensed that he was in greatest danger of losing everything he had built up over the last six years and becoming the helpless victim of the wily Sir Donald Mann. Only Sir William Mackenzie could rescue him. He "left without a word." He could not afford to wait for Mackenzie's return from Ottawa. Before leaving Toronto, Martin called on another friend for help, Sir William Mulock, who refused even to see him. Andrew Haydon in Ottawa was Martin's last resort:

> Andy listened to my tale of woe. "It seems to me that you are up against it. We shall see some Cabinet Ministers."
> We found two together. I told them the whole story, how ... Sir Wilfrid Laurier and his colleagues had welcomed me ... how many millions of dollars I had brought to Canada... how the mine was operating and providing work for many ... and that apparently Mackenzie, Mann & Company took our precarious financial situation as a welcome opportunity to enrich themselves....

Martin fought a desperate battle trying to rescue his personal and emotional investment in Canada. He also felt responsible to the German shareholders. He felt most uncomfortable when he had to explain that the man in Germany he was working for, Georg Büxenstein, was actively involved in the German war effort, having volunteered to create the Imperial Automobile Corps. Martin directed another highly emotional appeal to the two ministers through which shone his commitment and loyalty to Canada. He saw a faint glimmer of hope when one of the ministers suggested that they all go and call on William Mackenzie. But Mackenzie refused to see them, probably unwilling to offer the help he intended to give Martin under what looked like mediation forced upon him by the two ministers.

But early next morning William Mackenzie called for Martin.

> He was as friendly as ever and informed me that the mine would be kept going, that the notes given by the collieries would have to be prolonged, but all this under one condition: that I should go to Nordegg, stay there, run the mine and be responsible for all going well. "From now on, you can draw on the railway company for your payrolls and other necessary expenses. And we shall also take care of the notes." I was happy. Sir William Mackenzie smiled.

And Mackenzie even agreed "with pleasure" to Martin's request for telegraph privileges. This was one of several instances during the war years where Mackenzie showed himself more supportive to Martin than what one might expect from his tough reputation and the effect of the ever-present hostile mood against Germany.

Andy brought me to the station at midnight. "That was a bad fight with the old fox...." He gripped my hand firmly ... and the train rolled into the night.

After his experiences in the East, Martin did not expect a hearty welcome in Nordegg. The people at the station greeted him in as friendly a manner as always. But on Marcelle Avenue, the atmosphere had noticeably changed during Martin's absence. The doctor he had hired less than a couple of years ago avoided personal contact, and John Shanks, whom Martin had recently hired as mine manager, seemed less open and co-operative. Martin, who had always praised the mine manager for his competence and his excellent performance, began to feel a tinge of regret about having chosen John Shanks over the other applicants. Although Martin was still the undisputed boss of the Brazeau Collieries, he realized that under the current circumstances he needed Shanks and his loyalty more than ever. He could not suppress a sense of foreboding.

If his relationship with John Shanks, a comparative newcomer to Nordegg, was strictly businesslike, Martin was unprepared for the hostile reaction confronting him when he called on his neighbours Ernest and Marthe Gheur. In his eyes, the Gheurs were cultured Europeans. He treasured the many hours he had spent in their home; he considered the warm-hearted Ernest and the charming Marthe his friends. Although he tried to understand the reasons for the extreme anger that had displaced the warm feelings the Gheurs had always demonstrated towards him, Martin was deeply hurt. The Gheurs bitterly reproached him about the German invasion of their peaceful homeland and the occupation of their beautiful hometown, Liège. The Gheurs, who had no news from their parents, relatives and friends, feared the worst.

Liège was a heavily fortified city only 20 miles west of the German border. The conquest of Liège, which was encircled by German troops within three days of the beginning of hostilities, was the first manifestation of the might of the German war machine. After ten days of heavy fighting, the last of the forts of Liège had fallen on August 16.

Newspapers reaching Nordegg were usually a few days old. But Ernest Gheur, who spent part of each week at the company office in Red Deer, always received the latest news with the daily delivery of the Edmonton and Calgary papers. The fall of Liège figured prominently in the headlines. There were even more disturbing reports about the suffering of the civilian population. The German military authorities had taken a number of civilians hostage in reaction to the outbreak of "franctireur" activities, civilians [today's guerrillas] who had attacked and killed a number of German soldiers. The world press was also incensed by the news that a number of Belgian civilians, among them elderly women, had been transported to Germany and placed in internment camps.

With sadness, Martin accepted that he had lost the friendship of the Gheurs. He had earned the enmity of the doctor, who was finally fired after the lower town population complained about his services. And John Shanks caused him increasing worry. But Martin was able to draw comfort from the fact that the miners in the lower town had not forgotten his concern for their welfare.

> ... the miners and their families remained very friendly towards me, although relatives were fighting amongst the allies, and many reports of deaths had come in ....

The miners were, of course, aware of the hostile attitude prevailing against Martin in the upper town. They had never felt welcome there, but now the miners did not dare visit Martin's home under any circumstances. Only the two mounted policemen were frequent visitors; and once every two weeks, Father Voisin, who came from Red Deer to say mass, stayed at Martin's house. William Mackenzie sent reassuring telegrams, praising Martin's successful efforts to prevent strikes that plagued other mines in Alberta.

In some ways, Martin was not unhappy to spend these critical days in the remoteness of Nordegg. But the Christmas season turned into a very depressing time. There was no word from Berthe-Marie and Marcelle. Only Dutchie received a card from New York with Marcelle's Christmas greetings. Martin wondered whether his mail was being censored. With a heavy heart, Martin spent a lonely New Year's Eve in Nordegg. The reports of events in Europe were not encouraging. The Austrians were under great pressure trying to hold the front in the East. And the rapid advance of Germany's armies into France had come to a standstill. Would 1915 bring peace and a less uncertain life for Martin?

> The long winter passed slowly. The cruel war went on. All I knew about it, was contained in the regular bulletin telegraphed to me, which I posted at the mine and in town. My correspondence with abroad had stopped entirely long ago.

Martin read voraciously during the lonely winter evenings. Except for his daily visits with the Kidds, he had ceased socializing with his neighbours in the upper town. On Sundays, he took long rides, always stopping at Dutchie's cabin.

Martin had longed for this dreary winter to pass; but with the arrival of spring, a succession of events started that made Martin's position in town more and more untenable.

On May 8, 1915, Martin held the telegram from Toronto in his hand that reported the sinking of the British passenger ship *Lusitania* by a German submarine in the Atlantic. Among the 1198 lives lost were 139 citizens of the still neutral United States.

There was an outburst of hate against Germany and anybody German. Of course I could not help feeling that this also affected my relation to many who had still been very friendly.

Now Martin did not even feel at ease visiting the lower town, where more and more people stopped greeting him. The suspicious attitude of the entire town increased when, on May 14, word spread like wildfire that Martin's residence was being searched by the authorities on that day.

Officers of the Northwest Mounted Police arrived at Martin's door. While being very courteous and discreet, even apologetic, they did confiscate his hunting weapons and a number of papers, some of which Martin considered vital for his continuing safety and protection.

On the following morning, Martin dispatched a coded telegram to Mr. Ormsby, the Secretary-Treasurer of the Brazeau Collieries in Toronto, an urgent message that was actually meant for Andrew Haydon in Ottawa. It was a cry for help, which Martin did not dare send to Haydon directly. Not being certain of how his coded message would be received by Ormsby, Martin also advised Haydon by an open telegram:

"Have telegraphed today important message to Ormsby to be deciphered and communicated to you. Please take steps at once and let me know results."

But as Martin found out later, he did not have to worry. Ormsby proved sympathetic and immediately forwarded Martin's message to Andrew Haydon:

Following received from Martin Nordegg, Nordegg, Alberta: Please communicate immediately Haydon deciphered: following spitefully accused of correspondence with enemy I have been searched by the police naturally without results but my protecting letters General Sam Hughes and Immigration Chief Officer Scott have been confiscated. I am now entirely without protection and permission for crossing boundary and anticipate further trouble. What can you do for me. Shall I come east. Telegraph reply.

Martin received Andrew Haydon's reassuring reply within two days:

Advise remain there. Commissioner Dominion Police and Department immigration will endeavour straighten out matter. Telegraph me direct anything new.

Andrew Haydon followed his cable with a letter explicitly describing his attempts to help Martin. The letter arrived in Nordegg on May 28, with the date of opening stamped by the Western Office of Brazeau Collieries. Andrew Haydon had obviously found it safer not to designate his letters to Martin as "private" any longer. Besides, he was sure that everybody in the office would read his letter to Martin, which could only help in letting the townspeople know that Martin still enjoyed the goodwill and protection of the government in Ottawa.

Andrew Haydon's reassuring telegram and his follow-up letter had not come any too soon! Again arising from events in Europe, there was more trouble, this time literally on Martin's doorstep!

Although a member of the Tri-Partite Alliance between Germany, Austria-Hungary, and Italy, the latter had declared her neutrality at the outbreak of hostilities in Europe. During the following months, the Italian Parliament was the scene of heated debates as to Italy's further position in the war. News of the unrest in the country and the huge demonstrations in favour of entering the war on the side of England, France and Russia had also reached the Italian miners in Nordegg, causing noticeable excitement in the lower town, which had not escaped Martin's attention.

On April 26, 1915, Italy had signed a secret treaty with the Allied Powers, agreeing to enter the war on their side in return for the promise of territorial gains in Europe and in Africa after a victorious end of the war.

On May 24, 1915, Martin posted the bulletin announcing that Italy had declared war on Austria-Hungary the day before. The Italians, who formed the largest ethnic group among the Nordegg miners, constituting with their families about a quarter of the total population, immediately broke out in jubilation. As yet, no anger was turned against Martin, who good-naturedly received a deputation "...asking permission for a parade, to be headed by their band, and to hoist flags on the only high flagpole in town, which stood in front of my cottage. I naturally granted this request without any hesitation."

Little did Martin expect in what fateful outcome his permission would result. When he woke up the following morning, the flagpole was bare; and at the office, trouble was awaiting him.

> Perhaps I saw ghosts, but I imagined that the office staff did not return my usual greetings with the same warmth. The higher officials, of course, had shown great reticence since months.
> A little while later, a deputation of the Italian colony arrived.... The spokesman told me, that they would haul up new flags that afternoon and should they disappear, there would be trouble. I suggested that

they should place a man there to guard the flags, and they considered that a very good idea. That afternoon, the same procession and ceremony took place, and when I returned to my cottage, I saw two Italians, sitting peacefully under the flagpole, smoking. They jumped up, as in former times, took off their caps and greeted me, and I shook hands with them.

But there was trouble elsewhere. The policeman arrived at Martin's cottage reporting "quite a riot in town, evidently directed against me, accusing me of having hauled down the flags."

The policeman requested Martin's permission to stay with him overnight, and Martin accepted. Later, when the night turned cool, the two Italian "guards" asked "for a drop" and Martin obliged. Likely, the bottle of wine he gave them was not the only drop the two consumed overnight. When Martin looked out of the window in the morning, the two Italians were sound asleep at the foot of the flagpole and the flags had disappeared again! Soon, a group of Italians assembled in front of Martin's house. They confronted Martin with loud accusations and would not listen to his explanations. Shaking their fists at him, they left with angry threats—"...you will hear from us."

Wondering who the troublemaker in town might be, Martin thought of a particular person with pro-German sympathies. Without realizing the difficulties he was certain to create for Martin, he could have taken down the Italian flags. But the policeman "... suspected somebody who would have an interest in incensing the population against me for selfish reasons. We never found the culprit...."

The policeman offered to stay with Martin for a few more days, and Martin "gladly accepted."

With all the trouble erupting in Nordegg, Martin was still a free man. But had he been interned, he probably would have been protected from becoming embroiled in issues of potential damage to his reputation of being loyal to Canada.

On May 28, a telegram transmitted via New York from the Deutsche Bank in Berlin arrived in Nordegg. Arthur von Gwinner, the Chairman of the Board of the Deutsche Bank, was concerned about a German settler, Eberhard von Schmidt, who had not been in communication with his family in Germany for months. Could Martin make some inquiries?

This was a typical example of what occurred in every country during the war. An innocent attempt to help people unable to communicate because of hostilities between nations was readily interpreted as an act of espionage or a prelude to sabotage, causing immediate difficulties for the person who is a citizen of an enemy country. Had Martin, out of caution, simply ignored the telegram, the consequences would probably not have been very different. The mere fact of being approached by a highly placed person from an enemy country was enough to put him under renewed suspicion.

Martin, of course, could not change his nature. He immediately asked the North West Mounted Police in Calgary for information on Mr. von Schmidt and sent a cable to the representative of the Deutsche Bank in New York that "… the man was still on his farm and not anxious to communicate with his family. Little did I think that this innocent inquiry would be later held against me."

Martin knew he was under intensified observation when he was prevented from reaching Dr. Oskar Wassermann, a director of the Deutsche Bank in Berlin, by cable via New York. Martin's inquiry and request for intervention concerned the Honorable Dr. H. S. Béland, the former Postmaster General of Canada, who had been interned by the German military authorities in Belgium and later placed in a prison in Berlin. Although Martin was acting upon the request of Sir Wilfrid Laurier, his cable was returned to Nordegg as not being admissible for transmission. Again, Andrew Haydon's intervention became necessary. The reply from Berlin arrived without interference, and Sir Wilfrid conveyed his appreciation of Martin's assistance in a letter to Andrew Haydon.

On June 1, another letter from Andrew Haydon arrived in Nordegg confirming the coded telegram he had transmitted to Martin a few days earlier that "Commissioner Sherwood will give you permission travel anywhere and give orders to restore documents."

The sympathetic Haydon added that

> I am so sorry you are so disturbed over the situation but you will read-
> ily understand from the state of feeling generally in the country that
> people sometimes do things that are not entirely necessary. I am sure
> you can be taken care of by various offices here and if you will let me
> know at any time as to your movements, I will try to see that you are
> not unnecessarily disturbed…. The war, of course, drags on….

Anxiously, Martin began to wonder whether it was only Andrew Haydon's loyalty and his efforts to have his friend Martin "taken care of by various offices" in Ottawa that had saved him from internment. Once more, he read Andy's letter, the last one to reach him in Nordegg. Late in the evening of the same day, the station agent knocked at Martin's door:

> "Telegram for you, sir." I opened it and read that I should hold myself
> ready to leave the mine soon and come East. The agent thought it best
> to bring me the message as he did not trust anybody to keep it secret.

The notice did not come entirely unexpected. The dramatic events in far away Europe increasingly affected the mood of the townspeople. Too much had been happening to Martin to maintain himself in Nordegg and carry out his duties as vice president of Brazeau Collieries. More and more, Martin had been forced

> ... to lead a solitary life. I knew that the animosity against everybody German was growing to great bitterness, and I thought it best to become a recluse....
>
> I started packing my belongings. My heart was heavy with the thought that I should soon have to leave these mountains and also the place which I created with so much love and under so many difficulties. I had the feeling that I would never return, anyhow not for many years.

Sooner than Martin expected, the next telegram arrived in the afternoon of June 3, calling Martin back to Ottawa immediately. Martin could never forget the following day, June 4, 1915:

> The train left at 5 a.m., but in spite of this early hour, I had a great send-off, and when the train pulled out, a few tears ran over my cheeks. I just could not help it. Father Voisin happened to be on the train, I went with him into the caboose, and called with him at the convent in Red Deer.
>
> That was a sad journey. With a heavy heart I travelled over the same route which had taken me so often to the West, and I thought of the great joy and the expectations which I had felt every time ... of my feelings at the progress of the realization of my dreams—until my last trip when I saw this fulfilment and felt the pride of having created a great industry. And now ... the consequences of the great catastrophe in Europe, with so many thousands maimed and killed every day ... it seemed all so irrelevant, so futile, to think of that industry out in the wilds of the Rockies, compared to the happenings in Europe.

During the "long and dreary days and nights" on the train, Martin could only think of what he had been forced to leave behind in the West. But he also anxiously wondered what would expect him in Ottawa.

> Passing through North Bay in the late evening, I was happy that the mental agony of the long journey would soon be ended. Arriving in Ottawa early next morning, I could hardly wait for Andy to appear in his office. He knew already the questions which would have to be answered by me. The investigation started and lasted two days....

If Martin was ever made to feel not merely like an enemy alien, but like a hostile, untrustworthy foreigner who only faked his loyalty to his adopted country, it was during this fateful week. It was difficult now to believe how much at home he used to feel in Ottawa among the many friends he had made in government and business when now so many of them studiously avoided him. How would Martin have survived these days without the faithful Andrew Haydon, who stood by him throughout the investigation and urged him to stay off the streets! Not that Andrew Haydon worried about Martin's safety in public. But it was painful to watch the once proud, optimistic, and gregarious Martin Nordegg in his present vulnerable state. Andrew Haydon did his utmost to protect Martin from all possible situations, where his former friends and acquaintances would meet him with hostility.

Martin needed all his strength and presence of mind to survive the tense atmosphere of the sessions of the investigation and the pointed questions of the committee. He would never forget the accusations and suspicions:

> Had I shipped coal to Vancouver for a German cruiser for an attack on the city?
>
> I replied that not one pound of our coal had ever been shipped to the West … and that Sir William Mackenzie could corroborate this.
>
> Had I helped German officers to leave Canada to join the German army?
>
> The only man I had helped … was old von Uslar, and I mentioned the telegram from Her Royal Highness the Duchess of Connaught.
>
> Had I regularly transferred funds from Canada to Germany since the beginning of the war?
>
> Yes, I had—to support my sister there—but…always…through the Post office at Nordegg.
>
> Was I aware that my German secretary had also sent money to Germany?
>
> I did not.
>
> Did I try to help Eberhard von Schmidt leave Canada so that he could join the German Army?
>
> No, I had only forwarded the request from the Deutsche Bank to the Northwest Mounted Police.
>
> Did I use a secret code in transmitting messages to Germany such as "an anxious mother [Eberhard von Schmidt's mother] is wishing to hear from her son," anxious mother no doubt meaning Germany?
>
> This thought had never entered my mind, and I could not believe it.

Even Martin's connection with the Lazard Brothers & Co. in London seemed suspect to the committee. Was not one of their officials, Mr. Pusch, a German citizen?

"I did not know."

Only now did Martin realize how his spontaneous nature, his frank, forthcoming way of helping people at a time when his actions should have been guided by extreme caution, had placed him in a most endangered position. He was certain that he would lose his freedom for the duration of the war.

There were many other questions which made me very uneasy and I
thought I would be interned in a concentration camp.

When the examination was over, Andy said to me, on the way to
his office:

"You know, that I am your friend. You also know that I have to
defend you. I can only do that, if you tell me the whole truth and nothing but the truth. I want you to give me your word of honour."

"I assure you, that I told the whole truth and have not concealed
anything."

He took my hand, pressed it, looked straight into my eyes:

"I believe you."

His fate, Martin knew, was now in the hands of the authorities
and, thank God, also in the hands of Andrew Haydon. If anybody
could prevent his internment, it was his friend Andy. With very
mixed emotions, Martin received Andrew Haydon's advice at noon
of the following day. His case had been dismissed, but it was imperative that Martin pack his bags and leave Canada at once for the
United States. Reluctantly, Martin agreed to go to New York where
he had friends to help him get established for the duration of the
war.

Andrew Haydon obtained a letter of authorization from the Chief
Immigration Officer in Ottawa for Martin allowing him to leave
Canada but also to return when required "for the conduct of the
mine."

Andy ... fetched me from the hotel and never left me until the train
pulled out of the station. I asked him repeatedly why my case had been
dismissed. The only reply I got, was, I should be happy to have got off
and should not bother why.

The train rolled slowly out of the station. Andy still stood on the
platform and waved his hand. I fell back on the seat.

The Canadian Immigration Officer was surprised ... that I was a
German leaving Canada.... I gave the officer the letter from the Chief
Immigration Officer to let me pass and enter any time. The Officer
wished me ... bon voyage.... The train rolled over the boundary and my
heart was heavy.

The day was June 11, 1915.

There had been no time to advise Berthe-Marie of his impending
arrival in New York. Besides, after the ordeal of the Ottawa investigation, Martin did not wish to send another telegram or communication from Canada, not even to his family. The unexpected reunion
brought new worries. How much Martin could have used the support of a strong, loving wife. But he was shocked by Berthe-
Marie's appearance and her preoccupation with herself. Hardly listening to the reasons for his sudden departure from Canada, Berthe-

Marie nearly overwhelmed her husband with the unhappiness that had not left her since her arrival in New York. To Martin, some of Berthe-Marie's complaints seemed rather trivial. Although located in an elegant building on 74 Broadway, the rented apartment was so small that she had found it embarrassing to entertain some of Marcelle's friends from the Sacred Heart Academy. She herself had no friends whatsoever, and nobody came to see her except occasionally Martin's friend Herbert Brussel, but he always seemed too busy to stay. Although she utterly disliked her present home, she did not like to go out. New York's streets were too crowded, Central Park was too far, and the small parks of the neighbourhood were overrun by people.

Martin, who had already seen himself behind the barbed wire of a Canadian internment camp, found it hard to listen to his wife's complaints until she began to relate to him her worry about her declining health. Berthe-Marie had always been easily depressed and unhappy, but Martin realized now that Berthe-Marie was not well at all. His mind burdened with innumerable worries and things that needed to be taken care of immediately, Martin was sufficiently alarmed to take Berthe-Marie to a physician recommended by Herbert Brussel.

The physician's diagnosis was hardly reassuring. Berthe-Marie suffered from a definite weakness of the cardio-pulmonary system; and Manhattan was more than unsuitable a place for her to get better, physically and emotionally. A stay at the seashore would be most advisable, a place such as Atlantic City almost ideal. If Martin needed to remain in New York for business reasons, he could easily reach Atlantic City by train on weekends. The clean, bracing ocean air would favourably affect Berthe-Marie's health; and after the turmoil of Manhattan's life, the elegance of Atlantic City would without doubt raise her depressed mood.

Martin, who had so much on his mind these days, was grateful for the physician's practical advice. Berthe-Marie had no objections to any plan as long as it would mean her escape from the hated Manhattan. Martin looked at Marcelle, who had been so successful and happy at the Sacred Heart Academy. But the summer holidays were just beginning, and most of Marcelle's friends would leave the city anyway. As usual, Martin's daughter, who had been moved about so many times in her young life, voiced neither demands nor complaints. Martin assured her that there would be swimming and boating in Atlantic City; and remembering Marcelle's happy days of riding through the Rocky Mountains, a guilt-ridden Martin promised his daughter that she would have her own horse as soon as they were settled in Atlantic City.

On July 10, the family travelled to Atlantic City, where Martin rented a spacious suite at the Hotel Traymore. Her mood much improved, Berthe-Marie found nothing to criticize. Three days later, Martin returned to New York, where he moved to the Hotel Astor after terminating the lease of the apartment on 74 Broadway. Keeping the promise he had made, he visited Berthe-Marie and Marcelle every other weekend. He had no inkling that quite soon, there would be a new reason to visit Atlantic City more frequently.

With more time on his hands than during the past years, Martin realized how far removed he had become from the affairs of the Brazeau Collieries as a result of his move to New York. Addressing his concerns to Mackenzie in a detailed letter describing the unsatisfactory communication with the head office in Toronto as well as with the mine in Nordegg, Martin candidly explained the reasons for his temporary absence from Canada. He outlined the arrangements he had made in Nordegg prior to his departure, so "...that I could really carry on the management by correspondence; further that I had permission to return to Canada whenever needed."

A remarkably gracious reply arrived from Mackenzie within days! Expressing his sympathy for the fate that had befallen Martin, Mackenzie reiterated how essential he considered Martin's continued involvement "for the progress of our enterprise." According to his explicit instructions, from then on, regular statements and reports would be forwarded to Martin by the Toronto head office, which Martin was expected to return with his comments and recommendations. Martin was also encouraged by Mackenzie to correspond with the officials at Nordegg, but his correspondence should always be sent via the Toronto office.

Martin was greatly reassured by Mackenzie's letter, which was so much more supportive than he had dared hope after his recent negative experiences in Ottawa. Still, he was somehow offended by the directive to send all correspondence destined for Nordegg via Mackenzie's desk. Did Mackenzie not trust him after all? Certain of Mackenzie's good will, Martin decided to challenge the directive. In his next letter, Mackenzie patiently explained that he actually wanted to protect Martin from any future suspicions and misunderstandings. Considering his current situation, Martin could not ask for more understanding and support from Mackenzie. But he had become painfully aware how tenuous his position with the Brazeau Collieries was. Mackenzie was his last and only protector.

Fortunately, unexpected tasks arose that involved Martin in entirely new activities in the United States to such an extent that his worries about his waning influence with Brazeau Collieries were relegated to the back of his mind. For the next fifteen months,

Martin was occupied to the fullest with solving technical and financial and political problems that culminated in success but, unfortunately, resulted in a repetition of what had happened to him in Canada. Representing German interests, he came under strong suspicion as soon as the United States entered the war in 1917.

After his successful work on behalf of German investors in Canada, Martin's reputation with the Deutsche Bank in Berlin was such that their directors engaged him immediately after becoming aware of Martin's relocation to the United States. The Deutsche Bank held considerable investments and interests in the United States, which had increased in their importance since the onset of the war. One of the investments of the Deutsche Bank in Pennsylvania had been plagued with seemingly insurmountable problems resulting in serious financial losses. To the directors of the Deutsche Bank, Martin seemed to be the right person to solve these problems. Martin accepted the assignment from Berlin with gusto.

In November 1914, the Deutsche Bank had already sent one of its directors, Mr. Hugo Schmidt, to New York to act side by side with Mr. Edward D. Adams, who had represented the Deutsche Bank in New York for many years. This dual leadership only exacerbated rather than solved the existing problems not in the least for Martin himself, who immediately gained the trust and cooperation of Mr. Schmidt, while Mr. Adams remained his determined adversary. But Martin had learned a great deal during his Canadian years. Despite a confusing multitude of problems fraught with dangers and pitfalls arising out of personality conflicts, technical faults, mismanagement, and financial manipulations that reached the level of high finance and international diplomacy, Martin did a splendid job. Free of the emotional investment he had made to Canada, he immensely enjoyed this complex, but time-limited task about which he later gave a detailed account in his memoirs.

The problem that Martin was expected to solve involved three large companies in Pennsylvania: the Lehigh Coke Company in South Bethlehem, owned by the Deutsche Bank in Berlin; the Koppers Company in Pittsburgh; and the Bethlehem Steel Company, both owned by the powerful Mellon family.

After his appointment to the board of directors of the Lehigh Coke Company, Martin was asked by the Deutsche Bank to investigate the company. Martin went to work immediately,

> … happy to have such an appointment offered to me which meant great activity.
>
> Mr. Adams did not seem very pleased, but Mr. Schmidt welcomed the appointment most heartily, because he had great trouble with the management and did not understand the technical part of this industry.

> He also had continuous trouble with Mr. Adams who was the President
> of the company. That did not look good to me... .
>
> I started to work with the General Manager, and I foresaw that I
> should have an enemy in him who resented any question and investiga-
> tion. It seemed to me to be a passive resistance.
>
> The company was in a very bad state. It had been losing money
> since its start. Coke ovens fell in. As soon as one was repaired, another
> fell in....

Under contract to supply the Bethlehem Steel Company with gas
and coke, the Lehigh Coke Company failed to meet its obligations
because of the continuing collapse of its coke ovens. In defense, the
Lehigh Coke had already started a law suit against the builders of the
ovens, the Koppers Company, which Martin tried to rescind, as
Koppers belonged to the Mellon interests. It was Martin's job to
make the Lehigh Company "a financial success" and rebuild the
damaged relationship with the Mellon enterprises.

For Martin, returning the Lehigh Company to full productivity
was the first task, which he could only accomplish by identifying
the causes for the constantly collapsing coke ovens. But during a
special meeting in New York with Mr. Adams, the general manager,
and the company directors, all his ideas and recommendations were
met "with an icy reception." Only Mr. Schmidt supported Martin.
After the meeting, he agreed with Martin's impression that Mr.
Adams and the general manager "... actually wanted to see the plant
run down, in order to acquire it at a cheap price and sell it then with
a large profit."

It speaks for the reputation Martin had built up in Berlin that his
recommendations were fully accepted by the directors of the
Deutsche Bank. Over the objections of Mr. Adams, Martin received
unlimited authority to act as he saw fit, without any interference
from Mr. Adams, to solve the technical and management problems
and explore a profitable sale of the company.

How grateful Martin was that his work in Canada had taught
him so much about the properties of various types of coal!
Observing the burning ovens day and night, Martin discovered the
cause of their collapse: the type of coal. The walls of the ovens collapsed because of the enormous pressure of the rapidly expanding
"swelling coal" used. Martin ordered test loadings with "shrinking
coal," which showed complete success. One more time, the ovens
were rebuilt; they never collapsed again. "My happiness knew no
bounds."

Under Martin's leadership, the Lehigh Coke Company achieved
a reliable flow of production, fulfilling all its contractual obligations
to the Bethlehem Steel Company. Lehigh had become a profitable

company, Martin proudly cabled to Berlin. He suggested the time for its sale had arrived. Against the vocal objections of Mr. Adams who, to no avail, even appealed to Arthur von Gwinner, the president of the Deutsche Bank in Berlin, Martin and Mr. Schmidt began to look for interested buyers. Arthur von Gwinner had authorized the sale of the company for a cash price of $7 million.

Martin had also ended the lawsuit against the Koppers Company. Two days later, he received an invitation to meet Andrew Mellon in Pittsburgh. Martin was in his glory when he met one of the richest men in the world. Andrew Mellon

> ... was succinct. I could not help admiring him, because he showed a perfect grasp of intricate, highly technical matters which he seemed to master absolutely. I came to the conclusion that he was one of the greatest men I ever met in my life.... He was very well informed, perhaps better than I, and if I ever wanted protection against the machinations of people who wanted to benefit by these troublous times, I should not hesitate to call on him.

Martin and Mr. Schmidt still had to contend with the interference and intrigue of Mr. Adams and his allies among the Lehigh directors who were not ready to give up their sabotage of the sale of the Lehigh Company with which Martin and Mr. Schmidt had been entrusted. Victory was near when Martin received an offer of $8 million from Mr. Schwab, the president of Bethlehem Steel Company. But Mr. Schwab was not prepared to pay cash. When the Deutsche Bank in Berlin firmly insisted on a cash sale, Martin turned to Andrew Mellon, who at once offered to buy Lehigh paying cash, but for only $7 million. Martin felt in a terrible predicament and telegraphed to Berlin. He was surprised when the Deutsche Bank instructed him to proceed with the sale to Mellon immediately. On January 17, 1917, the sale was closed. Unsuccessfully, Mr. Adams tried to sabotage the sale to Andrew Mellon up to the last minute. To Martin, it was obvious that he hoped to drag out the proceedings until the entry of the United States into the war, which everybody expected within weeks. At that time, Lehigh Coke would have fallen into Mr. Adams' lap like a ripe plum.

The months of intense activities in Pennsylvania had come to a successful conclusion on the triumphal day when Andrew Mellon placed a cheque for $7 million into Martin's hand,

> ... the biggest cheque Mr. Schmidt and myself had ever seen. Then we thought it high time to celebrate this great event. We did not even take a taxi, but the subway in all modesty and went to Luechow's German restaurant, and did not know what to order appropriate to the great occasion.

To Martin's surprise, Andrew Mellon asked him to continue the management of the Lehigh Coke Company. Martin was exceedingly proud, but not for long. Only a few days later, the offer was retracted with great regret expressed by Andrew Mellon and his brother, Arthur. Martin could not ignore that war was imminent for the United States.

From the Deutsche Bank, Martin received a commission of $15,000 for the successful sale and, to his much greater surprise, the sum of $25,000 from Andrew Mellon with the words:

> "Mr. Schwab and I have decided to give you another check as our appreciation of your excellent work."
>
> I was elated, not so much for the money, but for the appreciation.

There were more sincere acknowledgments, some of them already under the shadow of impending war. After expressing his appreciation of Martin's successful efforts, Mr. C.A. Buck, vice president of the Bethlehem Steel Company wrote on February 13:

"... It is with regret that I recognize we will probably not have a very close association in the future...."

And on the same date, Mr. W.A. Wilbur, former vice-president of the Lehigh Coke Company wrote to Martin:

> My dear Mr. Nordegg:
>
> Your thorough and energetic analysis of the production and operating conditions, as existing when you first undertook your comprehensive investigations of the Lehigh Coke Company, brought about a reasonable and satisfactory solution of matters of controversy between the Koppers Company and ourselves, and were of untold value to the Lehigh Coke Company, and had that Company continued in its past ownership, would have contributed tremendously to the great earnings that the plant will inevitably show.
>
> It was indeed a great pleasure to me to be associated with a man of your ability in bringing about these results.
>
> If in the future you should have occasion to come to Bethlehem, please bear in mind that my latchstring is always out. ...
>
> Whilst our activities henceforth will probably be in diverging lines, I shall always think of you as a man bound to succeed in whatever channel and work of life you devote your energies.
>
> Believe me, as
> Very sincerely yours,
>
> W.A. Wilbur

How much Martin needed such kind words of appreciation and recognition during the following weeks when after international finance, politics with its machinations entered his life to his detriment!

Before Mr. Schmidt and Martin could carry out the instructions from Berlin to deposit the $7 million in three different banks, the German Ambassador Count Bernstorff called Martin from Washington.

> He said, he knew all about the payment and asked to let him have one million dollars. Mr. Schmidt asked for his authority.... Unfortunately, Mr. Schmidt had to pay him the million, after receiving the authority.

The one million dollars handed over to the German ambassador is one of the most mysterious items in Martin's account. Was it possible that the money had been dedicated for the political activities of the German Embassy in the United States and in Mexico? Martin was most disturbed about this transaction, which had brought him into direct contact with the highest placed German official in the United States. He was certain everything had already come to the attention of U.S. authorities. As a consequence, their surveillance of Martin's movements would only be intensified.

Martin resented his enforced connection with the German Embassy. He had met the entire senior staff on several occasions but did not care for most of them. In his memoirs, he particularly singled out Franz von Papen, the German military attaché in Mexico City since 1913 and from 1915 on in Washington, "... who was to play a most nefarious role in the future."

Like others in the early 1930s, Franz von Papen, although a staunch conservative, would act as "the one holding the stirrups" for Adolf Hitler on his ascent to the dictatorship of Germany.

Another person Martin thoroughly disliked was Dr. Heinrich Albert, the financial counsellor of the German Embassy. Martin was horrified to learn that Dr. Albert was occupying the suite next to his in the Astor Hotel. There was nothing he could do but avoid at all cost being seen in Dr. Albert's presence. He steadfastly refused Dr. Albert's invitation to join him for a drink in his suite, especially after Dr. Albert told him indignantly that he was certain his suite had been searched by the Secret Service in his absence.

In a dramatic sequence in his memoirs, Martin writes about the suspected activities of Dr. Albert, who never parted with his portfolio, and how the Secret Service men pursued him in a cat and mouse game until they finally succeeded in getting a hold of the prized portfolio.

> In the portfolio was found evidence of the negotiations by the German Government and its agents regarding the acquisition of war plants and

factories, of sabotage and bribes and reports of spies. In fact, the most incriminating documents possible....

On February 1, 1917, Germany proclaimed the beginning of unrestricted submarine war. Immediately, the number of ships belonging to hostile as well as neutral countries, lost while crossing the Atlantic, rose dramatically. By November 1917, 105 German U-boats had sunk a volume exceeding 8 million tons.

In an immediate response to Germany's declaration of unrestricted submarine warfare, the United States severed diplomatic relations with Germany on February 3. The German ambassador and his staff were requested to leave the country.

As Martin wrote,

The cup was full.... The German ambassador and his staff ... were to leave by the 'Bergensfjord' and with them sailed a great many Germans.

Among the passengers was Franz von Papen, who was carrying his personal papers in a trunk sealed by the Swiss Consulate. As von Papen did not enjoy diplomatic immunity, his trunk was opened by the search crew of a British cruiser when the *Bergensfjord* was sailing north along the Canadian coast. Within days of the seizure of von Papen's luggage, Martin was ordered to appear before Captain Burke of the U.S. Department of Justice, who showed him a copy of the cheque for $1 million that he had been ordered to give to Count Bernstorff. It bore the signatures of Hugo Schmidt and Martin Nordegg

Martin did his best to explain his part in the signing of the cheque to Captain Burke, who ordered Martin not to leave New York without his permission. In view of the political developments of the past few days, Martin's position had indeed become very precarious. But as yet, Martin was not classified as an enemy alien. While the unrestricted submarine warfare was considered a *casus belli* [cause for war], a tenuous state of peace continued. But public opinion in the United States clamored for war; and after the British Secret Service had intercepted and deciphered a diplomatic note from Berlin addressed to the government of Mexico offering that country a treaty of assistance, the United States declared war on Germany on April 6, 1917.

Martin expected his immediate internment. But it was Mr. Schmidt who became "... the first German to be interned when the United States went to the war."

On April 8, Martin received a call from his lawyer Herbert Brussel asking to meet him immediately at the flower shop in the Pennsylvania Station. Brussel refused to divulge over the telephone any reason for the urgency. When Martin arrived at the flower shop,

Herbert Brussel took him without a single word of explanation to a train on the easternmost platform. Guarded by soldiers, this was the first train to take German internees to Camp Oglethorpe and Hugo Schmidt was among them.

> I emptied all the money I carried with me into his hand. We then shook hands, and walking along with the train until it gathered speed, I waved him Goodbye. [Herbert Brussel] advised me to get all my things ready for my probable internment next week. On the way back to the hotel, I thought things over and came to the conclusion, that if I had to be interned, I would rather be interned in Canada where I still had friends.

Martin felt like a cornered animal. In great haste, he started sending letters in all directions. He received many kind, encouraging replies, although none of the persons approached found it possible to be of actual help to Martin. Sir George Bury, vice president of the Canadian Pacific Railway, closed his handwritten letter with the assuring sentence "While perhaps you may be considered by some an 'alien enemy' I at any rate feel that you are a friend of the Empire."

Equally reassuring was the reply from Sir Robert Kindersley, a senior partner of the Lazard Brothers Co. in London.

In desperation, Martin even considered the possibility of returning to Germany. He had written a detailed letter to Andrew Haydon, which was forwarded to Sir Percy Sherwood, Chief Commissioner of Police in Canada. In his reply addressed to Andrew Haydon's office on May 22, 1917, Sir Percy acknowledged that

> ... Mr. Nordegg's communication ... shows a very fine feeling and a high sense of honour, which I assure you is appreciated. You may tell him,... that there is no objection at all, so far as we are concerned, to his returning to Germany.

One must wonder whether Martin had indeed considered a return to Germany. He certainly felt greatly discouraged by the waning influence he was able to exert over his affairs in Canada. Neither did the United States offer him a safe haven any longer.

Martin decided to explore the attitude of the authorities in Washington and turned to an acquaintance at the State Department, Mr. Frank Polk, who always had been well disposed towards Martin. While written in obvious sympathy, Mr. Polk's response was noncommittal:

> I beg to acknowledge receipt of your letter. I appreciate the spirit in which it was written and think you are wise to consider appearances. It is very difficult at this time to advise you as to what course you should pursue. I think in matters of this kind you had better be guided by what

would or would not give grounds for suspicion under the particular circumstances as they may arise.

Undeterred by Mr. Polk's reply, a masterpiece of diplomatic language saying nothing despite the many words used, Martin decided to submit a formal application for permission to leave the United States to the Department of Justice.

The news from Germany was terrible. The war was no longer going well. This makes Martin's seeming intention to return to Germany all the more a mystery, especially in view of his increasingly ambivalent feelings about the country of his birth.

He was very well informed about the difficult living conditions in wartime Germany, where hunger was rampant and the mood of the population, one of depression and hopelessness. Even if he would eventually be interned in the United States, his lot and well-being in that country would certainly be preferable to life under the current conditions in Germany. One cannot help but surmise that Martin had hoped that, together with his wife and daughter, he would find a way to spend the remaining years of the war in a neutral country. Passenger ships were still sailing to Rotterdam from New York. Martin had some friends in Holland, and he and his family would be safe there. Berthe-Marie voiced no objection to the idea of returning to Europe. But Marcelle confided to her father that she wished she could stay in Atlantic City, where she had a gentleman friend.

Martin composed a lengthy submission to the Attorney General in Washington, presenting himself as a man who had demonstrated his loyalty to Canada as well as to the United States. Even though classified as an enemy alien now, his activities (enumerated by Martin in detail) over the past ten years, which had been of considerable benefit to both countries, should assure the government of his trustworthiness.

> My relations with numerous officers of the Canadian Government and their friendly attitude towards me and confidence in me, has been shown throughout the period of the war by numerous letters which I hold, relating in part to a proposal at one time made by me that I should be permitted to proceed to Germany; in part to my continuing as a director of the Brazeau Collieries, Limited, above referred to, which permission was expressly granted in April, 1917, by the Canadian Secretary of State; and in relation to my personal safety in travelling, and as to other matters, all of which letters I am prepared to submit to the proper authorities for inspection, if desired....

Martin also stressed the fact that he would never be a threat as a German soldier fighting against the United States

... being forty-eight years of age, and having suffered a compound fracture of my right arm, which resulted in my being dismissed in 1894
from any military service, I am wholly incapacitated for any military
service....

Martin also enlisted Berthe-Marie's origin in his cause:

My wife is a French woman, and desires to go, with my daughter, immediately to Holland, where I will leave them in case the application
above referred is granted.

The response from the Justice Department throws some light on
Martin's reputation at that time. His connections with German embassy personnel and with bankers and industrialists in Germany
during the previous months must have given him a higher profile
than actually warranted. Although Martin attempted to strengthen his
case by the inclusion of letters of support he had received from
Canada and from Great Britain, the curt letter of the Justice
Department leaves no doubt that Martin was considered a person of
potential danger to the interests of the United States:

... your application made to the Attorney General to leave the United
States and go to Germany has been denied.

There was still another possibility, Martin thought. He submitted
another application for permission to leave the United States, this
time for Canada. But within one week, he was advised by the
Department of Justice on June 6, that

... relative to your application for permission to leave the United States
and go to Canada ... the Attorney General advises that the Department
of Justice does not deem it wise to permit you to leave the United
States.

Martin could only conclude that he remained under severe suspicion. He had to accept that for the duration of the war he was
trapped in a hostile country. Perhaps there were other persons of ill
will who were trying to harm him? Martin's question was justified.
He never saw the letter that had been forwarded by the American
consul in Toronto to the Secretary of State in Washington:

I have the honour to inform you that Mr. H. E. Redman of the law
firm of Mulock, Milliken, Clark & Redman in Toronto...informed me
that prior to the outbreak of the war Mr. Nordegg claimed to represent
Imperial German interests in Canada and was quite active in several
companies in Canada.
    Mr. Redman is of the opinion that Nordegg is a man that it would
be well to keep under surveillance.

Martin would have been especially hurt, as one of Mr. Redman's partners was the son of Sir William Mulock, once a good friend of Martin. The day Germany entered the war, William Mulock let Martin know that he would never speak to him again, a promise that Sir William kept throughout two wars and the interwar years until his death in 1944.

Whether it was Mr. Redman's letter or Martin's unwise attempts to gain permission to leave the country, Martin no longer enjoyed an image of relative trustworthiness and cooperation with the authorities. Captain Burke ordered Martin to appear at his office to advise him that as of the following day he would have to restrict his movements to Atlantic City and report to the local police on a daily basis. A return to New York would only be possible with Captain Burke's explicit permission.

In his temporary exile in Atlantic City, Martin was, for once, in a more depressed mood than his wife. He realized the damage his banishment from New York would do to his position with the Brazeau Collieries. Too much had already been happening in Toronto and even in Nordegg that caused Martin enormous worry. He had every reason to fear that his town and his mine would slip out of his hands. What concerned Martin most were the constant rumours that the name of the town and of the post office were to be changed.

There was nothing else to do than appeal to people whose loyalty Martin was still quite sure of. Persistent inquiries and numerous letters produced some results. R. B. Bennett, the future prime minister, assured Martin in a letter dated September 27, 1916

> ... that every reasonable effort will be made to see what can be done on your behalf.... I note they are trying to change the name of Nordegg Post Office and you do not wish it done. I will do what I can to see that your wishes are met....

On September 22, 1916, the vice president of the Canadian Northern, D.B. Hanna, wrote to Atlantic City that

> I do not know of anyone who would take such action, and in fact your letter is the first intimation to me of same.
> We expect Mr. Ormsby back the first of next week from the West, and I will discuss the matter with him with a view of confirming the President's previous action on the matter....

The reference to Sir William Mackenzie in this letter is significant. Repeatedly throughout his memoirs, Martin referred to his indebtedness to Sir William for loyally protecting his interests. This might not have extended to protecting Martin's financial interests and his influence and position with Brazeau Collieries as much as

Martin had hoped. But preserve Martin's legacy on the town of Nordegg Sir William certainly did. On May 23, 1916, R.B. Ormsby, Secretary Treasurer of the Brazeau Collieries had already advised Martin that

> Sir William Mackenzie has instructed that any proceedings with regard to the change of name of Nordegg are to be stopped. I know you will be glad to hear this....

And in October of the same year, Ormsby sent another reassuring letter to Atlantic City. That Ormsby had been frank with him, Martin learned from a letter Ormsby had written to Stuart Kidd on September 26. Stuart had greatly relieved Martin's concern by sending him a copy of this letter in which Ormsby confirmed that

> ... there was some talk of having the name changed but Sir William Mackenzie, President of this Company, gave instructions to the contrary...
>
> I presume the recent letter you refer to is one from the Post Office Inspector at Edmonton, and that the petition is a petition to oppose the change of name. As soon as the petition has been signed by a number of people I suppose you will send it to the Post Office Inspector. If you do this you might tell him that you have been advised that although there was some talk of having the name changed you understand that the change of name is not now desired. I am writing other officials of the Railway Company on the subject....

Martin was grateful that he still had friends in Nordegg, foremost Stuart Kidd. Stuart had started the petition that stopped the proposed change of name of the Nordegg Post Office. But unexpectedly, attempts were made from another direction, telling Martin unmistakably that powerful enemies in Toronto and in London were determined to exploit his status as enemy alien to remove him from all positions of influence with Brazeau Collieries and destroy all assets of the German Development Company. Martin would have been realistic enough to accept a temporary seizure of the assets of his German Development Company by the Canadian government for the duration of the war. But what alarmed him most was a scheme concerning certain Brazeau bonds pursued by Lazard Brothers.

T.D. Regehr summarizes the content of documents held in the Legal Department of the Canadian National Railways relating to a bill before the Canadian Parliament:

> When war broke out in 1914 approximately half of the bonds had been actually paid for.... When war broke out only Wassermann [Germany] and José Allard [Belgium] interests were deemed to be enemy interests....

Lazard Bros. wanted this bond issue cancelled because the bonds had been held in a Belgian bank at the outbreak of the war and there was some danger that they might be improperly transferred or issued by the occupying German forces. The correspondence in the Canadian National Railways Legal Department files and the parliamentary records all indicate that Lazard Bros., rather than Mackenzie, Mann & Co., were the prime movers behind this bill.

The bill was not passed, but

The capital stock of the German Development Company and the shares held by this company were taken over by the Canadian government in 1918 to ensure that none of its assets would be used to the advantage of the enemy.

Martin was not ready to give up. In a letter to Stuart in January 1917, he raised the possibility of opening a mine in Harlech, the last railway stop before Nordegg. He asked Dutchie to determine the extent and quality of the coal seams around Harlech and proceed with staking if his explorations turned out to be promising. What was going to happen during the next few years was most intriguing, as it demonstrated the resurgence of Martin's indomitable spirit, even at the time of his worst troubles with the Brazeau Collieries head office. Despite the handicap of the great distance that separated him from Alberta, Martin proceeded rather successfully, thanks to the reliable work carried out by his two friends, Stuart and Dutchie.

A detailed letter of several pages from Stuart Kidd to Martin gives a picture of the surprisingly advanced planning for the mine and town at Harlech. Stuart's letter of January 2, 1918 also reports on the 'flu epidemic, which had taken 29 lives in Nordegg.

I have been at home nursing my family ... as they were all down with the Flu.

James McKelvie came in to see the sick and he and Dutch and I went down to see the mine to-day. McKelvie was very favourably impressed.... He is at present manager of the Premier Mine Drumheller and is doing very well.... I am confident he could make a success as manager here....

Of course as you know we are both almost absolutely ignorant in regard to shares and stocks and we look to you for a fair deal as that is and has been your life work....

I think Dutch should be retained to supervise prospect work as well as to have a seat in the Directorate. As to my opening a store there in the interests of the new Company I should certainly like to open one....

The first thing to be built is a boarding house for the construction crew to be used later for miners.... The townsite is a nice one.... We should build several rather good cottages something like the five roomed ones here as it is good policy to get in several good contented families as a nucleus of a good crew of men.... The houses should be farther apart than here to give more garden room as the climate is better there than here....

I would say that Dutch put in a lot of hard work on his prospecting and that he has studied and developed into a very intelligent prospector and I am sure he will prove a valuable man to the new company in that and in many other capacities....

As you can imagine I have been too worried to give business much attention lately and these rambling remarks are all I can think of now. I only wish I could talk to you two hours.

Yours faithfully,
Stuart.

A new vision arose in Martin's mind. Harlech, named after the ancient Welsh capital of Merionethshire, would become another model town, by necessity smaller than Nordegg, but more beautiful. After a depressing summer, planning work on the Harlech mine had put a fresh purpose in Martin's life.

One day I had a great joy ... a brief visit from Andrew Haydon.

Andy had obtained a permit for Martin to come to New York. But on the following day, Martin was ordered to return to Atlantic City immediately.

The summer dragged on and ... I refrained from making any acquaintances in Atlantic City. At last the autumn came, and I was anxious to return to New York. I wrote to Captain Burke for permission and received it with instructions to report to him immediately upon arrival. He instructed me in regard to my movements in the City which were very much restricted and forbade me to approach the waterfront; I had also to call at the police station of my district and had an alien enemy card issued and my fingerprints taken. My former circle of friends had become very small indeed; most Germans had been interned and the Americans did not seem very anxious to be associated with an alien enemy....

If in his memoirs Martin claimed to have been lonely and unhappy in Atlantic City, he was not entirely truthful; but he did suffer under the unhappiness of Berthe-Marie, who led a life of near seclusion. She had not made a single friend or acquaintance and rarely agreed to accompany Martin on his daily walks. There was only one emotion they both shared, the joy of seeing their daughter so happy and exuberant. Marcelle had fallen in love with Arthur Glover May, a young American who was spending a long vacation with his parents in Atlantic City. Arthur's parents, Louis and Susan May, had come to New York from Alabama, where Arthur had been born in 1891 near Birmingham. Louis May, a well-to-do stockbroker, had divorced his wife in 1914. Arthur, a bookkeeper for the Standard Oil Company, had recently been stationed in Shanghai, but had returned to the United States for a three-month visit. For both Arthur and Marcelle, the relationship must have been love at first sight.

After a brief courtship of less than two months, Arthur asked Marcelle to follow him to Shanghai where they would get married. Perhaps Marcelle wanted to escape the oppressive atmosphere in Atlantic City; perhaps she foresaw a happy, uncomplicated relationship in a marriage to Arthur May. She readily agreed; and after Arthur's departure at the end of February 1918, Martin started to explore the possibilities of obtaining an exit permit for Marcelle and also for Berthe-Marie who, for whatever reasons, wanted to accompany her daughter to China. We do not know what Martin's thoughts were. Being separated from Berthe-Marie once more was, perhaps, not an unpleasant thought.

Unexpectedly, the formalities required for obtaining an exit permit for Berthe-Marie and Marcelle were handled with great courtesy by the Department of Justice, the Secretary of State and the Commerce Department. Equally unexpected was Captain Burke's advice that Martin was free to return to New York City with the proviso to report daily to the police. He was required to give an account of his movements and of the names of persons with whom he had been in contact; further, he was not permitted to approach the waterfront.

The family took up residence in the Hotel Astor while Martin's friend and solicitor Herbert Brussel arranged for a hearing held on March 18, 1918, at the Southern District Court of New York, where Martin was asked to post a certified cheque for $10,000 as security. On the 23rd, the Swiss Legation in Washington, which represented the interests of Germany during the war, issued passports to Berthe-Marie and Marcelle "for travel to Shanghai." On March 27, the Department of Justice advised the Secretary of State that

... Mrs. Nordegg is a French woman by birth and is the wife of a German who now resides in this country having been refused permission to return to Germany because of indefinite suspicions concerning him. The object of the trip by Mrs. Nordegg and her daughter is the marriage of the latter to a Mr. May who represents the Standard Oil Company in China. You kindly investigated Mr. May's character and reputation, finding them excellent.

Mr. Nordegg has lodged with the United States Marshal in New York City a certified cheque for $10.000 which sum is to be forfeited in case either Mrs. or Miss Nordegg is guilty of any action injurious to the cause of the United States while abroad....

Under the circumstances and particularly in view of the substantial
security against misbehavior, this Department has the honor to advise
you that in its opinion licenses for the transportation of Mrs. and Miss
Nordegg may safely be issued....

On March 30, Martin took Berthe-Marie and Marcelle to
Pennsylvania Station in New York for their long journey to the
Pacific. In her purse, Berthe-Marie carried a copy of a letter from the
Secretary of Commerce to the effect that

This Department has granted license to transport German subjects Mrs.
Martin Nordegg and Miss Marcelle Nordegg on steamship ECUADOR
of Pacific Mail Steamship Company sailing San Francisco April 6th.
Please instruct Collector to permit departure.
(Lansing)

With tears in his eyes, Martin kissed his daughter good-bye. A
seasoned traveller since her early childhood, Marcelle was in the
happiest of moods, ready to cross yet another ocean and get married
in far away China. But that would not happen as quickly as she
wished.

Berthe-Marie and Marcelle arrived in Honolulu on April 10,
where unexpected circumstances forced them to stay at the Moana
Hotel for three months. On July 2, they were joined by Arthur May
who had travelled from Shanghai via Yokohama on the SS *Siberia
Maru*. Accompanied by Arthur, Berthe-Marie and Marcelle returned
to San Francisco on board the SS *Ventura* arriving there on July 15,
three months after their departure from San Francisco for Shanghai.
Without a valid visa and provided only with an alien identification
card issued in Honolulu, Berthe-Marie and Marcelle were held on
Angel Island Station in San Francisco Bay by the Immigration
Service of the U.S. Department of Labour.

After a hearing on July 22, the Commissioner at Angel Island
forwarded a letter to the Commissioner General of Immigration, together with a record of investigation of Berthe-Marie and Marcelle
Nordegg, describing both as "… aliens … highly intelligent and refined."

Prior to the hearing, Berthe-Marie and Marcelle were finger-
printed and photographed. The sombre faces of the two women
show the stress resulting from their unexpected delay in Hawaii and
the shock of being detained as illegal immigrants instead of being
readily readmitted to the United States. Berthe-Marie especially
looks tired, emaciated, aggrieved, and certainly much older than her
years.

Excerpts from the sworn statement given by Berthe-Marie and
Marcelle during the interrogation tell a heart-breaking story of con-

fusion, disappointment, and fear. Berthe-Marie especially must have been very distraught, as some of her statements given were incorrect, while others contradicted each other, jeopardizing her plea to be readmitted to the United States:

> ... my husband ...was Manager and Director of a coal mine in Canada and when war was declared the government took it over and since he has not been doing anything at all....
> We were going to Shanghai. The boy, Mr. May, was employed in Shanghai with the Standard Oil Company and the President of Standard Oil at New York stated that we should bring the daughter to China to marry Mr. May, as he could not get away ... we got from Washington a passport to go to Shanghai, but her father tried to secure visae of Chinese and Japanese consular representatives but found it was absolutely impossible, and therefore we proceeded to Honolulu with the idea of having her fiancé meeting us in Honolulu and returning to China.

It was Marcelle's turn to explain that

> ... if he came to Honolulu he was told by his employer that he would lose his position, and as he desired to enlist in the American Army he gave up his position, came to Honolulu and met us there and proceeded with us ... on the "Ventura" without our getting married, because I desired to wait to get to New York so that my father could be present and also as his [Arthur's] family resides in New York.
> ... (his nationality) is American; born in the United States. His mother is a cousin of Mr. Polk of the State Department.*

Confused and increasingly distressed, Berthe-Marie committed some unfortunate errors in her answers:

> Q. Mrs. Nordegg, after you arrive in New York is it presumed that you expect to take up residence with your husband and remain with him?
> A. Yes, surely.
> Q. Has your husband sufficient funds to live off of?
> A. No; we are going to live on the $2000 I have now.
> Q. Has he any other resources?
> A. No.
> Q. How does your husband feel in regard to the present world's conflict?
> A. He feels he owes all to America so long as he is in America.... he is thankful for the hospitality given to us.
> Q. And how do you feel in this matter?

---

* The relationship between Arthur's mother and Mr. Frank Lyon Polk claimed by Marcelle was not confirmed by Mr. Polk's descendants. The most interesting part in Berthe-Marie's final statement concerns her mention of Martin's brother and his two sons, none of whom Martin refers to anywhere. Only once does his brother's name Theodor Cohn appear, and that is as a witness at Martin's and Berthe-Marie's marriage in 1897 in England.

A. I feel very much in sympathy (weeping) with France, on account of being born a French woman. I have only one relative who is in the active service of Germany and he is a nephew of my husband's. I have three full brothers, and one half-brother in the French Army right at the fighting front, on the Western front. My husband has two nephews, his brother's sons, who are now in the English Army, one in Palestine and one in France. These are the sons of my husband's brother [Theodor] who has resided in England all his life....
Q. Has your husband ever made any application or effort to become a citizen of another country?
A. He wanted to be a Canadian because his business was there and then war was declared.

The case of two women with German passports [the Swiss passports had been issued for travel to Shanghai only] trying to enter the United States at that time of war must have been unique. Also unique and unfortunate was Berthe-Marie's statement as to her husband's lack of money, as the subsequent motion passed by the Board of Inquiry clearly confirms:

I have to advise you that, in view of telegraphic instructions to this office ... it is the unanimous decision of this Board that you be excluded and ordered deported as alien enemies ... and also as persons likely to become public charges....

A note appended to the report points to some confusion, perhaps even conflict between various authorities:

It is the belief of the Board that there must be some conflict of instructions.... The testimony and papers at hand would seem to indicate that all steps had been taken to entitle their admission to the main land ... yet instruction here is such that it is required that all alien enemies arriving shall be excluded as such and as persons likely to become public charges....

For the Department of Labor, which handled all immigration matters at that time, Berthe-Marie and Marcelle Nordegg were simply two persons among thousands trying to gain entry into the United States. There was no reason to accord them special treatment. The Justice Department, on the other hand, which normally did not get involved in ordinary immigration matters, treated the Nordegg ladies as a very special case. But its directive to admit the ladies to the United States was not immediately binding for the immigration officials at Angel Island.

This explains why on Berthe-Marie's file one finds a total of twelve letters or telegrams from various government departments, all of them confirming permission of entrance. Berthe-Marie also presented a letter from Martin's friend Warren R. Roberts, a Chicago lawyer, who was stationed in Washington as Lieutenant Colonel in the Quarter Master Corps of the National Army. Roberts had advised Berthe-Marie at the Moana Hotel in Honolulu that

"... she should apply to the District Attorney for permission to return to America ... and that no difficulty would arise in having permission granted...."

In two separate letters from the U.S. Attorney in Honolulu, both on file, Berthe-Marie and Marcelle were

"... granted permission to proceed from Honolulu, T.H., to New York via San Francisco on the SS *Ventura* on or about July 9, 1918."

Eventually, a letter from the Commissioner on Angel Island to Washington, dated July 22, 1918, confirms that

"The aliens are now en route to the Hotel Astor in New York City..."

What happened subsequently is shrouded in mystery. Available records do not indicate that Arthur May entered military service after his return to the United States. He likely remained in New York City, as municipal records reveal that a marriage license form was picked up by Arthur and Marcelle on December 27, 1918. But, as a notation attached to the record advises, "it was never returned." Neither could a record of a subsequent marriage in the State of New York be located.

However, some time in 1919, Marcelle did go to China and married Arthur May. The first postcard from "Marcelle Nordegg-May" was posted to Dutchie in Harlech on June 12, 1919, from the city of Tsinan. As on the earlier attempt to reach Shanghai, Berthe-Marie had accompanied Marcelle again. How long she remained in China cannot be ascertained. At any rate she never returned to the United States.

Once more, Martin took his wife and daughter to the Pennsylvania Station to see them off on their long journey to China. When would he hold Marcelle in his arms again? On her last day in New York, she had given him a portrait of herself. In gentle sepia, it shows Marcelle in a mink stole and a dark cap with a pompom in the same colour, according to the fashion of the day. Her head turned slightly sideways, Marcelle looks directly into the camera with somewhat septic, pondering eyes. Marcelle's beautiful features are striking, the expression of her face is gentle, but there is not a trace of a smile.

Did Martin have a presentiment that Berthe-Marie's departure was the beginning of the end, that they would never live together again? Martin realized how much he would miss his daughter. But the separation from his wife, he admitted to himself, would make life far less complicated for him.

Martin never left the Pennsylvania Station after waving goodbye to Berthe-Marie and Marcelle. He took the next train south to meet his lady friend, who appeared on the stage of Nixon's Apollo Theatre in Atlantic City.

VII

SONIA

On Saturday, July 28, 1917, Nixon's Apollo Theatre in Atlantic City opened with the pre-Broadway run of *The Golden Age—A Comedy of Youth* by Sidney Toler and Marion Short.

In view of the popularity of its authors, the play had received more than the usual publicity. Both had widely toured the United States and had appeared in Atlantic City several times, Marion Short also as an elocutionist, whom the *Atlantic Review* described as "charming ... and delightfully intellectual."

The premiere of *The Golden Age* was also eagerly awaited because of the appearance of Marion Abbott in the leading role, an actress of striking appearance. She had, in the words of the *New York Times*, "risen to prominence as portrayer of difficult character roles." Sharing the stage with Miss Abbott was the young Helen Hayes.

In 1917, Martin's mind was preoccupied with the unsettling news he was receiving from Toronto and from Nordegg. He was in no mood to go to the theatre and enjoy a comedy when Marcelle begged him to take her to the premiere of *The Golden Age*. Only after much urging did he agree to take Berthe-Marie and Marcelle to the Apollo Theatre. He paid no attention to the names prominently displayed on the brightly illuminated marquee.

During the intermission, a curious Martin remained in his seat to search the program for the name of the actress who played the part of Felice. Martin had been fascinated at first sight by her compelling stage presence. She was a woman of small stature with graceful movements. He was captivated by her dark, expressive eyes and her husky voice which, despite perfect diction, carried an attractive Eastern European accent. According to the program, Felice's part was played by Sonia Marcelle. What an incredible coincidence that the actress who had enthralled Martin so quickly carried the first name of his daughter. This must be a good omen, Martin decided, already intent on meeting Sonia Marcelle. For the rest of the evening, all night, and the following day, Martin could not banish the image of Sonia Marcelle from his mind. He decided he must meet her as quickly and often as possible before the play would take her back to New York at the end of the following week. For the rest of his life, Martin would cherish the memory of the evening when, without enthusiasm, he had gone to the theatre and discovered the woman destined to become his partner in life.

Berthe-Marie did not find anything out of the ordinary when Martin left her alone the next evening. Often feeling unwell, she resented Martin's abundant energy and perpetual restlessness. She usually declined his invitations for walks along the Boardwalk or the occasional brief sailing or fishing expedition. She never enjoyed going out, even in the early evening. She had come to accept Martin's habit of going out at night without her and never questioned him the next morning. Berthe-Marie did not suspect anything when Martin left the house after an early supper the day after their visit to the Apollo Theatre.

Martin could hardly anticipate that he was about to enter into a rapidly unfolding relationship that would raise new barriers between himself and his wife—barriers of pain and guilt about secrecy and deceit.

Martin had left his card and a bouquet of roses at the stage door. Without his wife and daughter sitting next to him, he was even more smitten with Sonia Marcelle than the night before. When he was admitted to Sonia's dressing room after the performance, he immediately felt a strong attraction to this beautiful woman's personality. He sensed a warmth and empathy that he had not experienced for many years. Sonia graciously accepted his invitation to a small after-theatre supper. Martin felt that she liked him and was attracted to him.

They sat together until the restaurant closed, telling each other about their lives. Time had run out far too soon, and they decided to see each other the next evening. They met day after day, until Sonia's engagement in Atlantic City ended after the weekend. Martin attended Sonia's performances every night; they met for walks; and one sunny, breezy day, they went out to sea for a brief fishing expedition. On the boat, Martin took his first pictures of Sonia.

Martin missed Sonia terribly and cursed the Secret Service for barring him from visiting New York. His mood restive and unsettled, he rented a horse and accompanied Marcelle on her daily rides. At home, he felt on edge in Berthe-Marie's presence. It is not certain whether Martin was able to hide his excitement and his compulsive preoccupation with Sonia. Berthe-Marie never asked a single question, but her physical and emotional health took a sudden turn for the worse.

Sonia was born on July 15, 1890, in the Russian city of Vilna as the youngest child of Isaac Meisel and his wife Rachel née Apator. All four Meisel children were given Biblical first names; Sonia's was Schefre or Schifra. Her two older brothers dropped their

Hebrew first names in favour of Harry and Louis after their arrival in the United States. Similarly, Sonia's sister Alte, the third oldest of the four Meisel children, changed her first name to Anna. Her younger sister, Schifra, eventually chose Sonia for herself, after being called Sophie by her parents as long as she lived in their household on New York's Lower East Side.

The Meisel family belonged to the middle class of Vilna's Jewish community. Isaac Meisel, who was born in 1855, was a well-respected optometrist, popular in the city's Jewish quarter. Like the majority of Vilna's Jews, the Meisels lived the life of a pious Orthodox family. This did not, however, exclude the children from receiving a secular education. The boys were enrolled at a trade school, while the two girls were sent to high school.

The vast majority of the Jewish population of the Russian Empire lived in the "Pale of Settlement," the area extending southwards from Lithuania through Poland and parts of White Russia to the western half of the Ukraine. This was the westernmost part of Russia to which, with few exceptions, the Jews of the Empire were relegated. It was the era of the Eastern European "shtetl," the Jewish ghetto, where especially in the smaller towns and villages, most Jewish families lived in often abject poverty. Only in the bigger cities such as Vilna, Warsaw, and Odessa would one find a larger Jewish middle class.

Whether poor or wealthy, though, education—first of all in the Jewish faith and later in languages, arts, sciences or trades—was foremost in the minds of most Jewish parents. Even the smallest and poorest of shtetls had not only their synagogue but also their cheders, where boys started their religious instruction years before their entry into regular school. Imbued at such an early age with the habit and discipline of learning, of acquiring knowledge and applying it, a high percentage of Jewish boys would do extraordinarily well away from the shtetls later in life in scientific, literary and artistic achievements.

Millions would emigrate to the West—to Austrian Poland with its more liberal and tolerant attitudes towards Jews, to Germany, France, England, and foremost to the United States, the promised land of freedom and opportunity. Most arrived in the New World in deepest poverty, but they worked hard, sacrificing everything for the sake of giving their children the best education. There were also those who had lived in comparative comfort in Russia but were determined to escape oppression, recurring pogroms, and the lack of educational and professional opportunities for citizens of Jewish descent.

The clan to which the Meisels and their relatives—the Tokars, Schafers, Krasners, Robinsons—belonged was representative of thousands of Jewish families who blossomed after their departure from Eastern Europe. The family tree drawn up by Sonia's nephew Leon Gamsa is witness to the unfolding of talent, showing scientists, physicians, artists, and musicians in great numbers. Leon Gamsa's godmother, Sonia's cousin, Sonia Tokar, became the personal physician to the female members of the royal family of Iraq. Several relatives who chose to remain in Russia were also successful. Maxim Robinson built up the largest chocolate and biscuit factory of the Empire, which he relocated to France after the Bolshevik Revolution of 1917. Aaron Schafer became a successful farmer on a large tract of land leased from a well-known Russian count.

This splendid family tree also includes a large number of tragic entries. When Stalin and Hitler divided Eastern Europe between them in 1939 and Soviet troops occupied Vilna and Grodno, several members of the family were deported and perished in Siberia. Some died during World War II, fighting as soldiers of the Red Army. Those who survived the Soviet occupation between 1939 and 1941 became the victims of Hitler, killed in the ghettos of Vilna and Grodno or taken to their death in the concentration camps of Treblinka and Auschwitz.

What was the city like in which Sonia spent her childhood and adolescence? Once an insignificant pagan settlement, Vilna only assumed importance with the building of a strong castle by one of the Lithuanian Grand Princes in the early fourteenth century. Its subsequent history was one of wars, sieges, occupations, and recurrent pillage and destruction. Over the centuries, Teutonic Knights, Tartars, Russians, Lithuanians, Swedes, Poles and Cossacks battled for its control. In 1794, Vilna was taken by the armies of the Czar. For more than a century, Vilna was a Russian city, although its citizens were predominantly Lithuanian, Polish, and Jewish. Indeed, by the end of the nineteenth century, its large Jewish community constituted 42 percent of Vilna's total population; and the city grew into one of the most important Jewish religious and commercial centres in the Russian Empire.

After World War I, Vilna never regained the level of prosperity it had gradually achieved during the relatively long peacetime that had ended with the occupation by German troops in 1915. The city was captured by Bolshevik troops soon after the end of the war, only to be taken within weeks by the army of the newly created Polish Republic. Although the Bolsheviks returned once more, they had to abandon the entire area after the creation of Lithuania, which declared Vilna the capital of the young republic. But in August 1920, the city was retaken by Polish armies and remained Polish until Hitler destroyed the Polish Republic in September 1939.

After Hitler and Stalin divided Eastern Europe, Vilna was turned over by the Soviet Union to Lithuania, which promptly moved its "temporary" capital of Kaunas to Vilna, now called Vilnius. Within a year, however, Stalin declared Lithuania a Soviet Republic and incorporated the country into the Soviet Union. A wave of deportations swept through the city, which were followed by the persecution of Vilna's Jewish community when German troops occupied the city in the summer of 1941 after Hitler's invasion of the Soviet Union. The entire Jewish population was herded into the old ghetto, where overcrowding, starvation, fear, persecution, and killings reined until the mass deportations to the extermination camps began. When Soviet troops recaptured Vilna on July 13, 1944, there were no Jews left in the city.

Despite its horrendous history of wars, destruction and persecution, Vilna (Wilno in Polish or Vilnius in Lithuanian as the city was called at different times) was a remarkably beautiful city. It was a major seat of the Roman Catholic, the Greek Orthodox, and the Jewish religions; all erected their impressive cathedrals and synagogues, giving the older part of the city its distinct appearance. Towards the end of the nineteenth century, Vilna had a flourishing university and other seats of higher learning. The old Jewish ghetto, although poor and decrepit, was still full of life. Increasing commerce and industrialization created large new districts, not only quarters of monotonous, overcrowded workers flats but also quarters of tree-lined streets and squares with architecturally pleasing apartment buildings for the well-to-do and middle-class citizens of Russian, Polish, Lithuanian, German, and Jewish descent. Isaac Meisel was prosperous enough to afford a flat in this part of town, the neighbourhood that Sonia, her sister and her brothers remembered from their youth.

When it came to the welfare of his family, Isaac Meisel set his sights high. He succeeded in moving his wife and children out of the ghetto to another part of town. There he quickly acquired a more prosperous clientele for his optometrist practice, which also included a number of non-Jewish patients. But this did not yet satisfy his hopes and aspirations. In 1902, at the age of 47, Isaac Meisel decided to emigrate to the United States. In May 1903, he left Vilna with his two sons for New York. As soon as he had established himself in the New World, he would send for his wife and daughters.

It did not take Isaac Meisel too long to acquire a license to practice as an optometrist and open an office on the main floor of

125 Forsyth Street on the Lower East Side. He was by no means the only optometrist in the neighbourhood, but Isaac was surprised how quickly he managed to acquire a clientele. Many of them were women and children complaining of eye strain from working long hours into the night on piece work taken home from clothing manufacturers. Besides, when word spread quickly that a new optometrist from Vilna had set up his practice, numerous recent arrivals from Isaac's home town brought their business to his office. Quite a few of them were still too poor to pay cash; but fortunately, Isaac's services were also sought by an increasing number of well-to-do patients. At the beginning of 1904, Isaac felt secure enough to rent one of the large flats on the second floor of 125 Forsyth. He was ready to call his family from Russia.

Isaac booked passage for Rachel and the girls for the month of August 1904 and with the tickets enclosed his recent photograph in the letter to his wife. The only surviving picture, it probably represents Isaac Meisel at his best, when he had achieved his goal of securing a better life for his family in the New World. Isaac looks modest, but proud, secure, and satisfied with himself and at peace with God and the world.

As an orthodox Jew, Isaac wears a cap; he is dressed in a dark-gray striped coat of obviously expensive cloth, a white shirt, and a dark tie. His already white beard is well groomed and trimmed. For a man of 49 years, his face looks surprisingly smooth, without a single line or crease. Accentuated by the small, wire-rimmed glasses, his eyes have a kind, warm expression. They dominate Isaac's face and, like his slightly prominent lower lip, show from whom Sonia inherited her facial characteristics.

On August 4, 1904, Rachel Meisel closed the door of the family's flat in Vilna for the last time in her life. Most of the furniture had already been sold. What was left was given to the Jewish Benevolent Society of Vilna for distribution to the poor. With tears in her eyes, Rachel sat in the carriage taking them to the Vilna Central Station. Would she ever see her home town again and the relatives who remained behind? Sonia and Anna, though, were filled with happy excitement, very different from their mother's ambivalent feelings. Their minds were filled with the descriptions of the wondrous life of New York that their brothers had enclosed in the letters Isaac had sent to his wife in Vilna.

Rachel and her two daughters took the train to Warsaw where they stayed with Rachel's cousin for a few days. From that time, the earliest photograph of Sonia and her sister Anna survives, a quite exceptional picture in its composition and technical quality. No wonder, for Rachel had taken her daughters to the most renowned photographer of Warsaw, Jan Mieczkowscz, whose studio was located at One Miodowa Street, next to the row of opulent palaces at the edge of Warsaw's Old Town. Mieczkowscz had been awarded the diploma of Russian Imperial Court Photographer and many medals.

The likeness of the features of the two girls is striking—the almond-shaped eyes, the slightly pronounced cheek bones, the straight but prominent nose, and the quite determined expression of the mouth. While Anna's hair is draped around her face, Sonia's is piled high on her head, hair stylings which, except for minor variations according to fashion of the day, either sister would retain all her life.

Accentuated by their dark dresses, both Sonia and Anna look astonishingly mature for their age—Sonia had just turned 14, while Anna was older by one year. In unintended symbolism, Sonia, who would always be the more intellectual, artistic, and worldly of the two, is holding a newspaper.

On August 20, 1904, Rachel and her daughters boarded the SS *Rotterdam* in Rotterdam. With the ocean being calm during the entire journey, the crossing to New York was very pleasant. While the majority of the passengers, poor emigrants from Russia, were confined to the crowded steerage, the Meisel women enjoyed a comfortable cabin and the freedom of the spacious upper decks. Sonia later remembered the excitement of being able to try out her still rudimentary English with the other passengers and of being admired for speaking German and French so well.

On September 1, 1904, on Ellis Island, Isaac took his wife and his daughters in his arms. During the ferry ride, Isaac pointed out the tall buildings at the southern tip of Manhattan, a sight already familiar to Rachel, Sonia, and Anna from the pictures he had sent them. A horse-drawn cab took them through Wall Street, jammed with carriages and men in business suits, before entering the dramatically different world of the Lower East Side. This was a world that at once seemed overwhelming and confusing to the three women, although strangely comforting. The teeming street life reminded them of their home town, even though they had never seen such immense crowds in the narrow alleys of the Vilan ghetto. Always surrounded by throngs of people, the cab made only slow progress; and by the time it reached 125 Forsyth Street, Sonia had realized that everybody without exception spoke Yiddish, although not always the way it was spoken in Vilna. Overwhelmed by the noise of the crowd, she momentarily closed her eyes. It was not hard to imagine being at home again. Where would she be able to learn proper English?

The people of the Lower East Side—their language, their garb, their daily life of trading and talking on the streets—gave Sonia a sense of being at home. But the tall buildings they filled, many of them to the point of total overcrowding, were very different from the Vilna Ghetto.

The large number of synagogues was striking. In every street, one could easily find several Jewish houses of prayer. The vast majority of the residents of the Lower East Side were referred to as "Russian Jews" and nearly all of them adhered to the orthodox way of their religion. It was not surprising that before World War I there were as many as 500 synagogues in the Lower East Side, ranging from large, impressive buildings to hundreds of tiny prayer rooms. Forsyth Street alone accommodated 17 synagogues along its 8-block length, including a tiny prayer room at 123 Forsyth and a large three-story synagogue at 126 Forsyth, across the street from the Meisel residence.

As Sonia soon learned, the Meisel flat at 125 Forsyth belonged to the small group of large flats with above-average comforts. But according to the census, the building still contained 18 flats on five floors, accommodating 74 persons. There seemed to be a constant coming and going, as overcrowded flats accommodating large families admitted additional newcomers, brothers, sisters, cousins, nephews and nieces, or friends. The numbers of "newcomers" arriving remained incredibly high, in some years swelling to 90,000 people, until the Jewish population of the Lower East Side would reach 600,000 around 1910.

No wonder the streets were teeming with life, with horse-drawn wagons, with peddlers' pushcarts, with sidewalks filled with people rushing about or standing in groups talking, while others were sitting on the front steps of their houses trying to catch some fresh air. Beneath the vitality and exuberance, however, an undercurrent of suspicion and anger could be detected. It was directed against greedy landlords, unscrupulous owners of sweatshops, and even against the city departments of health and education and their well-intentioned attempts to deal with the dangers of disease in the over-crowded tenement district.

Last but not least, among the "Russian Jews," there was often a sense of being offended by the benevolence of the "Uptown Jews," primarily the prosperous, assimilated German and British Jews who had arrived in New York a few generations before. They were said to be embarrassed by the poverty and seeming backwardness of the Jewish newcomers from Eastern Europe.

There were frequent rent strikes against slum landlords, who charged enormous rents while neglecting the most basic upkeep of the tenements they owned. The exploitation of men and women in factories and sweatshops, including the work taken home, was notorious. With newcomers desperately seeking work, which was always in short supply, wages were often cut, even for children's work, which was a pittance to begin with. When a local box factory reduced wages paid to children and adolescents by 10 percent, a "children's strike" was the result, which was readily supported by the protesting parents.

Nor were the public authorities always spared from becoming the target of the enraged population of the Lower East Side. The year 1906 became the year of the famous—or infamous—"adenoid strikes." Periodic vaccinations of all school children had already raised the suspicion of their parents, who quite willingly entrusted their offspring to the educational system, but they were incensed at the public health officials and nurses invading the public schools.

When routine examinations established a prevalence of enlarged adenoids in many children, school principals sent letters to the parents, advising that their children would have their adenoids removed at no cost. Unable to read English, many parents feared the worst, and a mood of near paranoia resulted in rumors of children having their throats slashed. All of a sudden, the mistrust of authority and the fear of its omnipotence, which had lain dormant since the departure from Russia, broke to the surface again. As much as parents valued the education of their children, they refused to send their children to school until the adenoid measures were called off.

Nevertheless, despite mistakes committed by eager public officials and well-meaning reformers who entered the ghetto full of fervent idealism, remarkable opportunities were created for tens of thousands of poor immigrants and their children as well. Starting with Lilian Wald's Henry Street Settlement in 1893, other settlement houses sprang up where the early social workers and volunteers helped newcomers of all ages acquire the skills that would open the doors for them out of the ghetto of the Lower East Side. Not only were survival skills such as language taught but time was devoted to literature, arts, music, and theatre. This liberal education no doubt contributed to the explosion of talent among the young of the Lower East Side; and many would soon become composers of popular music, the stars on Broadway, and the directors in Hollywood.

A towering figure among the Lower East Side reformers was Miss Julia Richman. Having been raised at Central Park West, she did not seek the fulfilment of her career in this well-to-do neighbourhood, but chose to dedicate her life to the children of the Lower East Side. One can assume that Miss Julia Richman also affected the future lives of Anna and Sonia Meisel in a most decisive way.

Of strong-willed character, Julia Richman had become a teacher against the wishes of her parents. Gifted and dynamic and possessed with a great deal of self assurance, Julia Richman had risen quickly through the New York Public School System to become its first woman principal, its youngest principal, and its only Jewish principal. Appointed district superintendent of schools in 1903, she chose the Lower East Side as the area of her major concern, immediately attacking the problems as she saw them with verve and incredible energy.

Twenty-three thousand Jewish children came under the tutelage of this powerful, dedicated woman who, with missionary zeal, decided to make these kids into "good Americans." In the process, Julia Richman changed from the proverbial "uptown do-gooder" into a well-organized administrator. While she never became "folksy" in her approach, she learned to understand the mentality of the ghetto inhabitants, their fears, and their aspirations. Above all, she was completely convinced that she always knew exactly what the thousands of her pupils needed, which, in retrospect, explains why her pronouncements always sounded so absolutely dictatorial. But as the future would show, Julia Richman was nearly always right, with her constant stress on the teaching and use of proper English, of perfect manners, of healthy outdoor activities, and numerous other items that she knew the children lacked in the deprived environment of the Lower East Side.

What Julia Richman introduced into the schools under her jurisdiction and continually monitored in person was the subject of endless, not always kind, anecdotes. While the school children alternately feared Miss Richman or ridiculed her behind her back, many of them would in later life freely admit that without Julia Richman's merciless preparation their adult life outside the ghetto would have never have been successful.

Typically, the girls of the Lower East Side schools rather than the male students seemed more amenable to Miss Richman's efforts. Although attending Miss Richman's schools for only a few years in the upper grades, Sonia and Anna were among those who obviously benefited from her progressive approach of educating children. Indeed, Anna seemed to follow directly in Miss Richman's footsteps!

Against much criticism from outside the ghetto and prejudice within the ghetto, Miss Richman had introduced free eye examinations and, if required, the provision of free eyeglasses to the children of her school district. True enough, it is possible that, as an optometrist, Isaac had inspired Anna to become an optometrist. But perhaps it was more than coincidence that Anna would eventually be in charge of eye examinations of all school children of the city of Newark and responsible for a program that Julia Richman had pioneered during Anna's school days on the Lower East Side.

Sonia was similarly affected by Julia Richman's educational aims. Nothing else received as much of Miss Richman's attention as the teaching of proper English, which she considered the primary prerequisite for a successful entry into the wider society outside the Lower East Side ghetto. Miss Richman exhorted her teachers not only to concentrate on vocabulary, grammar, and spelling but also on intensive coaching in correct pronunciation and diction, without which the ghetto inhabitants would never be able to shed the aura of the Lower East Side. Granted, Sonia never managed to erase completely the last touch of a foreign accent. But, without the benefits of three years of intensive tutelage by Julia Richman's teachers, would she have succeeded in her career as an actress?

Sonia must have been a delightful student to have in an English language class. Obviously, she had a gift for languages; she already spoke Russian, Polish and Yiddish fluently and was quite proficient in German and even more so in French. As Sonia later related to her nephew Hyman, her teachers were impressed with her rapid progress in English; they soon gave her books to read that were far above her grade level and also supported her interest in drama and theatre. Before she graduated from high school, Sonia was already on stage in several school plays. "At that time," she told Hyman, "I fell in love with the theatre and decided to become an actress."

Isaac and Rachel Meisel considered Sonia's love for the theatre simply a passing infatuation. They had not taken into account Sonia's drama teacher, who had encouraged Sonia to attend additional drama classes at the Educational Alliance, a Lower East Side institution that had grown from a small settlement house into a huge five-story building that offered numerous courses and activities in English, art, music, etc., to the gifted poor of the Lower East Side. The starting point for the careers of numerous famous actors, musicians and artists, the Educational Alliance also played a crucial part in the development of Sonia's acting career.

But life on the stage was not yet quite within reach. Isaac Meisel had already decided the further education of his daughters. His two sons were already working in the trades. There were opportunities for young men to earn a decent living and raise a family in the blue collar world. But without appropriate education, the options for Jewish girls were much more limited. The sweatshops, domestic work, or perhaps at best sales work in a store became their choices. Even secretarial work required attendance at a business school. Isaac Meisel, who had always felt he belonged to the middle class, was grateful that he could afford to pay for the continuing education of his daughters. His choice was the New York City College.

When Anna graduated from high school in 1907, New York City College already had a long-established reputation for providing the education young Jewish men and women needed to enter the mainstream of American society. This had not been the original intention of the founders of City College; but in 1903, 75 percent of its students were of Jewish descent, nearly all of them residents of the Lower East Side. And when Sonia graduated from New York City College in 1910, more than 90 of its 112 graduates were Jewish.

Sonia had entered the City College in 1908, one year after her sister Anna. Sonia took business classes according to her father's wishes, but concentrated mostly on English and French literature and language courses. After her graduation, she gently explained to her parents that, as an obedient daughter, she had faithfully completed her business training; but her future would not lie in commerce but on the theatre stage.

After Anna's decision to enter her father's profession, Sonia's choice of acting as a lifetime career came as a terrible blow for Isaac and Rachel. According to the Old World view, they both considered work at a theatre a rather disreputable occupation. This opinion was still prevalent among the older generation of the Lower East Side, although the Yiddish theatre had been flourishing there for years. For Sonia, it became the entrance to the world of professional acting. Without her parents' knowledge, Sonia had already spent much of her free time at Jacob Adler's famous Yiddish theatre, where Jacob and Sarah Adler soon began to take an interest in the young woman.

Upon his wife's insistence, Jacob Adler gave Sonia a start in minor roles. It was rather quickly established that in Sonia the Adlers had discovered a stage personality with the talent to succeed outside the Yiddish theatre of New York. They gave her increasingly more prominent parts in order to foster her self-assurance; and, rather confidently, they pushed Sonia onto the English stage. But they did so with much thought and empathy. Upon their suggestion, Sophie Meisel became Sophie Massel for her first appearance on the stage of the Forrest Theatre in Philadelphia as Elsa in *Hans the Flute Player—A Comic Opera in Three Acts*, taking place "in the rich capital of an imaginary country between Holland and Flanders."

Nothing is known about Sonia's acting career for the next few years. *Hans,* a short-lived, but popular play, did not bring Sonia any fame. But after the end of her Philadelphia engagement in

December 1910, her first step out of the Lower East Side, Sonia managed to land enough (though usually inconsequential) parts, which gave her confidence to move out of her parents' home on Forsyth Street into a tiny apartment on 23rd Street near Broadway.

By the summer of 1914, Sonia took aim at a career on the silent screen. An impressive portfolio was created by the theatre photographer F. Brunel, who presented Sonia Massel and the wide spectrum of her acting talent: the innocent young woman, the peasant girl, the mother, the nun, Ophelia, the Indian maiden, the Spanish gypsy, the young emancipated woman in shirt and tie, the cool intellectual, the Arab woman brandishing a knife—all characters in various poses—and, finally, the vamp, which landed Sonia her first part in the movies.

Placed in the portfolio, but originally not part of it was a mysterious picture of Sonia in a nurse's uniform, receiving a decoration from a French general in the presence of other officers and ordinary soldiers in the background. This picture looks so incredibly authentic that one cannot imagine it being part of a silent picture done in New York or Hollywood. But there is no record of Sonia ever having been sent to the European theatre of war. Some of her relatives, however, maintain that during World War I Sonia did entertain the troops; but did she go to France?

Some of Sonia's correspondence has survived from the years when New York was still the seat of the major film studios. One can find the signatures of some of the great names of the silent screen—John Cort of Cort Film Corporation, Carl Laemmle and Alex Koeppel of Universal Film, Samuel Goldwyn of Goldwyn Pictures, Lewis and David Selznick—and others whose names have since been forgotten.

In April 1917, Carl Laemmle wrote to William Fox introducing "Sonia Massell, the young lady who has had considerable experience on the legitimate stage as well as in pictures.... I know she will prove a valuable acquisition to your organization."

A year earlier, Sonia's agent had referred her to Carl Laemmle as "unusually clever in pictures of the Theda Bara type."[*]

While Sonia was working for various studios over the years, her name was changed again and again according to the producers' preferences. Letters refer to Sophie Massel or Mansell, Sonia Masselle, Sophie Marcel and, finally Sonia Marcel, the name used by Sam Goldwyn, which Sonia had already changed to "Marcelle" before adopting it as her permanent, legal name.

---

[*] Theda Bara (1890-1955), a popular actress in the silent movies, famous for her roles as predatory female, the "vamp."

Sam Goldwyn had become aware of Sonia after her success in *Behind the Secret Panels*. His studio had already been moved to Hollywood when he gave Sonia her great chance in the film *Hungry Hearts*.

If Sonia was in demand as an actress on the silent screen during and after the war years, nearly all of her pictures must have been less than memorable. Archives and histories of the silent film era show Sonia Marcelle's name only once in connection with the film *Hungry Hearts*, produced by Samuel Goldwyn in 1921, directed by E. Mason Hopper and released in 1922. This film, rare for its time because of the social issues it presented, has retained its reputation to this day. It was one of a few films with a social message that was released after the war when such topics had fallen out of favour with the public. Society was entering the Jazz Age and there was no more interest in films presenting social problems.

Based on a group of short stories titled *Hungry Hearts* by the prolific Russian-Jewish author Anzia Yezierska, who grew up on the Lower East Side of New York, the film *Hungry Hearts* tells the tale of a Jewish family that leaves Russia after much persecution and lands in the squalor of the Lower East Side. Struggling for a better life, the mother angrily damages the landlord's property after another raise in the rent and is forced to stand trial. The landlord's nephew, a successful lawyer, wins the case and falls in love with the mother's beautiful daughter and subsequently takes the family out of the ghetto into a better life.

As so often occurs in Hollywood pictures, the story was somewhat romanticized and prettied up, over the loud protests of its author Yezierska. Although no copy was placed in any film archives, the film retained its fame for the graphic and moving presentation of life in the ghettos of Eastern Europe and New York. Lost for more than sixty years, a copy was discovered some years ago in a house in London after it had been burglarized. This copy made it possible to enlarge on the history of the social problem film in the silent screen era. In *Film History* (1987), Kevin Brownlow published an article "Hungry Hearts: A Hollywood Social Problem Film of the 1920's", in which Sonia is mentioned. Brownlow illustrates "...what happened when a sincere effort to produce a realistic drama was sabotaged by producers who thought they could "improve it." Exactly the same thing happens today."

Once the production of *Hungry Hearts* was launched, the studio experienced immediate casting difficulties, especially for the roles of the daughter and the mother. Numerous actresses were interviewed for the role of the mother, but some looked "Irish rather than Jewish" or definitely lacked "Jewish mannerisms." Others, like the actress Mary Alden "...could not possibly acquire Jewish manner-isms in such a short time between now and starting of the picture."

As Brownlow continues, "...with the start of the picture loom-ing, Goldwyn took Yezierska's advice and settled upon stage actress Sonia Marcel."

Sam Goldwyn called Sonia to his office on Fifth Avenue and found her charming and suited for the part. Within hours, he sent a letter addressed to "My dear Miss Marcel." On September 17, 1921, Sonia signed the contract, which was found among her papers after her death. Samuel Goldwyn offered Sonia $300 per week "... to pose, act and appear in the motion picture entitled *Hungry Hearts* ... plus transportation from New York to Culver City and back."

It tells something about the rush under which Sam Goldwyn called Sonia and prepared the contract of her engagement. His letter to her is addressed to Sonia Marcel, likely in error, but this new spelling remained with Sonia throughout her involvement in the production of *Hungry Hearts*.

Casting problems continued, culminating in the suspension of the production. The young Ethel Kaye, chosen for the role of the daughter, was dropped after shooting had begun. As Brownlow writes, "If one member of the cast is replaced, the others fear for their jobs. For this is the time to make changes; soon it will be too late. And the axe duly fell on the actress playing the mother, Sonia Marcel."

A desperate Abe Lehr, casting director, telegraphed to Sam Goldwyn the disastrous recommendation:

> We have gone along from day to day with hope that ... Sonia Marcel would give us an improved performance but in spite of everything that Hopper can do and talks that I have had with her we feel she will kill our picture if we go on... She is photographically almost impossible for this part because of hard straight mouth and hawk nose that even in slightest profile gets over hardness which makes her repellent in her sympathetic scenes.... Her personality is negative and instead of giving us simplicity of peasant Jewess she is giving us intensity of an intel-lectual woman dressed in peasant's clothes.... We are apparently doomed with definite failure if we go on.... We are faced with extra pro-duction time it takes Hopper each day to get over Marcel's scenes even passably.

What had happened to the well-regarded actress Sonia Marcelle? She was Jewish, she looked Jewish, but she was incapable of por-traying a "peasant Jewess." The "hard straight mouth," and the "negative" personality do not remind one of the Sonia as she ap-peared in the photographs of her portfolio and in other, personal photographs of that time and of later years. One might assume that

Sonia could not come to terms with her director, which would account for the exaggerated complaints from Abe Lehr.

"E. Mason Hopper would have been one of the finest directors," said his former assistant William Wellman, "but he was completely crazy.… He was a little screwy, but he had great talent."

Hopper faced criticism from Sam Goldwyn who "…complained that Hopper was inclined to be 'too realistic' in his direction of the East Side characters (in other words they were too Jewish)."

Perhaps Hopper expected Sonia Marcel to portray the character in a way she was incapable of. Sonia had impressed everyone at all times as being very refined. Not even her own life experience would help her—she had grown up as a Jewish middle-class girl. We will never know. What we do know is that *Hungry Hearts* became a memorable film.

Again, according to Brownlow, "Hopper transferred Yezierska's story … with care and dedication. And he created one of the best, albeit one of the simplest, Jewish pictures of the entire silent period."

Sonia was not to be part of this or later productions. By her own choice, she ended her career on the silent screen and returned full time to the legitimate stage, which she had never entirely left during her years as a movie actress.

A number of playbills and reviews have survived and some of them deserve mentioning, as they trace Sonia's gradual progress to well-known stages in more substantial plays, alongside popular and respected actors. In January 1917, if not before, Sonia had reached Broadway and was, for the first time included in a *New York Times* theatre review of the play *Seremonda,* a play in four acts by William Lindsay, which had opened in the Criterion with Sonia Marcelle as Clara and Julia Arthur in the title role:

> … Handsomely mounted … a respectable attempt to restore the fairly poetic drama … with the queenly Julia Arthur in the title role.… Seremonda is lavishly and tastefully mounted.… Miss Arthur plays it regally.…

No comments were made in the *New York Times* review on Sonia's performance as an actress. Only her name and the part she played were mentioned.

During the summer of 1917 came the important engagement in Atlantic City with Helen Hayes and Marion Abbott, which led to Sonia's first meeting with her future husband Martin.

1917 was also the year of the Russian Revolution, an event which temporarily redirected Sonia's acting career away from the English stage.

On October 18, Sonia appeared as the main character in the Russian play *On the Eve of the Revolution* by A. Swirski. Presented by the Society of Russian Dramatic Artists at the North Star Theatre on 5th Avenue and 106th Street, the play was not a success. Hastily written and produced, it folded within a week.

The group of actors remained together, however, and was much more successful with its next production, *War,* by the Russian playwright Artzibasheff. Travelling across the country, the troupe called itself now "The Free Russia Stock Company" with "Sophie Marcelle" as its star. A poster from its performances in the Metropolitan Theatre in Chicago in both Russian and English survived among the possessions of Sonia's cousin Emma Gamsa who last lived in England:

"The famous emotional actress Sophie Marcelle in the great Russian drama *War.* Presented by the Free Russia Stock Company, this play has produced the greatest effect all over the United States."

After the disaster of *Hungry Hearts* in Hollywood, Sonia returned to New York, where she signed a contract with the Ruby Corporation for a part in the play *Rosa Machree* by Edward E. Rose. The original contract signed by Sonia indicates that she was to be paid, for the time, a quite respectable sum of $175 per week. An appendix stated that "... if Company moves to Broadway, the above salary to be $200.00."

The *Encyclopedia of the New York Stage* characterized the play as "...a melange of comedy, melodrama and sentimentality mixing ethnic ingredients of Jews and Irishmen in a tale about Rosa (Julia Adler), daughter of a Jewish mother (Sonia Marcelle) and an Irish father (Clarence Derwent). She travels to her anti-Semitic aristocratic grandfather's castle and wins over the irascible old gent to where he is praising the mating of Hebrew and Gaelic..."

Rosa Machree opened on January 9, 1922, at the Lexington Opera House in New York. The reviews were not kind to the play. Written and produced at the height of the controversy surrounding Henry Ford's anti-Semitism, the play was announced on the billboards as "A direct answer to Henry Ford"

The play's message was that through intermarriage reconciliation and harmony between races is possible, no matter how complex the mix.

"As such, it [the play] was cordially applauded by an audience that was in no sense a Ford House," reported the *New York Evening Post*, while in a rather caustic vein criticizing the play and all its actors except "Sonia Marcelle, a Russian actress, [who] did well as the mother," even though her part was most difficult, as

... the curtain went up on a Yiddish-American mother of an Irish-English-Yiddish-American daughter, who as time went on proved to everybody's satisfaction that despite the three hyphens the Yiddish was the predominant strain.

The part of Rosa, the daughter, was played by Sonia's friend Julia Adler. As the *Evening Standard* reported,

...the play also serves to introduce Julia Adler, daughter of Jacob Adler, to the English-speaking stage. Miss Adler is pretty and had no difficulty with the leading part inasmuch as good English speaking was not necessary.

It must have deeply hurt Sonia to read the sarcastic comments on Julia Adler, whose parents had given Sonia her start in theatre. But it did not matter that much any more. *Rosa Machree* turned into a "quick flop" and never reached Broadway. What mattered much more for Sonia was the time she wanted to spend with her future husband. She declined several offers for appearances in New York, as they interfered with Martin's travels on which she now liked to accompany him. She also declined all offers to go on tour. *Rosa Machree* was Sonia's last stage appearance.

VIII

NEW CHALLENGES
NEW BEGINNINGS
1919 - 1923

"My dear Stuart, I found myself again, and I am doing big things once more!

"Doubtless you will have been surprised not to hear from me for such a long time...."

This letter, dated Hotel Pennsylvania, New York, July 5, 1919, the first communication Stuart had received from Martin in more than seven months, ended on a cheerful note:

"You and Dutchie are still near my heart. ...Goodby, boys, I will yet camp with you at Harlech!"

Only years later, when Martin eventually did "camp at Harlech" did Stuart learn that his friend had gone through very trying times after the war had finally ended in November 1918.

In his memoirs, Martin related how on November 11, 1918, his friend Judge Waite, who did secret service work on behalf of the State Department, had taken him on an outing to the Catskill Mountains.

> It was my first excursion from New York in more than a year, and I enjoyed the beautiful scenery. Judge Waite told me that ... according to information received from London, Germany could not last another winter and the collapse were near.
>
> We returned late at night and the nearer we got to the city, the more excitement we saw in the streets of the towns and villages we passed. Judge Waite addressed a policeman, displayed his badge and asked for the reason. The policeman said only one word: "Armistice." We could not believe it. In the city the excitement knew no bounds.
>
> It all seemed a nightmare to me: the Emperor flown to Holland— the invincible army on the retreat.... The next few days I felt dazed, unable to think clearly.
>
> A few days later I received a telegram from Ottawa to come there.... I received another telegram from Ottawa, directing me to go first to Toronto.

If the war was over, its consequences for Martin and his position as Vice President of Brazeau Collieries were only now felt in full.

Sir Robert Kindersley had arrived in Canada and proposed to convert the 5% bond issue of the coal company into a 7% issue of preferred shares. I objected to the proposal, but was told that my objection, while recorded, would not affect the conversion, because the majority of shareholders, viz. Mackenzie, Mann & Company and the bankers, represented by Lazard Brothers, had already decided on the conversion.

[Thomas] Mulvey and Andy [Haydon] promised to vote the way of my liking. The comptroller [Clarkson] also agreed to it....

At the door of the office building in which my office was located, the comptroller turned to me, shook hands and said goodbye. I said:

"Am I not going to that meeting?"

"No. You are neither a shareholder nor a director any more" said the comptroller.

"We will meet you at the hotel and report to you" said Mulvey.

I felt as if somebody had hit me over the head. I had to stand still for a while to gather my senses again. Here was my child, my work, which I had created out of nothing, for which I had suffered so much mental and physical agony, taken away from me for no fault of mine. It was cruel. Like a drunken man, I staggered back to my hotel. My strength was gone. I threw myself on my bed and buried my head in my hands. I did not notice the passing hours....

T. D. Regehr explains in his edited version of Martin's memoirs that

The capital stock of the German Development Company and the shares held by this company, were taken over by the Canadian government in 1918 to ensure that none of its assets would be used to the advantage of the enemy.

What Nordegg apparently failed to realize was that Clarkson, Mulvey and Haydon were elected directors because they now controlled and administered the shares of the Brazeau Collieries owned by the German Development Company. Since Nordegg, an enemy alien, no longer controlled these shares he was ineligible for election to the Board of Directors.

After the adjournment of the crucial meeting, Thomas Mulvey and Andrew Haydon told Martin about

... the proceedings of the meeting, also that the comptroller suggested to Sir Robert Kindersley to see me who refused.

I took a third highball. Mulvey must have read my thoughts.

"Do not give up. Your work is not yet lost to you. Have courage and be a man."

And Andy said:

"By our long friendship, I beg you not to despair. Somehow you will come out on top again."

I left the same night with my friends for Ottawa and after a few days again for New York.

> What should I do now? I felt that I had also lost the war.
>
> A chapter of my life was closed. How would I open a new one, and where? And how?
>
> I tried to visualize the future of the enterprise in Canada.... My main object was to try to save ... what could possibly be saved. On the other hand, I knew and felt it at every visit there, that the hatred against anybody German ... would not abate so quickly, that I could take up work again in Canada.
>
> To return to Germany, to work there ... did not seem feasible to me. I had been too many years away from Germany to accustom myself to the country of my birth. No, Germany seemed out of the question.
>
> What then? Why not the United States?"

As the following years would prove, Martin had made the right choice, even though at least in certain circles in Ottawa he was soon to be welcome again to a degree that he had not expected.

No doubt to remain near Sonia must also have been an important consideration in choosing the United States as a country to live and work. But while they drew closer and closer, Martin and Sonia continued their separate careers.

Although Sonia liked to travel as much as Martin, she could only occasionally accompany him because of her engagements on stage and screen, while Martin feverishly attempted to rebuild his shattered career.

Despite the restrictions that had been imposed on Martin during the war years, he still felt sufficiently respected in financial and political circles in New York and Washington. True enough, he had no liquid assets at the end of the war, but he certainly considered his knowledge of the current situation on both sides of the Atlantic and his connections to financial circles in both the United States and Germany and the respect he enjoyed among them as important assets. Furthermore, he was a less controversial figure in the United States than in Canada. If his contributions to the post-war reconstruction were not wanted in Canada at this time, Germany certainly needed everything from capital, to food, to machinery.

> ... Whatever I would do, would have to be in connection with Germany. Why not try in the first instance to alleviate the sufferings of the German people?

And this meant, first of all, the provision of food to the German population. Although hostilities had ended, the hunger and deprivation that had gripped Germany since the winter of 1917 continued unabated. The British blockade was still in effect pending Germany's signing of the Treaty of Versailles.

Even though Martin was not a stranger in New York, he certainly was at a new beginning, not unlike after his arrival in Ottawa in May 1906. But now, he had not even a cent of capital to invest. Nevertheless, within weeks of the armistice, Martin had prepared a proposal involving millions of dollars "... to lend to the Deutsche Bank many millions of Dollars for the purpose of importing foodstuffs from the United States."

After receiving a sympathetic reply from a large New York Bank, Martin presented his proposal to the Secretary of Trade and Commerce in Washington.

No matter what hostile feelings against Germany still prevailed in Washington, Martin, with his humanitarian proposal that would also benefit the U.S. farmers, found open doors in the capital. His plan immediately appealed to Herbert Hoover, the Director General of the American Relief Administration who advised Martin by letter that "...your scheme for securing American capital might receive support from Paris [i.e., the Armistice Commission] if it was limited to the purchase of foodstuffs."

Martin played his cards with an open hand. But as the country was technically still at war with Germany—no peace treaty had yet been signed—Martin remained under intense surveillance. During the next months, even years, Martin more than once became the object of controversy between the Departments of State and of Trade and Commerce. Even at Westminster in the House of Commons, there was an inquiry from the floor what Martin Nordegg's true intentions were in trying to facilitate the transfer of millions of U.S. dollars to Germany while the British blockade was still in effect.

Greater mistrust was communicated to the State Department by the Alien Property Custodian's Office of the Department of Justice and its Bureau of Investigation. Regardless, Martin managed to obtain an initial exit visa and during the next two years crossed the Atlantic on numerous occasions while the various departments of the U.S. Government continued their investigations, trying to decide how to treat this strange man Martin Nordegg.

A flurry, at times a storm, of correspondence, cables, confidential memoranda and letters illustrate the controversial image Martin had gained among different circles in Washington. The question whether to grant him exit and entry visas continued unabated for two years.

It seems that in every department, Martin had friends and enemies concerned with his activities; contradictory directives and responses originated from all of them, as the following indicate:

"Mr. Nordegg will shortly conclude the mission on which he has been engaged in Germany...." [Attorney General, February 9, 1920]

"Mr. Nordegg...has very actively assisted our Government in matters in which we were interested ..." [Department of Justice, October 21, 1920]

"... Mr. Nordegg has rendered valuable assistance to the Alien Property Custodian's office, and has given considerable help in matters in which this office is interested." [Alien Property Custodian, December 3, 1920]

"... Mr. Nordegg has valuable and confidential information which it is expected will be extremely helpful and necessary...." [Alien Property Custodian, December 7, 1920]

Martin continued his trips to Germany. Invariably ahead of his detractors in Washington, he always managed to obtain his visa from U.S. authorities—sometimes in Berlin, at other times in The Hague, Rotterdam or Paris. But contradictory requests to keep Martin Nordegg out of the United States continued:

"... This Department has heretofore requested that such passport be withheld, but now wishes to withdraw its objection ... he can at this time render considerable assistance to the Government if permitted to go." [Alien Property Custodian, July 23, 1920]

"Mr. Nordegg should procure a passport from the Government to which he owes allegiance ... When he is ready to return he should present his passport to the American Consul nearest his place of sojourn, apply for a visa, and request that the matter be referred to the Department. The question of granting a visa to Mr. Nordegg can not be decided in advance." [Secretary of State, August 14, 1920]

"There are ... reports indicating that Nordegg deviated from the purpose of his visit abroad in behalf of the Government...." [Secretary of State, November 13, 1920]

"... There is nothing ... which necessitates the presence of Mr. Nordegg in America...." [Department of Justice, November 24, 1920]

"... no objection to Mr. Nordegg, who is now in Berlin, being allowed to return to this country." [Department of State, December 4, 1920]

"... you should not have granted Nordegg visa without direct authorization from Department. Action has caused great inconvenience. Observe regulations strictly in future...." [Department of State, December 20, 1920]

Of all the directives and inquiries, the most important message was:

"...it would be of value to facilitate Nordegg's return to this country." [Department of State, October 2, 1919]

What did Martin accomplish during this hectic period when he tried to alleviate the suffering of the starving people in the country of his birth, while at the same time offering some financial advantages to the United States? Did he use the opportunities of his mission to rebuild his shattered career? In these trying times, help often came from unexpected sources, but in Germany, the response to Martin's initiative to help the country of his birth failed to materialize.

Herbert Hoover must have succeeded in persuading the International Armistice Commission in Paris to drop objections against the Nordegg scheme of supplying food to the starving people of Germany. At any rate, whatever concerns might have been voiced in Washington or in London, Martin left New York for Rotterdam on May 2, 1919. He may not have been the first German national to be permitted to leave the United States for his homeland, as he claimed, but certainly one of the very first ones.

From Rotterdam to the German border, Martin shared an over-crowded train with hundreds of families returning from the German colonies in Africa. Oblivious to the changes of four years of war, a revolution, and a harsh peace treaty had wrought on their motherland, they began to sing patriotic songs as the train approached the German border. Even though Germany was now a republic, all of them were still staunch monarchists. When the train passed Doorn, the new home of the exiled Emperor who had been forced into abdication by the Allied powers, by his generals and finally by the revolution in his own country, Martin recalled, with mixed feelings, his audience with the German Emperor at the Palace in Berlin a dozen years before. Leaving peaceful Holland, Martin suffered a shock from which he did not recover for days. Conditions in the country and the mood of its desperate people were far worse than he had imagined. At the border station of Bentheim,

> ... after an hour's waiting, the German train pulled in and was rushed for seats. I was surprised to see that most windows were broken, the cover of the seats torn into shreds. The mob had just played havoc with the state's property.

At midnight, Martin arrived in Berlin, where all the better class hotels were filled, many of them occupied by wealthy refugees from Eastern Europe.

> After a sleepless night, I ventured into the street. It looked desolate, covered with filth and torn newspapers, and the formerly beautiful main street, Unter den Linden, looked worse. I walked there and saw...a taxi, without rubber tires, having instead steel tires with springs.

With the promise of an extra tip in dollars—the precious currency that would fetch its owner anything from food to pleasure—the taxi driver agreed to drive Martin to Georg Büxenstein's plant in the Friedrichstrasse. "He saw me from the window of his office, rushed down the stairs, kissed me on both cheeks, with tears in his eyes, and was too moved to speak."

After more than four years, the old friends were finally reunited. Martin had much to report on the events in America, while Büxenstein related his own war experiences and the events of the past November when the revolutionaries had occupied his printing plant and, on Büxenstein's equipment, had printed the "Büxenstein Lied," a rousing song popular among the members of the revolutionary Spartakus Bund.

In November 1918, Berlin and all other large German cities had been in the grip of a revolution of the radical left. Modelled after the Bolshevik Revolution of 1917, workers and soldiers councils were introduced, replacing the existing government authorities. At the congress of the Spartakus Bund in Berlin on December 30, the Communist Party of Germany was founded. There were battles in the streets of Berlin, which was already paralyzed by a general strike. By the middle of January 1919, the government had regained control of the German capital. But the "Büxenstein Lied" was not forgotten for many years in memory of the heavy fighting between the revolutionaries and government troops that stormed the Büxenstein printing plant. Georg Büxenstein was especially fond of the second, third and fourth of the seven verses of the "Büxenstein Lied":

> And with the rifle in his hand,
> The Spartakusman fights from behind the newspaper piles;
> The bullets fly around his head;
> But the Spartakus is not afraid.
>
> And the artillery is pounding,
> But the Spartakus has only guns;
> Grenades land all around him,
> The government dogs are storming Büxenstein.
>
> Oh Büxenstein, oh Büxenstein
> Spartakus means to be a fighter.
> We have fought at Büxenstein's,
> And now they are putting us in the penitentiary!

Because of its excellent printing facilities, the Büxenstein plant, which was used by the Spartakus for the printing of thousands of revolutionary edicts and propaganda material, was of strategic importance for both the revolutionaries and the government. Four years later during the inflation, the Büxenstein plant again assumed major importance as the printing press of the worthless German currency. At that time, though, Georg Büxenstein was no longer its owner.

On the day after Martin's arrival in Berlin, Büxenstein called a meeting of the board of directors of the Deutsches Kanada Syndikat. Praise was heaped on Martin, who was enthusiastically received by Arthur von Gwinner, the president of the Deutsche Bank, and the bank's directors. They had not forgotten Martin's services with the Lehigh Coke Company and its successful sale on behalf of the Deutsche Bank. Before leaving Berlin, Martin also met with Gustav Stresemann, one of the young republic's foremost politicians and soon to become Germany's foreign minister.

Martin felt in the midst of action, but none of the plans came to fruition. Neither he nor others had realized that times were not ripe for projects involving lending large sums to a country that had just emerged from a lost war. Germany was impoverished, incredibly indebted, and not yet accepted again by other nations. Thus, to Martin's deep disappointment, the Deutsche Bank declined the offer of credit from America, for it would be impossible to repay in the foreseeable future. Only the energetic Stresemann seemed optimistic; he urged Martin to found a German-Canadian Economic Company immediately. Now it was Martin who was cautious and pessimistic. But despite his advice that times were not ripe for a renewed German presence in Canada, Stresemann travelled to Canada in the summer of 1919, where to his dismay he realized that Martin's assessment of the mood in Canada had been correct. Nevertheless, Martin offered his good offices to Stresemann. "I introduced him everywhere, but he returned without any success."

During this first post-war visit to Germany, which had changed beyond recognition in almost every respect, Martin felt strangely homeless, almost as if abandoned. His immediate family was now living in China; and communicating with Berthe-Marie and Marcelle from Germany was almost impossible. All by himself, Martin visited his father's grave in the huge Jewish cemetery in Weissensee. He travelled to Hamburg, where his sister Malwine and her husband and their daughter Bertel lived in poor circumstances. During the war, Martin had managed to send small sums of money regularly to Malwine and her family. Now he was glad that he was in the position to give them a substantial sum before leaving for America. As he had promised, Martin also visited Dutchie's relatives in Hamburg to tell them about their brother Conrad. They were amused about his nickname "Dutchie," which they had not heard before. They realized that Dutchie, while leading a life as simple as theirs was probably happier than they were.

Martin returned to Berlin in September 1919, where the general meeting of the Deutsches Kanada Syndikat resolved to bring all activities in Canada to an end. "All I had to do, was to save what could be saved."

But Georg Büxenstein and Arthur von Gwinner of the Deutsche Bank were not prepared to let go of Martin's services. They urged him to embark on new ventures, namely to "...export German inventions. As the first invention, they suggested the Zeppelin airship."

Thus, it happened that Martin travelled by the Zeppelin airship *Nordstern* from Berlin to Friedrichshafen at Lake Constance, the centre of Germany's airship industry. On board, he wrote an enthusiastic postcard to Stuart Kidd, postmarked

> 1st Oktober 1919 An Bord des Zeppelin Luftschiffes [on board the Zeppelin airship]:
> Travelling on a Zeppelin from Berlin to Switzerland at 60 miles an hour. It is indescribably beautiful.... Kind regards to all of your family and Dutchie, Martin Nordegg.

But Martin did not like what he saw in Friedrichshafen. He was taken aback by the pathetic attitude expressed by Kapitän Lehmann.

> ...who had been flying his Zep to England during the war. I found him most sentimental and he had actually tears in his eyes, when he described to me how he was sure that many innocent people had been wounded or killed during his activity. But orders were orders and they were to be obeyed.

Martin felt manipulated and used when it became clear that Dr. Eckener, the director at Friedrichshafen, tried to sell the *Nordstern* and another airship under construction to the United States before both had to be turned over to France under the terms of the not yet signed Versailles Peace Treaty.

A depressed and discouraged Martin was eager to return to the United States. But Stresemann insisted on one more meeting.

> Stresemann spoke to me about the Constitution of the Republic of Germany, and about his own political party, further of his hope to play an important part in German politics. He added, that if I could get a sympathetic offer from financial institutions in the United States, I should let him know immediately, because that seemed to him the only way to put Germany on its feet again.

Martin concurred that it was important to get capital into the struggling young republic. Stresemann raised an idea, which Martin translated into action immediately after his return to New York. It had already been raised by Arthur von Gwinner, who suggested Martin found a syndicate in New York for the purpose of

> ... selling the most valuable German patents through my connections.

From then on, I crossed the ocean continuously.... I approached
several banking friends in New York and ... a syndicate ... was quickly
formed. But I must confess that my heart was not in this business. I
had never been a trader. While my gifts and education enabled me to
grasp technical matters quickly, I could not buy or sell.

Within days of his arrival in New York, the press interviewed
Martin for a story, which seemed sensational at the time. Who
would think of sending money to the defeated former enemy so
soon after the cessation of hostilities?

"Germany to Get Big Credit When Treaty Is Ratified," the *New
York Tribune* proclaimed after interviewing Martin,

...the German engineer and capitalist, who has been in the United
States since 1915, and who is said to be in the confidence of the
Canadian and American governments.
The amount will run from $100,000,000 to $250,000,000.
"Everything I am doing in the negotiations I am conducting," said
Mr. Nordegg, "is with the approval of the State Department at
Washington." He is also cooperating with the Federal Reserve Board.
"After the armistice was signed," said Mr. Nordegg, "I received au-
thority from Mr. Hoover, of the food administration in this country,
and from the Canadian government to go ahead and establish corpora-
tions in the United States and Canada, the purpose of which would be
to buy foodstuffs for the shipment to Germany. We hope to get at least
$100,000,000, but raise the figure to 350,000,000 or 500,000,000, if
possible...."

In this lengthy interview, Martin pulled all registers to identify
where he and his backers stood politically:

"... the banks here which will extend the first credits will be out and out
American institutions. No German-American bank or any institution
with a German-sounding name will participate."

The *Tribune* had for several days attempted to break "...the almost impenetrable veil of mystery ... thrown about the negotiations
which Mr. Nordegg is conducting."

Whatever, Martin displayed remarkable courage and, if he was
not immediately successful, he nevertheless managed to pry open
rigidly shut doors between the financial institutions of America and
Germany. This was no small feat from which Germany would
sooner or later benefit, thanks to Martin's determined efforts and
considerable diplomatic skills. As the *Tribune* pointed out:

... [on Wall Street], one of the difficulties in the way of making credit
advances to German interests has been the reluctance of American banking houses to take the first step owing to fears of hostile criticism by
the American public.

While Martin refers only briefly in his memoirs to his efforts to raise credits for the shipment of foods to Germany, reported in the *New York Tribune*, he never mentioned his later role in a huge financial project of which he was without doubt the originator. Started in 1922, the project takes on added fascination because of the involvement of Franklin Delano Roosevelt and of the Soviet emissary Gregory Zinovieff who tried to raise capital for the rebuilding of the impoverished Soviet Union.

On September 24, 1936, the *New York Sun* published a fascinating article after the news had reached the United States that Zinovieff had been sentenced to death and quickly executed in one of Stalin's show trials. The *Sun* summarized Zinovieff's revolutionary career as follows:

> Zinovieff was a close revolutionary associate of Lenin and Trotzky. Later he broke with Trotzky to work with Stalin, broke with the latter to conspire with Trotzky, and just before his sentence last week, again denounced Trotzky.

What makes this article even more interesting are the other names connected with Zinovieff and mentioned in the *Sun* article under the headline "Soviet Leader Acted as Agent for Roosevelt Company in 1922"

In that year Zinovieff visited the offices of the Financial Post in Toronto in the company of Martin Nordegg and Andrew Haydon

> ...to enlist the support of the Post for United European Investors Ltd., of which Franklin D. Roosevelt was then president. United European Investors Ltd. was a Canadian company with its head office in New York City.

In a rather complex scheme, the company tried to raise U.S. dollars "...to be exchanged for whatever they could get of the billions of German marks held in the United States and Canada." The marks obtained were to be invested in real estate in Germany. "In December 1922, Mr. Roosevelt announced that the first 100,000,000-mark investment in Germany had been made."

The company filed its last annual report in March 1927 and was dissolved three months later. By that time, Franklin D. Roosevelt was no longer president and all the directors were German-Americans, with the exception of Andrew Haydon and Martin, the only Canadians on the Board of Directors.

With some sarcasm, the *Sun* ended its article with the observation that Mr. Roosevelt was

> ...really anxious to help out the mark holders in the United States when he consented to head this company. It was a lovely plan on paper like a

lot of New Deal legislation which he has fathered since but signally
failed to realize the hopes inspired by the progenitors of the plan....

If nothing permanent evolved from Martin's frantic activities, he
was as inspired, energetic and busy again as he had been during his
successful Canadian years. And he did earn handsome profits. But
in what truly mattered to him, success and achievement now evaded
Martin in the United States and even more in Canada, where his renewed hopes turned to total defeat. Martin seemed to stand up to
these disappointments remarkably well, but nothing hurt him as
much as the final decline of his influence over the continuing development of his beloved Nordegg.

The benevolent attitude of several members of the Canadian
government, however, gave Martin a great deal of comfort.
Gradually, the office of the Secretary of State began to utilize
Martin's advice again, especially in matters concerning the reestab-
lishment of relations with Germany. Upon the directive of Martin's
friend Thomas Mulvey, the Canadian Secretary of State, a laissez
passer was issued by the Secretary of Immigration and Colonization
in Ottawa on July 14, 1920:

> The bearer of this letter, Mr. Martin Nordegg (whose signature and pho-
> tograph appear hereunder) is a National of Germany, aged 51 years;
> height 5'6"; weight about 128 pounds. Mr. Nordegg is well known to
> the Canadian Government and is called upon to cross the border from
> the United States into Canada at frequent intervals in connection with
> matters relating to the State Department. As Mr. Nordegg enters Canada
> always as a non-immigrant, there is no objection to these visits and the
> present letter is issued to relieve Mr. Nordegg of any difficulty on the
> boundary.

Aside from rescuing as much as he could of the investments of
the Deutsches Kanada Syndikat and, above all, his own position
with the Brazeau Collieries and the town of Nordegg, Martin had
not been entirely inactive in Western Canada. He had quietly formed
a new Canadian company, Cosmopolitan Development Corporation,
registered in Ontario, through which he managed to raise funds for
his new coal venture close to Nordegg. In between, Martin employed Dutchie in prospecting and staking in Northern Ontario and
in oil and gas exploration west of Toronto—ventures that were singularly unsuccessful. Although they had necessitated much hard
work and several trips to Ontario, Dutchie had enjoyed this assignment immensely.

In Alberta, Martin's helpers were the indispensable Dutchie who
did the prospecting and the trusted Stuart Kidd, who staked and
registered the claims. Martin formed the new company, Harlech

Coal Company Ltd., with Stuart, Dutchie and himself as the first investors in the stock of the new company. From New York, Martin enlisted additional investors, among them Andrew Haydon and Thomas Mulvey in Ottawa and R.B. Bennett (the later Prime Minister) in Calgary.

There is some correspondence left from these years that illustrates the solid friendship between Martin, Stuart and Dutchie. The letters also allow occasional glimpses into their personal lives. The early correspondence between Martin and Stuart reveals, however, that Stuart and Dutchie had been the actual originators of the scheme to develop a coal mine at Harlech, although Martin might have played his part in encouraging and advising the two men. Before the end of the war, they had enlisted Martin as partner in their venture, because, as Stuart wrote to Martin in New York on January 2, 1918,

… we are willing to have you go ahead and do the best you can for us along the lines you propose.…

Further correspondence with Stuart and other parties illustrates how involved Martin became in trying to bring the Harlech venture to fruition, from getting engineers' reports—including one from John Shanks, Martin's successor as mine manager at Nordegg—to contracts for selling the future coal mined at Harlech for which Martin provisionally engaged the United Grain Growers of Canada in Winnipeg, which, as he informed Stuart, was "…the ideal corporation…who have agents all over the prairie provinces, to interest more potential investors."

In between, there are constant warnings to Stuart and Dutchie, to be careful because "… there are not many honest people left in this world.…"

And to another investor, Martin confides that "… if the two present owners are left to their own resources, they will no doubt be harmed sooner or later by unscrupulous associates or buyers.…"

Operations of the Harlech Coal Company must have started in 1920, as can be seen from the audited report to the shareholders in February 1921 which, however, describes the mine as "…still in the development stage."

Unfortunately, things did not proceed as Martin had hoped. There was lack of capital and in early summer of 1921, Stuart and Dutchie were pleading for a sale of the entire property. That Martin was not quite ready to "jump ship" is indicated in his letter from June 22, 1921, to R.B. Bennett:

I am getting more sanguine about our property, but we should do some prospecting before coming to any conclusions. The matter of financing seems the difficult point right now. Were it not for this, as well as the difficulty of proper management, I would never give one thought of letting others into this valuable property.

At this date, the operations at the Harlech mine seemed to have been suspended, as Martin pleaded with Bennett, that

> Bernhard [Dutchie] should receive from Harlech his wages since the day we shut down, and should be further paid weekly wages. Were he not on the spot, we would have to engage a caretaker and pay him.

In a similar vein Martin wrote to Stuart and Dutchie on the same day, typed on the impressive stationery of his new office on 74 Broadway:

> Now as to your idea...to sell the property. I can only say, I will be the last one to sell out, as long as we have the slightest chance of finding the money.

Martin still hoped to rescue the entire operation, if he would come out West. He was making detailed plans which included his arrival in Nordegg on July 20, 1921: "Regarding our trip to the mountains. I would not dare to take my friend across the Saskatchewan in high water."

This was no doubt a reference to Sonia. There were also some other interesting personal news in the letter:

> Stuart will smile when I say, I want to take it easy this time. But I got so much older during the worries of the war and I am now a grandfather of a one year old!

Martin never managed to come West in 1921, as he was called to Europe on short notice. He was also eager to sail for China to see Marcelle and his little grandson. Martin's extended absence from North America seems to have contributed at least in part to the failure of Harlech. It also destroyed forever Martin's friendship with R.B. Bennett, something which Martin deeply regretted. He also felt guilty that Dutchie had received a raw deal. But in the end, Martin succeeded in securing a little piece of land near the railroad tracks across from the water tower in Harlech, where Dutchie built himself a cottage. A relieved Martin wrote to Dutchie:

"You have been treated rather badly formerly, but that is of the past ... we all like you and think more of you than yourself."

Stuart never failed to keep Martin informed about the developments in Nordegg. Shortly after his return from his first post-war trip to Europe, Martin received a disturbing message from Stuart that another rumor about changing the name of Nordegg was circulating in town again. On July 21, 1919, a worried Martin telegraphed

Andrew Haydon that "attempts are again being made to change the name of Post Office in Alberta. Stuart Kidd has communicated this already to Ormsby. Kindly see that all attempts are frustrated."

Another telegram sent by Stuart to Andrew Haydon is quoted in Haydon's reply to Martin, dated July 31, 1919:

> Post Office inspector at Edmonton again taking up matter changing name of Nordegg village. Nordegg asked me to wire you to do all possible to prevent. Answer me to Congress Hotel, Chicago.

Haydon responded:

> Nothing in department yet about Post office. Will watch situation. On further inquiry at the Department, I find nothing has as yet come to the notice of the Department in regard to any change, and it is likely nothing more will ever come of it.

Nothing further did come of it and Martin began to breathe easier. But the battle about the name change did not end in 1919. There was the town and the post office which indeed would keep their names to this day. But there was also Nordegg, the railway station, terminus of the Canadian Northern Western Railway, another of Martin Nordegg's creations. As part of the Canadian Northern Railway, the line to Nordegg had become part of the Canadian National Railways in September 1918.

Sir William Mackenzie's last triumph had been the official opening of the completed Canadian Northern Railway in September/October 1915. Members of Parliament, various dignitaries and the press lavishly treated by Mackenzie had been on a triumphal cross-country tour, which ended with the official ceremony at the small town of Gladstone in Manitoba, the birthplace of the Canadian Northern.

Since that time, the Canadian Northern (now referred to as the CNoR in distinction to the CNR, the newly created Canadian National Railways) had experienced rising financial difficulties. Despite government support extended throughout the following years, much of it due to the friendship between Sir William and Prime Minister Borden, the CNoR became mired in deeper and deeper difficulties. Refinancing schemes depending on support of Canadian and American sources did not materialize, and after several government-appointed commissions failed to find workable solutions to make the Canadian Northern solvent and profitable again, nationalization of the railway became inevitable. In September 1917, the CNoR Bill passed through the Senate; and in September 1918, both Sir William Mackenzie and Sir Donald Mann resigned from the CNoR, while D.B. Hanna was appointed the first president of the nationalized railway. When Martin met Sir William in Toronto, he found the former tycoon friendly but preoccupied and still in deep mourning after the loss of his beloved wife who had died of cancer.

Both the Canadian Northern Railway and its competitor, the Grand Trunk Pacific, had experienced years of financial distress to the point of insolvency, which resulted in the Canadian government's decision to take over both railways, amalgamating them into the Canadian National Railways. After Sir William Mackenzie's resignation as president, Martin knew he had lost his last protector in the battle of retaining his influence in Nordegg. His worst fears were confirmed when the new president of the Canadian National Railways, D.B. Hanna decided to change the name of the railway station from Nordegg to Brazeau. Martin, who had known Hanna for years, wrote a very personal letter of almost four pages imploring the new president of the CNR to leave the station's original name unchanged. Martin's letter begins with an invocation of Sir William Mackenzie, his power and his loyalty to Martin Nordegg who had served him and his enterprises so well:

Hotel Astor
New York

November 3rd, 1919

Dear Mr. Hanna:
    I am just informed that your railway is changing the name of the station "Nordegg" in Alberta. It received its name by the orders of Sir William Mackenzie, when the Stettler-Nordegg branch was constructed.
    Various attempts were made during the war to change the name, but they were always frustrated by orders from Sir William.
    Let me recall to your memory the services which I rendered to your railway.

The remainder of the first page of Martin's letter is filled with an enumeration of what he had accomplished for the benefit of the Canadian Northern Railway. On the following pages, Martin's words become more and more impassioned. It is clear that the news of the change of name hurt him deeply, that few things were as close to his heart as the recognition of his services to the company and to Canada by having a town and a railway station named after him.

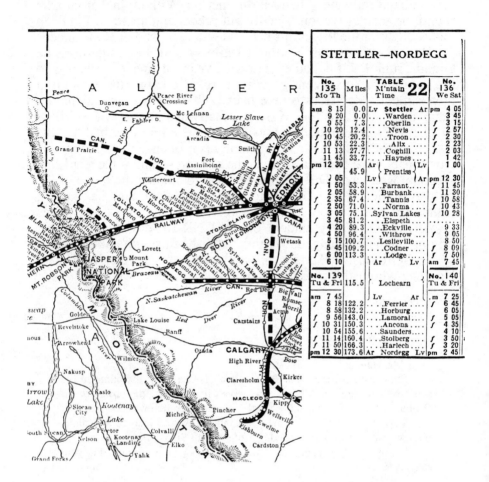

Canadian National Railways—Timetable and Map (Edmonton, Calgary, Nordegg area) Source: CNR Timetable, 1920s

It means nothing to you, and so much to me. I saw in that station the crowning of hard and arduous work of many years—years which I spent living with Indians, in the wilderness, in the heat of summer, in drenching rain and in the cold of winter, under great hardships, and then matching poor wits with the high financiers of Europe, for the benefit of your railway. Nothing was too much for me, and all hardships were forgotten, when my work was accomplished and bore my name as the only, but highest recognition.

Since then I organized and developed the coalfields, which enable your railways to run on the vast prairies at a huge saving in the price of coal.

What then can be the reason for the change?... I have not done anything against your interests.

Could it be possible that now, one year after the war, one official—whose services to your railway will never equal those which I rendered voluntarily—considers my being a German as such a disgrace to the railway and country, that my name has to be stamped out from the place which owes its existence to me?

During my recent stay in Germany—being the first German to be allowed to leave the United States and return—I spoke everywhere of Canadian justice and fairness, citing my own case ... and the benevolent attitude of great Canadians, Sir William Mackenzie, Sir George Bury and others, who enjoyed the confidence of the Governments of the Dominion of Canada and the United States.

Can the change then be anything but the spite of one individual?

What I created in Canada stands there and will be there, even when and if my name should be wiped out from the map where it stood for many years. It remains the work of Martin Nordegg whose education, intelligence and energy, overcoming continuous handicaps and obstacles, has created a monument, now to be hidden under a cover.

Whatever you decide will bear the stamp of D.B. Hanna who, together with Sir William Mackenzie and Sir Donald Mann created the Canadian Northern Railway system against the greatest obstacles and animosities....

It is true, Martin used dramatic words in order to once more demonstrate his accomplishments to D.B. Hanna. But his words largely reflected the reality of Martin's courage and successes against great obstacles and, last but not least, his pride which was being so deeply hurt now. Only after he received Hanna's reply did Martin realize that he had invoked Sir William Mackenzie's name in vain when pleading his case.

On November 29, 1919, Hanna's reply arrived at the Hotel Astor in New York. Martin, who had also reminded Hanna of "...the memory of pleasant relations and many charming conversations with you, my dear Mr. Hanna," was brought to tears when he read Hanna's distant, cool, unapologetic words, from which an uninformed outsider could easily conclude that the two men had never met each other, much less had shared work and decisions over many years:

Dear Sir:—

> I find, for one reason or another, I have delayed acknowledging your letter of third instant.
>
> The change of name of the station was made for the simple reason that 'Brazeau' on the time card indicated a mining development ... and no other thought was given to it.... "Brazeau" on the time card indicates just what it means—coal.
>
> I am sorry you have taken the change of name so much to heart, because, personally, I do not attach much sentiment to the calling of any place after any person and over-looking the local industries which would suggest a more appropriate name.

Other than "I am sorry" there was not the least expression of empathy on the part of Hanna for the deeply wounded Martin, who could not help remembering that in another part of Alberta, a sizable town and its station were named after D.B. Hanna.

Whatever was left of Martin's accomplishments in Western Canada was in danger of slipping out of his hands completely. Martin had to find his way back to Canada and to Nordegg where, he was sure, he would still have much support! That this was not just idle hope, that the loyalty of the residents of Nordegg to its founder would indeed remain alive for years to come was indicated almost four years later in the letter which Martin wrote on April 18, 1923, to Mr. D. Morgan, the Secretary of Nordegg Local Union No. 1087 of the United Mine Workers of America.

Dear Mr. Morgan,

> I received today copy of your recent resolution regarding the reinstating of my name on the railway station.
>
> I want to express to you and to the members of the local Union my sincere thanks.... No matter if your letter results in success or failure, I am proud to know that there are men who appreciate what I did or intended to do.
>
> But what pleased me more than that, was the evident expression of goodwill towards me. That is exactly what I tried to earn from all men with whom I come into contact. And it seems that I have succeeded with many at Nordegg.
>
> I succeeded in spite of the obstacle which somehow exists between employer and employee and which finds its expression in the word "gentleman" which you used. I have found many a gentleman in the highest sense of the word amongst workers and I am proud to earn their confidence and friendship. And I found many who do not deserve that title, amongst the class with white collars. For me, a man is a man. There is no class distinction in my own mind. The only distinction

which I make and permit myself, is that of character. And character does not depend on birth or education, least of all on the pocket book....
    And if in the future I should be able to see you all oftener, and provide you with better comforts in your daily life, I would be truly happy.

If, again, his words seem to be overflowing with sentiment, the document to which Martin responded in his letter to Morgan called for such expressive words of appreciation of unequivocal loyalty. On April 9, 1923, five months after Martin's first visit to Nordegg in more than seven years, Morgan had written to Sir Henry Thornton, Director of the Canadian National Railways in Montreal:

> Dear Sir:
>
> At a very representative meeting of the Miners Union of Nordegg held on Sunday afternoon last, the question was discussed of our depot being called Brazeau and the town itself Nordegg.
> You may be possibly aware of the fact that the town and depot were very properly named the same, until action of some kind caused the changing of the name of the Depot.... Mr. Martin Nordegg is to us nothing more or less than a Gentleman of our acquaintance, we mean "Gentleman" tho in the broadest and best sense of the term.

Referring to what the enforced absence of Martin had caused, Morgan's letter continues that

> We are well aware of the fact that were it not for the great World war with its devious disturbing influences we would be enjoying a far more up to date town than we have at present. We are confident that Mr. Nordegg was very desirous to have a camp here that would be an innovation from the point of view of convenience and comfort.
> Considerable could be said upon this matter.
> However, suffice it to state we feel it to be both fitting and proper that the depot should carry the name it had at first.
> Further, we are convinced that it is no more than justice to Mr. Nordegg for the energy and time he has devoted to the promotion of this coal field.
> Being a mining town, the miners and their families naturally form practically the whole populace.
> Therefore we respectfully request that you give this matter your early attention....

The world seemed to change for Martin when the Liberal Party was victorious in the 1921 federal elections.

> The Dominion elections were awaited by me with bated breath. I knew that if my friends would get into the saddle, my chances in Canada would be my resurrection.... Nothing kept me away from Ottawa on the day of election.... Andy ... took me to Mackenzie King's office in the house of Parliament.... We went into the streets

and saw the jubilation of the people ... and after midnight we went again to the house of Parliament for congratulations. William Lyon Mackenzie was Prime Minister of Canada.

Andy Haydon was tirelessly active on Martin's behalf, taking him to the ministers of the new cabinet and pleading his case for resuming his role in the Brazeau Collieries. Being certain now of the sympathy and support of the new Liberal cabinet, Martin returned to New York, dissolved his syndicate, and waited for word from Andrew Haydon.

On the 22 of May, 1922, I received a telegram from Andy, recalling me to Canada. There was only one thought in my mind. I was returning to Canada and was welcome again!

Everything seemed to have been well prepared for Martin's return. On Andy's urging, Martin had already applied for naturalization in March 1922; and one of the first memorable events after his return to Ottawa took place on June 8, when Martin gave his oath of allegiance to the King in the office of Judge Mulligan with Andrew Haydon and Thomas Mulvey present as witnesses. Two days later, Martin received his Canadian passport.

But there were still delays in implementing the plan which Martin had outlined in a letter to Stuart Kidd:

Confidential   120 Broadway,
                                            New York
                                            15th of February 1922.
Dear Stuart,

Ottawa just informs me that the Government is forcing Clarkson to resign in my favour as Vice-President etc. of Brazeau. As soon as the very complicated legal affairs connected ... have been settled, I take up my residence again in Canada.

I then contemplate coming West at the earliest possible moment and will meet you in Calgary ... and go to Nordegg for some time. How many official cottages are now there ... and is there anything free?... I don't want anybody there to know that I am coming. Maybe, that Shanks will find it necessary to resign. In that case I have to see that the entire organization does not quit with him. If he is clever, he will try to apologize for past behaviour. I was the man who started the whole business. I engaged Gheur and Shanks. If Shanks goes, the business will still go on under a different man. Rely on it....

Kindest regards
yours sincerely,

Martin Nordegg

Don't say one word even to Dutchie. You must remain the only one who knows.

An optimistic Martin saw the return to Nordegg and his former position with the Brazeau directorate within grasp.

With new energy I started now to regain my former positions within the coal companies, and had many meetings with Sir William Mackenzie [and] Sir Donald Mann. Sir William wanted me to take up again my former position. But Mr. F. Perry, the representative of Lazard Brothers ... told me point blank that it was the intention of his firm to eliminate the German interests in the companies which I had created.

Martin still felt hopeful, knowing that Sir William and Thomas Mulvey, the Secretary of State, were on his side. But Mulvey, who suggested Martin's re-election as Vice-President to the Board of Directors, also had to explain to Martin that "...the Government had no power to enforce this, as our companies were private companies, subject only to the decisions of shareholders."
Martin was still not ready to give up.

Mulvey proposed my election as Director. Sir William was absent.... Sir Donald Mann, however, represented the shares belonging to Mackenzie, Mann & Company, and voted against my election together with the representative of Lazards. I then heard that in the settlement between Mackenzie, Mann and Company and their financing bank, the Canadian Bank of Commerce, their shares of our companies had been used as collateral and passed into the hands of the Bank. It showed me that all hopes for regaining our property were shattered. The principle of my life was, never to enter where I was not received with pleasure. Therefore, I made no further attempt to force myself into my own companies, where on account of greed, antagonism, jealousy and private hate, I was not wanted.

With these bitter, angry words Martin closes his account of the crucial meeting in his memoirs. But his task was not yet finished. "...now I had to make careful plans to sell our shares at the greatest advantage. I had to bide my time—even if it should take years."
It was imperative that Martin personally assess the condition of the Brazeau Collieries at Nordegg, especially to gather his own "observations regarding the value of our holdings, independent of the reports from the head office which might be biased."
The return to Nordegg occurred under circumstances very different from the plan he had communicated in confidence to Stuart earlier in the year. But Martin nevertheless followed his original plan.

I travelled to Calgary and Red Deer and then by train on "my railway" to Harlech where Dutchie lived. Stuart Kidd had sent a saddle horse for me, and I rode to the bank of the Saskatchewan. Then I struck out over the hills towards Nordegg.

It was afternoon when we reached the water-tower overlooking the mine and town. I stopped my horse to take the view all in. It looked to me exactly as on the day when I had left. I cantered on the new road toward the mine office, jumped down, threw the reins to Dutchie and entered the building.

What happened during the private meeting with John Shanks is recorded only in Martin's memoirs. It appears that the meeting was polite; but it was used by Martin to impress Shanks with his [Martin's] status, even though it was no longer based on any power. Shanks and his superiors had won, but Martin made sure that Shanks recognized his moral superiority.

He was surprised to see me already ... and I should have had a more comfortable trip, if I had used the railway. I answered that I came on horseback out of the mountains as I did at the time when I discovered the coalfield which now afforded employment to him. And did he remember that I engaged him?

He said he never forgot it, and when the plebiscite was held to change the name of the town, he voted against it.

I replied that I appreciated his fairness. But if this were so, why did he antagonize me during the war? He maintained that he did not. I then asked him, which of the directors had visited the mine since my departure. The reply was, that none of them had ever visited the mine.

After the encounter with his successor, Martin was prepared to meet the townspeople. Perhaps it had all been carefully planned, perhaps it was coincidence—Martin had chosen the perfect moment:

I rode into town. On the way, I met the miners who were just leaving their cottages to go on night shift. My appearance created a sensation amongst them, as so many recognized me, they stopped the horse, reached for my hand and I saw joy in their eyes, and they shouted to the newcomers who I was. The news of my arrival spread like wildfire in the town, the women and children ran out of the cottages and I was greeted everywhere. I stopped at the store, the manager [i.e. Stuart Kidd] greeted me, invited me to stay with him and his family in their cottage on the hill and I accepted with pleasure.

During the following days, Martin took a hard look at every detail of the mining operations and the records in the mining office. John Shanks was very co-operative.

Martin was pleased to see that as a town Nordegg had not changed, but neither had the mine and its operations, which made Martin very angry and resentful.

> I found that the six years of my absence had not changed anything at all. All remained as I had left it. My intention had been to make this mine the nucleus of a large combination of mines ... providing the West of Canada.... Of course, as our mine was paying, and the directors and head office were 3,000 miles away, and the creative spirit existed no more, I could easily see, that there had not been the slightest attempt at enlarging the scope of the mine. Nor had any attempt been made to open the great Kananaskis field....

On November 1, Martin left Nordegg by train. Hundreds of people came to the station to say goodbye, asking Martin to come back soon. He knew he would, but the next time he would come strictly as a visitor. The long train ride back East gave Martin time to plot his further strategy:

> ...the management of our mine had been definitely taken out of my hands ... our interests were now subject to the good will of the majority, consisting of Mackenzie, Mann, respectively the Canadian Bank of Commerce and Lazard Brothers. But ... the time had not arrived. I must first see if I could not raise the output to show some larger profits and sell on a better basis of profits.

After receiving Haydon's and Mulvey's agreement "...to sell our interests under all circumstances," Martin had an amiable meeting in Montreal with Charles Vaughan, the vice-president of the Canadian National Railways who promised to do his best to increase the coal purchases of the CNR from the Brazeau Collieries. Martin happily reported a few months later that at the Brazeau Collieries in Nordegg,

> The tonnage increased rapidly and reached the possible maximum output. I offered our shares to Lazard Brothers for cash.... I applied to the Custodian for the release of all property belonging to my Development Company. After due consideration by Cabinet, the property was released. I cabled the great news of this sale to my President....

The time had come to dissolve the German Development Company Ltd., of which Martin had rescued more than he had expected. The cash value of the sale exceeded Martin's hopes, not in the least as the result of his intercession with the Canadian National Railways. Records indicate that during this crucial time the Brazeau Collieries employed over 800 men and had reached the highest coal output of all mines in Alberta.

In Germany, the Deutsches Kanada Syndikat would also be liquidated soon. Martin arrived in Berlin feeling victorious. Thanks to his hard work and skill,

...a profitable investment had been saved from a total loss in spite of the war.

Need I describe the excitement at the meeting when I appeared for the distribution in the hectic time right after the inflation, with many hundred of thousands of dollars?

One cannot help imagining this board meeting, and how Martin—literally or figuratively—opens his large attaché case and proceeds to throw handfuls of precious dollar bills in large denominations into the air in front of the stunned directors of the Deutsches Kanada Syndikat. It is indeed quite possible that Martin arrived with the profits of the sale in cash, as due to currency regulations, international monetary transfers to Germany were still very difficult.

The gratitude of the shareholders was enormous. The German economy was just beginning to take its first hesitant steps towards recovery after the years of devastating inflation, when at its height, one dollar was worth 400 billion marks. The shareholders of the Syndikat still considered themselves wealthy men, but everybody was short of cash. No wonder the profits of Martin's sale of the Canadian investments meant a great deal more than the "hundred of thousands of dollars" would be worth during normal times.

This was Martin's only happy hour in Berlin. He was too late to throw his arms around his old friend Georg Büxenstein who had never let Martin know of his fatal illness with cancer. Büxenstein had died just days before Martin's arrival in Berlin.

His widow told me afterwards that my cable was the last news he received and he said to her "my friend Nordegg is a real fellow." Next morning he was dead.

There was nothing else that would keep Martin in Berlin. He lived in comfort at the Hotel Bristol, which was now half empty. The German capital presented a picture of extremes: incredible poverty and lack of work; gray crowds of haggard, poorly dressed people filled the streets of the centre of the city; while the amusement districts, filled with the music of the suddenly popular jazz age, were throbbing with the hectic life of luxury, which only the newly rich were able to enjoy. They did so without shame.

Martin stopped at Wiesbaden for a few days, where Berthe-Marie now lived since her return to Germany a few months before. Martin was shocked to find Berthe-Marie in poorer health than ever. Even short walks in the park seemed to be too strenuous for her. She was certainly too frail to consider a return to Canada. But Berthe-Marie had no desire to follow her husband. She did not object, though, to going with Martin to Davos, Switzerland, famous for its climate beneficial for respiratory problems.

They spent Christmas with Martin's Swiss friends at a charming chalet at Bad Ragaz. Berthe-Marie seemed much better, her mood almost serene. Martin thought that during the next summer Berthe-Marie would enjoy a stay in this small, but elegant spa and benefit from the treatments offered. Even though the days in Bad Ragaz and Davos had been the most harmonious days Martin and Berthe-Marie had spent together in a long time, Martin left his wife with a sense of foreboding. It had not helped that Berthe-Marie had told him how distressed she had been about leaving the unhappy Marcelle, who was now contemplating a divorce from her husband in China.

On December 30, 1923, Martin rushed by express to Naples, where he boarded the SS *Conte Verde* on the following day. On his arrival at New York on January 11, 1924, he completed the questionnaire for the passenger arrival list entering "nobody" under the column requesting name and address of the nearest relative!

During the calm sailing to New York, though, Martin had many undisturbed hours to think over his life. What had brought him to Canada in 1906 had definitely come to an end. With sadness, but also with great pride, Martin relived his past years of great accomplishments and deep disappointments. He concluded that through trials and tribulations he had become a man who was well regarded on two continents. His services were again desired by the Canadian government. And, despite the great adversities of recent years, he was still a wealthy man. Fifteen years later, Martin closed the memoirs of his Canadian years with obvious satisfaction and pride.

> I had liquidated the Development Company and was once more a free man, free to devote my time to anything.
> There were two ardent wishes in my heart: to roam the world to my liking and to help and assist mankind. And I carried both through.
> I made many friends in Canada and I established my home there.

The German Development Company would not be the last company founded by Martin Nordegg, nor would Canada remain his one and only home for the remainder of his life, for he truly fulfilled his plans of "roaming the world and assisting mankind." Deep in his heart, however, the attachment to Canada and his memories of the West would remain alive forever.

"Often I longed for the Rocky Mountains, and travelled again over the trails and to the town which still bears my name."

IX

YEARS OF BLISS
1924 - 1936

The twelve years between 1924 and 1936 were personally perhaps the happiest years in Martin's life. After the affairs of the
Deutsches Kanada Syndikat and the German Development Company
had been brought to a relatively satisfactory conclusion, Martin
started several new business ventures, but none were of the all-con-
suming nature of his explorations and pursuits in Western Canada
prior to the war. Although advancing in years, Martin enjoyed excellent health, and his relationship with Sonia was happy and fulfilled.
For the first time in his life, Martin enjoyed a sense of constancy and
permanence, and that was reflected in the beautiful home that he and
Sonia created for themselves in Ottawa.

These were years of true, though not unmitigated bliss for
Martin, starting on a tragic note with the death of Berthe-Marie, and
ending with a frightening experience in Europe, which heralded the
rising tensions and hostilities leading to World War II.

During these years and, indeed, to his last days, Sonia was part
of Martin's everyday life. With the exception of Martin's last two
trips to Europe, Martin and Sonia were never separated. They
shared every experience, every problem, every decision.

In retrospect, the exceptional nature of their unique relationship
brings the tragic, unfulfilled first marriage of Martin into stark light.
One must wonder whether both Martin and Berthe-Marie would
have been happier had their paths never crossed.

When Martin met Berthe-Marie in England, he was just enjoying
the first successes in his professional life. He felt free, optimistic,
and sure of himself. No doubt Berthe-Marie saw in Martin the person who would lead her out of the restricted, uneventful life of a
governess in a small English country manor.

With fateful consequences, their decision to join their lives in
marriage came far too quickly, too soon to be able to appreciate each
other's character and outlook on life. No doubt the early arrival of
Marcelle contributed to the initial happiness of the marriage. But just
as her mother's did, the life of Martin's daughter would unfold in
the shadow of her father's unusual career.

After his return to Berlin in 1902, new and powerful forces began to take hold of Martin's imagination. They were opportunities challenging him to a degree that permanently displaced the well being of his family as the first consideration in Martin's plans for his personal life.

Had Berthe-Marie been a stronger personality, she might have insisted on the primary rights of herself and Marcelle in Martin's mind. Had she only possessed a fraction of Martin's physical health, of his energy and drive, she might have encouraged Martin to include her needs and her happiness in his own plans to a greater degree. With his thirst for adventure and risk, his openness and adaptability, Martin succeeded in feeling at home in every country where his personal aims or political circumstances took him. Berthe-Marie, on the other hand, never returned to the country of her birth except for brief visits as a married woman; she obviously remained a permanent expatriate, almost in exile, in whatever country Martin took her, Germany, Canada, or the United States. Her unhappy destiny seemed to fulfill itself in her lonely death in Switzerland, a country where she had neither friends nor any emotional attachments.

Over and above Berthe-Marie's unhappy marriage stood her poor health, which declined steadily over the years and would have never allowed her to follow Martin's peripatetic existence, even if she had wanted to. She could never fault Martin for not looking after her material needs and her precarious physical health. In that sense, Martin was a most responsible husband. Perhaps it had never been his intent to exclude Berthe-Marie from his exciting life. But whether he was driven by his dreams or whether he needed to escape from the unfulfilling relationship with a chronically depressed wife, he failed as the emotionally caring husband.

In the end, the temperamental incompatibility of Martin and Berthe-Marie, their totally different expectations on life and its rewards, and the political circumstances especially during the second part of their marriage when Berthe-Marie was trapped in exile in the United States, contributed to the personal tragedy that overshadowed Martin's otherwise so admirable life. Berthe-Marie's existence as a married woman remained one of disappointment, loneliness, and emotional deprivation. With her gentle, unaggressive personality, she was unable to struggle for her rights in this tragic marriage.

Can Martin be absolved from his failure as a caring husband who should have been more willing to share a greater part of his life with Berthe-Marie or as a father who loved his daughter deeply, but was so seldom present in her life? Perhaps one has to grant Martin that fate, which led him into such unexpected directions, failed him in the instance of his first marriage. That he had the capacity and desire to build a fulfilling marriage and be a responsible, loving and caring husband, Martin proved in his second marriage. Fate smiled on Martin again after he met Sonia. And it was also kind to him by enforcing a long period of friendship during which Martin and Sonia would get to know each other thoroughly. If anything, Martin's second marriage was not one hastily entered into as his first marriage had been.

It is impossible to fathom how much Martin valued his first marriage. But he never sought a divorce from Berthe-Marie. When he was finally free to marry Sonia, he married a woman who possessed all the traits of character and temperament that he had sought in vain or had failed to foster in Berthe-Marie.

Soon after they first met, Martin realized that Sonia had become the most important person he had ever had in his life. Indeed, Sonia's optimism, her positive outlook towards life and other people, her love of travel and curiosity about other cultures seemed to complement Martin's character perfectly. Where he was restless and tended to be overly active, Sonia was calm and secure in her own personality.

This exceptional constancy and stability is evident in the photographs of Sonia over a period of nearly fifty years. As a young woman in her early twenties, she did not look much different from the mature person in her sixties. Other than the evidence of a gradual maturing and gentle aging, Sonia never seemed to have changed during these decades. She never changed her hairdo, always wore large earrings, and always dressed according to the fashion of the day. Her clothes, made of the best materials, were quietly elegant.

Twenty-five years after Sonia's death, her great-niece Joyce Rothchild gave a delightful portrait of her aunt Sonia to the author. She remembers her aunt especially vividly from the 1950s, when Joyce was an impressionable teenager and Sonia already a widow.

> My aunt was of rather small stature, but she had a dramatic appearance. Her hair was always swept up in a large mass, sometimes with a thick braid crowning her head, and her eyes were warm and impressive. She always wore heavy, dangling earrings, and as a result, her earlobes were enormous and the piercing holes quite large, something which fascinated me when I was a child.
> My aunt had a wonderful, warm voice. Being Eastern-European-born, she always had a certain accent, but she spoke several languages fluently.
> Her home on Central Park West was filled with beautiful furniture and art treasures, which my uncle and aunt had collected during their many travels throughout the world. She was deeply interested in the arts, although not so much in modern, avantgarde art, and she loved for-

eign movies, the ballet and the theatre. She often took me to plays and ballet performances, also on my 16th birthday when she introduced me to alcoholic beverages by ordering a cocktail for me during a late dinner after a show.

This was the Sonia Martin loved and treasured. Still leading a peripatetic life and travelling to Europe again and again, Martin had found a home, physically and spiritually, even before his marriage to Sonia. During the early 1920s, Martin always stayed at the Astor Hotel while in New York, but he spent many happy hours at Sonia's apartment at 140 West 58 Street, just one block south of Central Park.

How different life in New York was for Martin now. There was Sonia's family. Her father and mother liked Martin very much and so did Sonia's sister Anna. A good number of photographs survive from these years, of outings in the country and visits to the country places of friends in the Hudson River Valley and at Water Gap in Delaware. Sonia always appears animated, while Martin looks quietly pleased and happy. Even Sonia's sister Anna looks cheerful, although her nephew Hyman Mizell describes her as a rather sombre person, dedicating herself to her work, seldom being lively company. Anna was a loner, never had male friends, and never married.

Martin had decided to travel the world, no longer primarily on business, but as a private person with some business concerns and a great interest in people and their cultures. He was now a British subject, while Sonia had become a naturalized U.S. citizen on June 13, 1922. Their first foreign trip took them to Ottawa, where Sonia was well received by Andrew Haydon and Thomas Mulvey and Martin's other friends. None of them could help but notice the striking difference between the charming, outgoing Sonia and Martin's unhappy wife Berthe-Marie. Everybody was happy for Martin.

Marcelle and her family had made their home in Tsinan, the capital of Shantung Province, approximately 150 miles south of Peking. Marcelle's husband worked as liaison staff for the U.S. oil company Socony. Tsinan was an important industrial city of some 500,000 residents, who were mainly employed in enterprises producing the famous Shantung silk. The city had a fairly substantial foreign colony consisting of some European and American merchants and the administrators and teachers of the American-endowed Cheelo University. So while living in, for its time, a rather exotic country, Marcelle was not entirely deprived of companionship of people of her own background.

At first, Marcelle had seemed happy enough in her marriage to Arthur May in China. After spending most of her life in countries that were the original home of neither her father nor her mother, Marcelle was able to take life in the utterly foreign China of the 1920s in good stride. In October 1919, she had given birth to "a sweet little baby boy," as Martin proudly reported to Stuart Kidd.

There are no reminiscences by or about Marcelle of her years in China, except a postcard to Dutchie from the early 1920s which is nothing more than a continuance of their correspondence since Marcelle's visit to Nordegg in 1912. It does seem to betray some nostalgia, perhaps even homesickness:

January 11th, 1920

Standard Oil Co.
Tsinan, China

Dear Dutchie —
The bear skin arrived here in fine condition. Many thanks for picking out such a beautiful skin for me. It was just what I needed in my home and furs are so hard to get out here. If you get some good photos of Nordegg I wish you would send me a few.

With best regards, Marcelle Nordegg-May.

There is no indication of how long Berthe-Marie had remained in China. But records of the payments she received every month from Martin's account in the Commerz Bank in Berlin reveal that by January 1923, Berthe-Marie had returned to Germany. Until Martin visited Berthe-Marie in Wiesbaden, he had felt quite reassured about Marcelle's happiness in her marriage. Nor had he been unduly worried about Berthe-Marie's health. There were no great worries about his family that would interfere with the increasing happiness he had found in his relationship with Sonia.

It seemed natural that on their first extended trip together Martin would take Sonia across Canada to Banff and Lake Louise and, finally, to Nordegg. This was Martin's second visit to Nordegg after the war. Decisions made in Toronto and in Berlin had terminated Martin's position at the Brazeau Collieries. Martin knew that there was nothing left for him in Nordegg other than many memories and a few loyal friends. Thus, this visit was of a quiet, private nature, but the old-timers of Nordegg remember to this day that in 1923 "Mr. Nordegg came to our town with a lady-friend."

Dutchie noted in his diary in March 1923, that "Mr. Nordegg and Miss Marcelle come March 10—stay to 19."

During this week Sonia made a new friend in the usually very reserved Dutchie, who immediately took to the spontaneous Sonia.

Always a conscientious correspondent, Dutchie notes from then on quite frequently "letter sent to Miss Marcelle—film sent to 19

Elgin Street [in Ottawa] for Miss S. Marcelle" and so on, later followed by entries about his visits to New York and Ottawa.

Dutchie became quite a traveller during these years, mainly in the employ of Martin, who for a while intensified his mining efforts in Northern Ontario. Working for Martin's Cosmopolitan Development Corporation, Dutchie spent nine months in the East. Martin had founded Cosmopolitan with Andrew Haydon, Thomas Mulvey and his German friends Hans Kramer and Hermann Danziger as partners.

Entries in Dutchie's diary tell about his adventures in the East:

> April 28, 1923—ready to stake claims
>
> May 23—Mr. Crook brings wire from Mr. Nordegg to go ahead to do assessment work ... see bear 1 mi south ... see first snake ... the black flies are terrible....
>
> May 29—wire from Mr. Nordegg. Dolph and I ... pick place for house....
>
> May 30—Dolph cleaned site for house and dug cellar....
>
> June 2—I go to town meet mr. Nordegg coming out.
>
> June 15—I go to town ... git my boat ... 1 pair of boots for Mr. Nordegg.
>
> July 13—waited around town for Mr. Nordegg and Mr. Vogel
>
> July 15—go to meet Mr. Nordegg and Mr. Vogel at Keerlake work for an hour ... stake claims...
>
> July 23—dig one shaft
>
> July 27—make road from wagon road top of hill to shaft ...
>
> Aug 11—strike rock quartzite ... letters to Vogel and Mulvey ... I go to town and drive car both ways.
>
> Sep 26—I start work on Ruby mine ... Stuart will be here at 2 pm
>
> Oct 27—wire to come to Ottawa
>
> Oct 30—arrive Ottawa 6:55. Talk to Mr. Nordegg and John B. Mulvey.
>
> Nov 1—Meet John B. Mulvey, talk to Steno; Meet Mr. Nordegg; to Dr. Dowling; Mr. Nordegg leave. National Gallery (later explore town) leave 1:20 after midnight.
>
> Nov. 16—write letters to Stuart—lots of prospecting, all minerals except gold and cobalt—letter to Miss Marcelle.
>
> Nov 21—letters to Jack, Ernest, Stuart, Mulvey, Miss Marcelle, Mr. Nordegg.
>
> Dec. 24—card from Miss Marcelle
>
> 1924
>
> Jan 19—see Mr. Nordegg and Mulvey—decide to go to Toronto and Oilfields—Cobalt to Toronto $10.00.
>
> Jan 22—arrive Toronto Union Station 7 am, breakfast with Mr. Nordegg—later train to Wyoming via Hamilton and London—examine 4 wells—find it too cold to do work.
>
> Jan 27—write ... asking Mr. Nordegg to come.

Jan 28—walk from Petrolia to Oil Springs, Morning Star and Oil City.

Jan 30—telegram to come to Ottawa; test made in Hotel Fletcher with oil limestone.

Feb 6—meet Mulvey and Mr. Nordegg; go to see Dr. Dowling and Dr. Cook; get check from Mulvey ... for Petrolia.

Feb 11—send $25.00 to Hamburg, mail letters to Otto, Liesbeth, Hedwig, Ida, Marie, A. Scharf and Miss Marcelle.

Report to Mr. Nordegg on Harlech. Leave Cobalt for $58.80 to Edmonton.

Feb 15—arrive 8:30 Nordegg

Feb 16—walk to Harlech.

These excerpts from Dutchie's diary help create the image of a man who had never received any formal education in North America, but who expresses himself very well in English. For most of his Canadian years, Dutchie lived in the bush, always making sure he had his privacy and socializing with people only on his own selective terms. His steady companions were his two dogs, Blitzen and Donner (reputedly direct descendants of the dogs Amundson had taken to the North Pole), that Dutchie had shipped from San Francisco. He managed to amass a remarkable amount of knowledge and expertise on mining matters; he knew how to prospect, handle legal claims, hire and employ people.

A wonderful photograph from 1912 has survived. It shows Dutchie in buckskins, slouch hat and a heavy belt with cartridges and his gun slung around his waist. He stands between Stuart Kidd and Wilfred Gray in front of a teepee somewhere in the bush between the Shunda Gap and Nordegg. The entire scene illustrates the frontier character that the Nordegg country still carried in the early years.

Dutchie was an avid letter writer, addressing his mail to locations in four continents, his correspondents ranged from simple workmen to the sophisticated Sonia Nordegg, and her cousin, Dr. Sonia Tokar-Lampert in Baghdad, to the faithful Marcelle in China. It included numerous friends and nearly all his relatives in Germany whom he never forgot, although he never returned to Germany for a visit.

Dutchie was also a voracious reader; the books he left behind after his final departure from Harlech represent a spectrum ranging from fine literature to historical, technical, and scientific texts. He was always curious about scientific and technical matters; and if there was one thing, perhaps the only thing, that made Martin impatient with Dutchie, it was Dutchie's "polarization machine." This was something he had designed and tried out in prospecting and assaying. From Martin's exasperated complaints to Stuart, one can only gather that in practical application Dutchie's "polarization theory" never worked out reliably, although he never ceased to believe in its potential.

Knowing that part about Dutchie, one is surprised to learn from his diary how physically tough he was. He could work like a horse for hours on end; he was oblivious to a tough climate; and he walked for hours through deep snow on snowshoes, or through rain and mud, worked all day far from home and still got back home on foot such as on September 24, 1924:

"There is coal south of Alexo between track and mine; try all along all day. Dinner at Stolberg, walked home at night." During this day, Dutchie covered more than 20 miles on foot with much work in between.

Dutchie's diary always tells us about the busy life Martin maintained during these years, especially his repeated trips to Germany. In February 1924, Martin writes Dutchie from Room 358 at the Bristol Hotel in Berlin.

In April after his return to New York, Martin announces another visit to Nordegg with Sonia, which, according to Dutchie's diary, took place in early June 1924.

Photographs show a happy, always smiling Sonia in front of Dutchie's neatly painted clapboard house at Harlech, or Sonia playing with Dutchie's dogs, or Sonia with Dutchie, who seems preoccupied with his dogs rather than looking into the camera, and with Sonia at the backdoor of the kitchen wearing, of all things, a white apron over her elegant dress. How the days were spent can be gleaned from Dutchie's diary:

> May 31—Mr. N. and Miss M on train.
> June 8— 'Conflap' with Mr. Nordegg and Stuart Kidd.
> June 13—in Edmonton 7 am meet Mr. Nordegg; and Kidd—go to university.
> June 14—meet Mr. Nordegg.
> June 15—meet Miss Marcelle at 10 am walk 1 and 1/2 hours; read the philosophers stone in the St. James Hotel.
> June 18—letters from Mr. N. and Miss M.
> July 3— letters from Mr. Nordegg
> July 10—letter from Mr. Nordegg from Montreal.

The last letter posted in Montreal advised Dutchie that Martin was on his way to Europe again, as his wife had died in Switzerland. During the following months, Dutchie continued to write to Sonia in New York—Martin had not mentioned that "Miss Marcelle" was accompanying him to Europe.

Martin had hoped that Berthe-Marie's stay at Bad Ragaz would be beneficial to her health. Bad Ragaz was one of the European spas that had the exclusive reputation as a source of healing as much as a place of social distinction. Its origin dates back to springs that were discovered in the Middle Ages and later developed into the insignificant Bad Pfäfers. How it became Bad Ragaz is described in a charming brochure of the Grand Hotel Quellenhof from 1995:

> There was a boy from Glarus, who wanted to be more than a shoemaker or farmer, the way his father was.... So he became an architect and went abroad ... to build the most beautiful palaces for the first families, and—being a workaholic—got an ulcer for his trouble. This brought him back to Switzerland, though hardly to relax: On March 9th, 1867, he acquired the domain of Hof Ragaz and the licence to utilize the Bad Pfäfers spring for 100 years from the Canton of St. Gallen ... and began building. On July 10th, 1869, the feudal inn opened its doors ... his hotel in Bad Ragaz, the QUELLENHOF.
>
> Whatever Bernhard Simon took in hand, was handled properly. Thus, Bad Ragaz—and in particular the QUELLENHOF—developed under his guidance into one of the leading addresses for royalty from all over the world and world-renowned literati.

This is where Martin had wanted his wife to seek rest and healing. Bad Ragaz was located in a beautiful countryside; the spa was elegant without being pretentious; it was not too large and was located somewhat off the beaten path. Berthe-Marie must have enjoyed the calm serenity and the elegant, but unobtrusive atmosphere of the Quellenhof. Perhaps her last weeks were serene and peaceful. One can only wish so for this unhappy woman who had battled physical illness and depression for much of her life.

After spending five weeks in Bad Ragaz to receive various treatments, Berthe-Marie died a lonely death as the guest of the Hotel Quellenhof. She was found dead in her room by the chambermaid in the morning of July 5, 1924. The death certificates give some scant data. The coroner, Dr. Freiburghaus, completed the personal data on the certificate and the attending physician, Dr. Kormany, determined "pneumonia" as cause of death. The entry in the town's civil register states Berthe-Marie's religion as Protestant and, not correctly, her date of birth as November 21, 1869, "as the daughter of Brandt [sic], Guillaume and an unknown mother." Her occupation was "housewife," her permanent residence Ottawa, and her civil status "married." Neither this entry nor the death certificate give the name of Martin as her husband. As the death was reported to the authorities by the director of the Quellenhof, Mr.Kienberger, one must assume that Berthe-Marie had stayed in Bad Ragaz without a companion. She was buried in the community's cemetery in Bad Ragaz. Her grave was levelled after twenty years, and there are no entries left in the cemetery books as to who arranged for Berthe-Marie's funeral or who was in attendance at the burial service.

Thus, with the death of the wife and mother, Martin's little family had ceased to exist. The husband and father was in Canada, the daughter and grandson in China. And Berthe-Marie was laid to rest in a location that had no meaning in her life nor in Martin's or Marcelle's.

On July 12, Martin and Sonia left New York by steamer for Rotterdam. A letter of condolence from David Rees, a retired union official, did not reach Martin until his return to Canada many months later. David Rees's words "Permit me to express my sincerest regrets, and sympathy to you in your bereavement, naturally made worse owing to its (apparent) suddenness… " are the sole reference to Berthe-Marie's death found in Martin's surviving papers. The original death certificates from Switzerland ended up in Martin's naturalization file in at the Department of Justice in Washington.

It was a sombre journey to Europe that took Martin and Sonia first to Wiesbaden. After closing Berthe-Marie's apartment, Martin and Sonia visited her grave in Bad Ragaz. Nor was the visit to Martin's sister Malwine Joel and her daughter Bertel in Hamburg free of worry.

Malwine had lost her first husband, a merchant of gentile origin, in 1910. A widower with a two-year-old son, he had married Malwine in 1902. After his death, Malwine left the Silesian city of Liegnitz with the two children, her ten-year-old stepson Martin and the two-year-old Bertel, to marry Louis Joel, who owned a small shop in a working-class district in Hamburg.

Although Martin had never been close to his older brother Theodor, who had lived in London with his wife and his two sons since the late 1800s, he held his younger sister Malwine very close to his heart. Now, Martin learned to his distress that Malwine's second marriage was in deep trouble. Louis had moved out of the family's apartment and was seeking a divorce. Malwine's step-son Martin had already left the family five years previously; after serious conflicts with his stepfather, he had returned to Liegnitz.

Malwine was not well at all, and Martin thought the best he could do was to take his sister and his niece for a holiday to Silesia, where they stayed at the comfortable Hotel Lindenhof in Schreiberhau, at the foot of the Giant Mountains. These were happy weeks for all. Bertel cherished her days with Uncle Martin and was enchanted by her new Aunt Sonia. She was in awe of what she heard from her about the fabulous life in the United States. How much she wished to live there herself, but her mother was in no condition to manage a move across the ocean to New York, even though Martin offered to make all the necessary arrangements and to look after her financial security.

A photograph from the days in Schreiberhau was found among Sonia's papers. It showed Bertel as a sixteen-year-old with long blond braids, wearing a short-sleeved dress with an intricate cross-stitch pattern, perhaps made by her mother. To her left stands her mother, a woman in her late forties, her dark brown eyes and her forehead reminding one very much of her brother Martin. Her facial expression is serious; her white dress is well tailored but somewhat plain. To the other side of Bertel stands Sonia, wearing a cream-coloured silk dress of expensive, but restrained elegance. As always, Sonia's regal pose is impressive. The difference between her and Martin's sister and niece is striking—the well-to-do, sophisticated lady from North America next to her husband's solid middle-class German relatives.

From the Giant Mountains, it was only an hour's drive to Liegnitz, where Malwine's stepson Martin lived with his young family. A tearful Malwine took Martin to the grave of her first husband. With her thoughts now focused on the past, Malwine begged Martin to take her to Reichenbach. Having psychologically established such a distance from his early years in Silesia, it would have never occurred to Martin to visit the town of his birth and childhood. Only because he wanted to fulfill every one of his sister's wishes did he reluctantly consent to Malwine's request.

The train ride through the rich Silesian lands along the foothills of the Sudeten Mountains at the height of summer was beautiful, but the hours in Reichenbach were painful for all. Malwine stood in tears at her mother's grave in the small Jewish cemetery at the edge of the town. Afterwards, plagued with very mixed emotions Martin took Malwine, Bertel, and Sonia to the synagogue where his father, from whom he had received his education in the Jewish faith, had been a preacher for so many years. Martin had consciously put this part of his life behind him many years before, at least as early as the day when he had decided to divest himself of his father's Jewish name and become Martin Nordegg. He refused to enter the synagogue and call on the Jewish preacher.

In vain, Malwine tried to find some of her girlfriends from school days. Martin did not even think of locating anyone. During lunch at the hotel on the Market Square, he was most uncomfortable when Malwine identified herself as a former resident of Reichenbach. But he could not ignore the excited greetings of Max Weil who happened to sit with his wife at a table next to Martin's and immediately recognized his former classmate. Martin and Max had attended the gymnasium together. Max had taken over the management and ownership of the Weil Textile Works in Reichenbach and proudly introduced his wife to Martin and Sonia. The two women quickly took to each other, striking up a conversation that planted the seeds for a lifelong friendship.

Martin was glad to escape from Reichenbach and leave his ambivalent memories behind. In Breslau, he and Sonia spoiled Malwine and Bertel for two more days. They stayed at the Monopol, the most elegant hotel in town; and Martin was at his most generous during their visits to the elegant stores in the Silesian capital.

After Malwine and Bertel returned to Hamburg, Bertel wrote a long letter of gratitude to her uncle and a few days later, on August 29, 1924, mailed a postcard written in German and in German script, addressed to

> Mr. Martin Nordegg,
> Hotel Fürstenhof,
> Potsdamer Platz,
> Berlin W

> Dear Uncle Martin,

> I am sure you will have received my letter. Yesterday, I visited the tailor who is so enthused about the wonderful material for my suit; it will fit me perfectly for sure—I will look most noble and elegant. You remember that I talked to you in Schreiberhau about Dr. Barbanelli, a relative of ours, the grandson of Nancy Krotoschiner; he would like to go to America and would only be too grateful for some of your advice, such as whether to go to California or stay in New York. He will give you a call, whether you would be free for 15 minutes or so. So, please, do it for me, Uncle Martin, and give him your good advice. You have tried and tested so many things yourself in America.

> Dear Mother's condition remains unchanged. Please write very soon!

> Faithfully,

> Your Bertel.
> [And in English and Latin script a footnote follows]:
> Many kisses, my dear Sonya! Don't forget your promise to see me again!

This was to be the first of many "trips through the world" Martin had envisioned for Sonia and himself. But the first two months in Germany had been entirely devoted to family matters. Noticing how emotionally exhausted Martin was, Sonia quietly dropped her own long-cherished plan to visit her relatives in Poland, whom she had not seen since the day she had left Russian Poland as a fourteen-year-old in 1904. It seemed much more important now to take Martin away from his troubling experiences of the past weeks in

Germany. As she would so often, Sonia placed Martin's welfare ahead of her own and proposed a trip to Switzerland to which Martin readily agreed. He suggested St. Moritz, where the two enjoyed happy, carefree weeks for the first time since leaving New York. Several photographs show Martin and Sonia sitting on bleachers in the midst of other guests, watching skating competitions, the ladies all dressed in elegant fur coats from white to gray to black, the gentlemen wearing jaunty sports caps on their heads, but always wearing white shirt and tie. In another photo, Martin and Sonia sit on deck chairs, bundled in blankets enjoying the bright sun and the dramatic, snow-capped peaks of the Graubünden Alps before going for a little hike with steel-capped hiking sticks in their hands. No wonder St. Moritz would always have a special meaning for Martin and Sonia, who would return to the beautiful resort more than once.

Two years later, their happy memories were complemented during another stay at St. Moritz over Christmas and New Year 1926, when Martin was happy to meet his friend Franz Petschek, who owned large coal mines near Aussig in Czechoslovakia. Sonia renewed their acquaintance with the Barcinski family from Lodz in Poland. As Franz Petschek's daughter, Mrs. Elizabeth de Picciotto, related to the author, their daughter was introduced by the always sociable Sonia to Franz Petschek who quickly fell in love with the lovely young lady from Poland. The engagement was announced on New Year's Eve and was soon followed by a happy marriage and a friendship with Martin and Sonia, which lasted to the end of their lives.

Sonia proved herself equally perceptive to Martin's need to do some work. After four weeks in St. Moritz, she sensed his restiveness and willingly followed him to Berlin, Hamburg, Paris, Rotterdam, and, as a last stop before returning home, to London.

Martin treasured Sonia's independence and wide range of interests. Neither in Germany nor in France did Sonia depend on Martin's company, leaving him free instead to pursue his business interests, while she explored art galleries and museums or went to the theatre on her own if Martin was not free to join her. It helped enormously, of course, that Sonia, who had never set foot on any European country except the Russian Poland of her childhood, was fluent in German and in French!

After a brief visit to Franz Petschek in Aussig, Martin and Sonia left for London. In England as in every other country they had visited, Martin had interviewed government officials and businessmen. He had profusely studied economic statistics and made pages of notes. On board the steamer from Southampton to New York,

Martin immediately went to work on a report to the Canadian government composed on his small typewriter, which always accompanied him wherever his travels took him.

As soon as he went on land in New York, Martin posted his "Memorandum on Canadian Exports to Central European Countries" to the office of Prime Minister Mackenzie King in Ottawa. In his covering letter, Martin referred to his memorandum which

> ...contains the conclusions arrived at after my repeated and thorough investigations of Central Europe.
>
> My personal motive in submitting them to you is primarily the wish to further the interests of Canada and secondary to enable the Liberal Party to act constructively in aiding Canadian trade and immigration....

Martin indeed presented a well-researched and documented submission, which analyzed the problems of Canadian trade which, to this day have not been fully overcome—one need think only of Canada's reliance on the export of raw, unfinished, products, trade barriers, and tariffs. Martin's observations, conclusions and recommendations can only be summarized in brief form:

> 1st. The export from Canada to Central Europe contains at present about 90% of cereals and cereal products.
>
> 2nd. Owing to the shipping manifests which are the basis of Canadian statistics, the ports of landing give their Country as importers (and by popular assumption, consumers). Consequently, the statistical figures do not disclose the actual Canadian exports to the respective Countries.
>
> 3rd. To prove this contention, it is only necessary to consider the Netherlands—a small country—which imported for the fiscal year ending March 1924, 4.3 Million bushels of wheat and 249,000 barrels of flour, which were landed at the port of Rotterdam.
>
> My investigation proved, that the very greatest part of this went up the Rhine to the German port of Mannheim and was distributed from there ... to a great extent to Switzerland!
>
> On the other hand, Canadian statistics show that Canada exported to Germany in the Calendar year 1923 1,828,271 bushels of wheat and 1,561,086 barrels of flour, most of which went to the port of Hamburg. From there it was trans-shipped to Czecho-Slovakia, Poland and other adjoining Countries—a part of the wheat having been milled in German mills.
>
> The German statistics for the Calendar year 1923 show a total import of 17 million bushels, and it is surprising to see that the United States contribute over 9 millions, Argentina over five millions, and Canada only 219,000 bushels.
>
> Of flour, Germany imported a total of 150,000 tons of which ... Canada supplied only 6000.

The probable reason is ... that Germany prefers those Countries which buy German goods on a large scale. The high rates of the Canadian general Tariff and the clause regarding importations from countries with depreciated currencies have greatly hampered this exchange of products. The depreciated German currency is a thing of the past.

The clause will have to be repealed.... A striking example of how commercial relations between two countries improve mutually—nearly automatically—are the figures for 1909 and 1913.

In 1909 Canada and Germany made a treaty ending many years of Tariff War. I take credit for having induced Sir Wilfrid Laurier and Mr. Fielding to open negotiations which were successfully concluded.

In 1909 Canada exports to Germany 4.1 million dollars, and in 1913, 16 Million, (Of this amount, wheat nearly 13 Millions).

In 1913 the total German imports of wheat amounted to 2 1/2 million tons of which Canada supplied 318,000 tons. The Canadian share in 1913 was therefore 12 1/2% as against only 1 1/2% in 1923 (see above).

The remedy which I suggest is twofold:

1. A Trade Treaty between Canada and Germany

... It seems hardly advisable to let the British Foreign office negotiate for Canada...

Germany is preparing ... a special tariff for cereals ... granted to those countries which conclude a trade treaty....

2. To establish a High Commissionership for Central Europe.

Canada is at present represented in central Europe only by trade and also immigration commissioners and officials. They have hardly the qualifications nor the position to influence either. It seems imperative for Canada to be represented in this very important market in an influential way. I believe, that a High Commissioner located in either Berlin or in Vienna can deal effectively in Germany, Austria, Jugo-Slavia, Czecho-Slovakia and Poland. It also should be his duty to ameliorate the present regulations there which prohibit effective propaganda for emigration. And it may be conceded, that emigrants from Germany, Austria and Czecho-Slovakia have formed a most desirable part of Canadian settlers.

An eloquent, precise document, Martin's memorandum points in a direction which, with many interruptions and setbacks, would be pursued for more than two generations before the problems Martin had so clearly elucidated would find a solution. Eighteen years after adopting Canada as his new home, Martin had once more served Canada—and the Liberal Party in government and in opposition—well!

Martin truly appreciated the interest Sonia was showing in his work. He knew he owed her much, first of all—and very soon—a travel experience to an exotic country.

On November 15, 1924, two days after his return to Ottawa, a rushed, but happy Martin wrote a long letter to Stuart Kidd in Nordegg.

Dear Stuart,

If I was ever rushed in my life, this is the time. After 4 1/2 months of absence, and now going to China, I don't know how to turn round. Today I must go to Montreal to await Mulvey who arrives from London, and I return here with him, so that we have time to talk quietly [about Harlech, no doubt]. On Thursday I got to go to New York, arrive in Montreal on the 28th and leave on the 30th by C.P.R. no.1 direct for Vancouver and embark at once for Japan and China. Impossible to say when I return. You can write me in the meantime, if you want. The last letter in Canada should reach Vancouver before December 5th, as the Empress of Canada sails at 11 a.m.

If you write after that, say until December 21st, address me c/c Astor House, Shanghai. Cable addresses I gave to Con [Dutchie], in case you have something good to let me know [about Harlech, no doubt]....

I was so happy to hear that Bena [Stuart's wife Robena] is her lovely self again. She better be, because I hate sick people, and I am so fond of Bena and her little brood. In summer, when you sent me the bad news [about Stuart's wife and her serious illness], I had to pacify Miss Marcelle, because she was so anxious about Bena....

On the Pacific Ocean I have 16 days to think what we will do. If Marcelle can stand the cold, we will return via Calgary. If not, we will sail via Honolulu and Frisco. In China I am going on pack horses to the great wall, wish you were along. But I got to do without you, and that is sad.

We will send a little thing to Bena and Peggy to remember us at Xmas. We dont forget our dear friends and count you two amongst the dearest....

P.S. [handwritten] This is all upset suddenly. Am invited by Mackenzie King for dinner and go only at 8 a.m. tomorrow to Montreal and return at once.

This was Martin at his best again. Busily setting up tight schedules, planning trips, and business meetings, and yearning for new adventures and challenges, readily sharing everything with his best Canadian friend Stuart. But one event, which no doubt contributed to the happy, excited mood of this letter, Martin did not share with Stuart: in between all his activities and his preparations for another long absence, he was rushing to New York not only to pick up Sonia, as Stuart assumed, but also to get married!

On November 22, 1924, Martin and Sonia were "joined in marriage" at the Municipal Building of the Borough of Manhattan. Martin's friend Warren R. Roberts, who had just opened his law office at the brand new, prestigious Wrigley Building on Chicago's fashionable Michigan Avenue, had come to New York to be Martin's witness, while Sonia's friend Arlen G. Swiger was the second witness. Sonia's sister Anna was there, and so were her parents, both of them regretting that Martin and Sonia had settled for a civil ceremony.

As her nephew Hyman Mizell explained, this was the first time that Sonia did not bend to family tradition and the wishes of her parents. According to Hyman,

> My aunt Sonia was a wonderful woman of strict moral standards; but she was not as one would say "a good Jew," although she always tried to be "a good Jewish woman" while with her parents.

But this time, Sonia followed the wishes of her new husband Martin, who had relinquished his adherence to the Jewish faith and the Jewish traditions so many years ago. In the marriage register, the data on Martin's father read "Moritz Nordegg, Government Official" rather than Hebrew preacher. But then, Martin was not entirely dishonest, for in Germany, Catholic priests, Protestant ministers, and Jewish rabbis had the status of civil servants and were paid by the state.

On November 28, Martin and Sonia left New York for Montreal, where they boarded the Canadian Pacific Transcontinental on the 30th for Vancouver. From there, on December 5, they sailed on the *Empress of Canada* to Shanghai.

In Shanghai, they were the guests of Sir Elly Kadoorie. Sir Elly's business interests were blossoming—he also owned the luxurious hotel where Martin and Sonia were staying. In conversation with Sir Elly, Martin could not help reflecting what had happened to the world and to him personally since they had last spent time together at the Banff Springs Hotel in Canada. Since then, his fortunes had gone up and down, finally returning to a level where Martin could be proud of his achievements and his financial independence once more. Martin had no regrets, but felt a tinge of envy when he met Sir Elly's sons. The last time he had seen them, they were children. Now young men, they were already employed in their father's enterprises. Martin had to think of his only child, whose marriage was apparently under considerable strain. He had not seen Marcelle since 1918 and had never laid eyes on his only grandson. Tsinan, Marcelle's home in China, was the next stop on Martin and Sonia's itinerary.

In the album of Martin and Sonia's travels, there are very few pictures of this journey, which is rather unusual, as Martin was such an ardent photographer. There are only a few pictures from the stay in Japan—a scene with village children and another one of the Ginza in Tokyo with Sonia in one riksha and Martin in another that is attached to the first and both being pulled by a short, emaciated man. But there are no photographs of Martin's five-year-old grandson or his father, and Marcelle is shown on only one picture. She must have accompanied her father and stepmother on a trip through China. In a bazaar in Nanking she stands next to Sonia, watching her father inspecting a precious Chinese vase. Marcelle looks very slim; she wears a smart, intricately knitted sweater; her hair is bobbed. In a letter to Stuart from Peking, Martin mentioned only briefly that Marcelle lived in comfortable enough circumstances, but she seemed rather melancholy, something which very much worried Martin, who was recalling the chronic depression of Marcelle's mother.

There is only one more picture from this trip, and it shows a number of people boarding the steamer at Tsingtao. It is a desolate scene, symbolizing a trip that had a disappointing end—Marcelle did not accompany her father and stepmother to Canada, as Martin had planned for her.

Railroad tracks and oil tanks form the background of the picture; an unpaved road runs on top of the levee from which crumbling stone steps lead down to a narrow plank laid across a muddy stretch of water to the ship that would take the travellers to Shanghai. The passengers are all Westerners; the men are in dark suits and coats, and the ladies are quite elegantly dressed wearing the cloche hats that were so in fashion in the mid-twenties. They all cast their eyes intently down to the rough stone steps, trying to negotiate the difficult path in their high-heeled shoes. Towering over the heads of the departing passengers are numerous, enormous steamer trunks carried on the shoulders of short, slim Chinese porters. Sonia is the first in the long queue; and a few steps behind her follows Martin in an elegant dark-gray overcoat with black velvet collar and gray pants and a gray Homburg on his head. He carries Sonia's hat box in one hand and a bouquet of flowers in the other—perhaps a farewell gift from Marcelle.

The return trip to New York must have been taken via San Francisco, as Dutchie did not note the hoped-for visit of Martin and Sonia to Harlech, an event that he certainly would not have failed to mention.

Instead, within three weeks of their return to New York, Martin and Sonia were on another journey, this time a cruise through the Caribbean to South America on the SS *Mont Royal*. From Port au Prince in Haiti, they mailed a postcard to Dutchie:

"Many kind regards from our cruise to the West Indies, Central & South America in tropical heat."

Sonia added a footnote that

"I will write to you soon again."

Martin and Sonia returned from their cruise on March 30, 1925. Not much else is known about their life during the remainder of 1925 or the following year. What did survive are large photographs of two oil paintings executed in New York by Fedor Zakharov in 1925.

The portraits are by no means the masterpieces of a great artist: Martin's features appear somewhat bland and certainly younger than his years; rather than gray as in real life, his hair is dark brown. But what does speak of Martin's life is the painting of the mine tipple in Nordegg on the wall behind him and the geological map he holds unfolded in his lap.

Sonia, although somewhat idealized, seems more alive. Her large dark eyes do speak to the viewer. As always, she wears long, precious earrings. Reflecting an important stage in her life, her years as an actress, Sonia wears a Spanish costume; she holds a fan in her right hand; and with her left hand, she gently presses a rich silk scarf to her chest, prominently displaying a precious ring on her delicately shaped hand. A beautiful mantilla of black Spanish lace cascades from her head across her shoulders and her arms.

Various records and letters begin to tell more again from 1927 on. Travelling fills much of the time as well as planning for Martin and Sonia's relocation to Ottawa. Incredibly, among the passenger arrival lists of the Port of New York for the year 1927, we find four landings of the Nordeggs—they had spent more than one and a half months of the year just crossing the Atlantic back and forth!

The passenger arrival lists from that year do contain some interesting data permitting some conclusions. Prior to their first trip to Europe in 1927, Sonia must have given up her apartment on 140 West 58 Street. When Martin and Sonia returned from Europe via Cherbourg on the SS *Columbus*, Sonia was listed "in transit to Canada" with her address in the United States as "c/o Mrs. Susan G. May, 38 East 38 Street, New York City," while Martin's residence was given as "Chateau Laurier, Ottawa, Canada." Mrs. Susan G. May, of course, was Marcelle's mother-in-law.

Martin and Sonia were now both residents of Canada, although they had not yet purchased a home in Ottawa, where they were temporarily living in a rented apartment. This might in part explain their restless existence during that year when they travelled to Europe four times. They also managed to squeeze in a visit to Nordegg, judging by a photograph of Sonia in front of Dutchie's house in

Harlech in early spring. Sonia is wearing a light wool coat, the sun is shining brightly, but there are still patches of snow around the house and among the nearby trees.

Stuart's son Fred Kidd remembers this visit very well. Martin and Sonia were spending quite a bit of time with the Kidds, who were enjoying their best Nordegg years. Fred writes that

> ... he [his father Stuart] was always busy being Postmaster and Justice of the Peace, and also was involved in laying away the dead. His word was his bond and his word was the truth—to my knowledge he never maliciously hurt anyone by word or deed. He was generous and kind— but had a hair trigger temper, which he kept under control most of the time.
>
> Dad bought 20 good type mares branded L7 on the left shoulder in 1921.... When I was big enough to ride, about 1931, the bush was full of our horses.... We outfitted a lot of tourists and oil company exploration parties.... Dad was made an honourary Chief in 1927 (to my knowledge the first to be so honoured by the Stoneys). Chief Peter Mark Wesley gave him his head dress and named him Chief Ta-Osa (Moose Killer). This was Chief Peter's own name....

During a visit with the author, Fred also related a charming little story from this visit of the Nordeggs.

> Mr. and Mrs Nordegg had stayed overnight at our house. As there was no train the next morning, my father borrowed a "jigger" from the stationmaster to take the Nordeggs back to Harlech. This little contraption on wheels seats at best four people and is propelled on the tracks by the pumping of a doubler leaver by two of its passengers. I was seven years old at that time. I was delighted that I could accompany my dad and his visitors. Standing between the legs of Mr. Nordegg, I thought this was a wonderful, adventurous ride. I also looked forward to seeing Dutchie again. I always liked being with him and helping with the chores around his cottage.
>
> But this time, just after lunch Mrs. Nordegg decided that it was time for my nap. I protested loudly that I never had a nap at home; besides I was far too old for such a practice and was not tired at all. But gently and firmly, Mrs. Nordegg put me to bed in Dutchie's bedroom and closed the door behind her. There was no way that I would fall asleep; and soon I heard a rather excited debate behind the closed door in Dutchie's kitchen. I remember Dutchie as always polite and courteous with Mrs. Nordegg, but now his voice was loud and belligerent. Nor was Mrs. Nordegg's dark, velvety voice as calm as usual. In rather loud, dramatic words, she accused Dutchie of having tried to seduce her maid Anni during his recent stay at their house in Ottawa. Anni was now madly in love with him, constantly in tears, and there was no other solution than for Dutchie to come to Ottawa soon, marry Anni and take her back to Harlech. Like Dutchie, Anni was German and would make a good wife for him.

Dutchie protested loudly, but after Mrs. Nordegg released me from
my nap and allowed me back into the kitchen, everybody seemed as
pleasant as always. I never let on that I had overheard the excited debate
and today I laugh about Mrs. Nordegg's idea to marry off Dutch who
was so independent and self-sufficient. Besides, he disliked women and
was about as far from being a lady's man as one could imagine.

There was a new reason for yet another trip to Europe during
1927. After deciding to settle in Canada and make Ottawa the permanent home for Sonia and himself, Martin had founded a new
company, Ultramares Limited, an investment company with the address of Room 420, Electric Building in Ottawa. Ultramares was incorporated June 18, 1927, with Martin as president, Andrew
Haydon as vice president and, as shareholders, his friends Thomas
Mulvey in Ottawa and Hans Krämer and Hermann Danziger, who
had been on the board of the now defunct Deutsches Kanada
Syndikat in Berlin. As real estate, the new company listed "three silver claims and polarization farm in Temiskaming, Ontario"—all
properties originally owned by Martin.

It is likely, at least in part, that the three further trips to Europe
were to assist Martin in raising funds for the new Ultramares
Company. Numerous photographs exist from the Atlantic crossings,
showing Martin and Sonia both looking well and relaxed, resting in
deck chairs, playing shuffle board, enjoying a party with costumes
and balloons, and Sonia placing her bets at the roulette table. One
picture from early July on the SS *Columbus* shows Sonia with Mr.
and Mrs. Frances Dubilier from New Rochelle, New York. This
was the beginning of one of Sonia's many friendships—Mrs.
Dubilier would be a great helper in Sonia's charitable projects in
later years, while Martin took on a directorship of a furniture company owned by Mr. Dubilier.

Passenger lists from the arrival on the SS *Columbus* on
October 22 give as "nearest relative" Martin's sister "Malwine Joel,
Fürtherstr. 5, Berlin." As Malwine is not listed in the Berlin directories during these years, she probably only rented part of an apartment on Fürtherstr 5. One must wonder about her personal circumstances after her divorce from Louis Joel.

There was the fourth trip to Europe in 1927 from which Martin
and Sonia returned on the SS *Berlin* on January 15, 1928. Six
weeks later, they started on another trip, this time circling the globe.

Sailing on the *Empress of Canada* again, they spent a week in
Japan and then visited Marcelle and her family, who had moved to
Tientsin. Martin had hoped that Marcelle would enjoy life at Tientsin
more than at Tsinan. Tientsin was a large, well laid-out city, a centre
of foreign trade with a colony of foreign residents numbering in the

thousands. There was an active social life among the foreigners in Tientsin, but if Martin had thought that Marcelle would be less lonely now, he was disappointed. Marcelle seemed very melancholy; and to his distress, Martin realized that there were reasons for Marcelle's unhappy state of mind. As he wrote to Stuart,

... physically, Marcelle is alright again. The trouble is somewhere else. She wants to divorce her husband who has an affair with another married woman.... I tell you this in confidence, so that you see that I do not keep any secrets from you and dear Bena, and that I have my own troubles....

For Martin, it was not easy to say goodbye to Marcelle and leave her behind in such unhappy circumstances while he and Sonia embarked on their trip of pleasure and adventure. But at least, he had elicited a promise from Marcelle that she would meet them in Berlin later in summer and, with her son, would visit Ottawa the next year.

A lengthy exploration of China followed. It took Martin and Sonia to Peking, to the Great Wall, and from Nanking on an extended river-boat trip to the Upper Yangtse and the famous archaeological sites in the interior of the country. In Nanking they again spent a good deal of money on Chinese antiques—there are pictures showing Sonia examining Chinese vases and other artifacts. They returned on the Yangtse River, staying on the boat all the way to Shanghai from where on April 2, 1928, Martin wrote a postcard to his friend and attorney Herbert Brussel in New York:

Dear Friend, we are having a very interesting time and are just leaving for Hongkong. I will write you from there a "professional" letter, registered, as I want you to do something for me in a legal way....

In Shanghai, Martin and Sonia boarded the German steamer *Trier*, a combined freighter-passenger vessel of smaller tonnage, which leisurely travelled to Europe with many stops along the coast of the Indian subcontinent, East Africa and Egypt before the Nordeggs went on land in Italy. It had turned out to be a rather exhausting trip. From Berlin, Martin reported to Stuart on June 2, 1928:

Dear Stuart,

We were 51 days on the ocean, from Tientsin on through the tropic until we reached Genoa on May 11th. It was hotter than Hell. We just melted away, but Mrs. Nordegg cannot sweat, so she suffered even more than I did, and now she is not at all well, and may have to go to a hospital next week....

The Nordeggs stayed in Europe for another three months, visiting friends in Germany, Austria, Czechoslovakia, France, and finally fulfilling Sonia's wish of seeing her relatives in Poland. From the comfort of Warsaw's Hotel Bristol, they travelled to Grodno, where Sonia felt like a queen from fairyland. She praised her fate and her parents for having taken her to the New World. While her relatives Boris and Fanya Wolgiel were not starving, Sonia was shocked about the plain, crowded living conditions of their home, the simple pleasures they could afford only occasionally, and the quite depressing situation under which they subsisted with little hope for a better future. Sonia became especially close to her niece Anna, their ten-year-old daughter. Anna seemed bright, modest, and hard working. In her mind, Sonia decided that she must help Anna towards a better future in the New World as soon as Anna was old enough to leave Poland on her own.

In August, 1928, Marcelle arrived in Berlin to stay with Martin and Sonia for nearly four weeks. She had crossed the Soviet Union on the Trans-Siberian Express, but had left her nine-year-old son behind in Tientsin. Martin thought it best to take Marcelle to Schreiberhau in the Giant Mountains. The less travel the better for Marcelle, who seemed terribly exhausted, more than seemed justified after her long train trip. A photograph shows Martin, Sonia and Marcelle standing at the window of the coach taking them from Berlin to Silesia. Marcelle's state of mind did not seem to improve, and even Sonia who had become truly fond of her step-daughter, seldom managed to reach Marcelle or make her smile. Back in Berlin, Martin made all the travel arrangements for Marcelle and her son's trip to Ottawa the following spring. That was all he could do for his melancholy daughter, who said goodbye without a smile and without shedding a tear when they took her to the Friedrichstrasse train station in Berlin. Two days later, Martin and Sonia left by train for Bremen and their return voyage to Canada, another of their long journeys ending again on a sad note. Martin wondered whether he had actually helped Marcelle by encouraging her to meet them in Germany.

On September 12, 1928, after an absence of more than half a year, Martin and Sonia arrived in Ottawa "to settle down for the entire winter," as Martin wrote to Stuart Kidd. And this time, they did settle down.

On October 1, they purchased a house on Range Road, at that time called Ottawa's Embassy Row. They bought their new home, which had just been completed by John R. Booth, the owner of a prosperous lumber business in Ottawa, for $35,000. Designed by the renowned architectural firm of Burritt & Kingston,

No. 28 Range Road was not only the newest, but without doubt also the most beautiful, tasteful, perhaps even the largest house on Range Road.

It is an indication of Martin's wealth and security that he purchased this elegant house and redecorated and furnished it most expensively into one of Ottawa's most glamorous, tasteful residences, for which the Nordeggs were soon widely admired among the upper circles of Ottawa.

Built on a double, possibly a triple lot, the house was two stories high, capped by an expansive low-angle, red-tiled roof. Designed in restrained Spanish-California style, the house had two slightly accentuated corner wings and a large two-story open verandah at its side. There were balconies on the second floor, adorned by stucco ornamentations around the railings and above the doors. Judging by the number of windows, the rooms must have been spacious. Aside from the elegant dining room and the huge living room, they included a rustic, expensively decorated wood panelled "country room" reminiscent of a Tyrolean "Bauernstube." Its furniture consisted of heavy, carved tables and chairs, which Martin and Sonia had purchased in Austria.

As photographs taken between 1928 and 1936 show, the large garden was carefully landscaped with trees and shrubs. Long rows of rose trellises, a fountain, and a white gazebo set special accents. The entire garden provided a sense of privacy and seclusion. Although extensive, it was of quite idyllic nature. At the front of the house, the view swept over the large front lawn to the open park across the street. Altogether, the house had the touch of a Southern home, at least on those summer days when the sun was shining brightly under a blue sky.

Martin and Sonia were most busy during their first months in their new home. But Martin always found the time to write to Stuart Kidd. While there was always business to discuss, Martin also needed someone to share his joy with. His friend Stuart would understand that he was not bragging but simply expressing delight in his good fortune of having Sonia. He shared his enjoyment, together with her, of finally creating a beautiful home after years of a restless existence spent to a large part in hotels, on board ships and trains or, earlier in his Canadian years, under the sky in the bush. This was his first true home, and he was already 60 years old! He deserved everything he could afford. On November 7, 1928, he wrote to Stuart:

"These are hectic weeks for Mrs. Nordegg and myself to settle down in our house which is far bigger than we need and want. All our furniture and belongings have arrived from New York, London, Berlin,

Vienna. Tokyo and Shanghai, and we are working like slaves. However, since today I can see the day ahead, when we will be in order....

Glad that dear Freddy is well again. I do hope that all your dear family are enjoying the best of health. When is dear Bena coming East? Mrs. Nordegg and I want her to stay with us and have a good time. Perhaps she could bring Betty along. We have a young girl friend here of Betty's age and they could amuse each other....

And on November 19, obviously excited about an announced visit by the Kidds:

Yours of the 14th just came in and I hasten to answer. You should know me by this time, and be convinced that I never bluff. You and Bena should also know that we are very fond of you two, and do not generally forget the good and bad times we spent together. Therefore we will be delighted if you two would come here and be our welcome guests, and we will try to make you comfortable and roll you into nice blankets, as you often did to me....

And more pride in the house and in what it was fast becoming:

You will of course, love our house. It contains the collection of beautiful things which we both made in all corners of the world. Ottawa is quite excited about it. After all, it is a little village, and they have never seen such things anywhere. So our house has already the reputation of being the finest. We can hardly save ourselves from visitors, and we are never alone.

The Prime Minister has invited himself for a dinner at our house in a few days hence. Charley Stewart was at dinner last Saturday and nearly missed the train. Bennett is also coming, and the rest of the political big pots, and they are all so kind with their compliments. But we know, that we have artistic taste and that it took many years of collecting and just knowing what would fit. We had hard trouble in the house with the workmen here, but we are nearly finished with them....

The renowned Ottawa interior decorator atelier of Bothe & Ehrmann had completed paintings of every room at 28 Range Road. Four of them survive from Sonia's estate. They show lavishly, but tastefully furnished rooms filled with antique furniture, large Chinese silk screens, paintings and sculptures. Precious Persian and Indian rugs find their counterpart in intricate ceilings. The salon, also called the Green Room, was furnished in English Regency, as was Martin's bedroom with its large portrait of Sonia in a white Spanish costume. Sonia's sitting room, the Chinese Room, was decorated with Chinese objets d'art throughout and black lacquered furniture. Her bedroom is executed in French rococo. Intriguingly, under the partial canopy over her bed, one notices an Italian seventeenth century painting of a Madonna and child.

This was a new world that Martin was creating for himself. There was nothing among the splendor of 28 Range Road that would remind the visitor of the explorer of the Canadian West. Martin had already donated the heads of a moose, an elk, a mountain sheep, and a mountain goat he had shot during his early years in the West to the Naturhistorisches Museum [Museum of Natural History] in Vienna. Perhaps it was no accident that Martin donated his collection of artifacts, which he had acquired from the Stoney Indians during his first trips to the Alberta Rockies in 1907, to the National Museum of Canada in Ottawa. On November 6, 1928, the Chief of the Anthropology Section of the museum, Mr. Diamond Jennings, gratefully acknowledged Martin's offer: "In the National Museum, here in Ottawa, we have a very incomplete section from the Plains area and are anxious to increase it.... "

In a short ceremony in the National Museum on November 23, Martin presented 30 pieces of Indian artifacts including, two donated by Stuart Kidd to the National Museum.

Perhaps Martin neglected his health during these months of decorating his Ottawa home. On January 13, 1929, he wrote to Stuart:

> While you had the mumps, I got the flu and so badly that one night Mrs. Nordegg thought I was dying. But I pulled around again, was 2 weeks in bed with an awful cough and fever and am now up again. But I must not leave the house for another week....
>
> My doctor wants me to go South. I don't. But it is possible that if I can get away before the snow begins to melt, we will sail for France and not return till the 1st of August. When is dear Bena coming? The bed is made for her already, and Betty will have her own room or sleep with her mother in the same room, as she wants.
>
> And you old Scout, when are you coming? ...

The Kidds did come to Ottawa, but Martin and Sonia did not leave for Europe until the fall of 1930. There were two reasons, one of them the impending visit of Marcelle and the other one, quite unexpectedly, Martin's decision to write a book on a topic he was concerned about as a citizen of his adopted country. It was also a topic in a field in which he considered himself an authority.

In August 1930, The Macmillan Company of Canada published Martin's book *The Fuel Problem of Canada*.

In its preface, dated July 15, 1930, Martin explains his decision to write this book: "The idea of presenting this economic monograph of the Fuel Problem originated from a casual remark to the Honourable R.B. Bennett, K.C., M.P., leader of the Conservative Party, to the author."

This was the time when Mackenzie King and Bennett were battling in the political arena, and it was not beyond the possibility that

R.B. Bennett would be Canada's next prime minister. Martin was concerned about this possibility as well as the increasing problems of marketing Canada's coal against foreign competition. These were problems that Martin blamed for the impending failure of his Harlech mine, in which R.B. Bennett had also invested. After a dinner at 28 Range Road, Martin had entered into a no-holds-barred debate with Bennett, passionately criticizing the Canadian government and its lack of energetic leadership in the economic development of the country.

Martin's book was widely reviewed in Canada and in the United States. He was invariably given credit for speaking from a position of authority in the field of coal mining and its distribution, of interprovincial and international trade practices, and his insight into the political system that governed Canada. A few excerpts from *The Fuel Problem of Canada* must suffice:

> Canada is the second largest coal importing country of the world and yet she possesses 17 per cent of the coal resources of the entire world.... The fundamental features for an independent supply are existing. The main handicap still is the long distance from the mines to the markets, resulting in an intense competition with foreign supplies. Apparently the industry has been unable or has made no attempt to overcome by its own efforts the present serious hindrance.

Without restraint, Martin lays bare the enormous profits middlemen derived from large-scale coal imports from the United States. Giving numerous examples of blatant dumping practices, he exclaims: "This surely must be known to the Dominion Department of Customs!"

And he appeals to the conscience of the Canadian government and its leaders:

> It seems ludicrous, that over 100,000,000 Canadian dollars should leave the Dominion annually, affecting adversely not only its currency, but also the country's trade balance—when every cent of this enormous sum might be used to great advantage in the country, safeguarding and advancing her industries, increasing the earnings of railways and paying a great number of workers, who in turn would consume agricultural home products and become users of her industrial products....
>
> At the present time, the rates for coal are arbitrary, absolutely unjustified and so prohibitive, that coal simply cannot move as far as it should.

Addressing the presidents of the Canadian National and the Canadian Pacific Railways, Martin questioned how they could stand idly by while permitting U.S. railways to reap huge profits from carrying coal into Canada.

Martin also offered solutions to meeting foreign competition, marketing and transportation:

Many domestic coal mines are not managed economically. There is not sufficient attention paid to the preparation of coal. Amalgamation of certain mines, forming of syndicates would be essential to improve productivity and reduce costs and pricing. Equally crucial is the formation of a Dominion Fuel Commission which should also give its attention to all other sources of fuel produced and consumed in Canada.

Turning to the root of the democratic process, Martin laid the blame for the government's lack of addressing Canada's fuel problem at the feet of public opinion. It was obvious that on this issue the lack of public interest and public concerns had permitted the government to let matters drift year after year. There had never been an outcry from the public at large, and the average Canadian was woefully uninformed to put pressure on the government to find a solution. What was required was a campaign of public enlightenment and education as to the existing conditions and their remedies. Without the public's pressure, the government would persist in letting the current conditions drift along as before.

It is astounding how Martin managed to complete this concisely written book in such a short time. Rightly, he received much praise in the press:

This highly interesting and instructive book will prove one of the most valuable contributions yet contributed for the development of our national life. The author proves himself an outstanding authority on the subject and tells its story in a straightforward and fearless manner.... He holds no brief for any government or corporate body connected with the fuel industry. His main purpose in writing this book is to enlighten the people of this country as to the immense value of their natural heritage now being wasted to the great benefit of foreign nations.

And a source Martin expected least to hear from, the *Drumheller Mail* wrote on August 26, 1930:

It will be a bitter pill for the coal operators of the Drumheller valley to swallow, but if we admit that the medicine with the most unpleasant taste is usually the most effective, all we can hope for is the best—because the medicine which Martin Nordegg administers to the coal industry at large and in particular to the operators of this delightful valley, is not even sugar-coated....

The *Queen's Quarterly* ended its review with the observation that "From beginning to end the book is thoroughly stimulating."

And the *Ottawa Citizen* agreed that "The Dominion Fuel Commission (strongly advocated by Martin Nordegg) is as neces-

sary to the needs of this great Dominion as the Railway Commission
and certainly should be brought into being with as little delay as
possible."

Perhaps trying to read Martin's mind, the *Ottawa Citizen* continued: "Who could fill the position of the first chairman better than the
author of the book under review?"

No other response was treasured by Martin as much as
Mackenzie King's letter:

> ... I have to congratulate you on your lucid presentation of an ex-
> tremely intricate problem.... In your book you make definite and, I
> think, vital suggestions. The book is worthy of wide and general read-
> ing if for no other reason than that it considers intelligently one of the
> greatest economic problems that the people of Canada even now are fac-
> ing and will have to face more definitely in the near future.

The letter was accompanied by a signed reproduction of
Mackenzie King's newest portrait, which found a prominent place
on Martin's desk.

Martin wanted to serve his country, especially the mining industry and the people of Alberta. But he was 62 years of age now and
cherished his personal freedom. Close as he was to the political
scene in Ottawa, he wanted to continue in his role as consultant on
specific issues, as conscience of government and corporations and
educator of the people. Publishing *The Fuel Problem of Canada* was
part of this mission. He would have felt honoured by the offer of
chairmanship but, no doubt, would have declined. Life with Sonia
was too precious and rewarding, and travel throughout the world
was now too much a part of his and Sonia's life.

While Martin was working feverishly on his book about the fuel
problem of Canada, Sonia entertained her cousin Sonia Tokar from
Berlin. Sonia Tokar, who at that time still called herself "Sofie," had
been born 1893 in Grodno to quite prosperous parents who could
afford to send their daughter to Berlin to study medicine.
Specializing in obstetrics and gynaecology, Sonia Tokar became one
of the first woman doctors in her field in Berlin.

Fortunately, the winter season of 1929-1930 did not bring cold
and snow to Ottawa at the usual time. Martin took a great number of
pictures during this visit, showing the two Sonias in elegant fur
coats standing in the park along Range Road, or Sonia Tokar in
front of the house, holding her cousin's cat in her arms. The latter
picture illustrates an interesting detail of the Nordegg house, the pa-
tio on the side of the house with its three large round-topped French
doors separated by crenellated pilasters.

Dutchie came to visit just before Christmas, and Sonia Tokar
must have enjoyed his company and his honest, straightforward

way, although later Dutchie must have had second thoughts whether he had conducted himself properly in the presence of this sophisticated lady from Berlin. But in early January 1930, he received a reassuring letter from Sonia Tokar:

> Dear Mr. Bernhard,
>
> I am not cross at all for your writing to me; just the contrary, was very glad to hear from you.
> And I thank you ever so much for your readiness to be me a helpful friend, when I need one.
> Wishing you once more a happy and healthy New Year, with kindest regards,
>
> your sincerely,
>
> Sofie Tokar."

And there is a last picture with Sonia Tokar and the Nordeggs with the Austrian Consul General, Dr. Ludwig von Kleinwächter and his wife, taken on the steps of 28 Range Road.

In early April 1929, Dutchie was delighted to find a letter from Marcelle among the mail Stuart handed him at the Bighorn Store in Nordegg:

> Dear Mr. Dutchie—
>
> I wanted to thank you for the Indian bracelet and trinket which you gave father for me—and which—although I haven't seen it yet—must be very nice. It was very kind of you to think of me! I hope to see you in the summer—I am looking forward to my trip to the mine and back on horseback to Banff where I haven't been for such a long time. I wonder what Nordegg looks like now—I heard that it has changed very much since I was there last.
> I shall never forget the lovely time I had on my last trip to the mine—and how all of you were so nice to me!
> But I'd better close now—thanking you again for those lovely trinkets and hoping to see you in the summer....

A genuine longing for Nordegg and the Rocky Mountains is expressed in Marcelle's letter, accompanied by the melancholy reminiscence of her trip with her father as a fourteen-year-old in 1912. But one can also glean from this letter that this was not the Marcelle of earlier years. Her handwriting, as intricate as ever, lacks the firmness one finds in her letters from earlier years.

In the late summer of 1929, Marcelle and her son, accompanied by a manservant, arrived in Ottawa. Martin was alarmed by the brittle state of his daughter's health. Marcelle had gained considerable weight and her face was pale and much fuller. Martin realized immediately that the promise of taking Marcelle once more across the Pipestone Pass from Nordegg to Banff would have to be broken. Marcelle would never stand up to the rigours of the trip, and all the precious, indelible memories of their journey in 1912 would be shattered. Nor did Marcelle's ten year-old son, who was a bit chubby, seem capable of meeting the challenges of a trip on horseback across the mountains. But Martin did enjoy the company of his grandson, a spontaneous, talkative boy, who seemed to cling to his grandfather. Martin was taken aback when he learned that Marcelle had thought it perfectly all right to leave her son in Ottawa in the care of Sonia's maid and her manservant, while she, her father, and her stepmother would travel West for a month.

Although Marcelle often seemed turned inward, she could also be very determined and stubborn at times. She no longer seemed eager to go to Nordegg. Martin began to fear the worst after Marcelle explained to him that all her plans were made. She would bring her son back to China, finalize her divorce—she had already arranged everything with her lawyer in Tientsin—and then leave immediately for Germany. Her husband was agreeable to everything as long as the boy would remain with him, to which Marcelle had no objections.

Martin took many pictures, some of them preserved in his album. One picture shows Sonia with her sister Anna, who had come for a visit from Newark, and Marcelle and her son, who looks like a typical student on holidays from boarding school. He likely attended the American school in Tientsin. Except for the beanie on his head, he is dressed like an adult, wearing a tweed suit, white shirt, and tie. A bit overweight, he is a nice-looking fellow, although with no resemblance to his mother. The serious expression on his face is notable, as Martin usually managed to make people look happy when in front of his camera. But neither does anyone else smile in the pictures from this visit; and in one picture taken by Sonia's sister Anna, Martin looks old and careworn as never before. Even Sonia, who always looks so charming and graceful on almost every photograph of hers that has survived, invariably carries a serious expression on her face.

Perhaps it is symbolic that eight of the ten pictures Martin chose for his album are about Marcelle's departure from Ottawa. Elegantly dressed with a enormous bouquet in her arms and a huge corsage on the lapel of her fur coat, Marcelle stands flanked by Martin and Sonia on the front steps of 28 Range Road. Another shows her by herself on the sidewalk with a lonely hatbox placed a few feet away at the curb; and yet another next to the automobile, ready to leave for the train station. It is a sunny day, but obviously chilly and windy and the trees on the other side of Range Road, once lush with green in summer, are now bare. Later, in the twilight of the Ottawa Union Station, Marcelle stands alone in front of the observation platform of the last coach, her face blank and lifeless like that of a mannequin. Did Martin think of the picture he took of Marcelle standing on a similar observation platform while happily and excitedly crossing the Prairies in 1912? There is a last group picture where with strained faces Martin and Sonia seem to wait impatiently for these painful minutes to pass. Only the Chinese manservant is wearing a perfunctory smile.

For a last time in her life, Marcelle crossed the Pacific Ocean, ordered her affairs in Tientsin, said goodbye to husband and son, and started the lonely week-long journey across the desolate, snow-covered plains of Siberia, Russia, and Eastern Europe. In Wiesbaden, where her mother had spent the last months of her life, she rented a small furnished apartment. There was not a single person she knew in the city. On New Year 1930, Marcelle failed to send her greetings to Ottawa. After a cable to Wiesbaden remained unanswered, Martin immediately booked passage to Cherbourg. On January 23, 1931, he stood, unannounced, on Marcelle's doorstep in Wiesbaden.

Martin broke into tears when he embraced his daughter. He felt as if he held a puppet in his arms. Marcelle had lost a great deal of weight, her hair was disheveled, and her dress rumpled and sprinkled with food stains. The entire apartment seemed in disarray, the kitchen full of dirty dishes, the bed unmade, and stacks of newspapers were piled up in the living room. Martin threw his arms around Marcelle again. Tears were still streaming down his face. He was caressing Marcelle's cheeks, but sensed hardly a response. Once or twice, Marcelle seemed to manage a weak smile when she told her father not to worry, that she was all right and glad to be back in Germany.

Martin spent a sleepless night in his hotel, mulling over in his mind what would be best for his daughter. Would she be able to stand the passage across the Atlantic? To that, Marcelle gave the answer the next day when she insisted on staying in Germany. Her mother did not like life in America and neither did she any longer. Besides, she needed to stay close to Switzerland, in case her mother needed her. She might call any day, and Marcelle must be ready to leave at a moment's notice, whenever her mother should ask for her. In terrible distress, Martin recognized that Marcelle was, at least at that moment, out of touch with reality. There was no point reminding her that her mother had died years ago.

If Marcelle was stubborn in refusing to even talk about another visit to Ottawa, much less to live with her father in Canada, she was in other ways frighteningly passive; she went willingly with Martin to a psychiatrist in Frankfurt. His diagnosis was severe depression with possibly the early phase of an acute psychosis. Immediate hospitalization was of utmost necessity; and travel to America, even if Marcelle were agreeable, was out of the question. When Martin pleaded with the psychiatrist to help him find the best clinic in the country—money would be no object—the psychiatrist made a telephone call to the Hertz'sche Privatklinik in Bonn. The medical director offered a period of treatment of six months, after which Martin would be requested to come to Bonn again to review Marcelle's progress and further care.

Next morning, an agitated Martin and a passive Marcelle boarded the train for Bonn. Martin did not succeed in engaging his daughter in any kind of conversation. Absentmindedly, Marcelle looked out the window across the River Rhine towards the bare hills of the valley, which looked so bleak on this cold, gray day. In Bonn, a taxicab took them to the Hertz'sche Privatklinik, which was pleasantly located in a park-like setting. Even though the buildings were not modern, they had an air of comfort and peace about them. While Marcelle was examined by Dr. Wilhelmy, the medical director, Martin used the time to peruse the brochure of the clinic. He gratefully realized that the psychiatrist in Frankfurt had indeed referred him to an excellent facility. Marcelle was admitted to the Hertz'sche Privatklinik on January 26, 1931.

The Hertz'sche Privatklinik had been opened as a modest establishment by Dr. Carl Hertz in 1849. Twenty years later, Dr. Hertz built an entirely new facility in the best district of Bonn on the Kreuzbergweg. The clinic quickly acquired the reputation of being one of the best facilities in the country and soon became well known beyond Germany's borders. The brochure referred to successfully treated patients who were members of Europe's foremost families, some of them of royal blood. It also stressed that the Hertz'sche Privatklinik was always in the forefront in adopting advanced treatment methods.

Dr. Wilhelmy gave Martin a relatively hopeful picture of Marcelle's condition, although he admitted that he had found depression one of the most difficult and stubborn conditions to treat. Martin took the suburban train to Cologne, where he booked a passage on the SS *Reliance,* scheduled to depart from Cherbourg in three days. By telephone, he asked his friend and business partner Hans Krämer in Berlin to cancel all appointments he had made by cable while on his way to Europe.

Martin dreaded the thought of entering Marcelle's apartment in Wiesbaden, his mind dwelling on the day almost seven years ago, when he had to close Berthe-Marie's flat after her death.

In Marcelle's living room, he discovered the album he had made for his daughter after their trip across Canada and the Rocky Mountains in 1912. It was the only item that Martin took with him to Canada. He stopped at the caretaker's flat, left the key with the caretaker's wife and paid her generously with the request to put Marcelle's apartment in good order. He also paid the rent for the forthcoming six months, picked up his suitcase at the hotel, and took the next train to Frankfurt, and from there the express to Cherbourg via Paris. If only Sonia were with him! Martin felt utterly dejected and alone.

Bad news was waiting in Ottawa. The Harlech venture was definitely coming to its sad end. Payments to the Canadian National Railways were far in arrears, and the Regional Superintendent had evicted Dutchie from the house Martin and Stuart had given him as a permanent home. Martin was very upset about what the CNR had done to his friend, especially after Dutchie wrote that after his bad experience with the railway, he was contemplating leaving Harlech for good. Nevertheless, the resourceful Dutchie had quickly built himself another cabin right in Harlech, but not without receiving the CNR superintendent's permission.

For almost fifteen years, Martin and Dutchie had sunk a great deal of money into Harlech; so had Stuart Kidd, but to a lesser degree. Both of them had taken heavy losses. Harlech never blossomed, one obvious reason being that, in contrast to Nordegg and its mine, Martin had never taken the time to take charge personally of the Harlech project. Like an absentee entrepreneur, he continually tried to get other parties interested and did raise substantial sums of money. But the day-to-day management in its various phases had never been in Martin's experienced hands. Only three times did Martin visit Harlech, but except for some intense discussions with Stuart and Dutchie, his days in Harlech and Nordegg had been spent as a visitor, twice in the company of Sonia.

Through Stuart, Martin had tried several times to get John Shanks to take over the management of Harlech, an indication of Martin's desperation. He still bore a grudge against Shanks and never really trusted him; but John Shanks did have the reputation of a competent mine manager, and there was no one else in sight. Shanks, probably wisely, ignored all overtures from Stuart.

The last known communication regarding the fate of Harlech is found in a letter to Stuart dated August 30, 1931. Martin and Sonia had just returned from Europe, both quite dejected, as Marcelle, although she had settled in quite well at the Hertz'sche Klinik in Bonn, had been far from ready to be discharged from care. With Marcelle's illness constantly preoccupying his mind, Harlech felt like an unbearable millstone around Martin's neck. He had few positive memories about this venture and now wanted more than ever to get rid of it all. This is clearly expressed in Martin's letter:

My dear Stuart,

I received your letter and the last statement of arrears....

I still maintain, that the Ry [the CNR] has no right whatsoever to prevent Con [Dutchie] taking out his private belongings. You must take the steps necessary for it....

I looked up the enormous file.... If we now abandon the coal leases and also the surface leases, we are given a certain time to remove all that is on the ground. Therefore naturally Con will also have to move, when the time is up.

You then say it is no use being bitter about Harlech. I quite agree with you, that Con and you are poorer and wiser. But you quite forget how much money I personally have sunk into Harlech, and how much my friends lost. I believe that over $150,000 were sunk in there. But what I regret more than the money, is the loss of confidence from my friends and specially R.B. Bennett. He will never forgive me for that, and every time he sees me, he jams it down my throat. The worry and time lost, I do not grieve about. As I see the business now, after so many years, we started on it, when prices for coal were high and supply short, we depended partly on people who were out there, and on managers who were either incapable ... or chucked the job as soon as they found something better. We should have made a greater success than Alexo or Saunders [two other mining towns East of Harlech that operated until 1954, the last phase of the closure of all Foothills mines including Nordegg]. In both places however there was a man who devoted all his time to it. That is, as I see it now. Nobody can be more sorry than I about the losses of all concerned. I have no reproaches to make to myself—I did all that was expected from me, and I held the company, sacrificing another $60,000 when everything pointed to throwing good money after bad. However, let us forget all about it now and try to save what can be saved.

I wish you would write to the lawyers ... the longer we keep the thing, the more rentals we have to pay....

This was the end of Harlech. Before the year ended, Martin also divested himself of all his other business operations upon the insistence of Sonia who was worried about the constant stress and its visible effect on Martin's health. There was no longer a need to pursue new ventures. Despite the world-wide economic slump, Martin and Sonia were well off, enjoying a secure financial return from the sound investments Martin had made. At the age of 63, he truly deserved to retire.

It did not seem too difficult for Martin to accept Sonia's advice. Before the end of the year, Harlech was wound up, and the Cosmopolitan and Ultramares companies were closed in the registers of the Provincial Secretary of Ontario. By the end of 1931, Martin was no longer an active entrepreneur, not even on a small scale. Photographs of the following years show him looking relaxed and smiling. His hair is no longer gray but silvery white, but his face is smooth and younger looking than during the preceding years. Martin had made the right decision.

Psychologically, Martin had overcome his losses without undue stress; but by the end of 1931, Martin and Sonia had to face another, more personal loss. Dr. von Kleinwächter was recalled to Vienna. There was no other family in Ottawa as close to Martin and Sonia as the Kleinwächters. Their two little daughters, Gunda and Ebba, were like grandchildren to them.

Dr. Ludwig von Kleinwächter had spent most of his career in the foreign service. He was born in 1882 as the son of a university professor in Czernowitz [today Czernowtsi in Ukraine], at that time a city of major cultural and commercial importance in the Eastern reaches of the Habsburg Empire. Kleinwächter began his studies at the University of Czernowitz and later obtained a doctor of jurisprudence in Berlin in 1909. He practised his profession for only two years before entering the foreign service of Austria-Hungary. First attached to the Austro-Hungarian consulate in Marseille, he was transferred to New York and later to Washington, where he remained until the entry of the United States into the war in 1917. Shortly afterwards, he was witness to the dramatic events in Petrograd [St. Petersburg], where he served as a member of the commission for the affairs of prisoners of war and civil internees in Russia. Between 1922 and 1925, Dr. von Kleinwächter was in charge of the Austrian Consulate in Chicago, where he and his young wife were introduced to the Nordeggs by Martin's friend Warren Roberts in 1925. In 1929, he was appointed Consul General of Austria in Ottawa.

There are several delightful pictures of Sonia with the blond Kleinwächter girls. The house on 28 Range Road became the second home for Gunda, born in 1925, and Ebba, born in 1927. Both remember the spacious house and the lovely garden where they were allowed to play and the kindness and love Sonia showered on them. Gunda Taylor-Kleinwächter, who now lives in Salt Lake City, describes herself as an extremely shy child, but she well remembers how much at ease and how carefree and happy she always felt while with the Nordeggs at their house, which she describes as "exciting, beautiful and comfortable." Both Martin and Sonia missed the Kleinwächters very much after their return to Vienna, but their close friendship endured.

There were more losses Martin would have to cope with. Andrew Haydon died on November 10, 1932; Thomas Mulvey would follow him on December 1, 1935. With these two men, Martin lost two of his best Canadian friends, who had also been his advisers and close business partners. Martin was deeply stricken with the loss of both men, without whom his life in Canada might have taken an entirely different direction. Both men not only advised and encouraged Martin in his ventures, but without their loyal support, especially Thomas Mulvey's as Under-Secretary of State, Martin might have never regained his foothold in Canada after the end of World War I.

In memory of his two friends, Martin wrote a eulogy, shared only with very few people and never published:

An Epitaph to Two Loyal Friends: Thomas Mulvey and Andrew Haydon

My thoughts during the long night did not let me sleep. They drifted from the sad facts to the human interest displayed by my dear friends Haydon and Mulvey—the best and closest friends I ever had.

To have gained their friendship was an accomplishment beyond value....

Mr. Mulvey was a devout Catholic; Irish to the core.... He had an intuitional judgment of people and facts and he expounded them in his ever condoning charming manner, interspersed with witty remarks—and his eyes smiled.... He rose quickly to the high Government position which he held for so many years.

But what I valued much more was ... that he was a true gentleman from top to toe ... of the old school, and so lovable for his excellent character.

What a genial host he was! It was a great privilege for me to hear his views and participate in the recital of his experiences of life.... His opinions were so mature, so well considered ...

It was a delight to travel with Mr. Mulvey in Europe.... These journeys are unforgettable—and the adventures we had together ... are so vivid in my mind.

Very frequently he gave me his elderly advice and I appreciated it as such and revered him.

Andy was my pal, my brother. How did our friendship grow so quickly?... How did it happen, how could it happen between two men so totally different from each other? Could it be just that attracting divergency in characteristics of birth, of locale, of surroundings, of education, of vocation? ...

He would have made an excellent judge—and he could have had a seat on any bench, or become Minister of Justice or Solicitor General, but this was against his inborn modesty, and he declined all such offers by Sir Wilfrid Laurier and Mackenzie King.

He possessed the great faculty of listening attentively and summing up the essential point of a complicated problem ... to come to a conclusion on regard to its solution.

He had undoubted literary gifts.... His favourite historical figure was undoubtedly Napoleon.... I knew that Andy was a sentimentalist and romanticist. When I took him on his first voyage to Europe ... I decided on a special Napoleonic tour.... In the Dôme des Invalides I showed him the sumptuous tomb and pointed out the inscription which Napoleon himself had written to be placed on his tomb; and Andy whispered to me: "Just think of that—ce peuple Français que J'ai tant aimé—and he loved them so much that he killed half a million of them to satisfy his own glory!'

Then, travelling through Germany, I took him to the hill on which Napoleon directed the battle of Jena. Andy stood still. One could see that he conjured up the whole battle in his imagination. Then he said, he wondered if on that hill the fruits of the revolution were not lost to mankind.

Andy read and reread the classics.... He lacked enthusiasm for sports and specially cards which he considered only a waste of time, and social functions were a horror to him.

He was the embodiment of scrupulous honor.... He trusted people too much.... He suffered in consequence large financial losses, but ... money actually meant nothing to him,... only the means for providing him and his family ... and the opportunity of helping others.

Andy gained in his professional and political life the love of all.... In politics he was a Liberal.... He became the organizer of the Party.... He was a most skilled and astute player in the political game ... as the great campaign strategist....

Finally he was actually forced to accept a Senatorship. He confessed to me that he did not know what to do with this honour, and he did not like the payment which went with it....

If there ever was a martyr crucified, vilified, far too noble to defend himself, or on account of his moribund illness incapable of answering unjustified charges, that was Andy.

A few days before his death a hurry call was sent to me as he wished to say Goodbye to me. During his coma in lucid intervals, while holding my hand all the time, he spoke of our friendship, our joys and sorrows, and when I was asked to leave he followed me with his eyes until the door closed. He died under great pain....

Martin would never forget his pal and brother Andy:

Maeterlinck in the Blue Bird makes the dead grandparents say to Myrtle and Tyrtle: "We are dead. But whenever you speak of us, we are alive again." And when our friends gather, dear Andy, they speak of you, and you are again alive amongst them.

In his relationship with the Liberal Party, Martin continued in the footsteps of Andrew Haydon, but communicated more closely with Mackenzie King than before Haydon's death. The Liberal Party was now in opposition, but Martin was convinced that the next federal election would bring Mackenzie King back to power. In the meantime, he felt he could be most useful in helping the Liberal leader shape the future policies of his party. Mackenzie King no doubt appreciated Martin's interest and contributions. His letters and notes sent to 28 Range Road sound generous and often quite informal, sometimes addressing Martin as "My dear Nordegg."

After another journey to Europe, Martin submitted a memorandum for Mackenzie King on Canada's role in world trade, dated December 14, 1934.

> There is no doubt in my mind that Canada is destined by her fortunate geographical position to play an ever increasing role in world trade.... The trend of trade will shift continuously and there will be still greater competition between producing nations in order to conquer new markets.
>
> It is not only an economic question for Canada, but also a political one in view of the coming elections ... no new idea has yet been mentioned in the coming appeal to the voters....
>
> I now take the liberty of suggestion to you ... a scheme which would undoubtedly bring great benefits to Canada ... and lastly take the wind out of the sails of the present government in its inaccurate statements and empty promises.
>
> This is the creation of free ports or free zones in our country.... I am familiar with the free ports of Hamburg, Danzig, Copenhagen, Singapore, Hongkong. We are locally better situated than most of the free ports.... The ports of ice-free Halifax with its new piers, then Montreal and principally Vancouver are ideally suitable. The sole mentioning of the intention should be an excellent political move. Even Fort William might be useful.
>
> The creation of free ports will not only influence shipping, but also result in a great advantage to the railways ... agriculture ... mining industry, exporting industry. Our banks will welcome the opportunity of financing transhipment of goods....
>
> The United States have recently passed a bill for the establishment of free zones. Political jealousy might prevent their coming into existence for some time. This gives us a chance to establish our ports firmly before Staten Island takes its place among the free ports of the world....

After receipt of Martin's memorandum, Mackenzie King promptly invited himself to dinner at 28 Range Road, sending a note of thanks to "My dear Nordegg" and "best wishes to Mrs. Nordegg and yourself for the New Year."

Martin also attempted to help Mackenzie King understand the intricacies of politics in the Prairies, where he wished the Liberals would take a greater interest to the benefit of the people. After the victory of the Social Credit Party in Alberta in August 1935, Martin passed a copy of a letter from Stuart Kidd to Mackenzie King. Stuart's (at times quite hilarious) report had nevertheless much relevance for the powers in Ottawa, which always lacked an understanding of the mentality of the Prairie people:

> ... A clean sweep almost for Aberhart.... I conceded about twenty-five seats to Aberhart but had no thought of this....
>
> What I mostly fear is that this gang ... will get us into some terrible messes.
>
> It has been the biggest bribery scheme at the least cost of any election ever run over the people and ... there is no hope of $25 per month ... they will crucify Aberhart....
>
> I think we will all have to vote Grit regardless of our previous affiliations....
>
> Here in Nordegg there were 10 votes for Labour, 158 for Social Credit and 23 for the Liberal. The women all voted S.C. as they wanted the $25 per month for their pin money.
>
> All the loose men voted for S.C. and all the bums....
>
> Well I must stop and go to work. Elections may come and Elections may go but we go on forever....

Martin had to chuckle when he read Stuart's comments. He was glad to see that his friend had regained his sense of humour after the terrible loss of two years ago when his wife had died as a result of a brain tumor. Stuart still managed to make a decent living in Nordegg and planned to send his boys to university. But like the rest of Canada, the overall situation in Alberta was desperate. The level of activity in industry and commerce had reached rock bottom. There were bread lines in the cities and government work camps in the country. Farmers had left their land after years of drought, which was even worse in neighbouring Saskatchewan. Thinking of the losses he might have suffered, Martin was grateful to Sonia again for insisting that he divest himself of all his business ventures.

On October 31, 1935, three days before her eighteenth birthday, it was time to say goodbye to Sonia's niece Anna from Grodno, who had spent a year in Ottawa "to learn English," as she had stated in her visa application. Like a mother, Sonia had been making plans for "Anushka, my foster daughter." Anna was very attached to Sonia, but she was terribly homesick. Had it not been for Sonia's overwhelming love and care, Anna might have returned to Grodno directly. Instead, she went with Martin and Sonia to New York, where she boarded a steamer for Haifa. Aware that under the poor circumstances Anna's parents subsisted in Grodno Anna would never enjoy an opportunity for a good education and a better life, Sonia had arranged for her niece to attend the university in Jerusalem for three years. She kept assuring the rather frightened Anna that she would never be lonely in Palestine, where several cousins on a kibbutz near Jerusalem were waiting for her.

Soon after Anna's departure, Martin and Sonia were ready for another journey, perhaps more strenuous and adventurous than all previous trips. This journey turned into one of Martin's special trips, which would take him and his wife to quite remote countries and places rarely visited by tourists. It also took them to some of the world's greatest sights.

The first leg of their journey started at Marseille, which they reached after a stay in Paris. Following a short stop at Mallorca, they landed at Alexandria on December 12, 1935, together with their Paris friends, Mr. and Mrs. Lamontagne. Photographs record the typical tourist excursions to the Pyramids, the Sphinx, and other sights. On their own, Martin and Sonia went up the Nile to Karnak and, by camel, to the royal tombs. A photograph shows Sonia at the entrance to King Tut's tomb. They continued past Edfu to Assuan and, turning north again, across the Suez Canal and the Sinai Peninsula to Jerusalem. Page after page of Martin's album is filled with his photographs of the famous sites in Egypt, in Palestine, and in Syria–from Jerusalem to Jericho to the Jordan River and finally to Baalbeck. There are also pictures of the visit to the kibbutz at Nahalal, where Sonia is photographed with her cousin, a young woman working in the fields. She looks optimistic and happy.

The reunion with Anna in Jerusalem was worrisome. Anna did not complain about her life, and she obviously worked very hard on her studies at the university. But when Sonia mentioned that towards the end of their long itinerary, she and Martin would visit Anna's parents in Grodno, Anna burst into tears and could not be consoled for a long time.

An overland bus took Martin and Sonia on an uncomfortable journey via Damascus to Baghdad. At the lonely desert crossing on the border between Syria and Iraq, Sonia is shown standing between two Syrian border guards. Baghdad brought a pleasant stay with Sonia's cousin Sonia Tokar and her husband Nahum Lampert. Both were respected physicians in Baghdad, Sonia as the gynaecologist, obstetrician, and personal physician to the female members of the royal family. During her years in Iraq, Dr. Sonia Tokar-Lampert helped several of the children of the royal family to enter the world.

Again, Martin took many pictures—in the garden of the Tokars, during an excursion with them to the ancient ruins in the valley of the Tigris and Euphrates, and of a day on the river with a large row boat belonging to the director of the Royal Museum, a German citizen.

Sonia Tokar cautioned her visitors to be careful with their comments about Germany, as the director was a well-known adherent of Hitler and the president of the local German association. The warning caught Martin and Sonia by surprise. They had not expected the need to be cautious so far away from Germany. During their stays in Germany, they had learned to be very circumspect in public. Although they felt protected with their foreign passports, Martin as a British subject and Sonia as an American citizen, they had more than once noticed hostile glances and angry mutterings from German people on trains and in restaurants. Both Martin and Sonia did look Jewish, but as foreign visitors now with a joint Canadian passport, they frequented without hesitation expensive hotels and restaurants from which Jewish citizens of Germany had long been barred. It was an unpleasant experience to realize that Hitler's arm reached as far as the Middle East.

The Tokars took Martin and Sonia to the Iranian border, where a hired car was waiting for them. In Teheran, Martin received permission to take a picture of the splendid peacock throne in the palace before meeting the Shah at his summer palace in Pahlevi. The day was extremely hot, and the Shah explained to Martin that he was continually thinking of his villa in the high mountains to the north in order to stand the pervasive heat.

The travel through Iran by car ended at a small harbour north of Teheran at the shore of the Caspian Sea, one of the important waters of the Earth but least travelled by Western tourists at that time. A small coastal steamer, crowded, hot, and not very clean, took Martin and Sonia to the Soviet Union, where they landed at Baku on January 31, 1936. Still not shying away from spending a fortune, Martin again hired a car and chauffeur and a guide from the Soviet travel service, Intourist. Most of the roads were terrible, and accommodations ranged from acceptable in the bigger cities to very poor in the country. But Martin and Sonia did see much of the country and its people; they traversed the wild mountains of the Caucasus and toured the city of Rostov and its spectacular theatre built in the modern Soviet style of the 1920s–a style that had experienced a brief period of fame before Stalin declared it "bourgeois and decadent."

After sightseeing in Kiev, the Nordeggs continued to Moscow, where Martin took some fascinating photographs of the interior of the Hotel Metropole: an elegant, walnut- panelled niche in the lobby with glassed-in display cases and a striking art deco table around which two of the hotel's chamber maids sit in drab coats of cheap material and, like Russian peasant women, wearing white kerchiefs tied behind their head. In another picture, five other maids, all in the same outfits, have their lunch around a table; not one of them has a smile on her face, and all studiously avoid looking towards Martin's camera. And there is the picture of the chambermaid making up Martin's and Sonia's beds placed against a wide double door.

These are the only pictures of Russian faces Martin seems to have taken during the weeks of travel though the Soviet Union. Their trip coincided with Stalin's show trials, which the Soviet press reported in great detail. Perhaps, it was not desirable or safe to preserve the likeness of the Soviet citizens.

One morning over breakfast, Sonia, who eagerly devoured the daily *Pravda,* discovered a familiar name: Zinovieff, Martin's business partner of years ago, was confessing to crimes he had never committed, as the ritual of the trials prescribed. In any other country, it would have been Martin's immediate inclination to rush to Zinovieff's help. But in Moscow, he had no influential friends. When he tried to "interview" the waiter in the breakfast room, the response was only a vacant stare, a shrug of his shoulders and a curt "Ya nye znayu [I do not know]."

It must have been a relief to enjoy the comfort of the elegant Hotel Europejski in Warsaw, where Martin and Sonia arrived on February 18, 1936. It was a bitterly cold winter in Poland, and Sonia felt more sorry than ever before when they visited Anna's parents in their small apartment in Grodno. At that time of the year, the city looked poorer and more neglected and bleak than Sonia could remember. She talked again with the Wolgiels about Anna's coming to America.

Martin and Sonia returned on the SS *Pilsudski,* the most luxurious of Poland's transatlantic steamers. They landed in New York on February 29, 1936. Upon their arrival in Ottawa, they found a letter from Dr. A. Kasen, director of a private psychiatric clinic in Jerusalem. Anna had been admitted there, suffering from severe depression.

Martin and Sonia were grief-stricken. It seemed utterly cruel that Martin's daughter Marcelle and Sonia's "foster daughter" Anushka were now both mentally ill and cared for in psychiatric facilities. Upon the advice of Anna's physician, Sonia arranged for Anna's return to her parents' home in Grodno. Anna left Haifa by boat on June 23. On the same date the Nordeggs sailed from New York to Bremen.

Martin and Sonia took the first train from Bremen to Cologne to see Marcelle in the clinic in Bonn. To their relief, Marcelle seemed much better than during their last visit. Marcelle's psychiatrist stated that she was well enough to take some shorter trips. Day-trips on a Rhine steamer for shopping to Cologne were followed by a week spent in the little towns along the Moselle and a three-day stay at Trier, where the three of them explored the Roman ruins. Marcelle is very slim, she is dressed in a silk blouse and a smart woolen skirt, a beret sits jauntily on the side of her head. She even manages a rare smile. On the stone steps next to her sits a relaxed Sonia with a very happy smile on her lips. But on another picture with Martin's step-nephew, Marcelle appears very serious again; the vagueness of expression on her face is sad and frightening. During the last day in Bonn, Martin took the last-known pictures of his daughter.

Martin was thinking of taking Marcelle back to Ottawa, if only for another visit. Quite at ease, Martin and Sonia left for Austria, where they met the Kleinwächters at Bad Gastein. When they returned to Bonn, Dr. Wilhelmy gently advised Martin that Marcelle had taken a turn for the worse and was not well enough to go even on a short outing with them. Any plans for taking Marcelle to Ottawa would have to be held in abeyance.

Back in Ottawa, there was going to be one last round of parties for which the Nordegg house had become so famous. Martin and Sonia had decided to sell their Ottawa home and return to New York. It must have been very hard to leave the wonderful house on Range Road with its history of happy visitors and guests, family members, friends from Canada and abroad, artists and businessmen, politicians and statesmen—two Canadian prime ministers among them. At the request of Prime Minister Mackenzie King, foreign dignitaries, especially from European countries, were often entertained, elegantly but without too much formality, in the unique ambiance of Martin and Sonia Nordegg's home.

To this day, Brigadier E. G. Beament of Ottawa, son of Martin's attorney and friend, remembers some of the parties on 28 Range Road and how the Nordeggs loved to entertain, especially the younger crowd. And there was the unforgettable evening when Mackenzie King had asked Martin and Sonia the near impossible— to entertain a delegation of military officers from Germany accompanied by the German ambassador, whom Martin had so far studiously avoided receiving as a guest. Sonia's nephew Hyman Mizell related the story of this event, which Martin had told him gleefully many times over:

> Not everything was pleasant or easy on that particular evening, especially the moment when Martin was forced to shake hands with the

German officers, realizing that this was the first time that someone had entered his home wearing the Nazi eagle with the swastika above the chest pocket of his uniform. But the Germans were full of praise for the elegant house, the good wine and the excellent food. They enjoyed themselves and were most cordial to Martin and chivalrous to Sonia. Obviously, nobody had told them that the Nordeggs were both Jewish. They certainly did not seem to notice Martin's and Sonia's Jewish features. Their reaction, or lack of it, speaks volumes: they would never expect to be placed in the position of being guests of a Jew, especially of one who had been born in Germany and become a rich man in North America.

Sonia was especially worried about her elderly mother, who happened to be staying with the Nordeggs. Old Mrs. Meisel was an impressive lady, who at the time was bound to a wheelchair after a recent fall resulting in a broken hip. Sonia had dressed her mother in an elegant gray-silver gown and placed a small tiara, which she had received as a gift from the Shah of Iran, on her head.

Like royalty, Mrs. Meisel sat on a heavily carved armchair in the corner of the Green Room. When one of the German officers asked Martin about the identity of the elderly lady, who looked like she belonged to royalty, Martin quickly replied,

Oh, she is our queen, but please, be kind and do not speak to her. Her mind is no longer clear and we want to save her from embarrassment.

Obediently, the German officers treated Mrs. Meisel with the greatest reverence, and both Martin and Sonia were immensely grateful that Mrs. Meisel did not utter a word, as she had promised. Instead, she played the role of a hard-of-hearing, mentally removed old lady. At the end of the evening, one after the other of the officers posted himself in front of Mrs. Meisel, clicked his heels and bowed to the grand lady.

On July 10, 1936, 28 Range Road was to sold to the Ottawa businessman Gordon Fleck for $35,000. That the value of the property had not changed in nine years, despite the vast improvements made by the Nordeggs, is a measure of the depressed real estate values prevailing since the world economic crisis of 1929. What emotions must have filled Martin's and Sonia's minds! They thought it best not to be present when their furniture and their art treasures were moved out of the house. In the morning of the 9th, Martin signed the final documents of the sale. Mr. Fleck had been most agreeable to look after the storage of the contents of the house. For the last time, Martin locked the front door of Ottawa home and turned the keys over to its new owner.

Once more, they sailed for Europe. Sonia wanted to visit Anna in Grodno, while Martin would stay with his step-nephew in Liegnitz in Silesia.

Had Martin only known what unpleasant surprises were awaiting Sonia at the German-Polish border upon leaving Poland, he would have accompanied his wife or, better, dissuaded her from taking this trip altogether.

From Liegnitz, Martin had taken Sonia to Breslau, where Sonia boarded the Prague-Warsaw express. All the doors to the carriages had been sealed at the Czech-German border, as the train was merely crossing German territory in transit with a short stop in Breslau. No German citizens were permitted to board the train. Two unsmiling German officials inspected Sonia's passport and travel documents, opened the door of a first-class carriage and resealed it immediately. Sonia was the only passenger entering the express to Warsaw after what to Martin felt like a foreboding ritual. As passengers were not permitted to open the windows while the train stopped at the station, Martin could not make out what Sonia was trying to say to him through the heavy pane of glass. The train pulled out of the station under the watchful eyes of the officials and a sole railway employee. Martin was the only civilian on the deserted platform under the grimy roof of the huge train shed. He wished Sonia had not gone to Grodno.

Martin boarded the next train for Liegnitz, which was overcrowded with happy families going to the Baltic Sea for their summer holiday. By the time he reached Liegnitz, Sonia had already crossed the border without any trouble, not expecting to be trapped in Poland at the point of leaving the country.

What caused the problem was a 50-pound British bank draft made out to Anna in care of a bank in Jerusalem. Anna had never cashed the draft, but had taken it with her when she returned to Poland. As this draft lacked the co-signature of Anna's psychiatrist Dr. Kasen and was therefore worthless in Poland, Anna had given it to her aunt just minutes before Sonia's departure from Grodno. Sonia had put the piece of paper in a folder that contained her correspondence with Anna and placed it in her suitcase.

Thirty-nine pages of documents found in the archives of the State Department tell the story of this incident and its consequences that involved the governments of both the United States and Poland. The file consists of various legal-size documents from the American Consulate General in Warsaw (8 pages and 6 pages respectively), from the State Department (6 pages), affidavits by Sonia (7 pages) and Martin (3 pages), a statement of claim against the Polish government by Sonia's lawyer Milton Diamond (4 pages), and various other missives.

The records begin with an urgent telegram from the Consulate General in Warsaw to the State Department:

August 28, 1936, rec.d 2:10 p.m.

Sonia Nordegg, American wife Martin Nordegg prominent citizen of
Ottawa, Canada, arrested and imprisoned at Rawicz, Poland, on charge
technical violation exchange regulations. Case reported Consulate
General this morning August 17th. Strong representations immediately
made appropriate authorities. Consulate General assured by high offi-
cials Ministries of Finance and Justice that orders have been issued to
State Prosecutor at Rawicz and customs authorities to release Mrs.
Nordegg immediately without bond.

The file concludes with a summation forwarded to the Secretary
of State in Washington, dated February 2, 1937, by Sonia's attorney, Milton Diamond, who requested the State Department's assistance in Sonia's claim against the government of Poland for an apology and an indemnity for moneys spent as a result of her arrest and
detainment in Poland. Excerpts tell part of the story:

Aug. 14/36 Mrs. Nordegg arrested at Rawicz ... for violation of
Poland's currency laws.... Mrs. Nordegg was then obliged to undergo a
most humiliating search and kept in custody at the Police Station, but
was allowed to telephone to Mr. Nordegg, then at Liegnitz, Germany,
who was expecting her.
Aug.15/36 12:30 A.M. Mr. Nordegg arrived at Rawicz in a hired
automobile. He engaged local counsel and was promised that Mrs.
Nordegg would be released on payment of ztl. 10,000. Later, however,
this promise was revoked.
Aug. 16/36 Mr. Nordegg continued his local efforts and wrote letter
to Embassy in Warsaw.
Aug.17/36 The Consul General, Mr. Thomas H. Bevan reported
the case to the Polish Ministry of Finance and the Ministry of Justice.
The latter informed the Consulate that instructions had been given to
quash the case.
Aug.18/36 Mr. Nordegg arrived at the American Consulate.... The
consul demanded, through proper channels, why the promise to him
that the case would be quashed had been broken;... on his protest the
case was actually quashed. Mrs. Nordegg was released, after four days of
continuous confinement.
Aug. 20/36 Mrs. Nordegg signed an affidavit, setting forth the case
in Warsaw.
Aug. 25/36 Return of passport to Mrs. Nordegg.

Sonia's affidavit is too lengthy to quote in full. But even in its
excerpts, it constitutes a fascinating witness to the precarious state of
European affairs at that time. In Rawicz, language problems added
to the already tense situation. Sonia requested that an English-
speaking person should be called to the train, as the customs inspector apparently did not understand the difference between a cashable
cheque and the draft in question. Sonia's baggage was removed

from the train for a further search, and when Sonia begged the inspector to please hurry, "... he told me that I was not leaving tonight... "

Sonia was present at the search of her luggage, watching her kimono being slashed because of a few suspicious scraps of paper found in its pockets. They turned out to be streetcar tickets from Ottawa, and "... it took quite some explanation to make him understand what they were."

Sonia's request to telephone her husband in Liegnitz was initially refused. Instead Sonia had to undergo what was probably the most humiliating part of her experience at Rawicz.

> He led me into a small room where a woman explained to me that I am to be examined. She made me take off my jacket, drop my skirt, took off my shirt waist, open my corset, drop my bloomers, and then gave me an almost medical examination.... She took my hat and gave it a thorough examination, put both hands in my hair to feel whether I had concealed anything under my hair, she also looked into my ears. After not finding anything, she let me dress....

Next, Sonia was asked to sign a protocol. She initially refused, but after being shouted at by the official

> that I understand Polish very well when I want to ... he made me sign it. Only then have I learned that I was under arrest and I was driven to the police station. I asked if I may go to the hotel to sleep,... but the police refused.... My husband succeeded in reaching me by telephone at 8 o'clock p.m. and told me that he would rush immediately by motor car to Rawicz and he appeared at 12:30 a.m. He also pleaded with the police to let me go to the hotel but without success.... I spent the night at the police station.
>
> Next morning I was taken before the local judge.... After my husband left for Ostrowo ... to speak to the prosecutor and engage a lawyer, I ... was taken to the prison in Rawicz and locked up in a cell.
>
> I stayed in this prison from Saturday, 15th of August, morning, until Tuesday evening at 7 p.m. when I was released under a bond of zlotys 1,500, and my passport was taken away from me and I had to sign a statement in which I obliged myself not to leave the country pending trial.
>
> I strongly protested against the unjust treatment ... as well as the humiliation I was subjected to.

The report by the American Consul General Thomas H. Bevan confirms Sonia's statements. It also throws some light on the machinations of government officials, some of them in highest positions and others, miserable little bureaucrats. Martin was frantically trying to engage reputable lawyers in Lodz and in Warsaw, but he had to ask for the personal intercession of the Consul General. After several broken promises on the part of Polish officials, he was finally successful. Mr. Bevan ended his report to Washington:

> Mr. Nordegg called at the Consulate General and reported to me the action he had taken. I was surprised indeed to hear that Mr. Kryczinski's assistant had ordered Mrs. Nordegg's release on a zls. 1,500 bond, when I had been definitely assured the previous day that she would be released without bond. I called Mr. Matecki and advised him that I would like to confer with him immediately.... During the interview ... he appeared very much surprised and did not believe the information furnished.... He reported the incident by telephone to Mr. Kryczynski who stated that he would countermand the instructions sent to the Prosecuting Attorney at Rawicz and instruct him to immediately return the bond and throw the case out of Court.
>
> Mrs. Nordegg's American passport ... was returned to her on August 25th....
>
> Both the American and British Embassies protested to the Foreign Office against the treatment received by Mrs. Nordegg at the hands of the Polish officials.

Sonia's case attracted a fair amount of attention in the press not only of the United States but also in Europe, especially in Germany. *The Völkische Beobachter*, the mouthpiece of the National Socialist Party, sarcastically commented on the inability of a country as huge as the United States to protect her citizens from the maliciousness of a country as small as Poland which, of course, as was well known, was suffering from a superiority complex. It is safe to assume that among German officialdom it was known that Sonia was Jewish. In this case, however, it was obviously to greater advantage for the increasingly hostile attitude of official Germany against Poland to deplore the fate of a poor U.S. citizen, while ignoring her Jewish origin. To set matters straight, the State Department published an official press release on August 25, which was immediately distributed to the embassies and consulates in Germany, Poland, England, and other European countries.

Both Martin and Sonia were severely shaken by this experience, Sonia deeply humiliated personally, and Martin angry and depressed by what had happened to both of them. Their visits to Germany during the past three years had been more and more overshadowed by the pervasive presence of the Hitler regime. But Martin had never expected such arbitrary treatment by another European country.

Martin and Sonia left Poland as quickly as possible on the shortest route. Sonia refused to return to Liegnitz, as this would once more require crossing the border at the notorious Rawicz station. Martin could not disagree and reserved a compartment in the Moscow-Paris Express to Berlin. The mood there was not reassuring. After the spectacle of the 1936 Olympic Summer Games, all of Germany still seemed to burst in national pride. Even months later, the daily papers were still filled with reviews of the Olympics, intending to keep the national spirit at the highest level. And one morning, Sonia discovered her name in the August 26th issue of the *New York Times,* which had just arrived at the Fürstenhof Hotel:

> Mrs. Nordegg of Ottawa, Canada, Citizen of the United States, was imprisoned August 17 on Technicality.

The story gave a slightly abbreviated version of the State Department's press release. Ironically, in the column to the left, the *New York Times* reported on the Paris visit of Dr. Schacht, the president of the German Reichsbank and Hitler's finance minister, according to the official announcement "... as a token of the desire of Germany and France to contribute to the peaceful improvement of the international situation,"

Martin could only laugh in disgust. He had known Schacht for a good number of years and considered him a true turncoat, who had successfully managed the transition from the Empire to the Weimar Republic and finally to the Third Reich. How could Schacht reconcile with his conscience the terrible fact that some of his former partners in business had been forced out of existence, including all Jewish banks. Among them, Schlesinger & Trier, which had been involved with the financing of Martin's Nordegg project, had been expropriated.

And again on the same page, the *New York Times* published an excerpt from Germany's last remaining Jewish weekly; the excerpt commented that the Zinovieff show trial in Moscow had finally proven that Jews no longer had a prominent role in the Soviet Union and that it was false for the German press to speak of the Soviet Union as "... an incarnation of Jewish Bolshevism."

This was a rather courageous statement; but since no one outside the Jewish community would read this paper, this comment was apparently tolerated by the authorities.

Sonia met Martin's distant relative Irene Jordan, who had taught underprivileged kids in Moabit, one of Berlin's poorest districts. Irene, whose husband was Jewish, gave Sonia a picture of the desperate situation and oppression of the Jewish citizens. Soon after Hitler's assumption of power, they had been barred from most professions, from universities, from the civil service, and from all branches of the arts. They had lost most of their rights as citizens and were no longer tolerated in swimming pools and other sports facilities, better restaurants, and cafes. Jews were subject to a constant barrage of vicious propaganda, they were frequently ridiculed on the street; and Jewish children were beaten up by Aryan kids. Only some Jewish stores were still in the hands of their rightful owners; but most were suffering badly, as the party promoted a constant boycott of Jewish stores. Nobody had thought this possible; almost every Jew had felt as good a German as anyone else in the country. But incredibly, too many Jews still believed that things could not get any worse. Irene Jordan was very doubtful.

There was no point in remaining in Germany. Besides, Sonia was emotionally exhausted. Martin suggested that they spend a month at Karlsbad in Czechoslovakia. There they would feel safe and welcome and also be close to their friends, the Petscheks in nearby Aussig.

Martin and Sonia returned to Liegnitz in early October, where they enjoyed a relatively peaceful two weeks. An entry in their joint passport indicates that Martin and Sonia reported their departure from Liegnitz to the police on October 22. Another entry refers to a bank draft exchanged at the Deutsche Bank in Liegnitz.

Martin, who did not feel well at all, saw a doctor in Liegnitz. He was short of breath and was plagued by a persistent cough. The doctor suggested a stay in a milder climate for the winter. Gentle, peaceful Meran on the southern slopes of the Alps would be perfect.

Well rested and in better spirits after the pleasant stay in Meran, Martin and Sonia stopped in Paris in December and sailed from Cherbourg to New York in January 1937. They avoided leaving from a German port, determined never to return to Germany as long as Hitler was in power.

Something extraordinary is notable in the passenger arrival list at New York, where the Nordeggs landed on January 14, 1937; both Martin and Sonia gave their race as "Hebrew." Was this entry accidental? Did Martin, who had stated his race as "German" for almost thirty years, no longer identify himself with the country of his birth, that country having taken on such threatening and radical characteristics?

The arrival at Ottawa on a bleak January day was sobering; the Chateau Laurier Hotel now their temporary home. Martin sat at the window in his suite, contemplating what was left for him in Ottawa, or even in Canada. For Martin, Canada had always meant working, planning, striving for success. But now, he felt old and tired. And he had Sonia's well being in mind. She was terribly unhappy staying at the Chateau Laurier, without a home to invite and entertain visitors.

Sonia convinced Martin that the move to New York could not come too soon. Martin had applied for the status of a permanent resident of the United States. Why should they not go to Europe again for the summer! There were enough countries left where life was still pleasant. They could avoid Germany and Poland completely. By the time of their return, Martin's residence permit would have been issued; and they could settle in New York, where Martin had more friends than were left in Ottawa. Depressed and feeling aimless as never before in his life, Martin knew that Sonia was right. There was nothing left for him in Ottawa.

And, for the first time since coming to Canada, there was nobody to bid him farewell at the Union Station. Again, he was immensely grateful for having Sonia at his side.

X

AN UNSETTLED RETIREMENT
1937 - 1939

After the bleak winter months of enforced idleness at the Chateau Laurier in Ottawa, Martin and Sonia departed happily from New York for Cherbourg on April 10, 1937. Martin had pulled up his stakes in Canada for good; but strangely enough, he did not feel any regret. Nor did it bother him that once more he and Sonia were without a permanent address. They had placed their furniture and art treasures in storage in Ottawa pending their return in the fall to take up residence in New York.

Except for a brief trip from Paris to Bonn to see Marcelle, Martin and Sonia had decided to avoid Germany altogether. The Canadian Legation in Paris was to be their forwarding address during their stay in Europe. Austria was still an independent nation and so was Czechoslovakia. They had many good friends in these countries; and, of course, they also planned to travel to Poland via Czechoslovakia to see the Wolgiels in Grodno.

The visit in Bonn was terribly sad and disappointing. Marcelle received her father and stepmother in quite a settled, though emotionally distant mood; but Dr. Wilhelmy's report was very distressing. He had observed Marcelle's increasing state of withdrawal from reality interspersed with episodes of acute psychosis, which required her separation from the other patients. Martin had planned a trip up the Rhine, where spring had arrived in all its beauty. But Dr. Wilhelmy asked Martin not to expose Marcelle to any change in her daily routine that would be very distressing to her and could easily result in another episode of acute psychosis. As tactfully as he could, Dr. Wilhelmy also explained the changed situation in Germany, where Jews had to expect to be insulted almost anywhere in public. He did agree to short outings in the city or perhaps a taxi ride to Bad Godesberg or strolls through the parks, although sitting on park benches should be avoided. Too many people were eager to point a finger at persons of Jewish appearance unless some type of Nazi insignia worn on their lapel would identify them as Aryan.

On their first outing, Martin and Sonia were already acutely aware that Dr. Wilhelmy had not exaggerated. Neither the charming restaurants along the Rhine River in the suburb of Bad Godesberg nor the better-class establishments in the centre of Bonn were accessible to them. The infamous signs "JEWS NOT WANTED" or "JEWS NOT ADMITTED" were posted at the door. Martin, Sonia and Marcelle finally had a rather poor meal in the waiting room second class of the Central Railway Station—the restaurant of the first-class waiting room was closed to Jews. The next two outings were more pleasant. Martin had followed Dr. Wilhelmy's advice to take a taxi to some of the villages in the countryside and stop at simple country inns.

Martin and Sonia left Bonn in deep emotional distress. It was clear to both of them that it would be impossible to get Marcelle out of Germany even if her condition should improve.

This was the beginning of Martin's full retirement. And this was to be the first trip to Europe where Martin would not combine pleasure with business activity. But against all expectations, their European summer had started on a depressing note for Martin and Sonia. Only after a three-week stay in Bad Gastein, which they had reached via Switzerland, did the sad memories of their days in Bonn begin to fade. Between Bad Gastein and Karlsbad, Martin and Sonia spent the next two months in the company of their friends, among them the Petscheks in Aussig and the Kleinwächters in Vienna. These must have been carefree days indeed. Martin took masses of pictures, all of them of near professional quality, in the Austrian Alps and the lake country of the Salzkammergut, of mountains and villages, of Austrian people in their colourful local costumes during a big country fair at Traunsee, and of old and new friends. There are photographs taken in the Vienna Woods and in Karlsbad, sitting with the Petscheks in elegant outdoor cafés or drinking the famous health-promoting but not very good-tasting waters of the Muehlbrunnen.

Both Martin and Sonia look exceedingly well, especially Martin, whose features are relaxed and animated. He is well tanned and happy. He was glad to see his step-nephew who had come from Liegnitz in Silesia to Aussig. His stepmother, Martin's sister Malwine, did not dare crossing the German-Czech border with her passport identifying the bearer as "Jewish." Martin could only communicate with his sister by telephone and was not at all sure that their conversation was not monitored by the German authorities.

Although a retired gentleman of means now, Martin remained the always curious, enterprising man. Not without difficulty, but with his usual persistence, he managed to secure two invitations to the opening of the Grossglocknerstrasse on August 3, 1937. This was a day of great pride for Austria, perhaps one of its last days of celebrating the achievements of the Republic. Famous as Austria's highest mountain, the Grossglockner was now accessible by car to ordinary travellers rather than mountaineers only; and the Nordeggs in their rented car were at the head of the long convoy that was slowly snaking its way up the mountainside, soon above the tree-line and later passing the glaciers before reaching the top of the Grossglockner. An enthusiastic Martin took many photographs of this memorable tour, of cars lined up along the bare mountainside for more than a mile, of views across unspoiled mountain scenery, and of Sonia dressed quite sportily and standing at the edge of a glacier.

On August 10, the Nordeggs crossed from Czechoslovakia into Poland at Cieszyn to proceed to Warsaw and Grodno. There were no complications at the border as in 1936. The Nordeggs were treated politely by the Polish border guards; the Europejski in Warsaw was as elegant and cosmopolitan as ever; and in Grodno, to her great relief, Sonia found her niece Anna in the best of moods and eager to come to the United States. Anna had already received a Polish passport and readily accepted Sonia's suggestion that they obtain the remaining documents from the local Polish authorities in preparation for their visit to the American Embassy in Warsaw. When she said goodbye to Anna at the Praga railway station in Warsaw, Sonia felt assured that she would soon welcome her niece in the USA.

There was nothing left for the Nordeggs to do in Poland. They departed for Vienna on the following day. One more stay at a popular resort, this time the Yugoslavian Opatia at the northern tip of the Adriatic Sea—Abazzia in Austrian times—concluded a sojourn through Europe of almost six months. It was the last journey to the Old World that Martin and Sonia took together; and despite its sad beginning, it was perhaps their happiest one.

In the last days of September, they took the Orient Express to Paris, continuing within a few days to Cherbourg, where they boarded the German liner *Europa*. Although the political horizon in Europe seemed to darken from month to month, neither Martin nor Sonia expected that within less than six months the Republic of Austria would cease to exist!

Looking back on their months in Europe, Martin could not suppress a sense of foreboding. No matter how beautiful Europe had looked during this exceptional summer of 1937 or how welcome they had felt in Austria, the atmosphere of unease could not be ignored. Everywhere, Martin and Sonia had met Jewish citizens who had managed to buy their way out of Germany into Austria or Czechoslovakia. But they were filled with fear, constantly worrying that Nazi Germany would extend its control beyond its borders into these countries too.

In November, the Nordeggs rented an apartment at 25 Central Park West. This was the prestigious address of a fifteen-year-old building of twenty storeys. But much of the furniture brought from Ottawa had to go into storage once more until a larger apartment could be located.

Sonia was happy to be close to her family, especially to her aged parents. Her father still lived in the Bialystoker Home for the Aged, while her mother had moved to the Jewish Home for the Blind. Sonia's sister Anna visited frequently. On New Year's Day 1938, Sonia excitedly informed her sister that in three months there would be another Anna living at her home, young "Anushka" from Grodno, who had so quickly received her immigration visa. Sonia had already booked passage for Anushka on the SS *Batory,* leaving from Gdynia on March 3, 1938.

While Martin and Sonia felt a little confined in their apartment, missing many of their art treasures and the fine furniture, Sonia's nephews and nieces and their children came from Brooklyn, from Queens, and from the Lower East Side to admire the elegant Nordegg apartment and precious furnishings the likes of which they had never seen. Sonia even persuaded her father to come and visit with the help of an ambulance. Her mother, too frail to leave the nursing home and nearly blind by now, would have loved everything, as she had during her visit a few years earlier to the much grander 28 Range Road in Ottawa. But old Isaac Meisel rather silently inspected everything; and before being helped by the ambulance attendants out of the apartment, he reminded Sonia not to forget to always be "a good Jew." He was very fond of Martin, appreciating that Martin had given his daughter a secure life and a happy marriage. But he wished very much that Martin were Jewish also, never realizing that such a wish was actually redundant—Martin had never shared the secret of his Jewish origin with anyone except his wife.

Sonia's father, though, became very fond of Anna Wolgiel, his great-niece from Grodno. For Isaac Meisel, young Anna was a true Jewish woman, modest, shy, and unpretentious. Anna always preferred plain, dark dresses with a white collar; her hair was parted in the middle and pulled back to a little bun; she never wore make-up. And Anna, always speaking Yiddish, warmed her great-uncle's heart with her stories of life at Grodno and its Jewish quarter, which had not changed all that much from the times when Isaac Meisel had visited Anna's relatives years ago. Anna, in turn, loved to visit Isaac at the Bialystoker Home. Overwhelmed by the hectic life of New

York, Anna felt safe in expressing her homesickness to old Isaac. And all the other old people at the home welcomed Anna like a messenger from the communities they had left so many years ago.

Anna was immensely grateful for all Sonia had done for her, but she never overcame a certain shyness and reserve towards her aunt. Perhaps Sonia was too spontaneous and demonstrative when she was pressing Anna against her bosom in genuine affection. It is not certain whether Anna was conscious of the fact that Sonia saw in Anna the daughter she never had; but because she was very close to her mother and missed her terribly now, Anna probably found it impossible to respond in the same way to Sonia's sincere affection. She appeared timid and a little insecure among the splendor of the Nordegg home, wondering how she deserved all the affection and attention and the expensive clothes Sonia showered upon her. It did not help that Sonia excitedly explained that it was for Anna's sake that they had moved to another, much larger apartment on 239 Central Park West so that Anna could have her own room and even her own bathroom. In Grodno, Anna had shared a tiny room with her sister, and there had not even been a bathroom for the family in their little house on Brigydzka Street.

Anna was, of course, a good "foster" daughter. She liked to accompany Sonia's maid Toni on her daily shopping to the grocery store around the corner; she helped with dusting and cleaning and worked hard on perfecting her English; and she responded very well to the private tutor Sonia had engaged for her. Still, Anna wondered how she would find her way through Hunter College, which Sonia wanted her to attend in the fall. At least she had learned how to use the subway to the Lower East Side so that she could visit old Isaac Meisel as often as possible. Sonia did not mind when Anna began to work as a volunteer at the Bialystoker Home.

There were also visits to Anna's other aunt, Sonia's sister Anna across the Hudson River. Anna always wished she could stay a little longer there. Anna Meisel had a small, modest house on 149 Spruce Street in Newark, where Anna Wolgiel felt much more at home than among the elegance of 239 Central Park West. Besides, while Anna Meisel was as loving an aunt as her sister, she was less exuberant than the emotionally expressive Sonia. Once in a while, Sonia took Anna to visit the Meisels in Brooklyn and Queens. Anna felt somewhat lost there with her age falling between the Meisel parents and their children, who were too young to be her friends and companions.

Towards Martin, Anna developed a respectful relationship. Martin was kind to Anna but quite reserved. Anna, who was politically naive and uneducated could not realize that in these days Martin was deeply preoccupied with the worrisome turn of events in Europe after Hitler's annexation of Austria.

When Martin and Sonia had been in Europe during the summer of 1937, Austria had still seemed relatively safe, although the outlawed Nazi groups there became more and more vocal in demanding Austria's inclusion in the German Reich. Italy, while a fascist state under Benito Mussolini, had always been seen as Austria's stalwart defender and protector of its independence; but after Italy had formed an alliance with Nazi Germany in November 1936, little Austria was unprotected and defenceless.

Anxiously, Martin followed the news from Germany and Austria; he worried about the intensifying crises and conflicts provoked by Hitler. Literally "ordered" by Hitler, the Austrian Chancellor Schuschnigg presented himself at Berchtesgaden. He was not allowed to leave until he signed an agreement on February 12 that proclaimed an amnesty for all members of the outlawed Nazi organizations and the inclusion of Austrian national socialists in his cabinet, among them Seyss-Inquart as Minister of the Interior. With this appointment, Hitler pursued for the first time a strategy that would place the fate of a country in the hands of his followers. Control of the Ministry of Interior meant authority over the police and the other organs of control, quickly leading to the assumption of power over the entire country and its people. This is how one country after another would fall into the orbit of communism, as Austria fell to Germany in the spring of 1938. It was a strategy that would later be successfully applied again and again by Joseph Stalin in the years following World War II, when the Eastern European countries lost their freedom and became part of the Soviet Bloc.

These were very tense days for Martin. His allegiance to the country of his birth and the German people was already deeply shaken, perhaps destroyed forever. No matter how undemocratically and ruthlessly Hitler acted, Martin could not deny that he had the enthusiastic support of the vast majority of Germans. And Martin was equally disturbed about the weak response of the Western democracies on both sides of the Atlantic to the threats uttered by Hitler not only against Austria but also against Czechoslovakia. Within days of Chancellor Schuschnigg's humiliation by Hitler in Berchtesgaden, Martin poured his anger, frustration, cynicism, disappointment and fear for the future of freedom and humanity into a remarkable (in parts cynical, in other parts prophetic) letter to his friend Agnes McPhail, a socialist and the first woman elected as member of parliament in the House of Commons in Ottawa.

316 Martin Nordegg

Dear Miss McPhail,   New York, February 17, 1938

Like a fresh breeze from the North, your letter blew in. We appreciated it the more, knowing how busy you are listening to debates which throw emptiness into nothing....

We miss talking and listening to you, to Mr. Woodsworth[*] and a few other friends—who have the dangerous habit of thinking and the sincerity of speaking. The latter is going quickly out of fashion, because that will be punished.

"Heads off," said the Queen of Spades.... People are being standardized into the same political creed.

I honestly believe, that democracy with its supposed tenets of liberty and freedom is doomed. Democracy has always an eye on votes, and while considering them, Fascism acts. Democracy is "laissez faire" in the highest potency; it is doomed because of its weakness. It was strong right after the war—but it weakened so rapidly, that political gangsters in other countries took the opportunities offered....

The chickens have now come home to roost. Fascism is the fashion. Nations and people who still have ideals, have no right of existence. It will soon be a crime to belong to another party or religious creed not sanctioned by the Government. You call the Fascist movement a flare-up in Quebec. Of course, that is how every fire starts; but this fire will not be extinguished.

Look at Germany.... The intelligent population pray to Hitler who makes Germany greater than she ever was—and prefer Hitler to God.... Hitler got into power, because he had penetrated into the German soul, and found there inherent brutality coupled with subserviency to the men above and bullyism to the man below; to give people a uniform, processions and other free entertainment.

The Romans did not go so far; they at least gave bread. Now the Germans prefer cannons to butter.[**] They are uniformed outside and inside and do not dare to speak, less to revolt. And the German army is better clothed and fed than ever before, and all demands for weapons ... are fulfilled at once. And the promotions! ...

We may come up soon to Ottawa. I do not intend to give up my Canadian citizenship. I still have faith in the country and its people and hope that Canada will be the last country to forbid thinking and speaking. But one can never tell.

Give our kindest regards to Mr. Woodsworth and his charming daughter. And our best remembrance to your dear self, and love from Mrs. Nordegg.

Yours sincerely

The Nordeggs.

---

[*] James Shaver Woodsworth (1874-1942) Parliamentary leader of the Co-operative Commonwealth Federation.

[**] Ironically, this was to be the phrase Hitler's minister of propaganda, Dr. Joseph Goebbels, would throw as a challenge at the German population seven years later at the proclamation of the "Total War" in 1944.

How prophetically right Martin was in the short run and in the long-term perspective! There were some protests. On February 20, Anthony Eden, the British Foreign Minister, resigned in protest over the conciliatory politics of Prime Minister Neville Chamberlain against Germany, where Hitler had given himself unprecedented power on February 4 by proclaiming himself supreme commander of the German armed forces and by taking over direct control of Germany's foreign policy. And on the 16th, the famous conductor Arturo Toscanini, a presence at the Salzburg Festival for years, announced his withdrawal from the festival in protest over the Nazi actions against Austria.

At the same time, the propaganda campaign against Chancellor Schuschnigg increased from day to day and so did the rapidly progressing chain of events leading to the demise of the Republic of Austria. On March 9, the defiant Schuschnigg announced a plebiscite that would enable the Austrian people to determine the future of their country democratically, either as an independent nation or as a part of the Third Reich. But the plebiscite was never held. Hitler ordered the Austrian Minister of the Interior, Seyss-Inquart, to cancel the plebiscite. Realizing that with the German troops massed at his country's borders, he had lost the battle and that his further resistance against Hitler's aims might promote strife and bloodshed in his country, Chancellor Schuschnigg announced his resignation on March 11. He was succeeded by the leader of Austria's Nazi organizations, Seyss-Inquart. On the following day, German troops crossed from Bavaria into Austria with Hitler following the advance parties of his troops. From his temporary headquarters in the district capital of Linz, Hitler started his triumphal progress through Austria to arrive on March 14 in Vienna. As the *New York Times* reported, after

> … a day of unparalleled glory for Adolf Hitler, the German leader who left Austria in his youth as a penniless artist, was cheered by thousands as he returned to Vienna today to proclaim the "Anschluss," or union, of the country with Germany….
>
> Forty tanks led the way, and police cars filled with officers brought up the rear. Along the route, Nazis from all over Austria cheered the man who once pledged that Austria's borders were inviolable.
>
> Hitler stood in the open car most of the drive … returning the nearly hysterical salutes of his ardent supporters….

Martin and Sonia had not taken the time to look at the morning papers, nor had they listened to the news on the radio. This was the day of Anna Wolgiel's arrival in New York. But when they returned with Anna from the pier, the maid, Toni, handed Martin the *New York Times*, which announced Hitler's annexation of Austria! What would Hitler's next move be? There were large German minorities in Czechoslovakia and in Poland.

Both Martin and Sonia took great pains to hide their shock about the news from Austria from Anna. This was supposed to be a happy day in her life! But after midnight, Martin tried to call the Kleinwächters, the Fliegels, and several other friends in Vienna. None of them answered the telephone. Next morning, the newspapers announced that Chancellor Schuschnigg and a large number of Austrian politicians and high government officials had been arrested. Over the next few days, more disturbing news reached the United States describing the terror the Nazis directed against Jews, Communists, Socialists, the prominent members of the Austrian government and civil service, and many other citizens known to have been loyal to the Austrian Republic and its institutions. By the end of March, the papers reported the arrests of more than 34,000 citizens. There was still no word from the Kleinwächters in Vienna, although Martin had sent several telegrams and had also forwarded a cheque to a non-Jewish friend, asking him to pass the money to the Kleinwächters.

It was time to renew acquaintances with Mr. George Messersmith, the Assistant Undersecretary of State in Washington. In better times, Martin had been introduced to Mr. Messersmith by the Kleinwächters in 1934 in Vienna, when George Messersmith served as United States envoy and minister plenipotentiary to Austria. Martin hoped to find an open ear in Washington, especially since the United States government had just requested Great Britain, France, and other democratic European nations to participate in a program to assist German Jews, especially those currently in great danger in Austria, to flee to safer countries. This request, issued on March 24, provoked a wild tirade by Hermann Göring during a public speech in Vienna. Göring warned all Jews to leave Austria immediately or face dire consequences.

On March 28 in Washington, Martin met with George Messersmith, who could not help at all. Messersmith explained that the U.S. government was not in the position to deal with the Nazi authorities in Vienna, as the United States had not recognized Hitler's annexation of Austria. There was no official communication possible between the U.S. Embassy in Vienna and the new authorities, especially in such delicate matters as inquiries about the whereabouts of former Austrian government officials, such as Dr. von Kleinwächter who had last been in charge of the Austrian Press Bureau and was no doubt in an endangered position.

Nor was the Canadian Ambassador in Washington, Sir Herbert Marler, able to help by getting information about the Kleinwächters from the British Embassy in Vienna. But Sir Herbert was most sympathetic when Martin asked for his support and protection—to whatever extent that might be possible—when he would be going to Vienna himself, a decision he had made spontaneously while Sir Herbert tried to reach the British Embassy in Vienna by telephone.

This was to be the first time in fourteen years that Sonia did not accompany Martin to Europe. She certainly could not leave Anna alone; and besides, Martin knew it would be irresponsible to take Sonia along on this difficult and risky journey. He knew that the protection American and British authorities could extend to him as a naturalized Canadian and former German citizen was limited and uncertain. He also suspected that the German authorities were by now fully aware that behind the very Germanic name of Nordegg, there was a Jew named Cohn who had been born in Germany. It was just as likely that the names of Martin and Sonia Nordegg had long been known to the Gestapo. Over the past five years, both Martin and Sonia had helped a number of German citizens, most of them Jewish, not only to leave Germany but also find entry into Canada or the United States. Martin now strongly felt the call to go to Europe and try to help his endangered friends.

Every day counted—the news from Austria about the plight of Jews and those known for their loyalty to the old regime was frightening. Martin booked passage on the fastest liner crossing the Atlantic, the *Queen Mary*, scheduled to depart from New York on April 4. He was nervous and anxious when he said goodbye to Sonia and Anna at the pier. But, like the Martin of earlier years, he also felt a sense of excitement in his veins, a determination to meet a new challenge. He was 70 years old and often did not feel well. But now he felt strong and ready to face the enemy and save at least some of his friends from a merciless, inhuman regime.

While crossing the Atlantic on the *Queen Mary*, Martin learned from the daily news bulletin that on April 6 the United States had recognized the annexation of Austria by the Third Reich—Great Britain had already done so on April 2.

Martin clung to the daily newscasts, and what he learned was more and more frightening. The pace of events leading towards confrontation and danger of war accelerated from week to week. Like background music to a drama leading towards death and disaster, these events accompanied Martin on his mission in Europe and his subsequent attempts to raise the awareness of politicians in the United States and in Canada.

On the day Martin arrived in Paris, a plebiscite was held in Germany including the former Austria. As during all previous plebiscites in the Third Reich, the outcome was predictable: 99 percent of all voters approved of the annexation of Austria!

In Spain the bloody civil war, which had started in 1936, was approaching its end. After the battle of Tortosa, where the majority of the Lincoln Brigade consisting of American volunteers fighting on the side of the Loyalists had been killed, General Franco proclaimed the virtual end of the civil war and the victory of the Fascist movement. Martin had never felt truly positive towards the left wing Loyalist government of Spain, but Franco's victory was to him, as it was to many others, another victory of Fascism and thus a further threat to freedom and democracy in Europe.

Even before his return to the United States, Martin began to worry about the safety of his friends in Czechoslovakia, especially the Petscheks in Aussig. While world opinion was still preoccupied with the events in Austria and Spain, Konrad Henlein, the leader of the Sudeten German national socialist movement in Czechoslovakia, aggressively demanded concessions for the German minority from the government in Prague. The war of words directed by Hitler against the small Czechoslovak Republic rose to a new level of denunciations and threats.

What Martin observed, witnessed, and personally experienced in Europe during the tense month of April 1938 is dramatically described in his 11,000 word report to the Canadian Ambassador in Washington, Sir Herbert Marler, and ultimately directed to the governments of Canada and the United States. In this unique document, Martin conveyed the fear, the pessimism, and the false hopes that had gripped much of Europe. His report is filled with accounts of meetings with strangers, officials, and ordinary citizens in France, Austria, Czechoslovakia, and Germany and, most movingly, with accounts of his visits to his friends in Vienna, who were not only living in fear but were already terrorized and in acute danger of being imprisoned. There was the sense of doom expressed by his friends in Prague and, in contrast, the naive hope among the Germans that everything would end peacefully, as "Adolf Hitler never wanted war." Nothing will convey the significance of Martin's observations and eye witness accounts better to the reader than quotes from Martin's report :

On board S.S.Hansa, May 5, 1938.

Dear Sir Herbert,

You knew the reason of my hurried trip to Europe after my visit with you....

The crossing on the "Queen Mary" was one of the worst of my many crossings.... We were late getting into Plymouth. Knowing that this meant reaching Paris only near midnight ... I telegraphed to our Legation in Paris ... everything was to be handed to me at the station in Paris.... I blessed the intelligence of our Legation.

But much went wrong and the papers and flight tickets to be handed to Martin at the train station in Paris by a man named Harris had been returned to the Legation.

I used very bad language, jumped into a taxi and drove to the Legation. I rang the doorbell furiously several times until at last a young woman opened the gate very carefully, and when I told her my name, she handed me a fat envelop. She was young and pretty and had not even taken the time to slip a wrap over her pink nighty.... To take the bus to the flying field at 6,30 a.m ... having no confidence in the night porter ... I sat with him and crossexamined him. He was sure that the Germans would attack France if Hitler could not obtain by peaceful means the mastery of Europe.... France would fight to the end and defeat the Boches....

Flying over Germany we met two German military planes and arrived at the Prague flying field at 11 a.m. A lady friend waited for me in her car.... She was worried about what would happen now since Hitler had taken Austria, and she expressed fears that his next step would be Czechoslovakia.... The people are terror-stricken, but ... hope for the protection of France, Great-Britain and Russia.

At the British Legation in Prague, Martin raised serious misgivings and was presented with

... a mimeograph sheet warning British subjects of entering Austria.... Subjects of the British Empire had to appear before ... the Gestapo, [be] examined and ... arrested for three days and then told to leave Austria immediately.

But Martin, undeterred, consulted with the U.S. Consul, asking whether there were any restrictions to be expected for travel to Austria but was told

... not for U.S. citizens....

Next morning I decided to protect myself, as Great Britain apparently could not do so. I telephoned the German Legation and wanted to speak to the minister Dr. Eisenlohr, an old friend of mine.... I was told that the Minister could not speak to me.... In the afternoon he called at my hotel and explained that he was being watched by the Gestapo ... a

laisser-passez as usual ... would be impossible, however he would be of
assistance to me in another way.... I felt quite safe after that....

In the evening, his friend Franz Petschek took Martin to his
home in Aussig. It was at that time that the Petscheks discussed with
Martin for the first time the possibility of being forced to flee
Czechoslovakia in the not too distant future. Martin assured them
that he would stand by to help them gain entry into the United States
and become established there. Perhaps they should prepare to leave
immediately; but for such a step, the Petscheks were not yet ready.

Martin left for Vienna the next morning on a large German
Junkers plane carrying only four passengers.

At the airfield in Aspern on landing I saw only German uniforms,
no more Austrian. When I handed in my passport, there was whispering
... until it reached the highest in command.... He saluted, clicked his
heels, said "Heil Hitler" passed my baggage ... and told me there was a
car outside ... to take me to my hotel. Apparently my friend in Prague
had been phoning....

For his entire stay in Austria, Martin was obviously under the
protection of Dr. Eisenlohr in Prague. Showing his place of birth as
Reichenbach in Germany and looking Jewish—everybody in
Germany, especially officials, had been trained to suspect a Jew in
every person with a prominent nose—Martin would no doubt have
been detained immediately or at least watched during his Vienna
days. But he met only courtesy from the men in German uniform.

Whether Dr. Eisenlohr assured Martin's protection only for
friendship's sake, however, remains open to question. Doing so
would have put Dr. Eisenlohr at considerable personal risk. Aiding
Jews, no matter of what nationality, was considered high treason.
While Martin believed that his friend was anti-Nazi, Dr. Eisenlohr
possibly acted with the permission of the government in Berlin,
which at that time still placed some priority on maintaining a positive
image among the American public. It could only help if Martin
Nordegg would return to the United States with the account that,
contrary to the horror stories in the press, he not only had moved
about Vienna unmolested but was treated with the utmost courtesy
by the new authorities in Austria.

Nevertheless, Martin demonstrated remarkable courage in
Vienna, where nearly everybody walked about in the street with the
swastika or another Nazi emblem prominently stuck in his or her
lapel. Any person without such overt display of allegiance to the
new regime was immediately suspect of being Jewish or an enemy
of Germany. Anywhere and anytime, such a person would be insulted, physically threatened, or taken to a police station. Martin was

only too conscious that he was moving about the streets without such identification of loyalty. He did not have a swastika to stick into his lapel, nor would he wear one if someone had given him such a stickpin. Yes, Martin thought, Vienna's character had changed beyond recognition since his last visit with Sonia.

> The airfield as well as the streets were decorated with swastika banners, still hanging from the triumphal entry of Hitler. Of course, there was also a swastika flag fluttering gaily on the cooler of the limousine!... At the British Consulate, the Consul wrinkled his brow.... The consulate had apparently nothing else to do than to get British subjects out of trouble.... He was curious to know why I had come to Vienna and . . . insisted on details. I answered that I intended to visit some old friends who were in trouble, especially Dr. von Kleinwächter of the Foreign Department. He said: "For God's sake, do not go near them, you will surely get into awful trouble. He as well as many high officials have been arrested and taken to the concentration camp in Dachau in Bavaria, and their families and apartments are constantly being watched." He then gave me the good advice ... not to walk the streets, take only taxis, avoid restaurants and cafes, because everybody who does not wear a swastika in his buttonhole, is being molested, sometimes even beaten and taken to do disgusting menial work....
>
> Then I drove through the former beautiful streets.... Few people were slinking by, and all the former gaiety on their faces had given way to gloom. Formerly the air was filled with music from restaurants and cafes—but now there were only German military marches to be heard. German uniforms of soldiers and police everywhere—at last my car stopped at the entrance of the hotel where we had made our home every year for months. At the entrance stood two stiff Prussian guards with bayonets on their rifles, and metal trench helmets.... I entered through the swinging door, while the guards presented arms, and I touched my hat, acknowledging this unsuspected salute ... not intended for me, but for a German general who followed me through the door. I smiled at him apologetically and he returned my smile with a stiff grimace.

As other observations and experiences related by Martin, this last one, reported with his usual gusto, does not lack irony and amusement. But after a mere moment, Martin was again confronted with the pervasive fear of the new regime.

> I had my room on the first floor assigned ... and there stood already the old maid and the valet to receive me. But nearly every door opened and officers looked out. The hotel was occupied by the staff of the Prussian 8th Army Corps.
>
> The maid ... asked me where the "Gnaedige Frau" was. I replied that she preferred to stay at home this time, and she said that this was good ... and she replied in a whisper "all is changed and we don't know how it happened and we are all very unhappy ... and we don't dare speak any more or else we may be arrested."

I felt unhappy myself and took the telephone off the hook to speak to my friends—the maid rushed to me, took the phone from my hand: "For Jesus Christ sake, don't speak, all is watched." I took a taxi. The friends whom I first called on, had received the $100 which I had sent them to deliver to Mrs. von Kleinwächter, but they had not dared to go near her or send the money to her, because her husband with his colleagues of the Foreign Office had been accused of high treason, being adherents of Schuschnigg. I spent the whole afternoon with my friends and heard many harassing stories....

After supper, Martin visited the elderly mother of his friend Dr. Leopold Frey, who had left Austria in 1928 and now lived in Chicago. The old lady exclaimed

"... the good lord has sent you." Then she broke down and ... amidst sobbing and sighing, she told me of the cruelties and indignities ... and that she wanted ... to go to her son in Chicago.... She related the investigation by the police, because she had signed the list of contributors to Schuschnigg's Fatherland Front. The police had again visited her two days ago, made a list of her furniture and belongings; the pension she got from her husband's factory had been stopped, her bank account blocked, also her son's....

In a touching but very practical way, Martin reassured the old Mrs. Frey that he personally would arrange for her to get a U.S. visa without queuing up at the U.S. Consulate for hours. He also gave her an introduction to the manager of the Canadian Pacific Steamships, Mr. King.

She called all the blessings of heaven on my head.... I walked through the dark streets to the hotel. There were no people ... only German patrols.

Next morning I called on another friend, an old aristocrat, and former high Austrian official. Here again, the old gentleman and his wife . . . broke down when they saw me so unexpectedly. They told me that one morning they were fetched out of bed by the Gestapo, hardly given any time to dress and taken for a cross examination. After suffering many indignities and threats, they were allowed to return home with the warning not to leave their home for longer than two hours at any time, as they might be called again.

They reported many cruel things.... The barbarity seemed to me unbelievable, but the couple is so trustworthy that one can and must believe them. They are devout Catholics and they tried to excuse their Cardinal[*] who advised his congregation to vote for Hitler. They said if

---

[*] INNITZER, Cardinal, Theodor (1875-1855): Archbishop of Vienna since 1932; encouraged Austrian citizens to vote for the "Anschluss"; soon after, he became very critical of the Nazi Regime.

he had not done so, then Schuschnigg would have been shot like the Minister Fey and others.

The mob of Vienna which is even more barbaric than the German, was now at last held in leash by the German army. One only hears abroad of the atrocities committed against the Jews, but nobody reports about the gentiles, especially not about the priests and nuns and members of the left parties and union leaders. Of the 120 reported suicides, not more than a few dozen died by their own hands, the others were killed. My head began to ache and I left them promising to do for them what I could.

What I could not understand, was, that if the couple was correct, that no more than 25% of the population had been Nazis before Hitler marched into Austria, and Starhemberg's adherents as well as the army had weapons, that Austria fell like a ripe fruit into Hitler's lap.

Martin's next call, the most important of his trip, was at the Kleinwächter residence. It was the main reason for taking the risk of entering Nazi-occupied territory as a foreigner and as a Jew. What Martin reported on almost three, closely typed pages must, unfortunately, be summarized and much of the tragedy, tension, fear, and drama of the lives of those loyal to the Austrian state such as the Kleinwächters, might be lost.

Walking in the streets, I noticed that everybody, even the children, wore swastikas. I seemed the only one who did not, and there was no doubt that people eyed me suspiciously, in fact they began to follow me. When I saw that the number was increasing, I went over to a policeman and asked him in broken German, where I could get a taxi. His suspicion was allayed by my hesitating and faulty pronunciation, and he walked with me to the next corner where I found a taxi. I thanked him, he saluted politely and I told the driver to take me to the Keilgasse. I had not given the number on purpose.... Reaching number 7, I saw on the third floor window two small faces peering out, flattening their noses against the glass. I had hardly entered, when the older girl, Gunda, flew down the stairs, threw her arms around my neck and would not stop hugging and kissing me.... I had to carry her some steps ... until my breath gave away, and there came already Ebba rushing down and repeated her sister's performance.

In the door of the apartment stood the maid, and I heard that Mrs. von Kleinwächter had a severe nervous breakdown.... The children dragged me into her bedroom and I saw Anny, aged by years, crying and sobbing.... She gave me the letter to read she had received from her husband only a few days ago, written from the barbarous concentration camp in Dachau. It had been written with a trembling hand ... that he had never received a line from her ... she had written many.

It required Martin's great persistence to persuade Mrs. von Kleinwächter to leave her bed, get dressed, and go out for dinner with him. The Gestapo had warned her not to leave the house, but after Martin's steadfast insistence, Mrs. von Kleinwächter agreed to accompany Martin and her two girls to the Schlossgarten. The four of them had an opulent meal at the restaurant, a place where he and Anny von Kleinwächter had only happy memories. Mrs. von Kleinwächter was finally able to give an account of the last weeks to Martin:

> Anny then poured her heart out to me. In the middle of the night they were woken up by two Gestapos, telling her husband to get up immediately, dress in their presence and she was told to pack some laundry in a small suitcase. Then she was left alone. In the forenoon she called at the police headquarters for information and was told that they knew nothing about the matter, but that she would hear very soon from her husband. Three days afterwards, a policeman called and asked her to pack more laundry for her husband. That at least was a sign that he was still alive. From her relatives she had received the news that he had been taken to the concentration camp at Dachau in Bavaria ... Immediately after his disappearance she called at the U.S. Legation....

Mrs. von Kleinwächter was received with the utmost courtesy. Her husband was well known to the U.S. authorities. Gunda had been born in Chicago and therefore had U.S. citizenship. As she was a minor, there would be no problem for her and her mother to depart for the U.S. immediately.

> Of course, she would never agree to a separation from her husband or her younger child, Ebba.
> I told her not to worry, because I had taken up the matter already with the former minister to Austria, Mr. Messersmith ... who expressed his most friendly feelings towards her husband who had been of great service to the U.S. but first of all, her husband would have to be released. I did not, of course, hint that I intended to call at the Gestapo in Vienna myself which I did later....
> We chatted until it was time for me to go....I had ordered a taxi to take them home and paid him; then I bought a large box of chocolates and had it sent to the girls.
> My next visit was to a doctor of medicine whose acquaintance we had made when Sonia consulted him.

This reference was to Dr. Otto Fliegel, the orthopaedic specialist who had treated Sonia's ailing hip years ago. For obvious reasons, Martin did not reveal his name until Otto and Carla Fliegel had reached the United States with Martin and Sonia's help.

> ... the doctor's wife ... was overwhelmed to see me, as she had written only a few days ago a postcard to Sonia, asking her for an affidavit for her husband and herself to immigrate to the U.S.... I had intended to ask the doctor why he was still in Vienna when it was clear to me that he would have to emigrate.

> From there, I called on a professor of medicine.... He took me to
> his private room and then broke down in tears. He told me of the many
> indignities he had to suffer and showed me a letter addressed to him by
> the authorities, exonerating him from cleaning the washrooms of the
> hospital because his services were needed. He told me that he would
> soon leave....

What Martin heard next was a harbinger of persecution to come
for all Jews in Germany after the pogrom of November 9, 1938.

> I visited several industrialists and business men. Some were Jews
> and they told me of the most harassing happenings. Their shops and
> houses had been ransacked for money and valuables, their autos confis-
> cated, their oriental rugs taken before their eyes. Their wives had been
> called out at night, ordered by those ruffians to dress quickly, come with
> them to clean the streets and the latrines of the barracks and sent home
> again. They had to scrub the pavement where Schuschnigg's name had
> been painted before the plebiscite which never took place. Just to listen
> to them, broke my heart—but when they told me how many prominent
> men were shot with their families, then my heart stopped beating. How
> were such things possible in the 20th century? The tortures committed
> brought me back to the inquisition in Spain and the middle ages.

It was time for Martin to leave. Had he accomplished anything
except extend his hand in friendship and solidarity and give comfort
to his endangered friends? Time would tell. One can only admire
Martin's incredible courage when

> ... next day I called at the Gestapo quarters and was received with
> the utmost politeness. The file of Dr. von Kleinwächter was sent for
> and the high official, after looking quickly through the fat volume, said,
> that he personally could not do anything but that he would report the
> matter to his superior officer and see what could be done to release the
> prisoner from camp.

The "fat volume" of the Kleinwächter file would grow considerably during the following year. Its complete content would not become fully known to the daughters of Martin's friend until 56 years
later. It would show that the Nazis had classified Dr. von
Kleinwächter as a prime enemy of the Third Reich. Did Martin fully
realize the danger he placed himself into by confronting the Gestapo
officials with his request for the release of his friend? Perhaps
Dr. Eisenlohr did keep his protective hands over Martin, no matter
what Martin decided to do for his friends.

> My mission was fulfilled, and I telephoned to the airport to secure
> passage.... The Nazi official in charge said, there would be no difficulty
> ... and that I should refer to him on arrival.

I paid my bill in the hotel, took a taxi, stopped at the British legation and reported my departure…. At the airfield in Aspern, the official
greeted me with clicking of the heels, raising his arm and shouting
"Heil Hitler", and I bowed to him, shook his offered hand and entered
the plane which had only two passengers…. We arrived in Prague at the
minute….

Franz Petschek waited with car and chauffeur at the airport to
take Martin to the German border near Aussig. Once more, there
were masses of swastikas on the German side of the crossing and
endless "Heil Hitlers" before Martin could proceed by taxi to the
Saxonian city of Löbau where his step-nephew waited with his car
to take Martin to Liegnitz.

It is significant that in his report Martin does not mention his
sister Malwine and her daughter Bertel with a single word. Indeed,
it is not certain that Malwine and Bertel were still in Liegnitz at that
time. Malwine's Aryan stepson and the relatives from his father's
side were still living in Liegnitz in fairly comfortable circumstances,
judging by the fact that Martin's step-nephew owned a car.

Martin had last seen his step-nephew and his relatives in 1936
after Sonia's harassing experience at the Polish border. He was astonished how, in the short span of less than two years, their attitude
towards the Third Reich had changed dramatically, perhaps as a result of the "Anschluss" of Austria, which had gained Hitler many
new admirers.

In spite of the preparations for war which I had seen myself, in
spite of the military establishments in Liegnitz which is not far from
the border to Poland, they did not believe in the possibility of war.
Anyhow, not in the near future. They maintained that Germany was far
from ready for it. According to their view, there was a great lack of raw
materials and a scarcity of officers. And if Hitler gets everything he
wants just by taking it without any interference from France and
England, why should there be any war? England and France will not
fight, that they knew for certain, and he does not want any more territory, only what belongs by rights to Germany. And Austria does belong to Germany. I did not argue, because I saw that it would be use-
less….

On his way to Berlin, Martin mused about the naiveté of his
relatives in Liegnitz. And just as in Liegnitz, Martin saw the same
evidence of growing military might in Frankfurt at the Oder, where
he left the train for a few hours before proceeding to Berlin.
Everywhere, new barracks were built and there was a huge, new
military airfield just at the edge of the city. He took a taxi and asked
the taxi driver

... if there would be any war. He said, of course there will be, against Poland, to do away with the Corridor* and to take back German Poland. Returning to town, he showed me the magnificent military buildings which had recently been constructed, and I wondered....

How could his step-nephew and his relatives refuse to believe that Germany was preparing for war! Did they reflect the opinion of the majority of Germans? Despite Hitler's threatening speeches whipping up the emotions of the entire country and his aggressive actions, they all believed him when he claimed to aim for nothing but peace! Would Martin find a more realistic view of Germany's strength and Hitler's aims among his friends in Berlin?

They were great industrialists, bankers, and also officials of the Foreign Office....

The general opinion was, that a considerable part of the population was strongly anti-Nazi, but nobody dared to speak out for fear. As to the Anschluss of Austria, they welcomed it—had not a plebiscite expressed the direct wish of Austria to be one with Germany?... No, there would be no war....

All the men I spoke to ... hoped that the Nazi Party would not last very long. Of course, since Hitler sent the army into the Rhineland** and took Austria, he had become very strong in power and even those who did not agree with his methods could not help admiring him. Of course, the rabid antisemitism was very bad—but it was highest time to curtail the Jews of Germany who had too much influence and were overbearing. But now, that they have been shown that they must be different, nothing else would happen to them.

Martin could not believe his ears. Years ago, Jewish citizens had lost all their rights; they had been barred from all professions, expelled from universities and the civil service. Many had taken the consequences and fled the country. Those who remained were living in fear, enduring an ongoing, vicious campaign intended to extinguish the reputation of German Jews as law-abiding citizens. Nazi propaganda declared Jews the enemies of the German people; they were accused of conspiring with the Western democracies and with Soviet Bolshevism to destroy the Third Reich and its people. Too many believed Hitler's propaganda and his claim that only he could secure peace and the survival of Germany and its people.

---

* In order to give Poland access to the Baltic Sea, the Versailles Treaty created the "Corridor" consisting of the former German provinces of Posen and West Prussia; as a consequence, the German province of East Prussia was separated by the Corridor from Germany proper.
** Until 1936 a "demilitarized zone."

Martin feared the worst for the Jews of Germany and those who "did not agree with Hitler." The immediate future would prove him right, rather than his friends in Berlin, some of them men of influence and power in the economy of the Third Reich. At least they ought to know better! In resentment and resignation, Martin wrote that

> I just listened without arguments. They, of course, knew it all and better—with typical German obstinacy.
>
> I was very happy to leave for Switzerland and my heart jumped with joy when I saw at the border the last stiff Nazi official and was greeted by the smiling and friendly Swiss customs officer.

From Zurich, Martin phoned a worried Sonia in New York—he had not dared to call Sonia since his first visit with the Petscheks in Czechoslovakia. How the world had changed in just a few years! Sonia remembered the day in Ottawa when, in the office of Prime Minister Mackenzie King, the first direct telephone communication by cable between Canada and Czechoslovakia was officially opened. The call from Martin and Sonia Nordegg to their friend Franz Petschek was the first communication over the new line between the two countries!

As glad as Martin was to escape from the overbearing presence of National Socialism in Austria and Germany, the few days in peaceful, serene Switzerland only increased his pessimism. Almost speaking like a mouthpiece of Hitler, using his arguments to justify his aggressive actions to the German people, Martin's Swiss friends

> ... were also of the opinion that there would be no war. After all, Germany had been very badly treated by the Allies in the Peace Treaty of Versailles and nobody could blame them if they now took back what rightly belonged to Germany.
>
> They admitted that Germany had become very strong lately in military matters, but they said it was the only way to cope with unemployment which was threatening to make more Communists. . .
>
> England and France ... should have prevented the military occupation of the free zone of the Rhineland by Germany, and England was to blame for it.

Discouraged and tired, Martin left Switzerland.

> I then flew to Holland, and then on to London where I had been laid off with a bad cold for days....

A week later, on the S.S. *Hansa*, Martin prepared his extraordinary report to Sir Herbert Marler in Washington, which, after pages of horrifying news and sometimes angry, sometimes resigned comments about those who should know better, ended with a sense of relief, how

> I was happy to return to our continent after an adventurous trip. I will come to Washington shortly to see you. With kindest regards,
>
> yours cordially,
>
> Martin Nordegg.

Martin also sent a copy of his report to Mr. Skelton in Ottawa who had been his friend for many years. Canadian Under-Secretary of State from 1925 until his death in 1941, Oscar Douglas Skelton was a man of power and influence in Ottawa, often referred to as "the deputy prime minister of Canada."

On May 20, 1938, Mr. Skelton wrote:

> ... your remarkable letter ... gives a very graphic and vivid account ... of the position and state of mind of the people.... I shall be glad to see both Mrs. Nordegg and yourself when you arrive in Ottawa....

Martin was forced to postpone his visit to Ottawa because of strict orders from his physician. Already confined to bed with a chest infection while he was still in London, Martin's heart problems had become more pronounced since his return to New York. Emotionally, he was very distressed, mulling over in his mind again and again the terrible memories he had brought back from Europe. Although there is no indication that he had seen Marcelle in Bonn, the worry about his daughter and the guilt of not being able to help her in any way must have burdened him terribly.

What happened to Martin's friend Dr. Ludwig von Kleinwächter did not become fully known until many years after the war. Meticulous lists of those to be arrested within 24 hours of the arrival of German troops and the Gestapo in Vienna have survived. That such lists were available immediately after the Gestapo's arrival in Vienna confirms that the occupation of Austria had been carefully prepared to the last detail. A "list of prominent persons," which included nearly all of the foremost politicians and civil servants, among them Dr. von Kleinwächter and the post-war Austrian chancellor Dr. Figl, was used to prepare the "first transport of prominent persons" [Prominenten Transport] destined for the concentration camp of Dachau near Munich in Bavaria. A few days later, Bruno Bettelheim, the famous child psychologist, was also taken to Dachau. No doubt, Dr. Sigmund Freud was destined for imprisonment in a concentration camp, but he and his family had left Austria for London on June 4.

In May, Dr. von Kleinwächter's wife was advised that the salary of her husband would be drastically reduced and that she was no longer permitted to employ any personnel in her household. Approximately once a month, a postcard would arrive from Dachau from Dr. von Kleinwächter that he was doing all right, but looking at the few words written with a trembling hand, Anny knew that this was not true.

Documents that survived in the Austrian State Archives illustrate how precarious Dr. von Kleinwächter's position had been. Periodic assessments by various Nazi authorities are characterized by increasing sharpness and cynicism. The preoccupation with Dr. von Kleinwächter's case seemed to rise and ebb at regular intervals of two to three months, possibly resulting from the repeated attempts by various persons to effect his release from Dachau. Gradually, the name of the General Staatsanwalt Welsch moves into the foreground. Obviously the only person in the hierarchy of government, party, and SS with some sympathy for the Kleinwächters, Mr. Welsch demonstrated great courage in repeatedly recommending Dr. von Kleinwächter's release.

His periodic activities on behalf of Dr. von Kleinwächter might have been connected with Martin's attempt to effect his friend's release from the concentration camp with the assistance and influence of Mr. Messersmith of the State Department.

The current Consul General in Vienna, Mr. Morse, was acting on behalf of Mr. Messersmith, who provided Martin with copies of Mr. Morse's reports, requesting each time that

> . . . after you have read it, it had better be destroyed and (my) name not be mentioned to Mrs. von Kleinwächter.

For a long time, there seemed to be no hope. But behind the scenes, there were political assessments, file reports, and letters indicating constant activity.

On August 1, 1938, the SS requested "a detailed political assessment" of Dr. von Kleinwächter from the highest office of the party headquarters in Vienna. On August 2, an identical request "of highest priority" originated from the office of the Commissioner of the Reich for the Re-unification of Austria with the German Reich, Gauleiter Bürkel. Apparently, the party authorities were overburdened with similar requests; on September 5, the SS again requested the Kleinwächter assessment ". . . in view of extraordinary urgency."

On the following day, Anny von Kleinwächter was called for an interview and signed the following statement:

> I beg for the discharge of my husband Dr. Ludwig Kleinwächter,
> 56 years of age, who has been imprisoned since March 12, 1938, since

April 2nd in Dachau. He was formerly Consul in Chicago, Ottawa etc. and since 1932 until March 1938 served with the press office of the federal chancellery. Perhaps this past service might be the reason for his imprisonment, any other reason was not know to me. My husband is half-Jewish, I am Christian ('fully Aryan'). We have two children.... My husband could not serve in the World War, as his arm was crippled due to an accident. If necessary, I would try to obtain residence in the United States—we have no relatives there but numerous friends.

On October 11, the Gestapo submitted a report stating that

Kleinwächter was one of the most active representatives of the Front of the Fatherland and is alleged to have influenced foreign journalists against National Socialism.... Emigration of Kleinwächter will not be permitted.

On November 18, the local party official completed a political assessment of Dr. v. Kleinwächter, stating that

K. is reserved towards the new authorities, had expressed no positive thoughts towards the party prior to the Anschluss, and was sympathetic towards Jews.

He did not participate in current political activities and was not worthy of any support of the national socialist state.... In view of his political past, K. is intolerable for party and state.

In the meantime, Anny von Kleinwächter was desperately waiting for a postcard from Dachau. On November 5, she gathered all her courage and requested—without success—information from the police, as she had not heard from her husband for more than five weeks.

Four days later, the infamous "Kristallnacht" occurred. Jewish shops and enterprises were destroyed throughout Germany, and 650 synagogues went up in flames. Apparently, the action of November 9 put a temporary halt on the review of Dr. von Kleinwächter's case and its further disposition. On November 20 and again on December 15, the Gestapo advised the office of the Generalstaatsanwalt that "... in view of the tremendous workload resulting from the action against Jews [Judenaktion] ... likely several weeks would pass before another review of the case would be possible."

On January 20, 1939, a telegram was received stating that

Dr. Kleinwächter's attitude was monarchistic—he is an absolute enemy of the Movement [i.e. National Socialism]. During his service with the Federal Press Service, he maintained intensive communication with Jewish correspondents of the local and foreign press [Pressejuden]. His status as an Aryan remains in doubt.

His discharge from the civil service has been requested.

On January 23, Anny von Kleinwächter was granted an interview with the Generalstaatsanwalt Welsch. The report of the interview stated that

> ... [she] advised that her husband's letters from the concentration camp indicated that he was severely depressed which caused her greatest anxiety. Her personal situation also became more and more difficult. She had been advised that her husband's salary would shortly be terminated altogether. She therefore would have to try and find some type of employment. Because of her husband's past contacts with the American Consulate, she would like to try to find some work there. But she was afraid that the Gestapo would hold this against her husband. She therefore asked to obtain the opinion of the Gestapo.

The following morning, a terrified Anny von Kleinwächter took a letter written the night before to the office of the Generalstaatsanwalt:

> May I add a comment to yesterday's interview which you were so kind to grant me. I remember having said that I had contacts to the local American Consulate. I did not express myself properly, as I have no connection whatsoever there, I do not even know the name of the gentlemen who might still be here from former times.
>
> I wanted to say that I wanted to try to find some type of employment through the consulate, should this become necessary. But I merely considered such a possibility....
>
> I beg you, Sir, to believe that I as much as my husband, whose character I know so well, want nothing else but to care together again for our two children.
>
> And may I express another wish: is it altogether impossible that my husband's status could be changed to that of a prisoner of the police so that he could be transferred to the local police prison?
>
> In trust and confidence, I place our fate in your hands. I know that you, Sir, whom a kind fate has sent to us, will do what is in your power.
>
> With the expression of deepest respect, your obedient
> Anny v. Kleinwächter."

Although likely written in great haste, Anny had chosen her words carefully. Perhaps she had detected a measure of compassion and sympathy in Mr. Welsch. As yet, she did not feel obliged to use the phraseology and etiquette of the Third Reich and conclude her letter with the obligatory "Heil Hitler."

Eleven months later, Anny's husband would feel forced to demean himself to the extreme in his letter asking for the release of his wife. Times had changed, Naziism was firmly established in Austria, and nobody dared to use terminology and salutations other than those prescribed by the party.

Anny had been right about Mr. Welsch. Three days after a meeting with the Gestapo on January 25, Mr. Welsch recommended in writing the discharge of Dr. von Kleinwächter. Three weeks later, Mr. Welsch was advised of the consent of the Gestapo, but no date for Dr. von Kleinwächter's discharge was set. Mr. Welsch could not provide any encouraging information to Anny when she called at his office on March 10. One week later, however, he received the official notification of Dr. von Kleinwächter's discharge from Dachau.

But this did not mean release from custody! Together with other Austrians in protective custody, Dr. von Kleinwächter was taken to the concentration camp of Buchenwald in Thuringia. Only on May 3, 1939, was he released from Buchenwald. On May 8, the discharge of the "Half-Jew Ludwig Kleinwächter" was officially communicated to the local party authorities. On May 31, he was dismissed from the civil service.

The Kleinwächters did not dare let Martin and Sonia know directly that Dr. von Kleinwächter had been released from the concentration camp. They had asked good friends who were travelling to Budapest to write to the Nordeggs and post their letter in Hungary. Martin was relieved about the good news about his friend. He had lived through a bad winter, and even the two months of rest in Lakeland in Florida had not fully restored his health.

Sir Herbert Marler shared Martin's relief about Dr. von Kleinwächter's fate. On May 24, 1939, he wrote from Washington:

My dear Mr. Nordegg:

Please accept my many thanks for writing me under date of 22nd May instant and sending me the copy of the letter to Mr. Messersmith. I am so glad to hear about Dr. Ludwig von Kleinwächter.

I marvel at the energy of yourself and Mrs. Nordegg and your never-failing kindness and kindly thought not of two or three but of hundreds. May the best of health and fortune ever attend you....

Unfortunately I have not been well for the past few months. I have reason to believe that I am recovering at the present time, but I will have to take a little care.

You and Mrs. Nordegg both of course will remember that you are always welcome at this Legation and that myself and my wife are entirely at your disposal. It is very little indeed to be able to do for two people like yourself and Mrs. Nordegg who are devoting their lives continually and unselfishly for the benefit of others.

With my affectionate regards,

yours very sincerely,

Herbert Marler.

Sir Herbert would never regain his health. He served as Canadian ambassador to the United States until his death in January 1940.

The news from Vienna were sparse. The Kleinwächters did not dare to correspond directly with anybody in a foreign country. Nor did Martin communicate with them, other than by letters addressed to trusted friends in Vienna. Aware of their financial predicament after Dr. von Kleinwächter's pension was reduced to a minimum following his dismissal from the civil service, Martin also regularly sent money through another friend.

Anny von Kleinwächter had been most cautious and carefully avoided any contact with the United States Embassy. It is not unlikely, however, that the indirect contacts of the Kleinwächter family with Martin and Sonia had become known to the authorities, leading to Anny's unexpected arrest on November 11, 1938.

A brief entry in the prosecutor's file of Anny Kleinwächter reports:

> The bookkeeper Josef Neschitz, Wien II, Streichergasse 7 presents himself and advises that his sister, the married Anny Kleinwächter, Wien 3, Keilgasse 7, had been arrested by the Gestapo on November 11th. For what reasons, he does not know. His sister has two children, aged 14 and 15 years. Her husband is Dr. Ludwig Kleinwächter who was released from protective custody on May 3rd.

Again, the family turned to Generalstaatsanwalt Welsch for help. On November 16, Ludwig von Kleinwächter addressed a three-page typed letter to Mr. Welsch first advising him that on November 11th

> my wife Anny ... was arrested by officials of the Gestapo after a search of the family's apartment lasting several hours, and then taken to the police prison....
> The reasons leading to her arrest are unknown to me.

Dr. von Kleinwächter then proceeds with a detailed description of his wife's family background beginning with the statement that "My wife is Aryan... "

He then appeals to Mr. Welsch directly:

> I trust that you, Sir, will remember my wife, one of many and perhaps the most grateful of all women who found consolation and hope from you during her frequent personal appeals to you while I was imprisoned in Dachau and Buchenwald. I am certain that you will not remember anything that would create a negative impression of her character.

In every way, my wife is so conscientious and correct that any illegal or dubious action would never enter her thinking.... Since my discharge from protective custody she has been so completely happy that she literally walked through life with a song in her heart. This is not the mood or attitude for subversive intentions or plans!

The letter continues to make a case for Anny von Kleinwächter. For an anxious fourteen months, her entire life had been dedicated in securing her husband's release from the concentration camp. She was far too intelligent and prudent to jeopardize her family and the freedom her husband had just gained or her own well-being for anything considered subversive. Her husband once more stated that

l can say that thoughts of such nature are very far from her mind.

My wife is truly honest, a decent, conscientious human being. It is certain that right now she suffers deepest emotional torture and she is consumed by deepest worry about her children.

Since my dismissal from the civil service, she takes care of everything in our household.... I regret to have to admit that since the arrest of my wife, our two children are not as well looked after despite my best intentions.

May I take the liberty of asking you to speak a kind word for the well-being of my wife with the appropriate authorities or most kindly to promote a hastening of the legal proceedings which must establish the complete freedom of guilt of my wife.

Heil Hitler!
Ludwig Kleinwächter.

How hard it must have been for Ludwig Kleinwächter to stress in his letter that his wife was Aryan ... and to conclude his submission to Mr. Welsch with "Heil Hitler!" Neither he nor his wife would ever be told why she had been arrested by the Gestapo.

Only a notation on Anny's file in the state prosecutor's office throws some light on her case:

As advised by the Gestapo, the arrests of November 8, 1939 were directed against persons who had been for some time under the suspicion of activities hostile to the state. Investigations are being conducted which, case by case, will determine whether the apprehended persons will remain under arrest or will be discharged from prison....

Once more did Anny enter the prosecutor's building, as noted in her file:

The married person Anny Kleinwächter presents herself to advise of her discharge from arrest on November 25th.

Martin Nordegg was furious when he learned of Anny's arrest. While visiting Ottawa with Sonia in December 1938, he stormed into Agnes MacPhail's office on Parliament Hill confronting her once more with the questions he had directed to her in a challenging letter on May 13, 1938:

> Perhaps you don't know that I had to go on a rush to Europe....
> The misery I saw and heard, is indescribable. I cannot think of it without ache of heart and deep feeling for so many unfortunates.
> You have always been an advocate for the underdog. What are you going to do about this terrible disaster over there? What is Canada going to do about it? Has the Committee been formed in Canada which the U.S. proposed to 30 countries? If so, why are you not in it? And if not, why don't you ask why Canada does not join this humanitarian move?....

Since Martin had written this letter to Agnes McPhail in May, Hitler had directed his aggression towards Czechoslovakia.

Martin followed the events in Central Europe with bated breath. With cynicism and resentment, he noted the weak, conciliatory responses by the Western democracies to Hitler's blackmail.

The demonstrations for Hitler in the Sudentenland, the area of Czechoslovakia that was predominantly settled by the German minority, became more shrill every day, reaching a pinnacle prior to Sir Neville Chamberlain's first visit to Hitler in Berlin on September 15. Another visit of the British Prime Minister to Bad Godesberg on the Rhine was the prelude to the infamous Munich Accord on September 30, when Chamberlain and the French Premier Daladier acceded to Hitler's demand for the relinquishing of the Sudetenland. The fourth power in the round was Italy, represented by Benito Mussolini. No representative of the Czech government had been asked to come to Munich! When the Czechoslovakian President Edvard Benes had advised his country's allies–France and Great Britain–that Czechoslovakia, with its quite powerful, modern army was prepared to resist an invasion of the Sudetenland by Hitler, he had been given the cold shoulder.

Returning from Munich, an exuberant Chambérlain stepped off his plane in London with the reassuring pronouncement of "Peace in Our Time." But as if in a fever, Europe continued to be shaken by events hardly anyone could have imagined only a few months before. On October 1, within hours of the Munich Accord, Poland took its share of Czechoslovakia by occupying the Olsa Territory, a strip of land with a mixed Polish and Czech population along the border between the two countries. On October 3, Adolf Hitler started his triumphal entry into the Sudetenland.

After the depressing months of endless news of Hitler's triumphs in Europe, a telegram dispatched in Budapest by a person unknown to Martin arrived at Central Park West on December 12:

LEAVING HAMBURG BY SS MANHATTAN DECEMBER 15 STOP ARRIVING NEW YORK DECEMBER 22 STOP OTTO AND CARLA STOP

The Fliegels belonged to the fortunate few who had succeeded in escaping from Germany before it was too late. With Martin's intercession through his friend Mr. Messersmith in Washington, the Fliegels had been issued a visa for entry into the United States much sooner than they had dared to hope. They had to leave all their possessions behind in Vienna; their bank accounts, valuables, and their jewelry had been seized by the Berlin government, and only with the deposit made by Martin had they been able to book their passage to the United States. Their gratitude to Martin and Sonia knew no bounds.

From the pier, Martin and Sonia took Otto and Carla Fliegel to a small furnished apartment at 55 West 57th Street. Fortunately, Otto was quite fluent in English. Martin was certain he would soon find a residency for Otto at one of the hospitals in Manhattan. On March 1, 1939, at the Mt. Sinai Hospital, Dr. Otto Fliegel slipped into a white physician's gown for the first time in the United States. He was on his way to becoming a respected pediatric orthopedic surgeon.

Martin had also been desperately worried about his friend Franz Petschek and his family in Aussig, which had now become a German city. There was no way he could help them at this time, as urgently as he wished. Only later did he learn that the Petscheks had managed to escape from Aussig to Prague, just hours before the entry of the German troops. Knowing that even in the rump of the Czechoslovak Republic their safety was probably short-lived, the Petscheks soon left for Poland. After an adventurous journey through several European countries, they arrived in Southern France from where they reached Brazil via Spain and Portugal. The odyssey finally ended with their arrival in New York on November 25, 1940. Their friends Martin and Sonia Nordegg were waiting for them at the pier.

The Petscheks had correctly anticipated Hitler's next move. After three months of fruitless diplomatic activities by the Western powers, Hitler ordered the Czech prime minister Hacha to Berlin and handed him an ultimatum. On March 15, 1939, German troops crossed the borders of the Czechoslovak Republic, and Hitler entered Prague. The angry, but helpless population watched in tears the raising of the Swastika above the ancient Prague Castle, the seat of the Czech government. The Czechoslovak Republic no longer existed. Its western half became the German Protectorate of Bohemia and Moravia, while out of its eastern half, Hitler created the pseudo-sovereign state of Slovakia under German control. A tiny section of the easternmost corner of the former Czechoslovakia became the short-lived Carpatho-Ukrainian Republic, while another part was annexed by Hungary. On March 22, within days of the occupation of Czechoslovakia, Germany also annexed the Memel district of Lithuania.

On March 28, Hitler sent a telegram to General Franco, congratulating him on the occupation of Madrid. With the fall of the Spanish capital, the devastating civil war came to an end and another Fascist regime appeared on the map of Europe. During the following weeks, another European country disappeared from the map. Italy's occupation of Albania created an immediate threat to Greece and Yugoslavia. In May, Hitler and Mussolini proclaimed the "Axis Berlin-Rome," a military pact that further changed the balance of power in Europe. Hitler was now ready to take on his next victim: Poland.

Focusing on Danzig and the "Corridor," the Polish territory separating Germany from its province of East Prussia, Hitler started a campaign of liberating Danzig and gaining direct access to East Prussia. As in Vienna 18 months before, the Nazi party took effective control of the governing powers in Danzig.

There seemed no way to stop Hitler's agitation for the amputation of the western parts of Poland, even though France and Britain had publicly declared that the occupation of the Free State of Danzig would constitute a *casus belli* [cause for war]; at the same time they reaffirmed their diplomatic and, if necessary, military support of Poland.

On August 23, Poland's security and survival seemed fatally threatened when a Treaty of Non-Aggression between Germany and the Soviet Union was signed simultaneously in Berlin and Moscow. The last remaining hope that the fear of the mighty Soviet Union, his declared arch enemy, would keep Hitler in check, had vanished. All of Europe now expected war.

After weeks of intensified propaganda, including a fictitious crossing of the German border by supposedly Polish soldiers, Germany invaded Poland on September 1, 1939, putting the entire world at awe with this first demonstration of Hitler's "Blitzkrieg." Within a week, German troops had reached the outskirts of the Polish capital. After continuous heavy, indiscriminate bombing, Warsaw surrendered on September 27. Hitler held his victory parade on the Aleja Ujazdowskie, part of the historic "Royal Mile" once the route of procession of the Polish Kings.

On September 16, Soviet troops entered Poland from the east; and two weeks later at Brest-Litowsk, a demarcation line was set by German and Soviet representatives. Another European country, Poland, had ceased to exist, even though France and Great Britain, contrary to their reaction to the occupation of Czechoslovakia, had stuck to their guns and had declared war on Germany two days after the start of the Polish campaign. Another of the small European nations came under attack at the end of November when the Soviet Union bombed Helsinki on November 29, starting its invasion of Finland.

On September 6, Martin had already written to Prime Minister Mackenzie King offering his services. On September 11, he received a reply from Ottawa, signed by H.R.L. Henry, the Prime Minister's private secretary:

> The Prime Minister has asked me to thank you for your letter of September 6th in which you have offered your services in the present crisis.
>
> Mr. King wishes me to let you know that your offer is being brought to the immediate attention of the appropriate authority.

The letter was accompanied by a signed photograph of Mackenzie King.

Sonia was overcome with anxiety about the fate of her relatives in Poland. She needed all her strength to reassure the disconsolate Anna, who now reproached herself for having left Poland instead of staying with her parents. At least Grodno was occupied by the Soviet army. In contrast to what was reported about the persecution of Jews and Poles by the Germans, there was no news about any mistreatment of the local population living in Soviet-occupied Poland.

Feverishly, Anna had been writing cards and letters to her parents and other relatives almost every day. But there was not a single reply for several months. Finally, in January 1940, a postcard arrived from Sonia's cousin Sam Tokar. It did not say too much other than that everybody was alive and well. There was no mention of Anna's family, but Sonia consoled Anna, that "no news is good news."

Not until May 1940 did Anna receive the first news from her mother in Grodno:

My Dear Child,

I have written to you so frequently. Yesterday, I finally received your first card written five months ago. What is new in your life? Are you working? Do you receive any letters from Poland? Here, there is nothing new. The weather is very good. Salinka rides her bicycle every day after school. Leva is working and comes home every day he is off, goes to movies and the theatre. He is satisfied with his job. His students respect and like him. I am doing worst of all. I am angry at Boris [Anna's father]. He works, earns money and I have to cook for him and serve him, but he gives me no money. Only my dear Leva gives me every penny. Isaac is very sick. Stay well and take good care of yourself. With love to you and everybody, your mother

Fania.

As short as her mother's card was, Anna was jubilant. At last, she knew that her loved ones were all safe, and everything at home seemed the same. She only noticed that the street where her family lived had been renamed from Ulica Brigidzka [Street of the Brigida Nuns] to Ulica Marksa [Karl Marx Street], while the Tokars still lived on [President] Hoover Street. But one year later, after the arrival of German troops, both streets would be given German names. Neither religious names nor the memory of Karl Marx were tolerated. And soon, Anna's family and many others who had lived on these streets for so many years would be taken away by the Germans, never to return.

XI

THE TWILIGHT YEARS
1939 - 1948

Gone were the days when trips to Europe and journeys to exotic places determined the rhythm of the year. With the beginning of World War II, the life of constant travel that Martin and Sonia had pursued for so many years came to a sudden end.

Martin foresaw only a gloomy future for Europe and expected the war to last for years, too long for him, as it turned out, to ever return to Europe and the country of his birth again. Having divested himself of all business interests, his life had suddenly become very restricted. Martin became obsessed with reading the morning papers, page after page; but not until 1943 did he find any news that promised him that the cause of freedom was not lost forever for the people of Europe. There was no word from the relatives in Liegnitz, nothing about the fate of his Jewish sister Malwine and her daughter Bertel, and nothing from Sonia's relatives since the last postcard had reached Sonia and Anna before the German occupation of Grodno in June 1941.

In April 1940, the neutral countries of Denmark and Norway had been attacked and occupied by Hitler's armies. On their advance into France in May 1940, German armies had invaded neutral Holland and Belgium. Paris was occupied on May 15, and three days later Marshall Pétain asked Hitler for an armistice.

With the bombardment of Belgrade on April 6, 1941, Hitler began his invasion of Yugoslavia and the subsequent occupation of Greece. On June 22, German troops crossed the borders of the Soviet Union. Even though the Red Army was considered the most powerful in the world, it failed to stop Hitler's armies in their rapid advance towards Moscow. Martin saw no end to this war. The defeat of Hitler seemed further away than ever.

It was Sonia who encouraged Martin to put his reminiscences of his Canadian years on paper to keep his tortured mind occupied and to return, at least in his memory, to happier times. Without much prompting, Martin delved with full force into what first seemed just a small project. Spending hour after hour every day, Martin progressed rapidly to a record of several hundred pages. With little reluctance, he accepted Sonia's idea that he should improve his reminiscences to the point where they could be published.

Sonia was elated to see Martin's former energy and enthusiasm return. She became his advisor, his quasi-editor, his partner in a new venture. At Martin's side, she was able to experience his Canadian years. What Martin prepared for the future readers of his memoirs was more than an account of the most rewarding part of his own life, he also created a vivid portrait of Canada and her people, of the men at the sources of power in the East and of the doers in the West among whom he counted himself. Even though Martin's memoirs carried all the characteristics of an autobiography, they were restricted to the story of Martin Nordegg, the explorer and entrepreneur; they did not completely portray the man Martin Nordegg and his private life. The reader might sense to a degree what drove Martin to seek adventure and success. His intelligence, his self-confidence and his courage, his self-discipline and his belief in himself and in people shine through the memoirs. What is missing, however, is the personal life of Martin Nordegg in its entirety, a description of his early years, of his parents and siblings, his first marriage, his first wife, his daughter, the change of name from Martin Cohn to Martin Nordegg. Only Sonia, his companion and wife for more than 30 years, is recognized in the dedication:

TO MY WIFE
who stood by me in loyal devotion
during the hardest days of my life
and encouraged me to write these memoirs.

There is little doubt that Martin refrained from bringing to light some of his private life and the people who were part of it in deference to Sonia, who had never been able to overcome a certain feeling of guilt towards Martin's first wife, dating back to the six years of her relationship with Martin while Berthe-Marie was still alive.

There is only one brief mention of Martin's sister without even including her name Malwine; and no reference whatsoever is made to his brother Theodor and his two sons in England. Nor does Marcelle exist in the memoirs, although Martin transferred to the memoirs several passages from the story he wrote for Marcelle commemorating their trip to Nordegg and through the Rocky Mountains in 1912. Martin wrote extensively about his many friends in Germany, in Canada, and the United States. But his family and relatives remain curiously absent. As a member of his family, Martin stands as a lonely individual throughout his memoirs.

In March 1940, Martin submitted the typescript of his memoirs to the Macmillan Company of Canada in Toronto. This seemed a logical choice, since MacMillan had already published Martin's book *The Fuel Problem of Canada* in 1930. Referring to the positive reception the book had received in Canada, Martin wrote to Macmillan on March 19, 1940:

> At the request of some of my old friends in Ottawa, I wrote my memoirs from my first visit to Canada, 1906 until 1924. But since reading some chapters to a few friends, they advise me to have them published, because they give a picture of Canada during this past period....
>
> Although the memoirs are in their intent an autobiography, I have written it in a popular style.... There are also many excellent photos ... and several maps....
>
> I am well aware, that at this moment there would hardly be sufficient interest in Canada for such a book, but I know too, that the preparation will take a long time, especially as I intend to revise the manuscript intensively ... consisting in its unexpurgated state of about 400 pages typewritten.... I suggest to condense this to about 300 pages....

As is not unusual in the publishing business, Macmillan's initial response was rather favourable. Martin's book "... would have considerable value as an historical revue of the period...."

But on May 31, 1940, Mrs. Ellen Elliott wrote from Toronto:

> Because these are difficult times for us, and Canada is at war ... the Director at present in charge ... and I do not feel we should make you an offer to publish the book. We know that it is a good book and we know it is the sort of book we should like to publish, but because of the present conditions we do not feel justified in making a commitment....
>
> You would be better advised to discuss the book with a New York publisher ... it is quite likely you could secure publication. Perhaps you would like to take the matter up with our New York House....

Mrs. Elliott's letter appeared genuinely complimentary, and Martin could not disagree that, at this time of war, Canadians would likely be preoccupied with other matters. But he had some other thoughts that he shared only with Sonia. While Canada was at war with Germany, MacMillan might perhaps be reluctant to market a book by a German-born author, no matter how fervently he had declared his loyalty to Canada. Martin also wondered whether Macmillan, which probably focused on its major market, Eastern Canada, could appreciate the potential size of the readership his book would find in the Canadian West, especially in Alberta.

Reluctantly, Martin went to a meeting at the Macmillan office on Fifth Avenue. He was very conscious of the fact that his memoirs were really a book about Canada and his love for that country. Only two chapters were devoted to the war years he had spent in the United States. After waiting for a decision for more than three months, Martin was only mildly disappointed with the response he received from the New York office of the Macmillan Company, dated October 25, 1940:

> As I told you during our pleasant talk ... we have been delighted to have this opportunity to consider your MEMOIRS about which our Canadian branch has written us so enthusiastically....
>
> I am extremely sorry to have to write you that we have finally decided against making you a publishing offer for the book. Our readers had many things to say of your life and work in Canada, but our sales people—who are inclined to be extremely conservative in these troubled days—could not feel completely confident of the sales possibilities of your book....

Martin did give some thought to Macmillan's suggestion of "self-publishing." He continued writing, rewriting, and incorporating Sonia's suggestions. With the editorial assistance of an English instructor from Hunter College, Martin's memoirs were ready for private distribution in fall of 1943. Martin, who would never do anything in less than perfect fashion, had his memoirs typed on top-quality paper and bound in two hard-cover volumes with leather backing. As title, he chose *Pioneering in Canada*.

With excitement in his heart, Martin proudly sent the first copy of his memoirs to the Canadian Prime Minister with the following dedication:

> To the Right Honourable William Lyon Mackenzie King, Prime Minister of Canada, in admiration and devotion. December 17, 1943, Martin Nordegg.

Mackenzie King's letter thanking Martin for the copy of his memoirs arrived shortly after the New Year 1944. Mackenzie King had maintained his correspondence with the Nordeggs. Neither birthdays of the Nordeggs nor New Year's greetings were ever forgotten. Mackenzie King was not known for being outgoing and generous with words of praise and admiration. The length of his letter, its—for Mackenzie King—unusual degree of spontaneity and feeling, and its expression of respect and near friendship are measures of the quality of the relationship between the two men. An excerpted copy was found among papers given by Sonia to her cousin Emma Gamsa in London:

Dear Mr. Nordegg:

I cannot thank you too warmly for your kindness in presenting me with your Memoirs. Your gift was brought to me from New York through Miss McCloskey of our Consular service....

Having been absent from Ottawa for some ten days, I found many pressing matters to which I had to give attention....

Since Christmas I have been enjoying at odd moments, your Memoirs. I have not as yet been able to read the Memoirs from cover to cover, but I found the pages which I have thus far read so fascinating that I must confess to you I have taken, in the enjoyment of them, more time from the affairs of State that I feel I was wholly warranted to take just at present.

For the books themselves, for your kind thought in having bound manuscript copies ... and for this gift as a birthday present I cannot thank you too warmly. What however touches me most deeply, is one of the many motives which I know caused you to go to all the trouble you have in making this presentation to me. It is what you knew it would revive of our mutual friendship and affection for Andrew Haydon. The pages of your book have lit up the past in a way which has brought it very vividly anew to my mind. They have revived many memories which I shall always cherish. For this I cannot thank you too warmly.

May I add that I have been deeply touched by the expression of your confidence and regard permitting me to have glimpses, not only of your exceptional experiences, but also of your inner life. These are so clearly revealed as one reads from page to page, and from chapter to chapter of the two volumes.

In all that I am saying of your kindness I of course include Mrs. Nordegg. To her, as well as to you, I cannot express too warmly my appreciation of your gift and all that it implies.

May I say that I think Mrs. Nordegg was more than justified in persuading you to make the contribution to Canadian development, history and literature, which the Memoirs when published will constitute.

Yours sincerely

W.L. Mackenzie King.

How much Martin needed such generous words of recognition! Mackenzie King's letter was a highlight at a time of stress, worry and anxiety. Martin's mood alternated between periods of depression about the war and excitement about the few happy events which occurred. He was also constantly worrying about his declining health and his never-before-experienced stages of listlessness and lethargy. Above all, the state of the world and its future filled Martin with increasing cynicism.

A letter to Stuart Kidd written on October 10, 1941, already gave a picture of Martin's mood at the beginning of the third year of

the war and how even small trivia bothered him greatly. This letter
also includes the last mention of Martin's friend Dutchie.

Dear Stuart,

Your letter of the 17th ult. [of the preceding month] reminded me
daily that I should answer it. But the troubles of moving into a new
apartment, then the catching of my usual head cold, then Mrs.
Nordegg's ailments produced by many worries and hard work, which resulted in a real breakdown, prevented me from writing. But now, that
all the trivial troubles, compared with what the people in Great Britain
and the continent are undergoing, are over, there is no excuse why I
should not pound the typewriter with two fingers.

So, here goes: You have many illusions about an army of helpers
in this "God's own country" under war conditions. You cannot get help
for love or money.... There are strikes everywhere.... To get a decorator, or a carpenter, is more difficult than one may believe. I remembered
some significant expressions, which I learnt from you when you were
addressing the cayuses, and I applied them, but they seemed to have
only a fleeting effect in the Rockies, while here people seemed to take
offense and became stubborn as mules....

But cheer up, it will be worse than that before the war is over.
Prices here for everything are rocketing ski high, and we have to curtail
our former way of living, and concentrate on bread and potatoes, beef
once a week, is a luxury....

We are gradually drifting into a socialistic state, where labour rules
and the families which live on an income from capital, are being impoverished. Well, my days or years are counted either in heaven or more
probably in the place below, and what happens after my riding into the
happy hunting grounds, does not seem to worry me any more.
Anyhow, I want to be cremated, to give me a taste of what I have to
face afterwards.

I was interested to hear from you something about Dutchie. I had
no letter from him for I believe, more than 3 years....

If money were not so expensive, I would like to come West once
more. That was my wish last summer. Perhaps we may carry it out
next summer.

At present I am busy coughing and take some syrup against it, but
that damned dry cough won't part from me.

And the cruel war goes on, God only knows how long the people
will have to suffer. The Russians make a much more formidable stand
than anybody suspected. I had not much faith in them when I was travelling there in 1937. They were very clever and fooled everybody with
their preparations for war.... Well, good luck to you and to the younger
generation.

Our kindest regards to you all,

your old friend

Martin Nordegg.

These excerpts are representative of the entire letter, in which Martin unburdened himself to his old friend who would understand him better than anyone else. There are several pieces of good news, but they are mixed with anger about the abnormal times; there is annoyance with health problems, which Martin should perhaps have taken more seriously; there is the longing for Nordegg and the West; and here and there again, Martin becomes descriptive in the best Martin Nordegg fashion. In every other paragraph or so there comes through what Martin called "Galgenhumor," the kind of grim humour that will make the reader laugh or chuckle while betraying the author's sense of helplessness. For Martin, this was an unusual reaction. He had always managed to tackle and solve numerous crises with determination, more often with good humour than frustration.

At least a few weeks later, Martin could write to Stuart how wonderful the new apartment had turned out after all the anger, annoyance and frustration of getting established. Martin and Sonia now lived at 145 Central Park West, one of the most prestigious addresses at Central Park. Called the San Remo, the elegant building of more than twenty storeys with its two huge corner towers dominated the western skyline of Central Park. Martin and Sonia's apartment on the ninth floor was reached by a private elevator, shared with only one other party. Their windows opened in part towards Central Park and in part towards 74th Street. Sonia's great-niece Joyce Rothchild remembers the apartment's spaciousness and the treasures it contained:

> The apartment entrance opened onto a large hall, which gave an anticipation of my great aunt and her husband's art treasures that one would find throughout their home. There were ample kitchen, larder, and maid's quarters, and two large bedrooms. Martin and Sonia shared one bedroom, while the other served as Sonia's "office and reception room." It also contained many art treasures from Europe and Asia. In one corner stood a huge block of malachite, bought by Martin in China, from which various art objects had been carved. Some of the furniture was Chinese, as were a number of vases and carvings.
>
> From the hall, you entered into the combined living room-library, where large portraits of Martin and Sonia hung—there was another portrait of Sonia in the master bedroom. A particularly precious piece of art seemed to be a sculpture of a horse kept under a glass dome. The dining room was enormous with its huge table seating 24 people. Along its walls, there were twelve oriental screens of precious silk.
>
> The Nordeggs seemed to entertain both on a grand scale as well as in a more intimate fashion.
>
> The live-in maid of the house was Toni, a woman Sonia had brought from Austria. Toni was a tall, serious, often rather stubborn lady. The two women seemed to have quarrelled incessantly over the

years—but my aunt Sonia kept tolerating Toni's moods and never sent her away.

A new acquisition was the summer house in picturesque Elizabethtown in the Northern Adirondacks in upstate New York, which Martin purchased as a retreat from Manhatten's oppressive summer heat. It was meant to substitute for the travel of former years, impossible then because of the war.

What Martin wrote about the cost of living and of being able to afford beef just "once a week," must have sounded a little pathetic to Stuart. But there were weeks when there was little cash in the Nordegg home. The investment income from Europe had completely dried up; income from Martin's U. S. and Canadian investments was shrinking; taxes had also been raised due to the war. As Martin wrote to Stuart, "... the last dividend was shaved off actually by as much as 25 percent."

Of course, Martin was still a wealthy man; but more than once, he and Sonia experienced a shortage of readily available cash.

Sonia's nephew Hyman Mizell remembered how his aunt gleefully and proudly related to him that she had decided to raise a large enough amount of cash to last for a good while by selling one of her numerous pearl necklaces. After much deliberation, she chose the most precious of all. It was the necklace she had received as a gift from Queen Wilhelmina of the Netherlands, who lived in Canada in exile at that time. Grateful for the help the Nordeggs had given to Jewish refugees who had escaped from Germany to the Netherlands and from there to Canada, Queen Wilhelmina had asked Martin what would give Mrs. Nordegg real pleasure. His spontaneous answer was "My wife always loves pearls."

He was quite embarrassed, though, when a few days later, the Queen presented Sonia with a huge strand of flawless pearls. As yet there had not been a sufficiently grand occasion to wear Queen Wilhelmina's pearls, but Sonia decided to part with them. As Hyman Mizell related with a chuckle,

My aunt chose one of her wealthiest acquaintances—because of her charity work, she knew some of the richest ladies in town—and invited her for dinner at the Ritz. Having chosen an elegant but plain black dress which set off Queen Wilhelmina's pearls in a most spectacular way, Aunt Sonia did not have to wait too long for the other lady's admiring remarks. Rather demurely, she replied that they were not hers, but they had been given to her by a once very wealthy lady, a refugee from Austria who had reached the United States with her and her husband's help. In gratitude, the Austrian lady made a gift of her pearls to my aunt, who found it impossible to refuse, as the Austrian lady was a very proud person. But knowing only too well that the Austrian lady had very little left to live on, my aunt had decided to accept the pearls and sell them privately and then send the money anonymously to the Austrian lady.

My aunt's story must have been very convincing. The dinner at the Ritz was a success in more than one way—the pearls were sold quickly for a substantial sum. My aunt used half of the money for her charitable work, while the other half kept her and Mr. Nordegg afloat for some time, certainly long enough until their temporary financial problems were solved.

Hyman Mizell, Sonia's favourite nephew, was also the only person who remembered a good deal about Sonia's charity work during the war years, when thousands of refugees from Europe arrived in New York, often after months or years of uncertainty and danger to their lives. Many reached the shores of the United States from the initially unoccupied southern France via Spain, Portugal, and sometimes Mexico. They arrived exhausted, malnourished, and ill and mostly destitute.

Although they were out of danger, they were filled with guilt about those they had to leave behind in the camps of France, who would now be at the mercy of the Nazis. In contrast to Sonia's generation, who had come to the United States as immigrants, ready for a life of promise and opportunity, the refugees Sonia dedicated herself to were physically exhausted and psychologically scarred. They were much better educated than the immigrants who had come from Europe 40 and years 50 earlier; but very few were prepared, by education or training or language, for starting a new life in a foreign country after years of facing terror and death. Unlike the immigrants of earlier years, they had never intended to leave their home country in search of a better life—their lives had been good until Hitler destroyed them.

With admiration, Hyman Mizell described to the author how the rich social life the Nordeggs had maintained in New York was utilized by his aunt Sonia as a tool for helping the destitute refugees from Europe. More often than before, the rich ladies were invited to 145 West Central Park, but no longer to drink tea, play bridge or listen to music, but to work for charity. Their husbands were well-known businessmen, and Sonia successfully enlisted their help. They owned large stores or wholesale businesses; their factories manufactured furniture, garments and many other articles needed by the refugees to start a new life.

Saturday was Hyman Mizell's day off. It was the Jewish Sabbath, but neither Sonia nor "Hi" lived the life of "good Jews" any more. After the meetings of Sonia's charitable circle during the week, Saturday was the day for Hi to receive his assignments from his aunt, run messages to place orders, and carry bolts of cloth from wholesalers to garment factories, all contributors to Sonia's charitable projects. Hi, a quick and clever man of comparatively small but strong stature, also picked up the ready clothing from the tailors to take it to a depot Sonia had rented near the garment district. He worked very hard and so did Sonia herself in different ways. As Hi remembered,

> My aunt Sonia often worked to the point of exhaustion. But she always remained the grand lady, she was always immaculately groomed, although she often looked very tired.

There were other worries that Sonia shared with Martin. There had been no word from Marcelle for more than two years. Long before the United States had entered the war against Germany, the regular letters from Marcelle's psychiatrist Dr. Wilhelmy had stopped. Martin was wondering whether Dr. Wilhelmy had been dismissed. As long as the United States remained neutral in the war, an occasional card had arrived from Bonn, written by a sympathetic nurse, letting Martin and Sonia know that Marcelle was well and thinking of them. For whatever such messages were worth, at least they assured Martin that his daughter was still alive and cared for at the Hertz'sche Privatklinik. Martin had been forwarding payments regularly to Bonn via his Swiss bank account. The receipts received periodically from the clinic in Bonn, again through Switzerland, were proof that Marcelle's care was paid for.

But when the United States declared war on Japan and its European allies Germany and Italy after the Japanese attack on Pearl Harbour on December 7, 1941, it was no longer legal for U.S. residents to transfer moneys from their Swiss bank accounts to Germany, no matter for what purpose. Marcelle's well being was in jeopardy, and Martin had to find a new way to assure the continuing care and safety of his daughter.

It helped Martin greatly that he was no stranger at the State Department in Washington, where he found a most sympathetic supporter in Mr. van den Arend, the Assistant Chief of the Special Division. He asked Martin to obtain an up-to-date statement from the clinic in Bonn through the offices of his Swiss lawyer. A letter from Switzerland arrived in early September 1942. Martin learned that a Professor Fischer had replaced Dr. Wilhelmy as the director of the Hertz'sche Privatklinik. His reply, forwarded by the lawyer in Berne, terrified both Martin and Sonia in more than one way. Martin immediately sent a translation to Mr. van den Arend in Washington:

> … we inform you of our communication to the Swiss Consulate in Cologne of a debt amount of RM. 1732.90. We have hitherto sent the

current bills to the Swiss Consul in Cologne. We are awaiting your news in which way Mr. Martin Nordegg intends to pay the debt. Mrs. Marcella May is at present very inquiet and we have been obliged to put her in a special room by which the former nursing attendance has been augmented considerably against our former charges. We should really raise our former charge, but at present we intend to keep the former charges. We are awaiting your immediate reply and we will send the bills as hitherto to the Swiss Consulate in Cologne....

Martin begged Mr. van den Arend for his assistance in finding a quick solution to the problem of transferring funds from his account in New York to the clinic in Bonn.

I am very anxious to pay the amount to the Klinik and I would be greatly obliged to you for information how to do it.

Mr. van den Arend worked out an incredibly intricate system, which eventually assured the flow of regular monthly payments to Bonn. Martin was requested to deposit the required moneys with the State Department, which would credit these amounts to the U.S. Legation in Berne, Switzerland, to be passed on to "... the Swiss government representative charged with the protection of American interests in Germany."

The funds would be then transferred from Berne to the Swiss Embassy in Berlin, where they would be exchanged into German currency before being sent to the Swiss Consulate in Cologne, which would hand the payments to the Hertz'sche Privatklinik in Bonn.

Martin was immensely grateful to the State Department, but he still worried whether this complex passage of moneys between two countries at war via a neutral country would be reliable. It took more than six months until Martin held the proof in his hand that the Hertz'sche Klinik had received the demanded funds for Marcelle's care. On June 26, 1943, Mr. van den Arend's successor, Franklin C. Gowen wrote to Martin:

My dear Mr. Nordegg:

I am in receipt of your letter of June 16, 1943 concerning your desire to ascertain whether funds have been advanced by the appropriate Swiss authorities on behalf of your daughter, Mrs. Marcelle Nordegg May, a patient in the clinic of Dr. Hertz at Bonn, Germany.

You will be pleased to learn that information received from the American Legation at Bern indicates that your daughter's case has been receiving the sympathetic consideration.... Since August 1942 they have advanced on her behalf the equivalent of $132 per month.... However, no vouchers evidencing these advances have been received

from enemy territory, doubtless owing to the disrupted communications....

Martin never felt truly reassured by the considerate letters he received from Washington. What would happen should the clinic in
Bonn decide to raise its charges again? Martin felt like a man being
blackmailed. Anxiously, he forwarded payments to the State
Department in excess of what he had been asked for. This created
new confusion in the accounts maintained by the Swiss representative in Berne. But on May 26, 1944, Mr. Gilson G. Blake,
Assistant Chief of the Special War Problems Division of the State
Department could give Martin some relief:

My dear Mr. Nordegg:

The Department has now received ... evidence of monthly advances
to your daughter, signed by a representative of the Dr. Hertz
Privatklinik ... totalling $1,879.71.... This amount exceeds your de-
posit.... Since it is assumed that financial assistance to Mrs. May is
being continued you may, should you so desire, include in your remit-
tance an additional amount to be deposited in her behalf....

The original documents ... are being retained in the Department's
files. There is enclosed for your information a detailed statement of the
advances made by the Swiss representative in Mrs. May's behalf from
July 1942 through August 1943....

Martin received Mr. Blake's letter on June 1, 1944, while the
period covered in the enclosed statement ended in August 1943. He
could only pray that the goodwill of so many different persons had
continued to operate faultlessly since August of the preceding year
and would do so until the end of hostilities. And hope was all he
had. No further proof of payment ever arrived.

And no information could be obtained from any source advising
Martin of Marcelle's state of health. Did he dare to hope that her
condition had improved after the alarming letter from Bonn in
September 1942, which gave such a terrifying picture of Marcelle's
condition?

During these painful years, Sonia stood by Martin when worry
and pain about Marcelle's fate consumed much of his strength,
when guilt about missed opportunities and regrets about wrong decisions were ever present in his mind. If he had only tried harder to
persuade Marcelle to come and live with him and Sonia before it was
too late because of the onset of Marcelle's mental illness!

Sonia had her own sadness and disappointment to contend with.
Her niece had lived with her and Martin for more than five years,
and Sonia had hoped so much that Anna would become a daughter
to her. But Anna remained shy and aloof, always preferring to stay

in her room studying. Sonia admired the industrious Anna. She also noticed that Anna never took the bus or the subway to or from Hunter College, crossing Central Park on foot instead. She knew that Anna saved every nickel, hoping for the time when circumstances would allow her to help her parents.

In the spring of 1944, Anna graduated with a bachelor's degree in pre-social work from Hunter College and immediately joined the U.S. Coast Guard. Sonia was pleased with Anna's decision, which perhaps was good for both of them. Right from her first days at the recruiting station at Palm Beach, Anna enjoyed life in the Coast Guard. As photographs taken at Elizabethtown show, she looked smarter and more comfortable in her blue and white uniform than in the dresses Sonia used to buy for her. These are the only pictures where Anna wears a spontaneous smile. With Sonia, she was now quite cheerful and more at ease.

Sonia herself was busier than ever with her charitable work for refugees. On April 10, 1944, Martin wrote to Stuart Kidd that

Mrs. Nordegg is doing such a lot of war-work that she impairs her health. But she considers it her patriotic duty and we must let it go at that....

Martin had much time to think and reminisce about his life these days in 1941. There had been the tragic mine disaster in Nordegg when an underground gas explosion killed 21 miners. Stuart had sent Martin press clippings reporting on the inquest, which had identified shortcomings and laxness in the observance of safety regulations. Martin wished he could be there to help with advice. He longed to see Nordegg again. But the times were not very suitable and his health not good. He wrote to Stuart:

... when they rebuild I wonder if they will use the same blueprint as before. You might suggest that they put up a couple of rooms for visitors.
One of the reasons why I don't come West any more, is, that you are not living there and I would not care very much to put up with Johnny! [John Shanks, the mine manager who had replaced Martin]....
We had a wretched winter here—you are quite right, why do I stay in this infernal climate for the last years of my life?

With Mackenzie King, Martin continued his lively correspondence. He closely followed the events in Canada, expressing his admiration for Mackenzie King's handling of the conscription crisis in the Province of Quebec. On December 15, 1944, Mackenzie wrote:

My dear Nordegg:

Your letter of the 15th instant [of the current month] has crossed one from me to you of the same or a nearby date. I thank you and Mrs. Nordegg most warmly for your good wishes on my seventieth birthday anniversary.

Let me thank you too for your words with respect to the recent crisis. It really was an appalling situation and as you say, with the forces what they are, perhaps inevitable. I do believe, however, that we not only managed to save the day but have possibly laid the foundation for a firmer bond of union between the different parts of Canada. Nothing could have been finer than the loyalty of my French-Canadian colleagues. Their part in maintaining the government at this time will yet be one of the brightest chapters in our country's history....

Mackenzie had included his recently taken portrait. Martin thanked him immediately, reviewing their long-standing acquaintance, which now had all the aspects of a friendship based on mutual respect and admiration:

New York, December 18, 1944

Dear Mr. King—

In the year 1923 you kindly gave me your signed photograph which I treasured ever since, and which stood between that of my dearest friends Haydon and Skelton.

Today you honoured me with your most recent photograph which I consider being excellent, and it will now replace the youthful one, taken when you first became prime minister.

Like a rapid moving film roll these 21 years by and the mental image displays your incessant work for Canada under the greatest difficulties, and in spite of two world wars, its enormous progress under your leadership in its politic, economic and financial life.

You have crowned and accomplished Sir Wilfrid Laurier's attempts to make Canada a nation, and his constant endeavor to conciliate the two races.

I wish I had seen Emil Ludwig[*] before he wrote his sketch, as from my observation I could have told many traits which he missed. But before long, I am sure, your biography will be written by somebody who knows Canada and yourself....

This letter illustrates again how close Canada remained to Martin's heart, even though he had applied to become a naturalized U.S. citizen immediately after the entry of the United States into the war. There is no record explaining the reasons of Martin's decision

---

[*] Emil Ludwig (1881-1948) German author of numerous biographies ranging from Rembrandt to Napoleon and Roosevelt.

to give up his cherished status of British subject and naturalized Canadian. One can only assume that he did not want to go through his personal experiences during World War I again, when he had been so vulnerable without holding the citizenship of the country he had chosen as his home.

It was not until February 8, 1944, that Martin finally received his certificate of naturalization. The file of his application contains a voluminous record of an incredibly detailed, meticulous investigation, which reveals some interesting details. It is noticed, for instance, that as his original first name, Martin was given his father's first name Moritz. At what stage it was changed to Martin cannot be ascertained. As it was extremely difficult and costly to legally change one's first name in Germany, it is likely that his second name was indeed "Martin," and that Martin began to use it as soon as he left home to become a student in Berlin.

Focusing on his political past, a file entry of December 14, 1942, states:

> ... It was learned that the subject and his wife are Jewish and were considered anti-Nazi. He was interested in Jewish refugee welfare in 1941. He is listed as the president of the International Furniture Corporation.... Nothing derogatory was developed....

In Martin's file, one also finds the account of the painful, hard-to-explain episode when Sonia, who was stayingin Lakeland, Florida, was asked to provide proof of death of Martin's first wife. In a pointedly worded, hand-written note, Sonia advised that "... you will find this certificate on my husband's file in Washington."

Few letters or notes of significance have survived from the years 1943 and 1944. Both Martin and Sonia must have anxiously waited for the end of hostilities and the opportunity to re-establish contact with Marcelle and the relatives in Liegnitz and in Grodno. By February 1945, Liegnitz and most of Silesia had been overrun by the Red Army. The papers reported that millions of Germans were fleeing from the advancing Soviet troops. As yet uncounted numbers had not survived the hundreds of miles of trekking on foot through one of the coldest and harshest winters on record. Thousands had perished under bombardments or the fire of Soviet tanks, which overtook the endless columns of refugees streaming along the highways leading westward. Grodno had been occupied by Soviet troops since the fall of 1944, but no reliable reports had reached the West, other than rumors of the discovery of death camps where hundreds of thousands, perhaps millions of Russians, Poles and primarily Jews had been killed by the Nazis–horrifying news, which Martin and Sonia could hardly grasp.

The first hopeful sign that the United States Army was preparing the final details of the occupation and military administration of Germany was a request Martin received from the US Army Foreign Positive Intelligence Section to assist "... with information on foreign territories."

Martin received this communication on April 26, 1945, when the Allied Armies had already deeply penetrated into Germany. On April 11, the first army units had reached the Elbe River near Magdeburg, 60 miles west of Berlin. On the 20th, Hitler's 56th birthday, Nuremberg, the scene of Hitler's annual party rallies, was occupied. A week earlier, Vienna had fallen to the Red Army. Each victory was welcomed by Martin, but at the same time, he spent sleepless nights worrying about Marcelle and his relatives and friends in Germany and the former Austria and their survival. The death toll among civilians seemed to rise as the end of the war drew closer.

On April 30, Hitler's suicide was reported. By that time, Berlin was in the throes of death, most of the city destroyed by the bombing over the past years and now by fighting from street to street. While Soviet soldiers conquered the city quarter by quarter, other units of the Red Army had completely surrounded the German capital. On April 27, the first units of the U.S. and Red armies had met at the Elbe River near Torgau. On May 7 and 8, 1945, Germany signed an armistice with the Allies.

Even before the end of the hostilities, millions of German soldiers had been taken prisoners, while the civilian population, although finally safe from bombs and grenades, remained in a state of shock. For others, the end of war meant liberation, especially for the millions of foreigners—most of them from Eastern Europe, who had been taken to Germany as slave labourers—and for the few who had survived the horrors of the concentration camps. Soon, however, the world learned that most had not survived. Millions had died from starvation and disease or had been killed by injection, by gas or by other methods imposed by the SS and their helpers. As the *New York Times* reported,

> American troops freeing the Buchenwald concentration camp April 12 were greeted by the dead....

And this was the scene found everywhere—in Bergen-Belsen liberated by the British, in Auschwitz liberated earlier by the Red Army, and in countless other camps.

As soon as the U.S. Army had occupied the Rhineland, Martin had written to the State Department in Washington asking for help in locating Marcelle. On May 14, Martin and Sonia were called to

Washington to peruse the lists of American citizens in Germany awaiting repatriation to the United States. Since the summer of 1944, the Swiss consulates in Frankfurt, Munich, and Cologne had quietly contacted citizens or former residents of the United States, who by choice or accident were spending the war years in Germany. The first lists had been forwarded to Washington by the American Legation in Berne in November 1944, followed by supplementary lists in April 1945 "... giving the names of Americans ... as well as those of their alien relatives in the United States, who desire or refuse to be repatriated."

With trembling hands, Martin turned page after page following the lists of names. There was no mention of Marcelle May-Nordegg. A grief-stricken Martin took Sonia to another section of the State Department to search for information on Sonia's relatives in Poland. What they were told destroyed their hopes forever. As in all other parts of Poland and Russia, practically all the Jewish inhabitants of the Grodno district had been killed in the Nazi concentration camps. Very few only had managed to survive and these were mainly younger males who had joined the guerrilla groups operating in the territories of former Poland and the occupied Soviet Union. Martin and Sonia decided against informing Anna, who was now stationed with the Coast Guard near Boston, of the terrible news they learned in Washington. Nor did they share their overwhelming anxiety about Marcelle with her.

Only in September 1945 did Martin and Sonia receive word that Marcelle had not survived the war. On September 20, 1945, Martin wrote to Stuart Kidd in Edmonton:

> I have to give you sad news today. You knew that Marcelle had been for years in a sanitarium in Bonn, Germany. Since March the State Department in Washington has been searching for her, although they knew the address. Every month they wrote that the U.S. Army over there cannot find her. A fortnight ago I cabled to young Beament of Ottawa who is now a Brigadier General, to make inquiries, and I just got his reply.
>
> The sanitarium had been repeatedly bombed last December and partly destroyed; Marcelle was taken to an air raid shelter where she lived some weeks and died from shock and exposure end of January last. May her poor soul rest in peace!
>
> You knew her well—she was such a delightful and clever girl, and she had to end that way.
>
> We had hopes of her recovery as long as she lived and now she is gone!—....
>
> Your old friend Martin.

In peacetime, Brigadier General George E. Beament was the junior partner in his father's Ottawa law firm of Beament & Fyfe, Martin's Canadian attorneys since the death of his friend Andrew Haydon. In the summer and fall of 1945, George Beament was stationed in Britain in the Canadian Army as dean of the Khaki University that offered university courses to Canadian soldiers serving in the European theatre of war. One of his friends, Brigadier David Strangway, was in charge of Deception with the Intelligence Section of the British Army of the Rhine. A journey to Bonn was easier for him to accomplish as a soldier than for a civilian, for nearly all of Germany was in ruin, its roads and bridges destroyed, and its railways just returning to limited operations.

In Bonn, Brigadier Strangway succeeded in getting a minimum of information only, but he was able to confirm Marcelle's death and communicated it to Brigadier Beament. Apparently, a telegram had been sent to the Swiss Consulate in Cologne, but it will remain a mystery forever why the notification of Marcelle's death had never reached Martin.

No doubt, had Martin felt well enough in fall of 1945, he would have found a way to get to Germany very quickly to ascertain what had happened to Marcelle during the last months of her life. Only 49 years later, 46 years after Martin's death, did a meticulous search of all possible sources in Bonn, conducted by the civic archives upon the request of the author, throw some light on the fate of Marcelle.

Combining the available information from the city, vital statistics, and the provincial psychiatric hospital, the City Archives of Bonn wrote to the author on March 2, 1994:

> Marcelle May née Nordegg ... died on January 28, 1945 in the Provinzial-Heil-und-Pflegeanstalt Bonn....
>
> She had been admitted on January 26, 1931 to the Hertz'sche Privatklinik, where she remained until December 31, 1944. This private clinic had been largely destroyed during air raids on December 21 and 24, 1944. On January 1, 1945, Mrs. May and other patients were transferred to the Provinzial-Heil-und-Pflegeanstalt [Provincial Mental Hospital]. According to medical records, Marcelle May died in that facility as a result of 'Erysipelas and circulatory disturbance' [acute inflammatory disease of the skin due to streptococcal infection].
>
> As the medical records state, her husband and son (around 1929 10 years old) lived in China. Marcelle May was a United States citizen and was therefore likely protected, when in 1941 five Jewish patients were deported and subsequently killed in 1942 in the Province of Brandenburg.
>
> On January 29, 1945, the Swiss Consulate General in Rhöndorf (near Cologne) had been advised by telegram of Mrs. May's death....
>
> During 1949, in a reply to an inquiry about Mrs. May, the American

Consulate in Bremen was advised by the Rheinische Landesklinik that
in 1929, her husband's address had been listed as L.O. May, Socony,
Tientsin [China].

Marcelle May was buried in a common grave on the Nordfriedhof
in Bonn. As the cemetery administrator advised, her grave was levelled
after 15 years as prescribed by regulations.

The Hertz'sche Privatklinik was rebuilt after the war, but razed on
March 31, 1952 to make room for another building.

As the Rheinische Landesklinik reported, it is likely that Marcelle
May's death was not necessarily due to "normal" circulatory distur-
bance; her medical record allows an entirely different interpretation.[*]
While this is an assumption which cannot be proven, it should not be
concealed at this time.[**]

The loss of his only daughter was perhaps the greatest tragedy in
Martin's life. Guilt and self-blame had never left him since his trip
with Marcelle to Nordegg in 1912. Never again had Martin been so
close to Marcelle. He always remained painfully aware how the unfulfilled marriage of her parents must have affected her, even during
the years when the family lived together in Atlantic City. That time
was also overshadowed by the illness and depression of Marcelle's
mother. Nor had Marcelle been blessed with a happy marriage.
Should Martin have warned her against entering into marriage so
quickly and immediately moving to a country as far and as foreign
as China? And should he have insisted that Marcelle return to the
United States after her divorce rather than to Germany? He had always expected that one day they would be reunited. But after
Marcelle became mentally ill, that hope vanished.

Now Martin had only regrets and sad memories. Sonia, as always, stood at his side; he had done his best for Marcelle as much
and as long as circumstances permitted. They still had Anna who, as
Martin and Sonia knew, had lost all her family in the concentration
camps. Anna would need them now more than ever. Soon she
would be discharged from the Coast Guard and would join them
again in New York.

Four weeks after receiving George Beament's letter about
Marcelle's death, a letter arrived from Washington advising Sonia
that her niece Anna Wolgiel had suffered a mental breakdown after
learning about the terrible fate of her family in Poland. She had been
admitted to the Chelsea Naval Hospital in Bethesda, Maryland, with
a diagnosis of severe depression.

---

[*] The writer refers to the distinct possibility that as a Jewish patient Marcelle
had been murdered.
[**] See also Addendum following the Epilogue.

Sonia and Martin's first visit to Bethesda was very distressing. Eager to give Anna all her love and support, her sympathy and compassion for having lost her family and all her relatives in the Holocaust, Sonia was taken aback by Anna's anger and hostility, which seemed exclusively directed against Sonia herself. Had Sonia not encouraged her to come to the United States, instead of leaving her with her parents for a few more years?

Anna blamed Sonia for interfering twice in her life; first by sending her to Palestine as a young woman, where she was consumed by loneliness and homesickness for her parents until she experienced a mental breakdown. How happy she had been after her return to Grodno, from where Sonia had taken her away a second time. There was no purpose in her life any more, and all she wished was to be dead and join her parents in a better world.

Helplessly, Martin stood at Sonia's side, filled with the terrible memories of Bonn, where at each of his visits Marcelle seemed to have slipped away from him a little more. He and Sonia had lost Marcelle. and now it seemed that they were losing Anna too.

That Anna's emotional health was not the best seems indicated by the mental breakdown she had suffered in Jerusalem at the age of 18. Facing the loss of her parents while she alone had escaped death would have been traumatic for a person much stronger than Anna. Too many of those who had survived the Holocaust as the only member of their family would struggle for years, sometimes for the rest of their lives, with a deep depression arising from the guilt of having been saved from the gas chambers. It seems clear that Anna suffered deeply under what was later defined as "survivor's syndrome."

For years, Sonia would visit her niece faithfully, finding her eventually more rational and controlled but very removed and expressing neither joy nor anger when greeting her aunt. In 1950, Anna would briefly return to live with Sonia after having spent almost five years in mental hospitals: at Mason General Hospital, where she was discharged from the U.S. Coast Guard with a certificate of disability; Bellevue Hospital in New York; again at Chelsea Naval Hospital in Bethesda; and finally at the Rivercrest Sanitarium in Astoria, New York.

More than ever, Martin and Sonia depended on their friends and their families, Otto and Carla Fliegel, who lived in the East 70s across Central Park; the Petscheks, only a few blocks north of 145 Central Park West; the Dubiliers and many others, among them the Jordans who were distantly related to Martin. Until 1933, Henry Jordan had been attaché at the German Consulate in New York. When Hitler came to power, Henry Jordan immediately resigned from the diplomatic service and remained with his family in the United States. He later taught at New York University and the New York School of Social Research, while his wife Irene was a lecturer of German at Rutgers University for some years. Martin was especially fond of their son, young Paul Jordan.

Many of their friends had been helped by Martin and Sonia in earlier years of distress and danger. Now, they were able and ready to return support to Martin and Sonia. A day of special joy was the reunion with the Kleinwächter family, who arrived in New York in February 1946. Dr. von Kleinwächter had been chosen by the Austrian government to represent his country in Washington, first as a diplomatic representative and later as the Ambassador of Austria.

In 1946, Sonia resumed her charitable work, which was now devoted to an orphanage in New Jersey, which her sister Anna was visiting regularly to conduct periodic eye examinations of the children. Deeply affected by a visit to the orphanage in the company of Anna, Sonia at once marshalled her influential, well-to-do friends and founded the "Sonia Nordegg Guild to Provide Clothing for Needy Orphan Boys and Girls." The Sonia Nordegg Guild operated "in cooperation with the American Committee for the Protection of the Health of Jews." This committee was a branch of OSE, a worldwide organization that was formed in Poland in 1927 under the name of TOZ. OSE devoted its work especially to the rescue and welfare of Jewish children.

Sonia was president of the Guild and Frank Petschek's wife its treasurer. Mrs. Justine Rothchild and Mrs. Emanuel Campe were vice presidents. The list of members showed many names well known in New York, among them the wife of John Weil, who had owned a large factory in Reichenbach, the town of Martin's birth.

Once more, 145 Central Park West was filled with visitors. As during the war years, there were frequent meetings of the members of the Sonia Nordegg Guild. Sonia's sister Anna visited often and so did Sonia's nephews and nieces, the Meisels and the Rothchilds and their children. There was much life in the Nordegg residence again, but it really centred around Sonia. Martin was described at that time as rather quiet and reserved, always quite formal with visitors, except with some of those who were his personal friends from old times. The Meisels and the Rothchilds and especially their children responded readily to Sonia's boundless affection, but as Hyman Meisel remembered, "we were always in awe of Mr. Nordegg."

In the hope that normal conditions would soon return after the end of the war, Martin had resubmitted the manuscript of his memoirs to Macmillan of Canada in the fall of 1945. He had thoroughly rewritten it and given it a new, more attractive title "The Possibilities of Canada Are Truly Great."

But Martin's memoirs received another rejection, although much recognition and respect were expressed in the letter of October 30, 1945, from Mrs. Ellen Elliott of Macmillan of Canada:

> We have given much careful thought and consideration to your manuscript, and I am sorry to tell you that we cannot find a way to publish it. We realize that it covers a very important period in the development of Canada and is, therefore, a valuable record. One might call it, with a great deal of truth, archive material....
>
> We have canvassed the potential market quite thoroughly, and the conclusion we have been forced to reach is that the total sales of a book of this kind in Canada at the present time would be disappointing. We regret ... because we have always planned our publishing programmes in such a way as to include volumes which reflect the growth of Canada in all its aspects....
>
> I re-read your script this time with as much interest as I did a few years ago, and I assure you that I personally am very sorry indeed that it falls to me to advise you that we cannot make a publishing offer at this time....

As disappointed as Martin was with receiving another rejection, he was glad to know that at least some copies of his memoirs had found their way to Canada, to some of his friends in Ottawa and in Alberta, to the library of the University of Alberta in Edmonton, and most important, to Prime Minister Mackenzie King. Some people would remember him and his work after all, his accomplishments and his record of the past life and of the people in Ottawa and in the West.

To a small degree, Martin returned to his financial interests, which had been dormant during the war years. But this activity seemed more like a way to occupy his time. He realized that not only had the world changed but he was no longer the man of boundless energy.

The winter of 1945/46 had been difficult for Martin. He had been continuously plagued with a stubborn cough and a shortness of breath. Worst of all, his eyesight had begun to fail. In spring of 1946, Martin decided to prepare his will, which he signed on June 13, 1946. He left his entire estate to ". . . my beloved wife Sonia Nordegg, if she survives me."

Should Sonia predecease him, Martin named as beneficiaries his wife's sister Anna; her nephew Hyman; her niece Ruth; her cousin Tevia, who had escaped the Holocaust and was now living in Brussels; and Anna, Sonia's niece from Grodno. One cannot fail but feel compassion for Martin. Not a single member of his own family was still alive to be remembered in his will! His sister Malwine and, apparently, his brother Theodor were no longer living. He had lost his only daughter and, one must assume, also his grandson who had remained with his father in China after his parents' divorce. It appears likely that he and his father perished in China during the Japanese invasion. Otherwise, Martin would have remembered at least his grandson in his will. This assumption seems logical, as no information of the fate of Arthur May and his son could be located in the records of various government departments in Washington. In 1948, the American Consulate in Bremen unsuccessfully conducted inquiries at the Provinzial Heil-und Pflege Anstalt and other civic departments in Bonn regarding the last known address of Marcelle's husband and her son. It is possible that prior to the preparation of his will Martin had once more tried to locate his grandson, who at that time would have been a man 28 years of age.

Martin's health and his mood improved much during the summer of 1947, which was spent entirely at Elizabethtown. One of the last photographs of Martin dates from this time. Dressed in a white summer suit and wearing white shirt and bow tie, Martin stands under the trees surrounding the Nordegg summer home. He looks quite well and tanned, but his advancing years are apparent. Another photograph taken at the same time shows Sonia in the best of health, slim, and looking younger than her years.

That some of Martin's old energy returned is reflected in the memorandum he prepared during the summer months on the matter of trade between Canada and a number of countries in South America, Europe, and Africa. Once more, Martin wanted to help his Canada in the difficult time of transition from a wartime to peacetime economy. On September 20, 1947, he wrote to Mackenzie King:

> After another long absence I am flying next Thursday to Ottawa in order to discuss with the Deputy Minister of Trade and Commerce the possibility of export from Canada to certain countries in South America, the Balkans and South Africa....
>
> I am further charged with an investigation of bringing to Canada an important new industry.
>
> As we want to see the few remaining friends, Mrs. Nordegg will accompany me, and we intend to spend several days, perhaps until the 30th in the Chateau [Laurier]. Then we go to Toronto and Montreal.
>
> Should your time permit it, I would like to pay my respects to you...

This letter sounds not unlike those of earlier years written by a purposeful, busy Martin Nordegg, full of plans and following a precise schedule. It was to be Martin's last journey to Canada, although he was talking again about the long-postponed visit to Nordegg.

The visit to Canada was not a success. Martin managed to attend the previously arranged meetings with the government officials in Ottawa, but every day, he felt ill and exhausted. Plagued with shortness of breath, Martin was worried about another flight and readily agreed to Sonia's suggestion that they cancel the rest of their trip and return to New York immediately by train. Sonia tried her best to lift Martin's depressed mood. He was unhappy with himself for not having been at his best during the meetings on Parliament Hill. He and Sonia had been received most cordially by Prime Minister Mackenzie King, but otherwise, there were few friends left in Ottawa. Too much time had been spent in their suite at the Chateau Laurier, which only brought up memories of old times when Martin had been at the height of his career and Ottawa was home to many of his friends. When the train stopped at the border crossing at Roose Point, Martin could not think of a reason ever to return to Ottawa—only Nordegg and the Rocky Mountains he wanted to see once more.

If the past winters had been hard for Martin, the winter of 1947-48 turned out to be his worst. Coughing and wheezing day and night and having no appetite, he began to lose weight. He also rarely left the apartment. More than ever, he depended on Sonia, who now typed all his letters, as his eyesight became poorer from month to month. Feeling lonely and shut off from the world, he longed for visitors, but was usually rather silent and uncommunicative when friends called. He loved the visits of young Paul Jordan, who would sit at Martin's side and listen to his reminiscences about his times in Western Canada. In true friendship, the Petscheks visited regularly, and Mrs. Petschek would read to Martin on many an afternoon.

Still, Martin was certain his health would improve once spring would arrive. In January 1948, he insisted that Sonia make reservations at the Jasper Park Lodge in the Alberta Rocky Mountains for the month of June. Although skeptical, Sonia fulfilled her husband's wish. But in early February, Martin suffered a serious heart attack. After three weeks in hospital, his condition improved quite rapidly, and he began talking more and more about the trip to Nordegg and the Rocky Mountains. What cancelled his plan was reported in Martin's letter to Ed Wilson on May 2:

> ... since the receipt of your last letter ... lie many weeks of illness. The last was the worst. You have probably read of the scare here of an epidemic of small pox, and everybody was inoculated. The poison from the vaccination got into my eye and it became a question if the eye should not be taken out in order to save the other.

But the doctors decided on a radical cure with 42 injections of penicillin and other new drugs and now after many weeks of suffering my eyesight is slowly coming back.

Under these circumstances we had to give up our reservations in Jasper Park Lodge for this year, and I regret that very much, as I had been hoping to come West and see my old friends again.

I hope that I may be able next year....

The sense of nostalgia and longing for his old friends and the people of Nordegg became even more pronounced in Martin's next letter to Ed Wilson on July 19, 1948:

... I am still very sick from my heart attack and also from near blindness....

I hope that the population will not entirely forget me although it is so many years since I have been there, and I don't know whether I shall be able to travel that long distance once again and see you all....

This was Martin's last letter to his friend Ed Wilson. It is filled with resignation and an acceptance that he might never be well enough again to travel, a feeling that death was coming nearer and that whatever he left behind in Western Canada might soon be forgotten runs through the paragraphs.

By August, Martin was completely bedridden. The last letter he received was read to him by Sonia. It came from the Prime Minister of Canada. One more time, Martin must have felt that what he had given to Canada was not forgotten:

Personal
Ottawa, September 4, 1948
Martin Nordegg, Esq.
145 Central Park West,
New York 23, N.Y.
U.S.A.

My dear Nordegg:

I have been long in writing to thank you for your exceedingly kind letter of August the 10th. I need not tell you, what my days have been like during the past month.

It is kind of you to speak as you do of my years in Canadian public life. Few men have followed their course with a kindlier personal interest than yourself. I am indeed happy to feel that I have not too greatly disappointed the expectations which you and our dear friend Andy Haydon held at the time I was chosen the Party's leader.

I am hoping now that the future may afford me the opportunity of following your example of doing a little in the way of writing Memoirs. I hope I may be as successful as you have been in remembering and in recording events.

With kindest regards to Mrs. Nordegg and yourself, and with renewed thanks for your letter,
Believe me,

Yours sincerely,

W. Mackenzie King.

P.S. I hope your health has improved since I last heard from you.

Martin Nordegg died at 2 p.m. on Monday, September 13,
1948, at the age of 80. Dr. Arthur Sonnenfeld, his physician since
1941, Sonia, and Toni, the Nordegg's maid of many years, were
with Martin during his last hours.

On September 14, the *New York Times* published Martin's
obituary captioned with his photograph from 1940:

MARTIN NORDEGG, 80,
A MINING ENGINEER

Martin Nordegg, financier and mining engineer, after whom the
town and river of Nordegg, Alberta, Canada, were named, died here yesterday, after a long illness, at the age of 80.

Mr. Nordegg, who was born in Germany, had lived and worked
most of his life in other countries. Shortly after the first World War the
State Department at Washington permitted him to make trips between
this country and Germany.

His schooling was in photochemistry and engineering, and he was
adventurous. His greatest success was in Alberta, where he explored the
foothills of the Rockies in a search for coal that proved successful.
Previously he had spent some time in England and Ireland.

In 1924, about the time he married Sonya [sic] Marcelle, an actress, Mr. Nordegg sold his coal properties. For a time he travelled
abroad on special missions for the Canadian Foreign Department.

Mr. Nordegg retired ten years ago and, with his wife, came to this
country. They travelled considerably. He devoted much time to his
hobby of collecting ancient Chinese art.

Several years ago the Nordeggs decided to settle in this city. Their
home was at 145 Central Park West.

Martin would have been pleased that the caption of the obituary
identified him as "mining engineer," the aspect of his career that he
was most proud of and where his greatest and most lasting achievements were accomplished. That he was not forgotten in his beloved
Canadian West was proven by obituaries in several Alberta newspapers, although his image had become already a bit legendary.
Confusing some events, while remembering others of importance

such as Martin's humanitarian work in the interests of refugees from Europe, *The Calgary Herald* wrote on October 6, 1948:

NORDEGG FOUNDER DIES IN U.S.

ROCKY MOUNTAIN HOUSE: Word has been received here of the death in New York of Martin Nordegg, 74 [sic], founder of the town of Nordegg and one of the principal shareholders in the largest coal mine there.

Born in Germany, he changed his name by order in council from Martin Cohen [sic] to Martin Nordegg. He was married twice. His first wife was Miss Marcelle [sic] of France and his second wife, who survives him, was of Polish birth. He was an accomplished linguist, speaking five languages. He came to Canada in 1905 [sic] and was interested in some of the silver properties developed in Ontario which brought that province to the fore as a mineral land.

Later he became associated with a British and Belgian group, who along with his German Development Company, provided funds for the project to be known as the Brazeau Collieries of Nordegg. Mr. Nordegg was one of the first from Ottawa to utilize telephonic communication with Europe and spoke to Edward Benes, who later became president of Czechoslovakia.

In later years, Mr. Nordegg spent his time between Ottawa and New York, and being interested in placing political refugees and displaced persons from Europe, he served on committees for this work. Besides his widow, he is survived by one daughter [sic] in New York.

The obituary in *The Calgary Herald* was identical with what had been published in *The Rocky Mountain Echo*, the weekly newspaper in Rocky Mountain House, the town closest to Nordegg and the centre for communications and supplies destined for the remote town that Martin Nordegg had founded at the foot of the Rocky Mountains.

On September 14, Martin's death was announced in the obituary column of the *Ottawa Journal*. In the same issue, the *Journal* published a brief obituary, which also appeared in the *Ottawa Citizen* and the *Edmonton Journal* on the same day:

MARTIN NORDEGG DIES IN NEW YORK

NEW YORK, September 13. (CP)

Martin Nordegg, emigrant from Germany, for whom Nordegg Alta. was named, died today. He was in his middle 70's [sic].

Nordegg left Germany for Canada at the turn of the century and became a prominent figure in the development of the Canadian West. He was widely known in Ottawa, and acquaintances said he occasionally exchanged letters with Prime Minister King.

The *Ottawa Journal* added a paragraph of local interest, again not entirely correct:

> Mr. Nordegg lived in Ottawa from the early 20's to the early 30's [sic]. His home, which had been built for J.R. Booth, Jr. was on Range Road.
> He had travelled widely, and about 1913 began coming to Ottawa from New York. where he returned after giving up residence in Ottawa. He was a great friend of the late Senator Haydon.

Martin's ashes were laid to rest in the mausoleum of the Ferncliff Cemetery in Hartsdale, Westchester County. The remains of Martin (and Sonia in 1970) were placed in a niche behind a marble panel with the inscription "MARTIN NORDEGG 1868 - 1948." While most panels show only names, the panel of Martin and Sonia's niche is distinguished by the carving of a map of Canada with the names of Alberta and Nordegg engraved. Whether this design was according to Martin's wish or a thought of his devoted wife, it is a meaningful memento to Martin's love for Canada and the town he had built in Alberta. Strangely, there is no evidence of the internment of Sonia's remains in this niche. Her name and her years of birth and death have not been engraved on the panel.

A memorial service for Martin was held at the Universal Funeral Chapel on 597 Lexington Avenue. Unfortunately, no record has survived of the service or of those who came to honour his memory. A large number of old friends, of business partners, of representatives of the State Department and the Department of Commerce in Washington, and of the Canadian government, perhaps even the Prime Minister of Canada, William Lyon Mackenzie King, must have assembled to remember Martin Nordegg. Unless he was absent from the United States on that day, Dr. Ludwig von Kleinwächter and his wife must have come from Washington. It is known that most of Sonia's relatives were present and that there was one Albertan among the mourners, Donald Kidd, the nephew of Martin's best friend in Alberta, Stuart Kidd.

XII

THE LAST CHAPTER
1948 - 1970

Guests at the reception that followed the memorial service for Martin remembered Sonia's dignified presence. For the last time, she was surrounded by Martin's friends, his acquaintances and his past business associates. Sonia had known almost everyone personally, often for many years. She had kind words for everyone who came to express condolences and share reminiscences. For Sonia, the reception was the last public celebration of Martin Nordegg and his achievements in Canada and the United States.

Sonia knew that she would miss Martin for the rest of her life. But as yet, she was incapable of appreciating how empty life without Martin would be. Theirs had been an untroubled love relationship from the first days in Atlantic City to the end of Martin's life. Their marriage was based on love and compatibility of character and temperament. It found its fulfilment in their never-failing mutual respect for each other and a remarkable congruency of interests, which always complemented each other.

It was only after Martin's affairs had been settled, his will probated, and the hundreds of letters and thank-you notes written, that Sonia acutely sensed the absence of Martin in her life. There was not only the emptiness of the apartment but also the loneliness of meal times and evenings. The telephone rang less frequently, fewer cables were delivered, and the volume of daily mail had shrunk noticeably. There was no one to talk with except her maid, Toni. Relatives and friends noticed how Sonia was becoming more and more critical of Toni. They wondered whether the aging maid was the undeserving recipient of Sonia's raging grief over the loss of her husband.

More than ever Sonia devoted herself to her charitable work with the Sonia Nordegg Guild and other projects. Time spent on her correspondence became part of her daily schedule. Letters and cards written to friends and acquaintances in North America and in Europe brought many replies. At New Year's and on Sonia's birthdays, hundreds of congratulations arrived. Sonia was particularly pleased that Prime Minister Mackenzie King always remembered her. She invited the Fliegels and other close friends to the summer house in

Elizabethtown for what too often became nostalgic weekends. The absence of Martin was intensely felt. In 1951, Sonia sold the property. No activity, no support from family and friends could replace Martin. Sonia never conquered the fear of becoming a lonely widow, of sooner or later being forgotten.

It was at this time that Sonia's sister Anna shared her observation with her niece Ruth Rothchild that Sonia almost frantically sought new friendships. This was indeed so; it is worth noting though that most of these new relationships would be of a lasting nature. Sonia also drew some of her nieces and nephews closer to herself; even the next generation took the courage to visit the famous great-aunt at her home on Central Park West.

Sonia's great-niece Barbara Deuty remembers how she and her cousin Irwin Rothchild explored Central Park on a hot summer day. Seeing the towers of the San Remo above the trees of Central Park, Irwin suggested on the spur of the movement that they visit Aunt Sonia. With pounding hearts, they tried to enter the elegant lobby of the San Remo, only to be shooed away by the doorman. Both Barbara and Irwin had barely reached their teens and were dressed plainly and simply as kids in their neighbourhood always were during school holidays. But they were persistent and caused quite a commotion when they finally managed to slip into the building. Nobody seemed to believe their story that they were related to Mrs. Nordegg. But finally, Toni was called downstairs to the reception desk and took them upstairs to the ninth floor.

Sonia seemed delighted to see Barbara and Irwin. She affectionately embraced the two and took them into the living room, where they were seated in huge armchairs, feeling terribly awkward and too shy to make conversation with their elegant great-aunt. To their great relief, Sonia asked whether they would like some refreshments. Barbara and Irwin nodded and waited eagerly for the delicacies their great-aunt would serve them. Sonia left, only to return empty-handed moments later. But after a while, the door opened, and Toni appeared with a huge silver tray. On small tables in front of Barbara and Irwin, she placed large, expensive gold-rimmed China plates and white lace napkins. In the centre of each plate was one delicious chocolate! The tiny treat was devoured quickly, but they did not dare to ask for more. Surely, there would be more food. After a while, Sonia asked her young relatives whether they would care for more refreshments. They, of course, nodded, expecting the "main course" to be served now. Sonia rang for Toni, and the earlier ceremony was repeated. Once more, golden China plates were placed in front of the visitors; and again, each plate had only one chocolate placed in its centre!

Barbara and Irwin left 145 Central West confused and disappointed, but also feeling victorious as if they had stormed a fortress. But they dared not repeat their unannounced visit at 145 Central Park West. What went on in Sonia's mind, one can only guess. She always had been so very fond of children. Perhaps she was no longer capable of mastering surprises like the unexpected visit of Barbara and Irwin.

In 1952, Dr. von Kleinwächter was called back to Vienna. When Sonia said goodbye to the family at the pier in New York, Mrs. von Kleinwächter took the firm promise from Sonia that she would come to Austria in the following summer.

In May 1953, Sonia took her first trip across the Atlantic without Martin. She spent the entire summer in Austria, revisiting all the friends and places she had enjoyed so much in Martin's company. But this became more than just a nostalgic journey, Sonia felt immensely lonely. After several weeks of travelling and visiting, she arrived in Bad Gastein in a state of emotional exhaustion.

The weeks in Bad Gastein did much for Sonia. From then on, she would return to Bad Gastein summer after summer, staying longer each time. Perhaps she never fully realized why she felt so carefree and so much at home in Bad Gastein. The beautiful countryside, the quiet elegance of Bad Gastein, the daily structure placed in Sonia's life through treatments, the daily promenades in the late morning and early afternoon to the sounds of the spa's orchestra, the quiet charm and elegance of the Hotel Astoria and its distinguished guests—all contributed to Sonia's attraction to Bad Gastein. Unlike in New York, Sonia never felt lonely. Here, she was among equals. They were all guests and what they were at home and what they had been in younger years seemed irrelevant.

Some of the postcards Sonia sent to her niece Ruth Rothchild from Bad Gastein have survived. They tell a tale of happy months in Austria:

> ... hope you received my card from the S.S. *Queen Elizabeth*. I came here with a cold but I am feeling much better. I love it here, nothing has changed, just as I left it here years ago....

And a couple of years later:

> ... I arrived here half dead on July 11th and was received with open arms. On the 15th had a surprise party, very gay. I am feeling a little more rested & a little stronger and wonder how Sam is. Please write to tell if he will have to be operated again.
>
> I love it here and my friend is just wonderful to me. My love to you all from
>
> Aunt Sonia.

> P.S. I made a cross to show you where my room is.

As the years went by, Sonia depended more and more on her relatives, wanting to be assured that they would always think of her:

> ... I received no mail since I left and wonder why. I wonder how Joyce is getting on. Please send me an air mail letter....

And always, she thinks of Anna. On September 30, 1955, Sonia writes:

> ... tell me how you all are and call up Anna before you write to me and ask her if she received the cheques for August and how she is. And if possible call up the Kings Park State Hospital Kings Park L.I., ward 441 and ask for the Dr. that takes care of the patient Anna Wolgiel and find out how she is before you write. I wonder if the boys went to camp.
>
> My love to you all.
> Aunt Sonia.

Sonia regularly wrote to Anna who had been admitted to the Kings Park State Hospital on Long Island. Sonia prayed that Anna would benefit from the care and get better. But Anna never answered Sonia's postcards.

When Sonia visited Anna at the hospital after her return from Austria in late October 1955, Anna was as distant and reserved as ever. Sonia was surprised by the report from Anna's psychiatrist of how positively Anna had responded to his suggestion that she would soon be well enough to leave the hospital. Anna had not mentioned anything to Sonia. On New Year's Day 1956, Sonia was shocked and deeply hurt when Anna called to tell her that she had been discharged from the Kings Park State Hospital three days before and was now living with a friend, an older widow who had been appointed her guardian. Anna lived on 107th Street, just off Central Park West, only a fifteen-minute walk from Sonia's home!

It took Sonia several months to realize that Anna had gained a measure of happiness and peace of mind since living with her guardian. Anna's termination of her dependency on Sonia had finally brought about the resolution of her unsatisfactory relationship with her aunt; it had been burdened with guilt about not having fulfilled Sonia's expectations and with Anna's anger at Sonia for having taken her away from her parents and her home in Poland. Anna was now much freer; she phoned Sonia almost every day and often came to visit at 145 Central Park West. Eventually, Anna began to share her worries and hopes with a grateful and delighted Sonia. In March 1959, she made her aunt incredibly happy when she announced her impending marriage to David Nathanson and asked Sonia to help with the arrangements for her wedding.

Anna's wedding on May 25, 1959, was the happiest day Sonia had experienced in many years. She liked David, a quiet, warm-hearted man; Sonia sensed he would take good care of Anna. A burden of unfulfilled hopes and of responsibilities that sometimes had seemed impossible to bear had been lifted from Sonia's shoulders. Anna seemed to have found stability in her life. She had been free of episodes of depression or self-absorption and had not needed any psychiatric help since her discharge from the Kings Park State Hospital's after-care clinic in January 1957.

Soon after Anna's wedding, Sonia left for Bad Gastein and did not return to New York until the following spring. After four months in Austria, she went to Belgium to visit her cousin Tevia Berkowicz, whom she had not seen since her last visit in Grodno before the war. Tevia had survived the Holocaust and now lived with her husband in modest circumstances in Brussels.

Another of Sonia's cousins, Emma Gamsa, had been more fortunate. She and her husband, a film producer, had left Berlin in 1935 and were well established in London when war broke out in 1939. From London, Sonia wrote to her niece, Ruth Rothchild on September 9, 1959:

> My dear ones—your letter followed me to London. Thank God all goes well with you.... I am leaving on September 17 for Israel.... My very best wishes to you all from Emma and myself. Lovingly,
>
> Sonia.

In Israel, Sonia's cousins, the Starowolskis and Amdurskis were waiting for her. The older members of the families remembered the visit of Sonia and Martin in 1936, when they were still living on the kibbutz near Haifa. When they asked about "poor Anna," who had left Palestine a sick person twenty years ago, Sonia was grateful that she could give her relatives good news about Anna and her husband David.

Sonia felt her best in years when she returned to New York in May 1960. With renewed strength, she returned to her work for the Sonia Nordegg Guild; she took care of others who needed her help; and she felt altogether less vulnerable than in past years. In the years before, there had been several events that had upset her deeply because they were part of Martin's past life. They concerned Nordegg and its mine.

In August 1955, Ed Wilson, son of Martin's friend, Tom Wilson, had sent Sonia press clippings reporting the imminent closure of the town of Nordegg. They were followed by two press reports about the closure of the Brazeau Collieries on January 14, 1955. Both were Martin's proudest achievements. Almost thirty years had passed since the days Sonia had spent with Martin in Nordegg. At that time, the town had almost 2000 inhabitants, and the mine was in full operation; Martin had been greeted by the town folks like a king returning to his country after a long absence. Sonia could hardly believe that the life of this town would come to an end only forty years after Martin had created it in the midst of the Western wilderness.

With many feelings racing through her mind, Sonia read the press clippings from Alberta. On July 26, 1955, the Canadian Press released a news item, which was published in *The Calgary Herald* under the headline

Once Bustling Coal Centre of Nordegg Joins Ranks of Ghost Towns Saturday

NORDEGG, Alta.(CP)—On Saturday this once bustling coal-mining community officially becomes a ghost town.

Not long ago Nordegg, nestled against the Rockies 130 miles southwest of Edmonton, had a population of almost 1,000. By the end of the week it will have dwindled to 25.

Brazeau Collieries owns the mine that supports the town, the houses its employees lived in, the Brazeau Hotel and supplies power and water. But since the mine was closed earlier this year, most of the 270 houses are vacant. The hotel doors are padlocked.

The Big Horn Trading Company is the only store still operating in Nordegg. Early this month it switched to a cash basis, cleared out clothing and hardware and now sells groceries only. Saturday it will serve its last customers.

The mine hospital is boarded up, and the doctor is preparing to leave.

Through the years, miners contributed one per cent of their pay to erect a recreation centre. It too is boarded up. The miners club with a library, pool room and dry and wet canteen, is wondering how to dispose of its cash assets.

The Nordegg United Church held its last service two weeks ago....

The postmaster will remain in Nordegg, at least until the post office is officially closed by the postal department. The station agent will still be there. Once he was responsible for the large daily traffic of coal cars in and out of the town. Today he dutifully posts the arrival time of the CNR train that arrives weekly from Rocky Mountain House, about 50 miles east.

About 25 others plan to remain in their old homes. Many of them are pensioners.... They say they will get their supplies at Rocky Mountain House.

The detailed report left little to Sonia's imagination. She had had such indelible memories of Nordegg. How rapidly things changed! Only six months after the closure of the mine, Sonia read a clipping from the *Edmonton Journal*:

> ... there are rows of empty houses, some with boarded windows and with panes bare of curtains and weeds thriving in front yards. Up at the mine head, we saw hundreds of empty coal cars, dusty and desolate. The cable-engines are quiet; so is the whistle that once timed men's shifts....

Even more heart-rending was the "Third Column" in the July 28 issue of the *Red Deer Advocate* by the Red Deer historian and naturalist Kerry Wood about

Nordegg's Dying Days.

> It was a sad thing, watching the death of a town in this happy year of Alberta's Golden Jubilee. Knotweed flourished on the main street; swallows nested in the middle of the quiet business section; and the fifty people left of the thousands who once lived there moved with a kind of dazed amazement, as they gathered in groups to discuss the end of their home town. On July 30, officially, Nordegg will die.
>
> A German pioneer named Nordegg discovered the rich seams of steam coal in the Chunga mountains west of Rocky Mountain House about the time this province was born....
>
> It used to be a busy place. The miners worked three eight-hour shifts day and night to fill coal cars with the shiny mineral that was shovelled into fire-boxes of locomotives all over Canada. Italian and Scottish and Welsh mining folk worked hard to wrest the coal from the inner core of the mountain. They played hard, when they were off shift, by hunting big game, fishing the rivers, enjoying ball games and hockey; and some did their best to grow flowers in the scanty soil in front of the squat, company-owned houses lining the hilly streets. There was always a thundering sound in the background, the endless rumble of coal cars coming out of the dark, dripping mines and speeding towards the tipple. Shrill screams of the whistle divided the day and night into three parts. Life was always busy and useful and people were happy there....

It was after receiving the sad news about Nordegg's demise that Sonia decided it was her duty to ensure that at least some of Martin's papers and copies of his memoirs be preserved for posterity to remain accessible to the public for future research. Her offer to the National Archives of Canada in Ottawa was gratefully accepted. On August 22, 1955, the *Ottawa Citizen* took note of Sonia's visit to Ottawa, her last trip to Canada, with a photograph showing Sonia at the National Archives:

GIFT FOR ARCHIVES

Mrs. Martin Nordegg presents her husband's memoirs to Dr. W. Lamb, Dominion archivist. Martin Nordegg, international financier, had a town, Nordegg, Alta., named after him. He and his wife were prominent in Ottawa social and diplomatic circles.

Two years later, Nordegg seemed to fade into history altogether for Sonia, when she received the news from Stuart Kidd's daughter Betty that her father had died. Stuart had been ill with Parkinson's disease since 1937 and had left Nordegg in 1939. As his son Fred Kidd wrote about his father's later years,

> In 1939 he left Nordegg and moved to Edmonton where Jim, and I were attending the University of Alberta—Betty kept house, and George attended school. He built a house and grew a big garden, something he had missed living in Nordegg. Dad made friends quickly—he was well liked.
> Unfortunately his health failed in the 1940's due to Parkinson's disease—probably contracted about 1937. However though not mobile he enjoyed reading and visits with friends for many years. He had a great memory, and was interested in many subjects....
> Dad died in 1957 at the age of 73 years.

On March 21, 1957, the *Edmonton Journal* wrote about Stuart Kidd

Well-known Pioneer Dies

> Born in Carlton Place, Ont. Mr. Kidd came to Alberta in 1903. He ranched in the Calgary district for several years and later became instrumental in the discovery and development of coal deposits in Nordegg and central Alberta Districts.
> He resided in Nordegg until he retired in 1939 when he moved to Edmonton. While living here he became interested in the Stoney Indian tribe and he was the first white man honoured by the tribe as honourary Indian chief.

Stuart, stalwart companion of Martin during the early years of Nordegg and his life-long friend, had maintained the friendship with Sonia after Martin's death. Now, there was only the next generation left, Stuart Kidd's and Tom Wilson's grown-up children.

Ed Wilson's letter at Christmas 1957 gave Sonia some comfort:

> ... Perhaps you knew that Mr. Stuart Kidd had passed on, it was just as well as he had been sick for many a year, which was hard on a person that liked to get around as much as he did.

We hear that the Government has taken Nordegg over, so perhaps they will be able to make something out of it. There are still quite a few of the people here in Calgary, also Edmonton, that go up there every chance they get. So many meet there and have a wonderful reunion. I don't think they will ever forget Nordegg and it is still a very beautiful place, even if it is closed down, which doesn't make any difference to the scenery....

One way or the other, Nordegg came up again and again in Sonia's life. In April 1961, the Canadian Broadcasting Corporation expressed interest in creating a television documentary on "... the town of Nordegg and the circumstances under which it was founded.

Robert Orchard, script editor at CBC Vancouver, wrote to Martin's former Ottawa law firm Beament, Fyfe, Ault & Hutton. George E. Beament, who in September 1945 had communicated to Martin and Sonia the sad news about Marcelle's death, was now the senior partner. He phoned Sonia immediately, and with her consent, forwarded his reply to Vancouver:

Mrs. Nordegg is most appreciative of the interest of your Mr. Orchard and his colleagues in these memoirs and the attitudes reflected in your last letter with respect to productions based on them. From my personal knowledge of the late Mr. Nordegg and his memoirs of the early days in western Canada, I feel sure that productions based upon them would reveal to the public a fascinating chapter in the early days of western development and the remarkable collection of personalities involved.

To Sonia, George Beament wrote that "... we must now keep our fingers crossed and be patient to see what develops...."

In spring 1962, Sonia was still waiting for the decision to be made by the Canadian Broadcasting Corporation. As she wrote Ed Wilson on March 2, 1962,

... I am still full of hope for work to start on the documentary, I even feel inspired to consider again a trip to Nordegg.... But first, I must go to Europe for a few months. I usually go for a cure, as my heart is not too strong....

The trip to Nordegg never materialized, and neither did the CBC documentary on Martin Nordegg and the town he built.

Sonia had good days and days when she felt rather poorly. But she always felt restless. She never slowed the pace of her charitable work and added new causes to her responsibility for the Sonia Nordegg Guild. She raised funds for several Jewish charities and for the Metropolitan New York Rehabilitation Association that her friend Milton Cohn had founded. Milton Cohn was the pioneering founder and first president of several organizations for the severely handicapped, among them the National Association of Homebound and Institutionalized Persons and the National Council of Work Centers for the Severely Handicapped.

Letters from the relatives in Israel were full of concern for Sonia's health. On February 28, 1961, Sonia's cousin Zhozia wrote from Ramat Gan:

Our dear Sonia:

Already two weeks and even more have gone by since I last wrote you. I worry when I do not hear from you. Moreover, you warned me that you would have much to do. I am sad and upset without letters from you. I am anxious to know everything about you and your health. That you stay healthy is the most important thing. You told me that you had a very severe winter with blizzards and much precipitation. Knowing you, I also know that you do not like to postpone anything until to-morrow, you will go out regardless of the weather, tiredness or feeling ill. May God protect you from every evil and all illness.... If it is too difficult for you, Sonia, to write a letter, we will be happy to just get a postcard.

I kiss you with all my heart and wish you all the best....

And again, on May 6, 1961, Zhozia writes an anxious letter in anticipation of Sonia's visit:

Our dear and beloved Sonia:

I have not heard from you for such a long time, and I am worrying about your health. My dear, you have undertaken such enormous humanitarian work to an extent that it has adversely affected your health. I like to hope for the best and expect to hear from you in the nearest future and soon be able to embrace and kiss our precious Sonia. Please let me know and we will be at the airport. I am already looking forward to the joy and pleasure of spoiling you and see you in the Land of Israel and in our home.

With much love,

Zhozia.

There is little that survived in letters or reminiscences from the following years. Sonia maintained her schedule of spending the greater part of the summer in Austria, stopping off to visit her cousins, Tevia in Brussels and Emma in London. Over the years, she had developed a firm circle of friends in Austria in Bad Gastein; in Schruns where she also took cures; and in Vienna. She liked the nearby spa of Baden, where she had once invited her friends Edith and Andreas Javor to stay with her.

Originally from Budapest, the Javors had fled from Hungary during the uprising in 1956 to Vienna, where Edith later worked for the Atomic Energy Commission. Sonia's friendship with the Javors dated back to the years when she felt extremely lonely and was eager to reach out to people she felt sympathetic towards. Sonia and the Javors had shared a compartment in the train from Zurich to Vienna and, as Edith Javor remembered, "we took to each other right away." Theirs became one of the friendships which endured to the end of Sonia's life. Gratefully, she remembered the Javors in her will.

Sonia took her last trip to Europe in 1967. A photograph survives from that year, which shows Sonia in an Austrian "Dirndl" dress. She is supporting herself with a cane and looks rather slim and somewhat drawn. She had just lost one of her friends, Otto Fliegel, who had died that April at the age of 69 years. More and more, Sonia had been feeling her age, although few of her friends recognized that her health was gradually failing. Sonia always remained charming, cheerful and sparkling with wit. In February 1965, she had already shared her worries about her health with her nephew, Hyman Mizell. Her letter of February 23, 1965 indicates how much she cherished—and expected—regular correspondence from her relatives.

Dear Hyman,

Many thanks for your detailed letter. I too received a letter from June with the happy news of their adopted son. I also hear now and then from Valerie.

I was very happy to hear how well your children are getting on. What a pity that the longshore men pulled you down so—this strike affected every one.

It made me sad to hear about your sickness, operations and other unpleasant things. I pray that the next operation will be very successful.

I too had plenty of sickness and am still not too well. But the Meisels are a tough lot and we can take it & you and I have to prove it. If you would see me, you would not believe how sick I am. I go to Europe for a cure every year & that does me a lot of good. Carla, Otto and Anushka are doing well & send their best to you.

My love to you all

Aunt Sonia.

In 1968, Sonia's sister Anna died unexpectedly at the age of 79. With a rising sense of loneliness, Sonia seemed more and more dependent on being included in the events and goings on in their families, on being honoured and recognized as the matriarch. She seemed extremely sensitive to even the slightest evidence of being forgotten. Her vulnerability in this regard was felt by her nephew Hyman and her grandniece Joyce. Without intending to, Hyman had somehow hurt Sonia deeply. Her reply to his long letter of explanation and apology was a curt note on May 18, 1967:

> ... Please forget all about the inconvenience that was created for looking for trouble. Just forget it.... I am leaving Sunday, 21 May, for Zurich....

But Sonia did not forget and excluded Hyman from her will. She also excluded Joyce because she felt slighted when, on the day of her wedding, Joyce did not find it possible to pick up her great-aunt at Central Park West and personally take her to the ceremony.

Sonia still loved children and young people. She never failed to remember the birthdays of Cornelia and Sabine, the daughters of Klaus and Johanna Brandt, who had arrived in New York in 1953. Distantly related to Martin, the Brandts had experienced the wrath of Hitler right after January 1933. Klaus Brandt was immediately forbidden to continue his work as a journalist. Until the move to Austria, he supported his family by writing the music to commercials for which Elli Heuss, the wife of the first post-war president of the Federal Republic of Germany, Theodor Heuss, wrote the words. But this activity was also outlawed. In 1940, Klaus Brandt found employment in an optical factory in Vienna. But while the family survived the war, Klaus Brandt lost his position with the optical factory when it came under Russian administration in 1946. In 1953 the Brandts moved to England and from there to New York, where the father found employment with a branch of his former employer in Vienna.

The family lived in the Borough of Queens, where Klaus Brandt died in 1966. Sonia tried to help his widow, Johanna Brandt, according to Sonia's relatives, Martin's niece by marriage.

Sonia's niece Ruth Rothchild pointed out to the author that

> Johanna Brandt was the only person from Mr. Nordegg's side mentioned in Sonia's will—how sad it was that Mr. Nordegg had practically no one left from his own family when he got old.

In her will, Sonia named 28 beneficiaries—all her nieces and nephews (with the two exceptions) and their children and her surviving cousins in the United States, England, Belgium, Australia and Israel. Also included in the will were four Jewish charities in New York, among them the Bialystoker Home for the Aged on the Lower East Side, the last home of Sonia's father Isaac; the Hospital of the Daughters of Jacob, where Sonia's mother spent the last year of her life; and the Zion War Orphanage in Jerusalem. Sonia also remembered several of her personal friends in the United States and in Austria.

In her last year, life became very difficult for Sonia. She no longer enjoyed going out or receiving friends at home. Johanna Brandt's daughter, Sabine Jordan, remembers how her mother told her that Sonia often complained that she was getting forgetful and could no longer concentrate for any length of time. She was terribly afraid of losing her memory. Sonia most treasured the visits of her close friend Mrs. Martha Froelich, whom she had appointed executor of her will. Living across Central Park, not too far from Sonia's apartment, Mrs. Froelich spent many hours keeping Sonia company and allowing her to reminisce about her life, which had been so remarkable as Sonia Marcelle, as Mrs. Martin Nordegg, and as the widowed Mrs. Nordegg.

Sonia Nordegg died peacefully at home in the afternoon of Tuesday, May 9, 1970. She was 80 years old.

"There had been no acute illness. Mrs. Nordegg just faded away," as Mrs. Martha Froelich related to the author.

Sonia's remains were laid to rest next to her husband Martin in the mausoleum of Ferncliff Cemetery. Joyce Rothchild remembers the memorial service at Campbell's Funeral Home on 1067 Madison Avenue:

> About 40 to 50 people were present. There was no eulogy, only very special music, which my great-aunt had apparently chosen before her death.

During Sonia's last year an unexpected request for her late husband's papers and memorabilia had brought Martin back into the centre of her activity. Professor T.D. Regehr of the University of Saskatchewan in Saskatoon had written to Sonia for permission to publish an edited version of *The Possibilities of Canada Are Truly Great*. He had discovered Martin's memoirs in the National Archives of Canada and asked Sonia for help in providing additional documentation.

Sonia asked Mrs. Martha Froelich to write to Professor Regehr to express her pleasure that her late husband's memoirs would finally become available to the public. She would gladly make some of his papers available.

Sonia never enjoyed the thrill of holding the first copy of Martin's published memoirs in her hands. The *Possibilities of Canada Are Truly Great* was published in 1971 by Macmillan of Canada in Toronto, one year after Sonia's death.

EPILOGUE

Even in our fast-paced age with its history of two world wars, readers of Martin Nordegg's biography might be curious whether traces of this unusual man can still be found in Europe, in Canada and in the United States.

Martin's birthplace, the once German town of Reichenbach in Silesia, became part of Poland in 1945 and since that time carries the name of Dzierzoniów.

The house in which Martin was born still stands across from the synagogue where his father served as preacher for many years. Miraculously, the Reichenbach synagogue was saved from the burning of Jewish houses of prayer by the Nazis in November 1938. But there has not been a Jewish congregation in town for several decades. The few citizens of Jewish faith attend services in the nearby city of Walbrzych, in German times called Waldenburg. Unused for decades, the Dzierzoniów synagogue is in a rather poor state. But, as documented by a plaque on its front elevation, the building is now protected as a historic site. Perhaps at some future date the synagogue, which also accommodated the apartment of Moritz Cohn and his family, will be restored to its old splendour.

The air raids of World War II left no trace of the building in Berlin's Leibnizstrasse, where Martin lived with his young family after his return from London in 1902. But the house in the London suburb of Gunnersbury, where Marcelle was born, still stands surrounded by a flower garden and is kept in good repair.

In Berlin, Georg Büxenstein's grand "printing palace," where Martin started his career, was totally destroyed in the air raids. On its site, a new building is rising in the again fashionable Friedrichstrasse, which had lingered in dust and destitution during the forty years of the existence of the German Democratic Republic.

The many elegant hotels where Martin spent much of his time—the Chateau Laurier in Ottawa, the Banff Springs Hotel in Banff, the Savoy in London—are still there in their old splendour. But the Astor in New York became the Waldorf-Astoria at a different location, and the Bristol and the Fürstenhof in Berlin have disappeared.

In Nordegg, a ghost town since the middle 1950s, Martin's house, the manager's residence, was razed. In Ottawa, the once widely admired home of Martin and Sonia, 29 Range Road, remains one of the most beautiful houses on the former Embassy Row. It serves now as residence of the High Commissioner of Sri Lanka. The Canadian Embassy in Washington, which Martin visited so often, was replaced by a spectacular new building in 1989. The original embassy building, one of Washington's architectural jewels according to the *Washington Post,* now houses the Embassy of Uzbekistan. The Sacred Heart Academy, which Marcelle attended before World War I, is still respected as one of New York's best private schools. In 1934, the school was relocated to the former Kahn mansion on East-91st Street next to Central Park. On the Lower East Side, 125 Forsyth Street, the first home of the Meisel family, was razed to make room for a park. The other buildings in Manhattan, where Martin and Sonia lived over the years, have retained their original function as elegant apartment buildings.

Many of the submissions and memoranda Martin prepared for the Canadian government and the Liberal Party are kept by the National Archives of Canada, together with part of his correspondence with prime ministers Sir Wilfrid Laurier and William Lyon Mackenzie King. His books *The Fuel Problem of Canada* and *The Possibilities of Canada Are Truly Great,* edited by T.D. Regehr can be found in libraries only. They are out of print. Only the story of Martin's trip to Nordegg with Marcelle in 1912 is readily available, having been published in 1995 under the title *To the Town That Bears Your Name.* Numerous letters, private and official, and hundreds of historically and personally significant photographs taken by Martin himself are scattered throughout various archives and private collections in Canada, the United States, and several European countries. Perhaps one day, the testimony and evidence of Martin's life and work will be centralized in one source. In Alberta alone, there are important reminiscences and documents in six different archives and several private collections.

What Martin created in Nordegg, the town and Alberta's largest coal mine, has largely disappeared since the closure of Nordegg and the Brazeau Collieries in 1955. Only a few buildings remain on Centre Street, while the traces of the crescents and streets laid out according to Martin's town plan, can be identified only with difficulty. Of the rows of miners' residences, a mere three cottages have survived. To appreciate the Brazeau Collieries of former times, requires some imagination. But the remains of the buildings and the layout and the size of the mine site are still impressive. The railway station building is gone. The railroad tracks from west of Rocky Mountain House to Nordegg were removed a few years ago. Only within the town limits and on the mine site were the railroad tracks left for historical reasons. What has survived of Nordegg and its mine has been protected as an Alberta Historical Resource since 1994. Preservation and restoration is carried out by dedicated members of the Nordegg Historical Society with the support of the Alberta government and the Municipal District of Clearwater. A small museum in the former school building of Nordegg keeps the memory of the Alberta pioneer Martin Nordegg alive.

It was the great tragedy of Martin's life that during his old age he had no relatives of his own family left. Thus it happened that Sonia's relatives became the family for Martin. He was very fond of Sonia's sister and her cousins, Sonia Tokar and Emma Gamsa. They predeceased Sonia, while her other favourite cousin, Tevia Bercowicz died in the 1970s. Sonia's niece, Anna Wolgiel-Nathanson lost her husband David on November 7, 1978, after 19 years of a happy marriage. As a widow, Anna was very lonely. In 1986, she gave up the beautiful apartment she had shared with her husband for many years at Park-View Towers in Elmhurst, Borough of Queens, and admitted herself to the Franklin Delano Roosevelt Veterans Administration Hospital in Montrose, Westchester County—whether for physical or emotional reasons could not be ascertained. At the end of November 1989, Anna was transferred to the Port Chester Nursing Home in Port Chester, where she died on April 5, 1990. Anna was 73 years of age when her tragic and often lonely life came to an end.

The administrator of the Port Chester Nursing Home remembers Anna as severely troubled mentally.

> She missed her husband David terribly and seemed lost without him.
> She was fearful of most people and constantly worried that someone might steal her money.

This might explain why Anna had not willed a share from Sonia's inheritance to some charitable cause, as her aunt had done so many times. Since she did not leave a will, Anna's estate, valued at well over $600,000, went to the State.

Anna's remains were interred at Ferncliff Cemetery, but not next to or near the remains of her aunt Sonia, as one might expect. Symbolic of her sad life and her lonely last years, the urn with Anna's ashes was placed in "PERMANENT STORAGE, Unit 8, Tier ST, Locker 1-5." Sadly, the public administrator did not find it appropriate to use funds from Anna's rich estate to assure a dignified burial site for her.

Somehow, Anna had lost contact with Sonia's relatives. Only Sonia's friend Mrs. Martha Froelich had kept in touch with Anna as a friend and had assisted her with her legal affairs. As the probate of Anna's will indicated:

> ... Mrs. Froelich emphatically stated that Anna Nathanson's family had been a victim of the Holocaust of World War II ... that Anna

Nathanson's parents were killed in Europe, that Anna Nathanson had no
siblings ... no aunts or uncles who survived the Holocaust.

Sonia's niece, Ruth Rothchild, died in 1994 in Tampa, Florida,
and her nephew Hyman Mizell in 1996 in Miami. Both remarkable
people, they were closest to Sonia among her relatives living in the
United States.

Not one of the many loyal friends Martin had in Canada and the
United States is still living. But his memory lives on among their
descendants. Only the fate of Martin's special friend Dutchie remains a mystery. In 1930, Dutchie asked Stuart to look after his
cottage in Harlech and left for Ontario. But he never returned to
Alberta and what happened to him after he stopped writing to Stuart
Kidd in the 1940s is not known.

Among the former residents of Nordegg and their children and
grandchildren, Martin Nordegg is not forgotten, although he is fast
becoming a legendary figure. Even though the town has been deserted for over forty years as a community of people, it is still very
much alive.

On November 5, 1957, the *Calgary Herald* reported on the former Nordegg residents:

Nordegg May Be Dead But the Spirit Lives On

Nordegg has been dead for two years, but it wasn't evident from the
faces of some 300 former residents of the abandoned mining town, 60
miles west of Rocky Mountain House, who came from all over
Alberta, Saturday, to renew friendships at their second annual reunion at
the Isle of Capri, owned by Louis Carloni, early Nordegg pioneer.

David Craig, active at 84, even came all the way from Fernie, B.C.
to say if Nordegg could be in any way activated, he'd move back to the
town in which he spent 40 years.

About 17 nationalities represented proclaimed Nordegg as a real
melting pot that never saw racial friction.

They were just one big family, even when the mine employees
reached a peak of 900 personnel in 1923, and they stayed that way even
when the mine personnel shrank to about 400 two years ago.

"We laughed together and cried together," said Mrs. Sarnia [Serena]
D'Amico Duncan, now of Calgary, who, together with her husband
Robert, were the first native-born Nordegg persons to marry and rear a
family in the mining town.

These qualities were recalled in four informal dinner addresses....

Said George Krause, retired RCMP constable who spent five years
in Nordegg, "It was the best place in the world to be stationed. I had
less juvenile trouble than in any of my other nine stations....

There is no greater testimonial to Martin's idealism and humani-
tarianism than the two annual reunions of the former Nordegg

residents–the dinner in winter and the camp-out on the outskirts of the old townsite in August. When the hundreds of people—original Nordeggers and their children, grandchildren, and even great-grand-children—congregate for a happy weekend of games, campfires, and reminiscing at the foot of Coliseum Mountain, which overlooks the town and mine nestled in the charming valley, Martin Nordegg seems among them.

When Martin created his town, he was determined to provide his miners with an environment that was humane and dignified. If he were able to listen to the old-timers reminisce about "Mr. Nordegg," he would know that his work and dedication had not been in vain. Even though the town he built is no more, Martin's idealism and humanity left a great legacy—the human spirit of kindness and of community that has remained so strong among the people who used to call Nordegg home—the town that to this day bears Martin Nordegg's name.

ADDENDUM

After the biography of Martin Nordegg had already been completed and edited, the author had an opportunity to view the medical record of Martin's daughter during a visit to the Rheinische Landesklinik in Bonn.

A deeply troubling document, the medical record of "Marcelle May née Nordegg" covers the years 1929 to 1945. It reveals that Marcelle was the victim of chronic schizophrenia, which progressed from intermittent phases of mental illness to its final state of total depersonalization. The author was shocked to learn that Marcelle's condition was much more serious than information received from various sources indicated. The medical history also states that Marcelle had attempted to commit suicide while still living in China and that her mother had experienced "periods of mental illness."

The admission of Marcelle to the Hertz'sche Privatklinik in January 1931 was preceded by four short-term hospitalizations in private clinics in Berlin and in the Frankfurt area, beginning in March 1929. Only between July 1929 to March 1930 was Marcelle well enough to live on her own and visit her father in Ottawa.

From the early stages of her illness, Marcelle was suffering from intermittent stages of delusions and paranoia. She believed she was the oldest daughter of the last czar of Russia, or the daughter of Emperor Wilhelm II—Martin was only her guardian, as she claimed. At other times, Marcelle was convinced that she had been sterilized while in Egypt in 1912; that she had been deceived when another child was given to her after her son died shortly after his birth; that Sonia had killed her real mother, Berthe-Marie. For a certain period, she insisted that she was a queen imprisoned in a hospital; she wrote numerous letters to various scientists—she would not take revenge on the world, which had persecuted her. She also worked on a book about the reorganization of Europe. Among the many delusional thoughts she expressed, there was only one item of truth: Marcelle claimed that she was related to the French philosopher Henri Bergson, which Sabine Jordan née Brandt confirmed as correct.

At her first admission to hospital, Marcelle was totally emaciated, a state which often reoccurred. She required frequent periods of forced feeding. She was often agitated and heard voices.

Between stages of severe confusion, Marcelle enjoyed weeks of complete lucidity. During such periods, she was charming, dressed very well, played the piano, made crafts, among them a series of dolls in folk costumes from various countries that she had visited during happier years. She wrote very warm letters to her father, while at other times condemning him as "that Jew who claims to be my father."

Treatments consisted of various methods of hydrotherapy, insulin, sedatives, and other medications. Attempts of psychotherapy were not successful.

Martin's visits always made Marcelle very happy, resulting in a temporary improvement of her mental and emotional state. But after her father's last visit in 1937, Marcelle's condition deteriorated rapidly. Her memory of her father and other persons once close to her faded completely. In preparation for the extermination of mentally ill persons, Marcelle was reported, as required by law, to the authorities in Bonn as suffering from schizophrenia. In February 1941, of the 6 Jewish patients of the Hertz'sche Privatklinik, Marcelle was the only patient not removed from the clinic. In that month, 50 Jewish patients from various mental institutions in the Rhineland province were taken to the province of Brandenburg to be killed in a special facility.

Marcelle's last seven years were characterized by the most severe symptoms of schizophrenia. The medical record reports frequent states of catatonia; of periods of prolonged screaming "like an animal" while otherwise being totally mute; of constant tearing up of clothing. Eventually, Marcelle was kept in a bare room with only a mattress and a blanket. She was no longer capable of personal hygiene and had open sores on her back and legs.

When Marcelle was transferred to the Provinzial Heil- und Pflegeanstalt on January 1, 1945, her personal records were lost. The closing summary following her death on January 28 stated "parents or relatives: unknown."

The last document on Marcelle's file is the reply to an inquiry by the United States consulate in Bremen regarding Marcelle's estate and personal belongings. On August 17, 1949, the Provinzial Heil- und Pflegeanstalt in Bonn advised that

> At her transfer from the Hertz'sche Klinik in Bonn, Mrs. May brought only one dress along which was used for her burial, as no clothing for dead persons to be buried could be otherwise obtained.
> Neither is there an estate, money or valuables.

PHOTO CREDITS

Author's Collection(C): frontispiece, 1,2,3,4,5,7,8,10,11,12,13,14, 15,16,17,18,22,23,27,29,32,33,34,35,36,37,38,39,40,41,42,47, 50,53,80,82,85,86.
Brigadier E.M. Beament: 45.
Bruno & Ursula Büxenstein: 64,65.
Canadian National Railways Archives(C): 75,76.
Culver Service: 77.
Der Spiegel: 66.
René van Damme: 25,26,
Leon Gamsa: 9,31,48,54,55,56,57.
Bernard Gheur: 69.
Glenbow Archives(C): 62,68,70,72,81.
Andrew S. Haydon: 63.
Sabine Jordan: 51.
Fred & Helen Kidd: 61.
Hyman & Runelle Mizell: 59,60.
National Archives of Canada(C): 73,74.
Nordegg Historical Society(C): 19,20,24.
Ottawa Citizen(C): 46.
Elizabeth de Picciotto(C):67.
Red Deer Archives(C): 6,21.
Reichenbacher Heimatbund: 79.
Ruth & Joyce Rothchild: 43,44,49,52,58,71,83,84.
U.S.National Archives, Pacific Sierra Region (Record Group 85, Records of the Immigration and Naturalization Service San Francisco District, Arrival and Investigation Case Files 1884-1944; Immigration file 17318 #7-5 & #7-6)(C): 28,30.

SELECTED BIBLIOGRAPHY

Alan, John A. and Rutherford, Ralph, *Saunders Creek and Nordegg Coal Basin.* Ottawa: Kings Printer, 1923.

Alberta in the Twentieth Century, Volumes 2-5. Edmonton: United Western Communications, 1992-96.

Albrecht, Hans et.al., *Pfäfers, Bad Ragaz, Valens.* Amriswil: Amriswiler Bücherei 1986.

Birmingham, Stephen, *The Rest of Us.* New York: Berkley Books, 1984.

Blücher, Princess Evelyn, *An English Wife in Berlin.* London: Constable, 1920.

Brownlow, Kevin, "Hungry Hearts: A Hollywood Social Problem Film of the 1920s." in *Film History,* Vol.I.

Chronicle of the Twentieth Century. Mount Kisco, N.Y.: Chronicle Publications, 1987.

Churchill, Winston. *Amid These Storms—Thoughts and Adventures.* New York: Scribners, 1932.

Cornwallis-West, Mrs. George, (Lady Randolph Churchill). *Reminiscences of Lady Randolph Churchill.* New York: Century Company, 1909.

Dowling, D.B. *Rocky Mountain Coal Areas between the Bow and Yellowhead Passes.* Geological Survey of Canada. Summary Report, 1906.

_____ *Coal Fields South of the Grand Trunk Pacific Railway, in the Foothills of the Rocky Mountains, Alberta.* Geological Survey of Canada. Summary Report, 1910.

Fleming, R.B. *The Railway King of Canada—Sir William Mackenzie 1848-1923.* Vancouver: UBC Press, 1991.

Fryer, Harold. *Ghost Towns of Alberta.* Langley, BC: Stagecoach Publishing, 1976.

Gheur, Bernard. *Retour à Calgary.* Paris: Éditions A.C.E., 1985.

Green, R. *Brazeau Collieries Limited, Nordegg, Alberta.* Edmonton: Alberta Research Council, no year.

Hanna, D.B. *Trains of Recollection.* Toronto: Macmillan of Canada, 1924.

Hower, Charles. *Report on Rocky Mountain Collieries Ltd, Brazeau Collieries, Ltd. and The Sixth Meridian Coal Lands.* Berlin: W. Büxenstein, 1910.

Israelowitz, Oscar. *Lower East Side.* New York: Israelowitz, 1996.

Life and Letters of Sir Wilfrid Laurier, The. Carleton Library Series; Toronto: MacClelland & Stewart, 1965.

Koch, W. John, *Daisy von Pless.* Berlin: Ullstein, 1990.

Lower, J.A., *Canada.* Toronto: McGraw-Hill Ryerson, 1973.

Ludwig, Emil. *Wilhelm der Zweite.* Berlin: Rowohlt, 1926.

Mann, Golo. *Deutsche Geschichte des neunzehnten und zwanzigsten Jahrhunderts.* Frankfurt: S. Fischer, 1969.

Masur, Gerhard. *Imperial Berlin.* New York: Dorset Press, 1970.

MacGregor, James G., *A History of Alberta.* Edmonton: Hurtig, 1972.

Melnyk, Brian. *Nordegg Historical Resources.* Edmonton: Alberta Historial Resources, 1981.

Meltzer, Milton. *Taking Root.* New York: Dell Publishing, 1976.

Morison, Samuel Eliot, Commager, Henry Steele, and Leuchtenberg, William E. *Concise History of the American Republic.* New York: Oxford University Press, 1977.

Neckarsulmer, Ernst. *Der alte und der neue Reichtum.* Berlin: F. Fontane, 1925.

Nordegg, Martin. *Pioneering in Canada, 1926-1924;* unpublished, no date (ca. 1938).

_____ *The Possibilities of Canada are Truly Great.* unpublished, no date (ca. 1945).

_____ *The Fuel Problem of Canada.* Toronto: Macmillan of Canada, 1930.

_____ *To the Town that Bears Your Name;* translated by Maria Koch, commentary by W. John Koch. Edmonton, Brightest Pebble, 1995.

_____ *Zur Stadt, die Deinen Namen trägt;* Vorwort und Epilog by Maria and W. John Koch. Edmonton, Brightest Pebble, 1995.

Petry, Ludwig, and Menzel, Josef Joachim. *Geschichte Schlesiens* Vol. 2. Sigmaringen: Jan Thorbecke, 1988.

Pless, Princess Daisy of. *Daisy Princess of Pless by Herself.* London: John Murray, 1929.

Radziwill, Princess Catherine. *Memories of Forty Years.* New York & London: Funk & Wagnall, 1915.

Regehr, T.D., ed. *The Possibilities of Canada are Truly Great! Memoirs 1906-1924 by Martin Nordegg.* Toronto: MacMillan of Canada, 1971.

_____ *The Canadian Northern Railway.* Toronto: Macmillan of Canada, 1976.

Schütz, Hans. *Juden in der deutschen Literatur.* München: R. Piper, 1992.

Stevens, G.R. *Canadian National Railways,* Vol.I *Sixty Years of Trial and Error.* Toronto: Clarke, Irwin & Comp. Ltd., 1960.

Young, Bigadier Peter, ed. *World Almanac Book of World War II.* Englewood Cliffs, NJ: Prentice Hall, 1981.

Zedlitz-Trützschler, Graf Robert, *Zwölf Jahre am deutschen Kaiserhof.* Stuttgart: Deutsche Verlagsanstalt, 1924.

INDEX

Italicized page numbers refer to illustration numbers